THE NATIVE LANDSCAPE READER

THE NATIVE LANDSCAPE READER

Edited by Robert E. Grese

UNIVERSITY OF MASSACHUSETTS PRESS   AMHERST AND BOSTON

IN ASSOCIATION WITH

LIBRARY OF AMERICAN LANDSCAPE HISTORY   AMHERST

A volume in the series
Critical Perspectives in the History of Environmental Design
Edited by Daniel J. Nadenicek

LC 2011015592
ISBN 978-1-55849-884-6

Designed by Jonathan D. Lippincott
Set in Fairfield LT Std Light
Printed and bound by Thomson-Shore, Inc.

Library of Congress Cataloging-in-Publication Data

The native landscape reader / edited by Robert E. Grese.
     p. cm.—(Critical perspectives in the history of environmental
design / edited by Daniel J. Nadenicek)
  Includes bibliographical references and index.
  ISBN 978-1-55849-884-6 (pbk. : alk. paper)
 1. Landscape protection. 2. Natural areas. 3. Landscape design.
4. Essays. I. Grese, Robert E., 1955– II. Nadenicek, Daniel Joseph.
III. Library of American Landscape History. IV. Series: Critical perspectives in
the history of environmental design.
  QH75.N315 2011
  712—dc23
                                                                2011015592

British Library Cataloguing in Publication data are available.

Frontispiece: Lady's Slipper. Photograph by Jens Jensen.
Courtesy Bentley Historical Library, University of Michigan.

Generous financial support for *The Native Landscape Reader*
was provided by Edsel and Eleanor Ford House.

Contents

Series Editor's Preface

The *Native Landscape Reader* edited by Robert Grese is the inaugural volume in the series Critical Perspectives in the History of Environmental Design published by the Library of American Landscape History and the University of Massachusetts Press. The aim of the series is to offer incisive commentary on issues concerning environmental design at this moment of unprecedented change. Global warming, a burgeoning aging population, peak oil, international economic tumult, technological advancements, and other factors ensure that the world our grandchildren will inhabit as adults will differ significantly from ours today. A probing retrospective of environmental design practices can provide the important insights of history, showing us approaches that are timelessly effective which can enrich our present and future innovative environmental strategies.

In his 2010 book *The Great Reset: How New Ways of Living and Working Drive Post-Crash Prosperity,* the urban planning theorist Richard Florida delineates three major eras of economic crisis in the United States during the past 150 years—the Panic of 1873, the Great Depression, and the current recession. In the years after the first two crises, he notes, Americans systematically transformed the national landscape through several interventions. Following the crash of the 1870s, large industrial cities were built, and by 1920 the United States had become an urban rather than agricultural nation for the first time. Entrepreneurs (or robber barons) supported by government incentives connected these burgeoning cities to the resource-rich hinterlands by an extensive network of rails, hastening extraction at an unprecedented scale. After the Great Depression, Americans again substantially altered the national landscape. The post–World War II era witnessed massive highway construction and the explosive growth of residential suburbs, enabling greater freedom of movement and making the American dream of home ownership available to millions. But the decentralized pattern of landscape change has also caused harm to the environment, and it is increasingly difficult to sustain. The seeds of our current economic downturn, Florida demonstrates, were sown during these past decades of suburban and exurban development.

Florida predicts that the current severe recession will lead to an era of revolutionary changes which will create a more environmentally sound and socially equitable landscape. But his prediction does not take into account that it will be up to generations of Americans increasingly disconnected from physical place to make these critically necessary changes. Grese astutely describes this broken connection in his epilogue. Other writers including Bill McKibben in *The Age of Missing Information,* Maggie Jackson in *Distracted: The Erosion of Attention and the Coming Dark Age,* and Richard Louv in his award-winning *Last Child in the Woods: Saving Our Children from Nature-Deficit Disorder* have elucidated the grave consequences of a distracted and environmentally detached populace. In this moment of urgent need for reconnection and innovation, we hope that Critical Perspectives in the History of Environmental Design will foster a cross-disciplinary dialogue on timeless lessons to be relearned about the human/nature relationship, which will inform the decisions we make and the places we design today and in the future.

A consideration of the words in the series title (critical / perspectives / history / environmental / design) illuminates how forthcoming volumes will help readers to better understand their place in natural and built landscapes. *Critical* can mean either a negative appraisal or clear and discerning judgment. Series authors will not only bring clear and discerning judgment

to bear on a wide variety of topics in the history of environmental design, but they will also offer commentary on negative critiques which will reveal the sources of different *perspectives.* Just as the composition of a perspective drawing can vary greatly depending on the location of the station point and number and location of vanishing points, so too here analyses of various perspectives will uncover the station points, or beliefs, from which critiques are leveled.

Kate Soper, in addressing the question asked in her book *What Is Nature?,* explicates three different perspectives on nature: the lay, the metaphysical, and the realist. The lay perspective, shared by many average citizens, holds that those things which appear different from human artifice (plants, for example) are the most natural (or, put more simply, green is natural and gray is unnatural). This seems a particularly unreflective point of view, but it is nevertheless widely shared. The lay perspective, which so completely disconnects nature from people, also leads readily to the commodification of nature. The metaphysical perspective suggests that nature is a human construct and, as such, can be manipulated in various ways (even rhetorically) for political or social purposes. The realist perspective, according to Soper, is the scientific point of view, nature as understood by an ecologist, for example.

The debate over native plants, introduced in *The Native Landscape Reader,* offers us an opportunity to put an analysis of perspectives to work in understanding the issues. In years past, realist scientists, with apparent lack of awareness of the social connotations of the words they chose (*native, alien, alien invader*) sought to educate a larger public (holding the lay perspective) about the negative consequences of various actions, including planting invasive exotic species. In recent years, writers and scholars operating from a metaphysical perspective have offered critical commentary about how nature and the idea of nature may be manipulated to control human populations. As Grese points out in his introduction, the landscape historians Joachim Wolschke-Bulmahn and Gert Gröning identify a clear linkage between native plant advocacy and a quest for ethnic purity in Nazi Germany. Banu Subramaniam, a women's studies scholar, argues that globalization has led to a backlash of nationalistic tendencies and rhetoric. She sees the anti–native plant rhetoric as part of a larger cultural reaction to outsiders including immigrants. Like other scholars who discuss biofear and environmental anxiety, Subramaniam, too, suggests that the campaign against "alien" plants often leads to words and actions extending well beyond any rational scientific approach.

Subramaniam's argument is supported by my personal experience of having witnessed colleagues aggressively uprooting alien plants as though waging a heated battle to save planet earth. On the other hand, there is still considerable realist evidence of the harm caused by invasive exotic species. Moreover, Douglas Tallamy's *Bringing Nature Home: How You Can Sustain Wildlife with Native Plants* provides compelling evidence that even non-invasive exotics can harm the environment when planted in large quantities in suburban settings. The problem is that native insects prefer to eat native plants. When insect populations decline it affects all species further up the food chain. In some places a dis-

cernable decline in bird populations due to shifts in native insect populations has been observed. Thus both the realist and the metaphysical perspective on nature have merit, as do critical analyses developed from those vantages.

Through probing *history* we can gain valuable information about the development of interpretations and context for understanding contemporary issues and debates. In the introduction to this volume, for example, Grese explains how the meaning of the word *native* and understanding of the concept of "naturalness" changed over time. The essays he includes express views of nature prevalent at their time of writing—the sense of loss with encroaching development, the idea of nature as pleasure ground, the notion of grounding in place, the healthful benefits of country life, the dawning awareness of ecology—which clearly influenced landscape theory and design.

In my own research on Frederick Billings, I have experienced how history can open the way to a multifaceted interpretation of an era or person. Billings was president of the Northern Pacific Railroad and an ardent conservationist in Vermont, what we would consider polar opposite trajectories, both savior and despoiler of the natural landscape. But by analyzing his many writings, I discovered that those seemingly contradictory perspectives were not disjunctive in the context of his own time and station in life.

In its use the word *environmental* is often limited to apply only to ecology, ecological systems, or natural landscapes. The Critical Perspectives series, however, embraces a broader view that includes the totality of our surroundings and both social and natural factors influencing land-scape interventions and interpretations. The word *design* connotes forethought and intention related to this broad understanding of the environment. In his introduction Grese provides an overview of Eric Higgs's *Nature by Design: People, Process, and Ecological Restoration* and discusses the importance of both ecological systems and cultural reflection. That balance will be sought as well in forthcoming volumes.

The Native Landscape Reader includes an essay by the nineteenth-century landscape architect Horace William Shaler Cleveland. In writing the introduction with Lance Neckar to LALH's reprint of Cleveland's *Landscape Architecture as Applied to the Wants of the West*, I was struck by Cleveland's acute observations of the past as he contemplated the immense environmental design challenges facing the American nation in the years following the Civil War. Cleveland's book was published in 1873, the year of the financial panic that led to the first "reset" described by Richard Florida. Today, as we face unprecedented environmental design challenges with life-and-death consequences, we must be equally diligent in discovering and applying the revelations our history has to offer. I hope that the *Native Landscape Reader* and each succeeding volume in this series will provide readers with awareness, insight—and hope—as we face those challenges together.

Except in a few cases, *The Native Landscape Reader* does not include the original illustrations that accompanied the historical articles, and occasional references to these illustrations have been deleted from the texts. A new illustration program was supplied by the editor, whose photographs appear throughout, supplemented by a few other examples, both contemporary and historical. Most of the original footnotes to the articles have been retained; notes to the Introduction and Epilogue appear at the end of the book.

We are extremely grateful to the Edsel & Eleanor Ford House for generously underwriting this important book. The estate's commitment to the stewardship and interpretation of the landscapes of Jens Jensen benefit thousands of people every year. Our most sincere appreciation also goes to John K. Notz Jr. for doing so much to further interest in Jensen and also for his generous support of this project. We thank Bob Grese for conceiving of this collection and working so diligently to see it through to completion. We are grateful to Carol Betsch for her editing on the introductory essays, to Mary Bellino for managing the project, and to Jonathan Lippincott, for his elegant design. Our gratitude also goes to Bruce Wilcox and the staff of the University of Massachusetts Press, publishers of this volume. We thank all these individuals, as well as the Trustees of the Library of American Landscape History.

Daniel J. Nadenicek

Preface

Assembling this book has given me the opportunity to revisit many of the authors whose writings have helped to shape my views and approaches to landscape design and conservation. One of the writers whose work greatly influenced my initial appreciation of and curiosity about natural and cultural history was May Theilgaard Watts. As a young student in architecture, I was assigned portions of *Reading the Landscape of America,* originally published in 1957. Watts's lively text describing the landscape of Illinois, Indiana, Michigan, and the Great Smoky Mountains in Tennessee and North Carolina inspired me to want to explore and learn the stories behind the landscape patterns I saw. Shortly thereafter, I decided I no longer wanted to be an architect and began the journey that eventually let me to landscape architecture.

While a graduate student at the University of Wisconsin, I began researching the work of the landscape architect Jens Jensen. That research grew into the book *Jens Jensen: Maker of Natural Parks and Gar-*

dens, published in 1992. Through my study of Jensen and mentoring by my professors at Wisconsin, Darrel Morrison, Evelyn Howell, Wayne Tlusty, Arne Alanen, and William Tishler, I was made keenly aware of the work of Jensen's contemporaries Wilhelm Miller, Elsa Rehmann and Edith Roberts, Ossian Cole Simonds, and Frank A. Waugh, who also advocated for a style of design that celebrated the natural landscape and emphasized the use of regionally native plants. Aided by a grant from the National Endowment for the Arts in 1987, I was able to do further research on these designers and writers. I began to realize that there is a long history of individuals who were urging greater attention to native flora and ecological processes and patterns in design. I also began to see a strong interplay between design and conservation efforts. At least some of these landscape architects intended their work to awaken people to the natural beauty of their region and inspire them to become involved in conservation activities.

In the years since those initial studies, I

have continued to look for articles on these topics. Because I found many of these writings in fairly obscure publications or deeply buried in popular ones, I began thinking about bringing them together in a collective volume. *The Native Landscape Reader* is the result. As I sorted through my collection of articles to decide what to include here, my goal was not comprehensiveness but rather to showcase the variety of writings advocating for native flora and the native landscape from the early 1800s through the mid-twentieth century.

My hope is that the reader will keep in mind the contemporary context of these authors and reflect on what in their work is pertinent to today's challenges. If you're like me, you'll discover much that is as valuable now as when the words were first written.

I have many people to thank for their help in producing this book. Robin Karson, executive director of the Library of American Landscape History, provided untiring support for the project from the very beginning and patiently offered advice and suggestions throughout. I am also grateful to the LALH Board of Trustees for their critical support.

Daniel Nadenicek and Robert Ryan reviewed draft versions of the manuscript and offered insightful advice for sharpening and reworking my text. I feel honored that Dan has made *The Native Landscape Reader* the inaugural volume in his Critical Perspectives in the History of Environmental Design series. Carol Betsch and Mary Bellino provided essential editorial help.

Many colleagues throughout my career have shared articles and leads on some of the historical figures I have included in the volume. For this I thank in particular Arne Alanen, Julia Bachrach, Ron Block, Alfred Caldwell, Carol Doty, Leonard Eaton, Barbara Geiger, Bruce Johnson, Karen Marzonie, Eric McDonald, Arthur Miller, Darrel Morrison, Jo Ann Nathan, John K. Notz Jr., Emma Pitcher, Dean Sheaffer, Robert Simonds, Roberta Simonds, William Tishler, Christopher Vernon, and Donn Werling. Early conversations with George Thompson helped me think about this collection as a distinct possibility. My students over the past two and a half decades have also inspired me with their endless curiosity and questions.

Finally, I thank my wife, Susan, for all her support as I've sequestered myself in libraries and archives and worked long hours at home amid my piles of papers to bring this book together. Without her love and patience, I would likely have given up the idea long ago.

THE NATIVE LANDSCAPE READER

Introduction

Growing concerns about the depletion of resources and global climate change have propelled many people, from landscape architects to professional stewards to home gardeners, to reexamine how we design and manage the land. From backyards to national parks, many have clamored for more "naturalness," a reconnection with our environment, which could guide us in both the aesthetic and the ecological realms. Although some people believe that longing for naturalness is relatively new, perhaps originally spurred by Earth Day in 1970, there is in fact a rich history of thought about the native landscape and the design and management of American gardens, parks, and national preserves. That history is revealed in the writings collected in this volume.

Through the nineteenth and early twentieth centuries—roughly the same period that the profession of landscape architecture and many American conservation movements were in their formative stages—the native landscape was the subject of intense interest, as a focus for scientific study, as a model for design, and as the focus of preservation (or restoration) efforts in the man-made landscape. Aesthetically, philosophically, practically, and politically, the native landscape served as inspiration and guide, as a source of plants and as instructor on how to plant, and as something to treat with wonder and awe. In addition, our relationship to the landscape generated much thought, as writers, designers, and others noted the calming influence of nature, gardens, and parks on the human spirit and fought to provide such places as refuges within and around developing cities and towns. Increasingly the native landscape was seen as a resource requiring ongoing management and care—or active stewardship, in today's terms. During this period some of the earliest efforts in ecological remediation were begun, as individuals sought to restore integrity to damaged ecosystems, to manage roadsides, forestry tracts, and parks, and to create arboreta and botanic gardens as reserves of native flora and fauna.

The Native Landscape Reader is a collection of writings from the 1830s through the 1930s which address these various themes. The choice of dates is somewhat subjective, but during this period garden and design publications paid ever greater attention to the native landscape. Literary interest in the native landscape began to decline by the late 1930s (only to pick up again after Earth Day and surge in recent years). Many of the articles were published in relatively obscure places, professional journals or reports; others appeared in widely read popular magazines. Together, they provide a rich record of the collective thinking about America's native landscape heritage and the celebration of that heritage in parks and gardens. Designers varied in their adherence to native flora and local ecological conditions: some were strict, but many were quite eclectic in their choice of plants, occasionally using plants that horticulturists have considered to be weeds. They all, however, advocated for greater attention to the rich beauty of our native flora and its "fitness." Their writings also provide a base from which we can continue to explore ways of designing and managing landscapes that help preserve biotic diversity in the face of climate change, continued habitat loss, and other forms of degradation. And I believe that they can give us hopefulness and optimism, as we recognize that people have been struggling with issues of conservation and restoration for at least 180 years.

The use of so-called native plants in both practice and rhetoric has at times generated controversy. In a 1994 article in the *New York Times Magazine*, Michael Pollan raised questions about garden styles re-

stricted to native plant species.[1] Pollan was responding to the current "natural garden" movement that, as many of the writers in this volume did, celebrates the value of native flora over imported species, particularly those non-native species such as Japanese honeysuckle, kudzu, purple loosestrife, and tree-of-heaven that have threatened the integrity of wild ecosystems. Those non-native plants and animals causing ecological harm are frequently labeled "aliens," "invaders," even "monsters," and the use of such fear-laden terminology evokes uncomfortable parallels with xenophobic attitudes in our society at large, particularly directed toward human immigrants.[2] In her article "The Aliens Have Landed! Reflections on the Rhetoric of Biological Invasions," the historian Banu Subramaniam has suggested that much of the battle rhetoric about alien plants and animals "misplaces and displaces anxieties about economic, social, political, and cultural changes onto outsiders and foreigners."[3]

The landscape historians Gert Gröning and Joachim Wolschke-Bulmahn have shown how native plant advocates in Germany developed strong ties to that country's National Socialism and Nazi ideology and politics from the late 1930s through the 1940s.[4] They document how the concept of the "nature garden" in Europe and specifically in Germany was developed through the work of the Irish garden writer William Robinson and the German garden architect Willy Lange. The nature garden concept as promoted by Lange fostered an emphasis on the exclusive use of native plants as part of the Nationalistic fervor that swept Germany during the Nazi era. They note that the "Reich Landscape Law," promoted by the landscape architect

Alwin Seifert, would have purged foreign plant species during the Hitler regime, in concert with its social policies.[5]

Wolschke-Bulmahn also points to articles by the Danish American landscape architect Jens Jensen published in the German magazine *Gartenkunst* as evidence of "his close connections to Nazi landscape architects."[6] Jensen was indeed one of the most fervent advocates of native gardens in the late nineteenth and early twentieth centuries, and Wolschke-Bulmahn suggests that his writings "confirm racism as an underlying motive for his plea for the exclusive use of native plants."[7] But a convincing rebuttal has been made by Dave Egan and William Tishler, who point to Jensen's support of immigration as contributing to the American national character, his disgust with the Hitler regime, and his belief that native plants were valuable as key contributors to a sense of place and to ecological integrity.[8]

Much as we do today, Jensen and many of the authors in this volume lived during a period of increasing immigration pressures and backlash in the United States. Policies of exclusion were put in place, leading to the National Origins Act of 1924, which favored immigrants from western Europe, limited numbers from southern and eastern Europe, and virtually excluded immigrants from Asia. Danish-born himself, Jensen deeply valued the diversity that immigrants brought to the United States, a belief he expressed in a talk he gave to a meeting of the Women's International League for Peace organized by Jane Addams in Chicago in 1924.

Now I will say one word about immigration, and that is this: That I believe in everybody coming to America. I do not believe in any restriction of the yellow races or black races or any other races. I am willing to take my place in this country with the rest of the world, and if I am to be defeated then I will go down in defeat after I have tried heroically to hold my own. I think it is absolutely wrong to make restrictions against anyone. . . . Either you must be so selfish that you bring in yourself only, or you must admit everybody, and I am for everybody.[9]

While Jensen admired the growing interest in native gardens in Germany, he was suspicious of the Hitler regime's political agenda. In a letter to his colleague Frank Waugh, he noted that he'd been invited to speak at the Twelfth International Horticultural Congress in Berlin but hesitated to participate because of Hitler's recent attack on Austria.[10] In the end, Jensen did send a paper, but it was read by Franz Aust, a professor of landscape architecture from the University of Wisconsin.[11] In a 1945 letter to the landscape architect Genevieve Gillette, Jensen remarked that Hitler had brainwashed the minds of 80 million Germans.[12]

Egan and Tishler demonstrate that Jensen's advocacy of the use of native plants was based not on exclusionary ideology but rather on his empirical observations of what grew best in the areas where he worked and on his deepening appreciation of the beauty and fitness of these plants to the midwestern landscape. As he recalled in his essay "Natural Parks and Gardens" (1930): "There were two reasons why I turned away from the formal design that employed foreign

Wetland, Pinckney State Recreation Area, Livingston County, Mich. (Photograph by Robert E. Grese.)

plants. The first reason was an increasing dissatisfaction with both the plants and the unyielding design—I suppose dissatisfaction with things as they are is always the fundamental cause of revolt—and the second was that I was becoming more and more appreciative of the beauty and decorative quality of the native flora of this country."[13] In truth, he was not a purist. He clearly recognized that many non-natives—such as lilacs, hollyhocks, roses, and peonies—had long-held associations in people's lives. He would regularly include them in his client's gardens near the house or in special formal planting areas.[14] Near his own family's cabin at The Clearing in Ellison Bay, Wisconsin, Jensen planted hollyhock seeds that were a gift to him and his wife from a friend. Of these plants, he noted:

> Hollyhocks, although not a true product of native soil, has truly become a part of our rural countryside as the immigrant, for the pioneer so loved the hollyhock that he brought it with him and planted it at his cabin and dugout door. Traveling through out our western plains, a clump of hollyhocks, or a lilac bush and a few apple trees, are all that remains to tell of the struggle of some early settler, who later, for some reason or another, had to give up the struggle and move onward.[15]

Jensen was, however, aware of the potential invasive qualities of non-native plants, noting how he had once planted oriental bittersweet before he realized it would become a problem.[16]

Defining what constitutes a native plant is part of the challenge of working with native flora. Although no single definition is accepted by botanists across the board, the presence of two features is crucial. The plant must occur naturally without human intervention and must occur naturally in a specific area or region. The existence of a plant prior to the period of European settlement (to the best of expert knowledge) is often considered the defining feature of a native plant for a particular region.[17] This definition clearly disallows those plants that have naturalized since European settlement (i.e., taken to their new home and spread as they did in their old), whether moved from one region of North America to another (such as from the Southeast to the Midwest) or imported from abroad.[18]

Advocates of their use frequently argue that native species are better adapted to local ecological conditions than non-natives. Stephen Jay Gould, however, has disputed the biological argument for the fitness or superiority of native species, suggesting instead that "'natives' are only the plants that happened to arrive first and [were] able to flourish." Nevertheless, he acknowledges the potential threat of introduced species to preserving native biodiversity:

> I do understand the appeal of the ethical argument that we should leave nature alone and preserve as much as we can of what existed and developed before our very recent geological appearance. . . . I would certainly be horrified to watch the botanical equivalent of McDonalds' uniform architecture and cuisine wiping out every local diner in America. Cherishing native plants does

allow us to defend and preserve a maximal amount of local variety.[19]

Fortunately, the number of non-native plants that become invasive is relatively small compared with the number actually grown horticulturally.[20]

In his review of the debates over the use of native vs. non-native plants, the biologist Daniel Simberloff has noted the challenges of supporting a preference for native vegetation on aesthetic grounds, as many writers, including those represented in *The Native Landscape Reader,* have done. He concludes that "the strongest ethical bases, and possibly the only ethical bases, for concern about introduced species are that they can threaten the existence of native species and communities and that they can cause staggering damage, reflected in economic terms, to human endeavors."[21] The garden writer Janet Marinelli and the

ecologist John Randall note in their book *Invasive Plants: Weeds of the Global Garden* (1996) that roughly half of the three hundred plants known to be invasive in North America were imported for their horticultural use.[22] We continue to learn about the dynamics of these invasive plant species and the challenges of controlling them.

In his article "Invasive Species as Ecological Threat: Is Restoration an Alternative to Fear-based Resource Management?" the social scientist Paul Gobster suggests that the "fear" and "threat" factors so often emphasized in discussions of invasive species may, in fact, have negative repercussions, alienating the public and losing vital support for important conservation aims. Gobster suggests changing the terms of the discussion to focus on the positives associated with conservation efforts: the "health" and "diversity" of landscapes, their "heritage" and "authenticity," their

Savanna near Dexter, Mich. (Photograph by Robert E. Grese.)

"sustainability," their value for people's "use and enjoyment," their value in providing a "sense of place," and their value as places that nurture "stewardship" and involvement.[23] These notions apply across the conservation continuum, from backyards planted in native species to large-scale ecological restoration efforts.

The term "native landscape" as used in the title of this volume refers both to the wilder nature that became the focus of conservation activities and to parks and gardens designed in a naturalistic style, particularly those emphasizing regionally native plants and plant communities. Some authors, such as Jensen and Frank Waugh, typically restricted their use of the term to those lands where human influence was minimized. They characterized designed places based on the native landscape as being done in the "natural style" or as "natural parks and gardens."[24] The

more comprehensive use of the term in the title allows for the inclusion of a broader cross section of writings about American nature, conservation, and design.

Today, the interest in native landscapes and conservation is as great as or perhaps greater than during the period covered by *The Native Landscape Reader*. Clearly, our need for conservation has not diminished—rather, it has become more pressing. Leading threats to biodiversity include our burgeoning human population, habitat destruction and fragmentation, introduction of exotic invasive species, and the pressures on natural systems exacerbated by climate change and environmental disasters such as oil spills and wars.

In addition, we are facing the loss of traditional knowledge about local ecosystems. As we have become a more high-tech society, we have become increasingly disconnected from the natural world around

Wetland, Illinois Beach State Park, Zion, Ill. (Photograph by Robert E. Grese.)

us. Few people can name more than a handful of the native species found in their region. Children are described as suffering "nature-deficit disorder." Many advocates for native gardens believe that bringing nature back into our lives through our gardens can make a huge difference, not just through their ecological value but also through teaching us the unique natural history of our region. National organizations such as the Wild Ones and the National Wildlife Federation (NWF) advocate for wilder gardens through their educational and certification programs like the NWF's "Certified Wildlife Habitat" program.

Native gardens help reduce energy and water use, encourage infiltration of stormwater runoff, provide habitat for regional wildlife, and encourage working *with* rather than *against* nature. As the late Craig Tufts, a naturalist for the NWF, explained: "These new gardens are nurtured by individuals who want to invite the natural world back into their lives; to see butterflies dance from flower to flower, frogs splash across a water garden, turtles sunbathe on rocks and to hear the trill of songbirds fill the air. It's a way to connect with the natural world. And while occasionally an unwanted critter may venture in, the vast majority of wildlife species that are attracted to these refuges are welcomed."[25] Bringing nature home can help us build our environmental literacy about the natural world and strengthen our connections to broader conservation issues.

AN EMERGING SENSE OF LOSS

Just as American philosophers, painters, and writers in the later eighteenth and early nineteenth centuries began to appreciate the vast beauty of the North American continent, they also realized that it was in danger of being irrevocably lost through human activity. The "axe" became the symbol of destruction, signaling the tension between advancing civilization and pristine wilderness.[26] Nowhere was this tension articulated more profoundly than in Thomas Cole's "Essay on American Scenery," read before the National Academy of Design on May 16, 1835, and included in Part I:

> The most distinctive, and perhaps the most impressive, characteristic of American scenery is its wildness. . . . It is the most distinctive, because in civilized Europe the primitive features of scenery have long since been destroyed or modified. . . . And to this cultivated state our western world is fast approaching; but nature is still predominant, and there are those who regret that with the improvements of cultivation the sublimity of the wilderness should pass away: for those scenes of solitude from which the hand of nature has never been lifted, affect the mind with a more deep toned emotion than aught which the hand of man has touched. Amid them the consequent associations are of God the creator—they are his undefiled works, and the mind is cast into the contemplation of eternal things.

Cole's view, this sense of wonder but also of impending loss, was shared by many American naturalists, writers, and artists of his generation. In *Wilderness and the American Mind* (1967), the environmental historian Roderick Nash describes how the flowering of Romanticism in Europe fostered in the United States a new perspective on the American wilderness. The Romantic notion that wild places reflected God's grandeur led to the embracing of places that would previously have been considered wastelands. Ralph Waldo Emerson took this idea a step further, suggesting that the landscape was, in fact, a holy text, contemplation of which could bring one closer to God.[27] American explorers, poets, and painters inspired appreciation of scenic wonders such as Niagara Falls, the Adirondacks, Catskills, and southern Appalachians in the East and, later, the Yellowstone region, the Rockies, and the Sierra Nevada in the West.[28]

Throughout the eighteenth and early nineteenth centuries, the journals of travelers who had experienced firsthand the natural wonders of the North American continent provided glimpses of the wild beauty, open spaces, and diversity of the broad landscape. The naturalist William Bartram, who traveled throughout the southeastern United States from 1773 to 1777, expounded at length on the beauty and sublimity of the American wilderness in his *Travels,* published in 1791.[29] The book quickly made him one of the foremost authorities on America's natural history.[30] Other explorers included Meriwether Lewis and William Clark, whose expedition of 1804–6 was commissioned by Thomas Jefferson to explore the lands acquired in the Louisiana Purchase of 1803. The American geographer and ethnologist Henry Schoolcraft learned the Ojibwe language from his wife, who was Ojibwe and Scotch-Irish, and traveled throughout much of the upper Midwest from 1822 to 1841, serving as an Indian agent, making maps of the Lake Superior region and the headwaters of the Mississippi River, and recording many Native stories and legends. Similarly, between 1838 and 1841 the American artist and author George Catlin traveled through the territories west of the Mississippi River, painting and learning the customs of the Native tribes living there. He exhibited his collection of portraits and artifacts in major U.S. cities and later in European capitals as well. These early descriptions of the North American continent are filled with wonderment and awe. They make us painfully aware of what has been lost.

Many of the earliest writers on the "native landscape" felt compelled to debate whether American scenery (and art) could compete with Europe's. Thomas Cole's "Essay" might seem strange to today's reader familiar with the varied scenic wonders of the North American continent. But in the early nineteenth century, many citizens of the new republic felt culturally inferior to Europe, and that feeling extended to their new country's "savage" landscape. Cole became one of the champions of the beauty, magnificence, and sublimity of American scenery.[31] European landscapes, he noted in his "Essay," are invested with long-appreciated legends and stories, whereas "American associations are not so much of the past as of the present and the future."

Cole is considered the founder of the Hudson River school of painters, which included his close friend Asher B. Durand, Frederic Edwin Church, Jasper Francis Cropsey, John Frederick Kensett, Sanford Gibson Robinson, and others, whose work celebrated the region of the Hudson River valley as well as the Catskills, the Adirondacks, and the

White Mountains. The concerns of the Hudson River school artists intersected with those of the Knickerbockers, a group of New York–based Romantic writers of the period, which included William Cullen Bryant, James Fenimore Cooper, and Washington Irving. Bryant became associate editor of the *New-York Evening Post* and used the daily to share etchings and writings extolling the virtues of the American landscape. Cooper's novels *The Pioneers* (1823) and subsequent volumes of his *Leatherstocking Tales* and *The Last of the Mohicans* (1826) illustrated that "wilderness had value as a moral influence, a source of beauty, and a place of exciting adventure."[32] Irving's *Sketchbook,* published in 1819–20, included the short stories "The Legend of Sleepy Hollow" and "Rip Van Winkle" and infused the Catskill region of New York State with a sense of magic and wonder. Through his writings, Irving endowed the American landscape with the "stored and poetical association" many people felt was lacking in comparison with Europe.[33] Collectively, the books, poems, articles, and exhibitions by these writers and artists helped to establish firmly an American tradition of literature and art.

The Hudson River region was also home to Andrew Jackson Downing, the most influential early American landscape designer.[34] In his 1851 article "The Neglected American Plants" (Part II), Downing further challenged the view that American scenery and flora were deficient, noting the popularity of American plants among the gardeners of Europe and pointing to the "apathy and indifference of Americans to the beautiful sylvan and floral products of their own country." In "A Few Hints on Landscape Gardening," also from 1851 (Part III), Downing claims that approximately one-half of the trees planted ornamentally during the previous ten years were tree-of-heaven (*Ailanthus altissima*) from Central China and Taiwan and silver poplar (*Populus alba*) from Europe. "It is . . . one of the characteristics of the human mind," he remarks, "to overlook that which is immediately about us, however admirable, and to attach the greatest importance to whatever is rare, and difficult to be obtained." Downing advises aspiring gardeners and designers to "study landscape in nature more, and the gardens and their catalogues less."

Similarly, the sculptor Horatio Greenough criticized American architecture for its imitation of classical European styles. In a series of essays, Greenough noted that the "organic beauty" found in nature provides an infinite source of inspiration for artists and designers. Although not heeded at the time, Greenough's essays were collected and republished in 1947 as *Form and Function: Remarks on Art by Horatio Greenough* and have been read by artists, architects, and designers ever since. His ideas on the relation of form to function were later celebrated in the work of Louis Sullivan and Frank Lloyd Wright.[35]

NATURE AS PLEASURE GROUND

From the mid-nineteenth century on, Frederick Law Olmsted and Calvert Vaux advocated tirelessly for the salubrious value of naturalistic scenery to the city dweller. Their work in New York's Central Park and Prospect Park in Brooklyn, the residential

Wetland flora detail, Waterloo State Recreation Area, Washtenaw County, Mich. (Photograph by Robert E. Grese.)

suburb of Riverside outside Chicago, and Chicago's South Park helped to establish a tradition of naturalistic design that was promoted by many of the practitioners and authors in this volume.

Wherever possible, Olmsted and Vaux worked with the existing conditions to enframe views of beautiful scenery, orchestrate sequences of meadows and woodlands, and provide dramatic and serene bodies of water. Their carefully designed urban parks, where existing conditions were sometimes unfavorable, often required more deliberate engineering. These landscapes included masses of trees and shrubs, ponds and streams, and ever-changing patterns of light and shade, intended to provide people living in the crowded, chaotic city an oasis of calm and coherence for passive recreation and enjoyment—in essence a piece of the country in the city.[36] In Olmsted and Vaux's

view, such places would have a powerful restorative influence on park users.[37] Their landscapes transformed nature into pleasure ground.

In creating these landscapes, Olmsted and Vaux pulled from both native and exotic plant palettes. For example, in Olmsted's design for the lagoon at the World's Columbian Exposition in Chicago, he gave primacy to the flora of Illinois wetlands but also enriched the palette with plants from other regions. He did emphasize, however, that they should blend into the overall landscape composition.[38] When Olmsted used exotics in his planting designs, he avoided the gardenesque style, with its plant novelties and showy flower beds or the museumlike display of botanical collections with widely spaced specimens, which had become immensely popular in the United States by midcentury.[39] As

Olmsted noted in his report for Boston's Franklin Park in 1886,

> The urban elegance generally desired in a small public or private pleasure ground is to be methodically guarded against. Turf, for example, is to be in most parts preferred as kept short by sheep, rather than lawn mowers; well known and long tried trees and bushes to rare ones; natives to exotics; humble field flowers to high bred marvels; plain green leaves to the blotched, spotted and fretted leaves for which, in decorative gardening, there is now a passing fashion.[40]

Horace William Shaler Cleveland, a contemporary of Olmsted's, developed his ideas of naturalistic design in his work with Robert Morris Copeland at Sleepy Hollow Cemetery in Boston in the mid-1850s; various projects in the Chicago area, including Highland Park (in collaboration with William M. R. French), which artfully preserved many of the scenic ravines along Lake Michigan, and work on Graceland Cemetery; and designs for park systems in Omaha and Minneapolis.[41] Cleveland advocated an integrated approach to landscape design and planning through a series of brochures and reports. He suggested that the western United States offered new opportunities for urban design which could integrate sensitivity to the natural topography, vegetation, and water features and provide for the social needs of people. Rather than singular large parks in a town or city, he promoted the idea of a continuous "green ribbon" of parks and boulevards running through and linking communities.[42] Notable among his expressions of this philosophy are his *Landscape Architecture as Applied to the Wants of the West*

Beaver dam, Oakland County, Mich. (Photograph by Robert E. Grese.)

(1873), *Culture and Management of Our Native Forests for Development as Timber or Ornamental Wood* (1882; reprinted in this volume), and "Suggestions for a System of Parks and Parkways for the City of Minneapolis" (1884).

By the late nineteenth century, a broader dialogue was emerging in landscape gardening, forestry, and conservation which emphasized greater appreciation of America's native flora and scenery and their value in recreation. The botanist Charles Sprague Sargent, director of Harvard's Arnold Arboretum from 1873 to 1927, created a prominent platform for discussion of these topics in the journal *Garden and Forest*, which he established in 1888. For nine years, *Garden and Forest* provided a forum for exploring the relationship between nature and art and for celebrating American flora and scenery, advocating for their protection and arguing their value to the general health of the American public. Sargent and William Stiles, an editorial writer for the *New York Tribune*, were able to attract many of the leading thinkers in the nascent field of landscape architecture as well as in horticulture and forestry to write for the journal. Contributors included Frederick Law Olmsted, Mrs. Schuyler (Mariana Griswold) Van Rensselaer, Liberty Hyde Bailey, and the young Charles Eliot, whose essays in *Garden and Forest* were pivotal in the development of the Metropolitan Reservations around Boston.[43] A number of articles from the pages of *Garden and Forest* are brought together in this volume, including several written by Sargent (or, more likely, by Sargent and Stiles together).

A LONGING FOR GROUNDING IN PLACE

The idea of the "wild" garden was immensely popular in the literature of the late 1800s and early 1900s. Magazines such as *Country Life in America, The Craftsman, The Garden, House Beautiful, House and Garden,* and *Ladies' Home Journal* routinely carried essays about gardening, particularly on wildflowers, wildflower gardens, and conservation efforts. The garden historian Virginia Tuttle Clayton has noted that the plethora of articles about wild gardens during this period coincided with a growing concern about the disappearance of native vegetation that people remembered from their youth. Many people saw wild gardening as a way of participating in conservation, protecting the native species that were being lost, and, ultimately, preserving a defining force in the American national character.[44] Increasingly, a call was sounded for a new style of landscape design, one that was truly "American" and grounded in place, to countermand the dominance of Italianate gardens so popular at the time.

Nowhere was the call more fervent than in the pages of Gustav Stickley's magazine *The Craftsman.* For instance, in 1906 one contributor, Charles Barnard, in an article titled "The Commercial Value of the Wild," noted that books about returning to nature were "on the shelves of every bookstore." Suggesting a "back to the land" sensibility, Barnard advocated for a rustic approach to building a country home, one with a minimal impact on wild nature.

> Too fast, too unwisely we have cut down the trees, plowed up the wild flowers

and driven away the wild things of the woods and fields. We have destroyed a native garden of surpassing variety and beauty to make a formal exhibition of foolish double monstrosities and mere overgrown wonder flowers. It is not yet too late to save our lovely wild places—not too late to transform our remnants of the wilderness into reservations and homes that shall be of surpassing beauty, because sweet, wild, natural and free from the conventional improvements of the landscape gardener.[45]

The interest in native flora in landscape design, in ecology, and in conservation was particularly strong in Chicago at the turn of the century; two of the region's most noted practitioners, Ossian Cole (O. C.) Simonds and Jens Jensen, were deeply involved with these ideas. Wilhelm Miller, who had worked at Cornell's Agricultural Experiment Station as a writer and editorial assistant under Liberty Hyde Bailey, the prolific professor of horticulture, botany, and agricultural science at Cornell, and served as an editor for *Country Life in America,* became fascinated with the work of Jensen, Simonds, and their colleague Walter Burley Griffin, which he perceived as a new regional style. In his role as extension landscape architect at the University of Illinois, Miller wrote the circular *The Prairie Spirit in Landscape Gardening* (1915) as well as several magazine articles (one of which is included in Part III), in which he described this "prairie style," based on flora and landscape forms common in the Midwest.

Simonds was the senior practitioner of the three and had built his early reputation on the enlargement and reworking of previous designs for Chicago's Graceland Cemetery by William Saunders, Swain Nelson, H. W. S. Cleveland, and William Le Baron Jenney. Simonds initially began this work as an employee of Jenney's design office, shortly after joining the firm in 1878. Over the following years, he reshaped the landscape of Graceland as superintendent and then as consultant, transforming it into one of the most celebrated "rural cemeteries" in the country.

From Graceland, Simonds went on to design parks and park systems in many towns throughout the Midwest, numerous country estates, college campuses, and at least two arboreta—Nichols Arboretum in Ann Arbor, Michigan, and the Morton Arboretum in Chicago. Although he did accept many introduced plant species, in his designs he emphasized common plants of the region that often were considered weeds—hawthorn (especially *Crataegus crus-galli* and *C. mollis*), wild crabapple (*Malus ioensis*), sumac (*Rhus glabra* and *R. typhina*), hazelnut (*Corylus americana*), elderberry (*Sambucus canadensis*), Indian currant (*Symphoricarpos orbiculatus*), asters and goldenrods (*Aster spp.* and *Solidago spp.*), and others. In his book *Landscape Gardening,* originally published in 1920, Simonds suggested that one of the goals of landscape design ought to be to "teach [people] to see the beauty of nature" and "to take pride in their surroundings."[46] He also saw a link between design and conservation: Landscape design "will teach [the city-dweller] to respect the wooded bluffs and hillsides, the springs, the streams, river banks and lake shores within the city boundaries and preserve them with loving care."[47] In "Nature as the Great Teacher in Landscape Gardening," which originated as a lecture at the University of Illinois in 1922 (included in Part III), Simonds urged landscape architecture students to study nature as a model for design.

Jens Jensen's career had many parallels to Simonds's. His first major design was the American Garden in Chicago's Union Park, for which he collected native wildflowers from the surrounding countryside, hoping to remind urban dwellers of the natural heritage of their region. Jensen continued throughout his career to experiment with native plants in horticultural gardens, and his work increasingly involved what today we call ecological restoration. In fact, Jensen's last public project, Lincoln Memorial Gardens in Springfield, Illinois, begun in 1936, can be counted as one of the earliest experiments in ecological restoration, comparable to Edith Roberts's work at the Vassar College Out-of-Door Botanical Laboratory that began in the early 1920s and the groundbreaking work by professors Aldo Leopold, John Curtis, G. William Longenecker, and others at the University of Wisconsin Arboretum (founded in 1934 and described in the article by Paul Riis in Part V).

Jensen learned a great deal about native plants of the Chicago region from the noted botanist/ecologist Henry Chandler Cowles (1869–1939) of the University of Chicago, who pioneered many of the concepts of ecological succession through his study of the flora of the dunes of Lake Michigan, which he initially published in 1899.[48] With Cowles and others, Jensen explored the prairies, wooded ravines, and wetlands of the Chicago area and studied ecological and spatial patterns which came to inform his landscape designs. Like Cowles, Jensen was fascinated by the biogeography of

plant distributions around the Great Lakes and published one of his earliest papers on the topic.[49] As a member of Chicago's Special Park Commission, organized in 1899, Jensen headed the inventory of the physiography and vegetation of the region which resulted in a proposal to create a large band of preserves, many of which were ultimately protected as part of the Forest Preserve system developed for Cook and surrounding counties.[50] Jensen's report from that study is included in Part VI.

THE PROGRESSIVE ERA—COUNTRY LIFE AND COUNTRY PLACE

The era of social activism and reform which spanned the 1890s through the 1920s also left an indelible mark on the American landscape. Providing fresh air and outdoor activities for children and for all social classes was considered imperative.[51] The work of reformers such as Jacob Riis, whose influential photographic exposé *How the Other Half Lives* (1890) depicted the brutal living conditions of New York City's tenements, brought attention to the need for playgrounds and parks in New York's slum neighborhoods. Reformers in other cities soon took up the cause. Chicago's Special Park Commission documented the need for small neighborhood parks and playgrounds throughout the city's densely populated areas, and individual districts quickly responded.[52] In addition to these inner city movements, concern arose about the welfare of people living in rural areas—their access to modern-day improvements in health and sanitation as well as to education. Underlying all these reform efforts was the idea of the importance of nature in the daily lives of citizens, whether in urban tenements, "country places" in the suburbs, or on rural farmsteads.

Jensen was interested in the role his "natural parks and gardens," as he liked to call them, would have on their visitors. He believed, as Olmsted did, in the calming influence of nature, particularly on people who led stressful lives.[53] Today, environmental psychologists have aptly noted the restorative value of natural scenery and the outdoors to human health and well-being.[54]

Much like Simonds, Jensen was also motivated by conservation values; he wanted his designs to cultivate a greater appreciation of nature and sense of responsibility for its stewardship.[55] To this end, Jensen helped found two environmental organizations—the Prairie Club and the Friends of Our Native Landscape. The Prairie Club was organized as an outgrowth of the Chicago Playground Association's successful "Saturday Afternoon Walking Trips," which routinely offered city residents the opportunity to explore the wilds around Chicago with Jensen and other nature enthusiasts that included Henry Cowles, William M. R. French, Walter Burley Griffin, Dwight Perkins, the prairie school architect and crusader for the Cook County Forest Preserve system, the sculptor Lorado Taft, and others.[56] The Friends of Our Native Landscape was a politically active group whose goal was to conserve areas of important scenic, natural, or cultural value across the region.[57]

A desire to foster socially shared appreciation of nature also informed Jensen's park and garden designs, in which he often provided settings for a variety of outdoor performances—including nature's. In his book *Siftings,* Jensen compared the scene of a patch of goldenrod illuminated by the sun's afterglow to an operatic performance. In an article on Chicago's Columbus Park, he describes the composition of sunset views, brilliant fall colors, and appearances of birds as evoking Schubert's Unfinished Symphony. Years later, he recalled walking with Henry and Clara Ford along the Great Meadow he had designed at Fair Lane, their estate in Dearborn. The linear space was oriented to the setting sun on the summer solstice, and Jensen remembered Henry's remark about the beauty of the sunset which few took time to see despite its costing nothing.[58]

Jensen created formal settings for outdoor performances as well, including council rings, circular stone seats on which groups could gather for poetry readings, discussions, and celebrations, and outdoor theaters, or Player's Greens.[59] Raised in the tradition of Danish folk schools with their strong immersion in outdoor celebrations, Jensen believed that participation in such outdoor activities, even as spectator, would foster an emotional attachment to nature.

Liberty Hyde Bailey, one of the seminal figures in American horticulture, plant science, landscape gardening, and conservation in the twentieth century is represented in *The Native Reader* by a chapter from his book *The Outlook to Nature* (1905). Born in South Haven, Michigan, in 1858, Bailey studied under the botanist William J. Beal at Michigan Agricultural College (now Michigan State University) and with Asa Gray at Harvard University. He then returned to Michigan Agricultural College, where he organized the country's first department of horticulture and landscape gardening in 1885. A short three years later, in 1888, he moved to Cornell University, where he spent the rest of his career in research, teaching, and public service and in organizing the Cornell Plantations, a botanical laboratory and arboretum for the campus. In 1908, Bailey was appointed by Theodore Roosevelt to head the president's Commission on Country Life, whose research and report provided a foundation for agricultural extension and social improvement in rural areas across the United States and drew on the work of other authors here, especially Frank Waugh's in rural conservation and planning.[60]

From 1896 to 1904, Bailey promoted the *Cornell Nature-Study Leaflets,* appealing to the teachers of New York to incorporate nature study into their curriculums. He summarized the effort in his book *The Nature-Study Idea: Being an Interpretation of the New School-Movement to Put the Child in Sympathy with Nature,* published in 1903. An eager student of nature from his early childhood, Bailey wrote the first four leaflets himself, touting the value of nature study for many fields and as the basis for fostering responsible land stewardship.[61] Bailey's own philosophy of nature was recorded in part in *The Outlook to Nature.* Later he would expound further on his ideas about our ethical and religious responsibilities to nature in *The Holy Earth,* published in 1918 and widely regarded as one of the seminal books in American conservation.

APPLICATIONS OF MODERN ECOLOGY

During the first decades of the twentieth century, practitioners and conservationists began to inform their work with the emerging ideas of ecology. Frank A. Waugh was a key early advocate for applying ecologi-

Yellow lady's slipper, Skegemog Marsh, Torch Lake, Antrim County, Mich. (Photograph by Robert E. Grese.)

cal principles in landscape design. Born in Wisconsin, Waugh studied horticulture at Kansas State University and taught at Oklahoma State, then moved east to the University of Vermont and finally to Massachusetts Agricultural College, where he served as chair of the landscape architecture program for some thirty years. A close friend of Jens Jensen (he was one of few academics Jensen truly admired), Waugh, like O. C. Simonds, urged students to study the natural landscape as a source of inspiration and, in 1917, he published *The Natural Style of Landscape Gardening*. During the late 1920s and early 1930s, Waugh conducted field studies in natural landscape aesthetics and ecology with his students. Articles based on these were published in *Landscape Architecture*, including "Ecology of the Roadside" (January 1931), "Natural Plant Groups" (April 1931), "The Physiology of Lakes and Ponds" (January 1932), and "Running Water" (July 1932). "A Juniper Landscape" (November 1931) and "Pine Woods" (February 1932) were published in *American Landscape Architect*. (He intended to collect these studies in a book which he tentatively titled "Guide to the Landscape: A Textbook for Motorists, Boy Scouts, and All Lovers of the Native Landscape, Especially for Painters and Landscape Architects," though he never did publish the volume.) Waugh also did extensive consulting work with the U.S. Forest Service, successfully arguing that recreation was a legitimate use of the National Forests and that landscape architects should be a part of the National Forest management teams.

Elsa Rehmann and Edith Roberts made a convincing case for an ecological approach to gardening and landscape design in a series of articles under the general title "Plant Ecology," published in *House Beautiful* between 1927 and 1928. They noted the ecologically and aesthetically distinctive character of different plant associations, such as the oak woods, an open field, or a juniper hillside, and suggested that each of the major plant associations of the northeastern United States could be used as a theme for an ecologically based garden. In the first piece, they urged readers to look around them to discover "the intimate scenes of your own environment, for it is these that you can preserve and re-create for yourself."[62] Roberts had studied under Henry Cowles at the University of Chicago, where she earned her PhD, and then taught at Vassar College in Poughkeepsie, New York, as a professor of botany. In 1920, she began converting what was described as a "four acre plot of poison ivy" to an outdoor ecological laboratory.[63] With her colleague Margaret Shaw, Roberts surveyed the flora of Dutchess County, gathering the information that provided the basis for their publication *Native Plants of Dutchess County*. "Knowledge," they noted in their foreword, would lead to "conservation," and conservation meant "greater utilization through wiser utilization."

Roberts's association with Elsa Rehmann led to a course on landscape gardening at Vassar in 1923–24. Following the publication of their plant ecology series in *House Beautiful*, they revised the articles as a book, *American Plants for American Gardens*, published in 1929.[64] Rehmann, who had written broadly about landscape architecture, in her article "An Ecological Approach," included here, called for integrating scientific understanding of ecology with appreciation for the aesthetics of natural associations in landscape design.

Among the individuals who were deeply influenced by Liberty Hyde Bailey's writings, particularly *The Holy Earth,* was Aldo Leopold, who would later produce another classic of American conservation, *Sand County Almanac,* published in 1949. Leopold studied forestry at Yale and after graduation went to work for the U.S. Forest Service in the Southwest. Over time he became the ardent champion for soil conservation, game and wildlife management, and wilderness preservation he was widely known as. Leopold's influence was also extended through the founding of the University of Wisconsin's Arboretum, which pioneered ecological restoration. His article "The Last Stand of the Wilderness," included here, was originally published in October 1925 in *American Forests and Forest Life* but was reprinted and widely distributed by the American Civic Association as part of their call for wilderness preservation on public lands.

Another influential book relating to conservation and land preservation in the 1920s was Victor Shelford's impressive *Naturalist's Guide to the Americas,* published in 1926. Shelford, also a student of Henry Cowles at Chicago, became a biologist at the Illinois Natural History Survey and professor of zoology at the University of Illinois in 1914. In 1915 he helped organize the Ecological Society of America, serving as its first president the following year. The organization's Committee on the Preservation of Natural Conditions sponsored *A Naturalist's Guide to the Americas.* The book, which provided a review of the natural conditions of each state together with a list of significant natural areas and a description of their conditions, was a pre-

cursor of natural heritage programs found in most states today. In addition, Shelford included a series of introductory essays by different authors which explored the value of natural areas to various fields, including literature and art, landscape architecture, silviculture and forestry, fisheries, geography, biology, and agriculture. This set of essays is included in *The Native Landscape Reader.* Other essays explored the threats to natural areas at the time and suggested policies for land preservation. Shelford helped to found the Ecologist's Union in 1946, later renamed The Nature Conservancy.[65]

This collection of writings on the native landscape would be incomplete without a piece by May Theilgaard Watts. The daughter of Danish immigrants, Watts grew up in Chicago, studied with Henry Cowles, and partnered with Jens Jensen to save a prairie remnant in Highland Park, Illinois. In 1940 she began a more than twenty-year association with the Morton Arboretum, where she worked as an ecologist and naturalist, crafting innovative programs in environmental education and building a well-deserved following among their participants. She was instrumental in establishing the Illinois Prairie Path in 1963, now a sixty-one-mile recreational trail, the first "rail-to-trail" conversion of its kind. Her witty writings about nature were found in "Nature Afoot," her regular column in the *Chicago Tribune.* Her short piece "A Story for Ravinians" and a poem, "On Improving the Property," are included here.[66]

ORGANIZATION OF THE VOLUME

The Native Landscape Reader is divided into five thematic sections. The first, "Appreciation of Nature" includes articles on various ways of looking at the native landscape and noting its value. Part II, "Our American Flora," explores nineteenth- and early twentieth-century attitudes toward the native flora, particularly their usefulness in parks and gardens. The essays in Part III, "The Native Landscape as a Source of Inspiration," show how the native landscape has been viewed as an inspiration for designers. Part IV, "Natural Parks and Gardens," further explores how parks and gardens connect people with local nature or distance them from it. Finally, Part V, "Restoration and Management of the Native Landscape," demonstrates the broad foundation built by these early practitioners and writers for the conservation and restoration efforts that continue today.

PART I

APPRECIATION OF NATURE

The authors in this section explore various ways of appreciating the native landscape at different scales, ranging from measured critiques of landscape scenery to fascination with an individual tree. Together, these essays demonstrate an evolving recognition of the native landscape as a source of national pride, as critical to scientific and artistic endeavors, and as essential to our own daily personal health and well-being. The attitudes promoted by the authors here helped to lay the groundwork for many of the conservation efforts undertaken in the late nineteenth and early twentieth centuries as well as for our awareness today of humans' psychological connections to nearby nature.

The first essay is by the artist Thomas Cole, considered the founder of the Hudson River school of painting, an influential American art movement of the mid-nineteenth century that portrayed wilderness and landscape in realistic, detailed scenes. In 1829, the English-born Cole traveled to Europe to study the great artworks of the past. On returning to the States, he painted American scenery with much greater authority, and it was during this period that he wrote this essay. In 1849, Cole's close friend Asher B. Durand painted *Kindred Spirits,* depicting Cole standing with William Cullen Bryant in a Hudson River landscape, in tribute to Cole as a tireless champion and interpreter of the beauty of American wilderness. The works of the second generation of Hudson River school painters, including Cole's student Frederic Edwin Church, Jasper Cropsey, and Sanford Robinson Gifford, were used to promote protection of landscapes in the Northeast. In the latter half of the nineteenth century, the painters Albert Bierstadt and Thomas Moran and photographers Frank J. Haynes, William Henry Jackson, and Carleton Watkins drew attention to scenic landmarks in the West such as Yellowstone and Yosemite that became icons of our national identity and heritage (see Nash, *Wilderness and the American Mind,* 78–83; and Huth, *Nature and the American,* 43–53, 140–47, 152–53).

The second essay in this section is a

much more lighthearted look at nature, through the eyes of the poet Danske Dandridge. Her short piece "In the Company of Trees," published in 1892 in *Garden and Forest,* invites us to let our imaginations go while lying under a tree and looking up into its branches with wonder. Dandridge was born in Copenhagen, where her father served as the first U.S. ambassador to Denmark, but she spent most of her life in Shepherdstown, West Virginia. She wrote poetry, books on American history, and gardening articles such as the one included here.

The third article, "Love of Nature," was also published in *Garden and Forest* in 1892 and urges our cultivating a childlike fascination with natural scenery. The piece, though unsigned, is generally attributed to Charles Sprague Sargent, the co-founder of *Garden and Forest,* and William Augustus Stiles, the journal's "conductor." Both were interested in botany, horticulture, and the emerging fields of landscape architecture and forestry and helped to build support for many of the nascent conservation efforts of that time. The son of a wealthy Boston merchant and banker, Sargent grew up on his family's farm in Brookline, Massachusetts. In 1872, he was appointed the first director of Harvard University's Arnold Arboretum. Stiles was born in New Jersey and graduated from Yale in 1859. As an eloquent and forceful editorial writer for the *New York Tribune* he advocated for the creation of small neighborhood parks accessible to the poor. Like Frederick Law Olmsted, Stiles firmly believed in the salubrious value of parkland, and the articles here demonstrate a remarkable depth of understanding of the role that nature and gardening play in people's lives. Together,

Sargent and Stiles launched *Garden and Forest* in February 1888.

O. C. Simonds's short piece "Appreciation of Natural Beauty" is a call to recognize the quiet beauty of nature close at hand, an idea he would express throughout his career as a landscape designer. The essay was read at the second meeting of the American Park and Outdoor Art Association in 1898. The association, organized in 1897 through efforts of Warren H. Manning and others, provided a professional forum for discussion of landscape art, public parks, and the growing need for outdoor recreation spaces in American cities. The organization merged in 1904 with the American League for Civic Improvement to create the American Civic Association, which worked for the creation and protection of parklands and contributed to the broader efforts to improve cities and villages, later playing a role in the City Beautiful movement (see Wilson, *The City Beautiful,* 36–50).

H. W. S. Cleveland's essay "Influence of Parks on the Character of Children" was also written for the 1898 meeting of the association. Cleveland apparently did not attend, so his essay was read by Charles M. Loring, a successful businessman, civic leader, and the first president of the Minneapolis Park Commission, who had hired Cleveland in 1883 to design a connected system of lakes, parks, and parkways for Minneapolis. Here, Cleveland addresses the role of parks and nature in social reform, particularly for children in tenement neighborhoods.

Liberty Hyde Bailey's *Outlook to Nature* explores the restorative value of nature in our lives. In this first chapter, he investigates an idea that environmental psychologists endorse today: that spending time in nature, particularly as a break from the stressful routines of our daily lives, helps people cope. Bailey suggests that taking the time to enjoy the out-of-doors either directly or by reading nature-based literature cultivates greater efficiency, hopefulness, and repose.

Six introductory essays from the landmark publication *A Naturalist's Guide to the Americas,* edited by the ecologist Victor Shelford (1926), are included in this section. For this project of the Ecological Society of America's Committee on the Preservation of Natural Conditions, Shelford asked authors from a variety of fields to address the value of natural areas to their field. Besides Shelford, contributors included Seldon Lincoln Whitcomb, a professor of literature, the teacher and landscape architect Stanley White, William W. Ashe, a botanist and forester, the zoologist Arthur S. Pearse, and the geographer Stephen Sargent Visher. Collectively, these essays demonstrate an impressive breadth of support, ranging from the humanities to the natural sciences, for the appreciation and conservation of wild lands.

THOMAS COLE

Essay on American Scenery

(1835)

It is a subject that to every American ought to be of surpassing interest; for, whether he beholds the Hudson mingling waters with the Atlantic—explores the central wilds of this vast continent, or stands on the margin of the distant Oregon, he is still in the midst of American scenery—it is his own land; its beauty, its magnificence, its sublimity—all are his; and how undeserving of such a birthright, if he can turn towards it an unobserving eye, an unaffected heart!

Before entering into the proposed subject, in which I shall treat more particularly of the scenery of the Northern and Eastern States, I shall be excused for saying a few words on the advantages of cultivating a taste for scenery, and for exclaiming against the apathy with which the beauties of external nature are regarded by the great mass, even of our refined community.

It is generally admitted that the liberal arts tend to soften our manners; but they do more—they carry with them the power to mend our hearts.

Poetry and Painting sublime and purify thought, by grasping the past, the present, and the future—they give the mind a foretaste of its immortality, and thus prepare it for performing an exalted part amid the realities of life. And *rural nature* is full of the same quickening spirit—it is, in fact, the exhaustless mine from which the poet and the painter have brought such wondrous treasures—an unfailing fountain of intellectual enjoyment, where all may drink, and be awakened to a deeper feeling of the works of genius, and a keener perception of the beauty of our existence. For those whose days are all consumed in the low pursuits of avarice, or the gaudy frivolities of fashion, unobservant of nature's loveliness, are unconscious of the harmony of creation—

Heaven's roof to them
Is but a painted ceiling hung with lamps;
No more—that lights them to their
*   purposes—*

From *The American Monthly Magazine* 1 (January 1836): 1–12.

They wander 'loose about'; they nothing see,
Themselves except, and creatures like
*   themselves,*
Short lived, short sighted.

What to them is the page of the poet where he describes or personifies the skies, the mountains, or the streams, if those objects themselves have never awakened observation or excited pleasure? What to them is the wild Salvator Rosa, or the aerial Claude Lorrain?

There is in the human mind an almost inseparable connection between the beautiful and the good, so that if we contemplate the one the other seems present; and an excellent author has said, "it is difficult to look at any objects with pleasure—unless where it arises from brutal and tumultuous emotions—without feeling that disposition of mind which tends towards kindness and benevolence; and surely, whatever creates such a disposition, by increasing our pleasures and enjoyments, cannot be too much cultivated."

It would seem unnecessary to those who can see and feel, for me to expatiate on the loveliness of verdant fields, the sublimity of lofty mountains, or the varied magnificence of the sky; but that the number of those who *seek* enjoyment in such sources is comparatively small. From the indifference with which the multitude regard the beauties of nature, it might be inferred that she had been unnecessarily lavish in adorning this world for beings who take no pleasure in its adornment. Who in grovelling pursuits forget their glorious heritage. Why was the earth made so beautiful, or the sun so clad in glory at his rising and setting, when *all* might be unrobed of beauty without affecting the insensate multitude, so they can be "lighted to their purposes?"

It *has not* been in vain—the good, the enlightened of all ages and nations, have found pleasure and consolation in the beauty of the rural earth. Prophets of old retired into the solitudes of nature to wait the inspiration of heaven. It was on Mount Horeb that Elijah witnessed the mighty wind, the earthquake, and the fire; and heard the "still small voice"—that voice is YET heard among the mountains! St. John preached in the desert; —the wilderness is YET a fitting place to speak of God. The solitary Anchorites of Syria and Egypt, though ignorant that the busy world is man's noblest sphere of usefulness, well knew how congenial to religious musings are the pathless solitudes.

He who looks on nature with a "loving eye," cannot move from his dwelling without the salutation of beauty; even in the city the deep blue sky and the drifting clouds appeal to him. And if to escape its turmoil—if only to obtain a free horizon, land and water in the play of light and shadow yields delight—let him be transported to those favored regions, where the features of the earth are more varied, or yet add the sunset, that wreath of glory daily bound around the world, and he, indeed, drinks from pleasure's purest cup. The delight such a man experiences is not merely sensual, or selfish, that passes with the occasion leaving no trace behind; but in gazing on the pure creations of the Almighty, he feels a calm religious tone steal through his mind, and when he has turned to mingle with his fellow men, the chords which have been struck in that sweet communion cease not to vibrate.

In what has been said I have alluded to wild and uncultivated scenery; but the cultivated must not be forgotten, for it is still more important to man in his social capacity—necessarily bringing him in contact with the cultured; it encompasses our homes, and, though devoid of the stern sublimity of the wild, its quieter spirit steals tenderly into our bosoms mingled with a thousand domestic affections and heart-touching associations—human hands have wrought, and human deeds hallowed all around.

And it is here that taste, which is the perception of the beautiful, and the knowledge of the principles on which nature works, can be applied, and our dwelling-places made fitting for refined and intellectual beings.

If, then, it is indeed true that the contemplation of scenery can be so abundant a source of delight and improvement, a taste for it is certainly worthy of particular cultivation; for the capacity for enjoyment increases with the knowledge of the true means of obtaining it.

In this age, when a meager utilitarianism seems ready to absorb every feeling and sentiment, and what is sometimes called improvement in its march makes us fear that the bright and tender flowers of the imagination shall all be crushed beneath its iron tramp, it would be well to cultivate the oasis that yet remains to us, and thus preserve the germs of a future and a purer system. And now, when the sway of fashion is extending widely over society—poisoning the healthful streams of true refinement, and turning men from the love of simplicity and beauty, to a senseless idolatry of their own follies—to lead them gently into the pleasant paths of Taste would be an object worthy of the highest efforts of genius and benevolence.

The spirit of our society is to contrive but not to enjoy—toiling to produce more toil—accumulating in order to aggrandize. The pleasures of the imagination, among which the love of scenery holds a conspicuous place, will alone temper the harshness of such a state; and, like the atmosphere that softens the most rugged forms of the landscape, cast a veil of tender beauty over the asperities of life.

Did our limits permit I would endeavor more fully to show how necessary to the complete appreciation of the Fine Arts is the study of scenery, and how conducive to our happiness and well-being is that study and those arts; but I must now proceed to the proposed subject of this essay—American Scenery!

There are those who through ignorance or prejudice strive to maintain that American scenery possesses little that is interesting or truly beautiful—that it is rude without picturesqueness, and monotonous without sublimity—that being destitute of those vestiges of antiquity, whose associations so strongly affect the mind, it may not be compared with European scenery. But from whom do these opinions come? From those who have read of European scenery, of Grecian mountains, and Italian skies, and never troubled themselves to look at their own; and from those travelled ones whose eyes were never opened to the beauties of nature until they beheld foreign lands, and when those lands faded from the sight were again closed and forever; disdaining to destroy their trans-atlantic impressions by the observation of the less fashionable and untamed American scenery. Let such persons shut themselves up in their narrow shell of prejudice—I hope they are few, —and the community increasing in intelligence, will know better how to appreciate the treasures of their own country.

I am by no means desirous of lessening in your estimation the glorious scenes of the old world—that ground which has been the great theater of human events—those mountains, woods, and streams, made sacred in our minds by heroic deeds and immortal song—over which time and genius have suspended an imperishable halo. No! But I would have it remembered that nature has shed over *this* land beauty and magnificence, and although the character of its scenery may differ from the old world's, yet inferiority must not therefore be inferred; for though American scenery is destitute of many of those circumstances that give value to the European, still it has features, and glorious ones, unknown to Europe.

A very few generations have passed away since this vast tract of the American continent, now the United States, rested in the shadow of primæval forests, whose gloom was peopled by savage beasts, and scarcely less savage men; or lay in those wide grassy plains called prairies—

The Gardens of the Desert, these
The unshorn fields, boundless and
*   beautiful.*

And, although an enlightened and increasing people have broken in upon the solitude, and with activity and power wrought changes that seem magical, yet the most distinctive, and perhaps the most impressive, characteristic of American scenery is its wildness.

It is the most distinctive, because in civilized Europe the primitive features of

scenery have long since been destroyed or modified—the extensive forests that once overshadowed a great part of it have been felled—rugged mountains have been smoothed, and impetuous rivers turned from their courses to accommodate the tastes and necessities of a dense population—the once tangled wood is now a grassy lawn; the turbulent brook a navigable stream—crags that could not be removed have been crowned with towers, and the rudest valleys tamed by the plough.

And to this cultivated state our western world is fast approaching; but nature is still predominant, and there are those who regret that with the improvements of cultivation the sublimity of the wilderness should pass away: for those scenes of solitude from which the hand of nature has never been lifted, affect the mind with a more deep toned emotion than aught which the hand of man has touched. Amid them the consequent associations are of God the creator—they are his undefiled works, and the mind is cast into the contemplation of eternal things.

As mountains are the most conspicuous objects in landscape, they will take the precedence in what I may say on the elements of American scenery.

It is true that in the eastern part of this continent there are no mountains that vie in altitude with the snow-crowned Alps—that the Alleghanies and the Catskills are in no point higher than five thousand feet; but this is no inconsiderable height; Snowdon in Wales, and Ben-Nevis in Scotland, are not more lofty; and in New Hampshire, which has been called the Switzerland of the United States, the White Mountains almost pierce the region of perpetual snow. The Alleghanies are in general heavy in form; but the Catskills, although not broken into abrupt angles like the most picturesque mountains of Italy, have varied, undulating, and exceedingly beautiful outlines—they heave from the valley of the Hudson like the subsiding billows of the ocean after a storm.

American mountains are generally clothed to the summit by dense forests, while those of Europe are mostly bare, or merely tinted by grass or heath. It may be that the mountains of Europe are on this account more picturesque in form, and there is a grandeur in their nakedness; but in the gorgeous garb of the American mountains there is more than an equivalent; and when the woods "have put their glory on," as an American poet has beautifully said, the purple heath and yellow furze of Europe's mountains are in comparison but as the faint secondary rainbow to the primal one.

But in the mountains of New Hampshire there is a union of the picturesque, the sublime, and the magnificent; there the bare peaks of granite, broken and desolate, cradle the clouds; while the vallies and broad bases of the mountains rest under the shadow of noble and varied forests; and the traveller who passes the Sandwich range on his way to the White Mountains, of which it is a spur, cannot but acknowledge, that although in some regions of the globe nature has wrought on a more stupendous scale, yet she has nowhere so completely married together grandeur and loveliness—there he sees the sublime melting into the beautiful, the savage tempered by the magnificent.

I will now speak of another component of scenery, without which every landscape is defective—it is water. Like the eye in the human countenance, it is a most expressive feature: in the unrippled lake, which mirrors all surrounding objects, we have the expression of tranquillity and peace—in the rapid stream, the headlong cataract, that of turbulence and impetuosity.

In this great element of scenery, what land is so rich? I would not speak of the Great Lakes, which are in fact inland seas—possessing some of the attributes of the ocean, though destitute of its sublimity; but of those smaller lakes, such as Lake George, Champlain, Winnipisiogee, Otsego, Seneca, and a hundred others, that stud like gems the bosom of this country. There is one delightful quality in nearly all these lakes—the purity and transparency of the water. In speaking of scenery it might seem unnecessary to mention this; but independent of the pleasure that we all have in beholding pure water, it is a circumstance which contributes greatly to the beauty of landscape; for the reflections of surrounding objects, trees, mountains, sky, are most perfect in the clearest water; and the most perfect is the most beautiful.

I would rather persuade you to visit the "Holy Lake," the beautiful "Horican," than attempt to describe its scenery—to behold you rambling on its storied shores, where its southern expanse is spread, begemmed with isles of emerald, and curtained by green receding hills—or to see you gliding over its bosom, where the steep and rugged mountains approach from either side, shadowing with black precipices the innumerable islets—some of which bearing a solitary tree, others a group of two or three, or a "goodly company," seem to have been sprinkled over the smiling deep in Nature's frolic hour. These scenes are classic—History and Genius have hallowed them.

War's shrill clarion once waked the echoes from these now silent hills—the pen of a living master has portrayed them in the pages of romance—and they are worthy of the admiration of the enlightened and the graphic hand of Genius.

Though differing from Lake George, Winnipisiogee resembles it in multitudinous and uncounted islands. Its mountains do not stoop to the water's edge, but through varied screens of forest may be seen ascending the sky softened by the blue haze of distance—on the one hand rise the Gunstock Mountains; on the other the dark Ossipees, while above and far beyond, rear the "cloud capt" peaks of the Sandwich and White Mountains.

I will not fatigue with a vain attempt to describe the lakes that I have named; but would turn your attention to those exquisitely beautiful lakes that are so numerous in the Northern States, and particularly in New Hampshire. In character they are truly and peculiarly American. I know nothing in Europe which they resemble; the famous lakes of Albano and Nemi, and the small and exceedingly picturesque lakes of Great Britain may be compared in size, but are dissimilar in almost every other respect. Embosomed in the primitive forest, and sometimes overshadowed by huge mountains, they are the chosen places of tranquillity; and when the deer issues from the surrounding woods to drink the cool waters, he beholds his own image as in a polished mirror, —the flight of the eagle can be seen in the lower sky; and if a leaf falls, the circling undulations chase each other to the shores unvexed by contending tides.

There are two lakes of this description, situated in a wild mountain gorge called the Franconia Notch, in New Hampshire. They lie within a few hundred feet of each other, but are remarkable as having no communication—one being the source of the wild Amonoosuck, the other of the Pemigiwasset. Shut in by stupendous mountains which rest on crags that tower more than a thousand feet above the water, whose rugged brows and shadowy breaks are clothed by dark and tangled woods, they have such an aspect of deep seclusion, of utter and unbroken solitude, that, when standing on their brink a lonely traveller, I was overwhelmed with an emotion of the sublime, such as I have rarely felt. It was not that the jagged precipices were lofty, that the encircling woods were of the dimmest shade, or that the waters were profoundly deep; but that over all, rocks, wood, and water, brooded the spirit of repose, and the silent energy of nature stirred the soul to its inmost depths.

I would not be understood that these lakes are always tranquil; but that tranquillity is their great characteristic. There are times when they take a far different expression; but in scenes like these the richest chords are those struck by the gentler hand of nature.

And now I must turn to another of the beautifiers of the earth—the Waterfall; which in the same object at once presents to the mind the beautiful, but apparently incongruous idea, of fixedness and motion—a single existence in which we perceive unceasing change and everlasting duration. The waterfall may be called the voice of the landscape, for, unlike the rocks and woods which utter sounds as the passive instruments played on by the elements, the waterfall strikes its own chords, and rocks and mountains re-echo in rich unison. And this is a land abounding in cataracts; in these Northern States where shall we turn and not find them? Have we not Kaaterskill, Trenton, the Flume, the Genesee, stupendous Niagara, and a hundred others named and nameless ones, whose exceeding beauty must be acknowledged when the hand of taste shall point them out?

In the Kaaterskill we have a stream, diminutive indeed, but throwing itself headlong over a fearful precipice into a deep gorge of the densely wooded mountains—and possessing a singular feature in the vast arched cave that extends beneath and behind the cataract. At Trenton there is a chain of waterfalls of remarkable beauty, where the foaming waters, shadowed by steep cliffs, break over rocks of architectural formation, and tangled and picturesque trees mantle abrupt precipices, which it would be easy to imagine crumbling and "time disparting towers."

And Niagara! that wonder of the world! —where the sublime and beautiful are bound together in an indissoluble chain. In gazing on it we feel as though a great void had been filled in our minds—our conceptions expand—we become a part of what we behold! At our feet the floods of a thousand rivers are poured out—the contents of vast inland seas. In its volume we conceive immensity; in its course, everlasting duration; in its impetuosity, uncontrollable power. These are the elements of its sublimity. Its beauty is garlanded around in the varied hues of the water, in the spray that ascends the sky, and in that unrivalled bow which forms a complete cincture round the unresting floods.

The river scenery of the United States is a rich and boundless theme. The Hudson for natural magnificence is unsurpassed. What can be more beautiful than the lake-like expanses of Tapaan and Haverstraw, as seen from the rich orchards of the surrounding hills? hills that have a legend, which has been so sweetly and admirably told that it shall not perish but with the language of the land. What can be more imposing than the precipitous Highlands; whose dark foundations have been rent to make a passage for the deep-flowing river? And, ascending still, where can be found scenes more enchanting? The lofty Catskills stand afar off—the green hills gently rising from the flood, recede like steps by which we may ascend to a great temple, whose pillars are those everlasting hills, and whose dome is the blue boundless vault of heaven.

The Rhine has its castled crags, its vine-clad hills, and ancient villages; the Hudson has its wooded mountains, its rugged precipices, its green undulating shores—a natural majesty, and an unbounded capacity for improvement by art. Its shores are not besprinkled with venerated ruins, or the palaces of princes; but there are flourishing towns, and neat villas, and the hand of taste has already been at work. Without any great stretch of the imagination we may anticipate the time when the ample waters shall reflect temple, and tower, and dome, in every variety of picturesqueness and magnificence.

In the Connecticut we behold a river that differs widely from the Hudson. Its sources are amid the wild mountains of New Hampshire; but it soon breaks into a luxuriant valley, and flows for more than a hundred miles, sometimes beneath the shadow of wooded hills, and sometimes glancing through the green expanse of elm-besprinkled meadows. Whether we see it at Haverhill, Northampton, or Hartford, it still possesses that gentle aspect; and the imagination can scarcely conceive Arcadian vales more lovely or more peaceful than the valley of the Connecticut—its villages are rural places where trees overspread every dwelling, and the fields upon its margin have the richest verdure.

Nor ought the Ohio, the Susquehannah, the Potomac, with their tributaries, and a thousand others, be omitted in the rich list of the American rivers—they are a glorious brotherhood; but volumes would be insufficient for their description.

In the Forest scenery of the United States we have that which occupies the greatest space, and is not the least remarkable; being primitive, it differs widely from the European. In the American forest we find trees in every stage of vegetable life and decay—the slender sapling rises in the shadow of the lofty tree, and the giant in his prime stands by the hoary patriarch of the wood—on the ground lie prostrate decaying ranks that once waved their verdant heads in the sun and wind. These are circumstances productive of great variety and picturesqueness—green umbrageous masses—lofty and scathed trunks—contorted branches thrust athwart the sky—the mouldering dead below, shrouded in moss of every hue and texture, from richer combinations than can be found in the trimmed and planted grove. It is true that the thinned and cultivated wood offers less obstruction to the feet, and the trees throw out their branches more horizontally, and are consequently more umbrageous when taken singly; but the true lover of the picturesque is seldom fatigued—and trees that grow widely apart are often heavy in form, and resemble each other too much for picturesqueness. Trees are like men, differing widely in character; in sheltered spots, or under the influence of culture, they show few contrasting points; peculiarities are pruned and trained away, until there is a general resemblance. But in exposed situations, wild and uncultivated, battling with the elements and with one another for the possession of a morsel of soil, or a favoring rock to which they may cling—they exhibit striking peculiarities, and sometimes grand originality.

For variety, the American forest is unrivalled: in some districts are found oaks, elms, birches, beeches, planes, pines, hemlocks, and many other kinds of trees, commingled—clothing the hills with every tint of green, and every variety of light and shade.

There is a peculiarity observable in some mountainous regions, where trees of a genus band together—there often may be seen a mountain whose foot is clothed with deciduous trees, while on its brow is a sable crown of pines; and sometimes belts of dark green encircle a mountain horizontally, or are stretched in well-defined lines from the summit to the base. The nature of the soil, or the courses of rivulets, are the causes of this variety; —and it is a beautiful instance of the exhaustlessness of nature; often where we should expect unvarying monotony, we behold a charming diversity. Time will not permit me to speak of the American forest trees individually; but I must notice the elm, that paragon of beauty and shade; the maple, with its rainbow hues; and the hemlock, the sublime of trees, which rises from the gloom of the forest like a dark and ivy-mantled tower.

There is one season when the American forest surpasses all the world in gorgeousness—that is the autumnal; —then every hill and dale is riant in the luxury of color—every hue is there, from the liveliest green to deepest purple, from the most golden yellow to the intensest crimson. The artist looks despairingly upon the glowing landscape, and in the old world his truest imitations of the American forest, at this season, are called falsely bright, and scenes in Fairy Land.

The sky will next demand our attention. The soul of all scenery, in it are the fountains of light, and shade, and color. Whatever expression the sky takes, the features of the landscape are affected in unison, whether it be the serenity of the summer's blue, or the dark tumult of the storm. It is the sky that makes the earth so lovely at sunrise, and so splendid at sunset. In the one it breathes over the earth the crystal-like ether, in the other liquid gold. The climate of a great part of the United States is subject to great vicissitudes, and we complain; but nature offers a compensation. These very vicissitudes are the abundant sources of beauty—as we have the temperature of every clime, so have we the skies—we have the blue unsearchable depths of the northern sky—we have the upheaped thunder-clouds of the Torrid Zone, fraught with gorgeousness and sublimity—we have the silver haze of England, and the golden atmosphere of Italy. And if he who has travelled and observed the skies of other climes will spend a few months on the banks of the Hudson, he must be constrained to acknowledge that for variety and magnificence American skies are unsurpassed. Italian skies have been lauded by every tongue, and sung by every poet, and who will deny their wonderful beauty? At sunset the serene arch is filled with alchemy that transmutes mountains, and streams, and temples, into living gold.

But the American summer never passes without many sunsets that might vie with the Italian, and many still more gorgeous—that seem peculiar to this clime.

Look at the heavens when the thunder shower has passed, and the sun stoops behind the western mountains—there the low purple clouds hang in festoons around the steeps—in the higher heaven are crimson bands interwoven with feathers of gold, fit for the wings of angels—and still above is spread that interminable field of ether, whose color is too beautiful to have a name.

It is not in the summer only that American skies are beautiful; for the winter evening often comes robed in purple and gold, and in the westering sun the iced groves glitter as beneath a shower of diamonds—and through the twilight heaven innumerable stars shine with a purer light than summer ever knows.

I will now venture a few remarks on what has been considered a grand defect in American scenery—the want of associations, such as arise amid the scenes of the old world.

We have many a spot as umbrageous as Vallombrosa, and as picturesque as the solitudes of Vaucluse; but Milton and Petrarch have not hallowed them by their footsteps and immortal verse. He who stands on Mont Albano and looks down on ancient Rome, has his mind peopled with the gigantic associations of the storied past; but he who stands on the mounds of the West, the most venerable remains of American antiquity, *may* experience the emotion of the sublime, but it is the sublimity of a shoreless ocean un-islanded by the recorded deeds of man.

Yet American scenes are not destitute of historical and legendary associations—the great struggle for freedom has sanctified many a spot, and many a mountain, stream, and rock has its legend, worthy of poet's pen or the painter's pencil. But American associations are not so much of the past as of the present and the future. Seated on a pleasant knoll, look down into the bosom of that secluded valley, begirt with wooded hills—through those enamelled meadows and wide waving fields of grain, a silver stream winds lingeringly along—here, seeking the green shade of trees—there, glancing in the sunshine: on its banks are rural dwellings shaded by elms and garlanded by flowers—from yonder dark mass of foliage the village spire beams like a star. You see no ruined tower to tell of outrage—no gorgeous temple to speak of ostentation; but freedom's offspring—peace, security, and happiness, dwell there, the spirits of the scene. On the margin of that gentle river the village girls may ramble unmolested—and the glad school-boy, with hook and line, pass his bright holiday—those neat dwellings, unpretending to magnificence, are the abodes of plenty, virtue, and refinement. And in looking over the yet uncultivated scene, the mind's eye may see far into futurity. Where the wolf roams, the plough shall glisten; on the gray crag shall rise temple and tower—mighty deeds shall be done in the now pathless wilderness; and poets yet unborn shall sanctify the soil.

It was my intention to attempt a description of several districts remarkable for their picturesqueness and truly American character; but I fear to trespass longer on your time and patience. Yet I cannot but express my sorrow that the beauty of such landscapes are quickly passing away—the ravages of the axe are daily increasing—the most noble scenes are made desolate, and oftentimes with a wantonness and barbarism scarcely credible in a civilized nation. The wayside is becoming shadeless, and another generation will behold spots, now rife with beauty, desecrated by what is called improvement; which, as yet, generally destroys Nature's beauty without substituting that of Art. This is a regret rather than a complaint; such is the road society has to travel; it may lead to refinement in the end, but the traveller who sees the place of rest close at hand, dislikes the road that has so many unnecessary windings.

I will now conclude, in the hope that, though feebly urged, the importance of cultivating a taste for scenery will not be forgotten. Nature has spread for us a rich and delightful banquet. Shall we turn from it? We are still in Eden; the wall that shuts us out of the garden is our own ignorance and folly. We should not allow the poet's words to be applicable to us—

Deep in rich pasture do thy flocks
    complain?
Not so; but to their master is denied
To share the sweet serene.

May we at times turn from the ordinary pursuits of life to the pure enjoyment of rural nature; which is in the soul like a fountain of cool waters to the way-worn traveller; and let us

Learn
The laws by which the Eternal doth
    sublime
And sanctify his works, that we may see
The hidden glory veiled from vulgar eyes.

DANSKE DANDRIDGE

In the Company of Trees

(1892)

If one wishes to be taken into the intimate confidence of a great tree, and to get the full enjoyment of its strength and beauty, he should lie upon his back on the greensward beneath it, cross his arms under his head by way of pillow, and let the eye climb slowly up the mighty trunk from root to topmost limb. Thus have I lain beneath an ancient White Oak; thus watched the infinitely varied play of light and shade through the dense foliage; thus noted the delicate tracery of the leaves against the blue of the sky, and learned by heart each wrinkle of its rugged bark. This is the way to study the varying characteristics of trees, and to learn many a sylvan secret only revealed to the real lovers of nature, upon whom she has graciously bestowed eyes to see and the heart to feel her beauty and her mystery. I have spent a summer afternoon moving slowly from trunk to trunk, from Oak to Maple, from Maple to Sour Gum, from Gum to Walnut, and then to Ash, to Poplar, and back again to the old White Oak, most satisfying of all.

From *Garden and Forest*, July 20, 1892, 340.

Sometimes as the sun would smile upon me through an opening in the boughs, or a light-hearted vireo warble a lullaby; the orioles whistle plaintively; the friendly squirrels pretend to scold, and scurry away from branch to branch, only to hasten back to peep again and drop a tiny acorn on my cheek. The great white clouds sailing far overhead; a distant hawk leisurely cleaving the air on his strong wings; a few drops from a flying scud—all these become stirring incidents, fraught with healing and refreshment to the heat-worn nerves and weary brain of the house-dweller. Should the eyes close into delicious slumber the great tree stands guard over its puny visitor, filling one with a sense of security and of being cared for as by a mighty and gentle nurse.

Thus has it chanced to me to be overtaken by a summer shower, and to be awakened by the first cool splash of raindrops upon my brow. The Oak had no need of mackintosh and umbrella; it was only necessary to turn the water-proof side of its varnished leaves uppermost,

Old oak, Vilas Circle Park, Madison, Wis. (Photograph by Robert E. Grese.)

and stand quietly to take whatever came, strong in the security gained by a hundred years of storm and sun. The foliage of the tree protected its sleeping guest as long as possible, but now, with a gentle warning splash, the drops fell more and more quickly; little streams ran down the trunk, following the corrugations in its rough bark; the leaves twinkled merrily as they shed their burden of moisture in my face. Then the sun came out a moment, and the whole tree sparkled joyously like the countenance of a friend who is bringing you welcome news.

CHARLES SPRAGUE SARGENT AND WILLIAM AUGUSTUS STILES

The Love of Nature

(1892)

One of the noticeable characteristics of this century is a growing love of natural scenery, but it may be questioned whether the love of nature is also growing, for a distinction must be made between the two. The first is a simple emotion—an instinct rather than a faculty—and, like all primitive instincts, it lies at the very foundation of being, having its roots somewhere in that mysterious region below consciousness. Perhaps it is stronger among the savage than it is among the civilized races of the world, but it is yet the birthright of every healthy child.

The appreciation of natural scenery, on the other hand, is a complex emotion which involves thought, memory and imagination, and as it rarely manifests itself in childhood it probably did not exist in the childhood of the race. Wherever this appreciation is found, whether among modern nations, among the Hebrews as indicated in their literature, or among the Greeks and Romans, as is evident from the skillful way in which their architectural creations were placed with reference to their natural surroundings, it is the outcome of an advanced, perhaps of a decaying, civilization. The towering mountain stirs the imagination of the boy, but it is to deeds of exploration and adventure. The dense forest lures him, but its chief attraction is the game it covers. The brook which sparkles through the meadows delights him, because it turns his water-wheel or excites his hope as an angler. And yet, blind as he may seem to the grandeur of the one or the beauty of the others, mountain, grove and stream, each plays its part in molding the boy's taste and character, and in after years he will be drawn to them by a deeper love, because they are inseparably blended with the careless happiness of childhood and youth. It is through some experience like this that the race has passed. Earth first ministers to man's necessities; in so doing it develops his faculties and awakens new powers, until at last, when he has gained

From *Garden and Forest*, July 20, 1892, 337–38.

dominion over it, the ability to discern its beauty comes with the leisure to enjoy it.

The pleasure which springs from the contemplation of a beautiful landscape differs in kind with each spectator. It may have no deeper source than the mere love of beauty, and it is then refreshing to the jaded spirit simply because the beauty is pure and appeals to no sordid or material interest. But when to the beauty of a landscape is added the charm of romantic and historic association, the pleasure it awakens is lifted above the region of the purely sensuous into the realm of sentiment and imagination. To the man of religious spirit, to whom the visible universe is but the thought of God made manifest, the mountain gloom and the mountain glory speak first of the majesty and dominion of the Most High; while the smiling landscape, with its suggestion of happy homes and sheltered lives, brings tender thoughts of Him who notes even the sparrow's fall. Among the same scenes the man of science, if he has not sacrificed all the poetry in his nature in the search after material truth, will be lost in wonder that the tumultuous and conflicting forces which have lifted the mountains from the depths of the sea and crowned them with everlasting frost can yet in obedience to the same immutable laws subdue their might to offices of tender grace, can stoop to paint the lily and add perfume to the violet. And so to each the landscape has its mission; to the dilettante it brings a fresh sensation; to the man of feeling a noble emotion; to the man of religion, thoughts of devotion and gratitude; to the man of science, reverent wonder at the mystery and majesty of natural law.

The love of nature, at first an instinct, springs from a deeper source than the admiration of scenery, and it may, when disciplined and chastened, awaken a still more profound delight. The heaven which lies about us in our infancy may be at first only a dim consciousness of the universal life of nature, that life which throbs in every tree and shrub, the instinct in every clod "which comes to a soul in grass and flowers." It may be an inheritance from some far-off age, when man was nearer nature's heart than now, some memory of which haunts the mind of the growing boy and brings much of the unconscious joy of childhood. Most of us know too well how this "vision splendid" fades into the light of common day, but in some fortunate individual it is retained through manhood, is assimilated by the intellect and shaped by the imagination, it becomes "the vision and the faculty divine," the rare gift of the poets of the race. Everyone who retains it as a conscious possession is at heart a poet though he may lack the poet's gift of expression. The lover of natural scenery is wont to talk with eloquence of the pleasure he finds in the contemplation of landscape beauty, but the true lover of nature says little of his joy. He cannot measure or describe it, but when alone in the dense forest or in some sunny glade a mysterious sense of kinship with the silent forces working all about him, or a dim consciousness of a haunting presence, comes to him unbidden and ravishes his soul with suggestions of a more awful beauty some day to be revealed, and after such hours of communion with nature he can return to the noisy world refreshed in spirit and strengthened for the inevitable conflicts of life. It is only the chosen few whose early affection for nature has become a controlling passion who enjoy in full measure this vivifying power.

Since the love of natural scenery may be cultivated, why may not the child's love of nature be preserved? Like other fine instincts, it requires delicate handling. It too often vanishes early, crushed out by hard necessity or crowded out by the insincerities of an artificial life. Nature does her utmost to retain her hold upon the child, the flickering sunbeams tempt him, and every moving shadow has a charm even in his mother's arms. The flowers of the field are his chosen playfellows as he grows; trees whisper to him their secrets; all the myriad sights and sounds of earth and air woo him with their promises of happiness, and while the enchantment lasts the little traveler needs no other guide through the labyrinth of beauty about him than his eager curiosity. But as this begins to wane would it not be wise to direct his attention a little deeper to the infinite variety of leaf and flower, the endless diversity of form and structure in bird and insect, shell and crystal? As his mind expands why not take him into Nature's workshop to note some of the slow and mysterious processes of growth, the circling of the sap, the perfection of the flower and fruit? Surely some dim wonder at the miracle which binds all the forces of the universe to each tiny germ in fulfilling its destiny, will fill his awakening soul with as deep a delight as that which in his earlier years greeted his keen and eager senses. In this way the study of natural science could begin without its drudgery; the child's powers of observation would increase with their exercise, and the closer investigation of nature about him would keep his interest as fresh as it was when he first began to look and listen. And

so as his faculties one after the other are enlisted in the delightful work, he "hearing gains who had but ears, and sight who had but eyes." Is it too much to say that if the original love of nature, which is every child's inheritance, was thus fostered and cultivated, that he would never lose that instinctive delight in the natural world, but that this delight would be slowly transmuted into the possibilities of a deeper and richer joy as maturity was reached?

To speak of gardening as an occupation for children in connection with a subject of such profound philosophy would seem at first to detract from its dignity, but nature has been before us and has implanted in the child the impulse to dig, which awakens almost as early as the desire to catch the sunbeam, and which is quite as vital, perhaps, to its perfect development. It is the law of our growth, that the finer gifts or graces can only be gained on the condition that their acquirement is not the object sought. Thus the child who is set to work in a garden of his own as soon as he has the moderate amount of strength and skill to begin the work, will glean a much richer harvest than the flowers or fruit which will be one reward of his toil. We most love that for which we have made some sacrifice, and, therefore, the growing things upon which the child has spent his tiny strength will be far dearer to him than the finest blooms of his father's greenhouse, while his interest in their relatives of the field and forest will be retained and strengthened by many associations.

This diversion in the garden, therefore, will help to keep fresh and strong the original love of nature which is the child's inheritance, so that he will be more likely to carry it with him into the strenuous work of manhood. So much has been said already in these pages of the influence of gardening upon character, that there is no need of enlarging upon this branch of the subject, but it may be worthwhile to invite attention to one among the benefits to be derived from early familiarity with the garden and its cultivation, which is rarely, if ever, taken into account. The child will love his garden and be happy in it. When early manhood comes, and during the busier years when he must test his strength in the world of men, his garden, like other pleasures and interests of boyhood, will take a subordinate place, but in the evening of his days, after the stress of his life's work is over, there will inevitably return the longing to possess and transfigure some portion of the earth's surface. This desire comes naturally to almost every man. The idea of rest in declining years seems to be inseparably connected with rural scenes. The paradise to be regained is never within the walls of cities. This is true even of the city-born and city-bred, and it is doubly true of one reared in the country, and when such a one takes up with renewed interest the occupations of his boyhood he finds, to his surprise, that in addition to the flowers or fruit which reward his care there is an ideal harvest of associations which may make his closing years rich with a beauty and a pathos all their own. Every leaf and flower touches some mystic chord of memory and association, and as he rests under the shelter of his Vine and Fig-tree the glory of that far-off time gilds his downward pathway with a tender radiance and revives the spirit of that early day when,

—*meadow, grove and stream,*
The earth and every common sight,
To him did seem appareled in celestial light

OSSIAN COLE SIMONDS

Appreciation of Natural Beauty

(1898)

If people could realize and enjoy the beauty around them, they would be happier and better, and the earth would gradually improve in appearance. They would see with pleasure the brightening tints of the willows and dogwoods that come with the first warm days of March, the tinge of brown caused by thousands of blossoms which a little later show in the distance, the graceful shape of the elm, then the reds and yellows that mark the place of the maples, and the varying shades of green as every gain in warmth and sunlight pushes out the young leaves from the swelling buds. They would note that the colors of spring are almost as varied as those of autumn. The little velvety leaves of the white oak are worth going miles to see when in May they hang like half-open umbrellas from the ends of the branchlets, and range from yellowish-white through pink to the deepest purplish-red. At the same time, the large, yellow buds of the shag-bark hickory,

with their red bracts, are as showy as most flowers. There is also a wonderful wealth of beauty in our native thorn and crab-apple trees, with their spreading shapes, their varying shades of foliage, and their profusion of blossoms. Later still, other members of the rose family, the spiraeas, raspberries, blackberries, and the wild roses themselves, supply bloom and color. Although during the latter part of summer, and through the autumn months, our trees and shrubs do not produce flowers in abundance, there are nearly always some to be found until those of the witch-hazel, remaining as a yellow mist after the golden leaves have fallen, fill the November air with perfume. Before the blossoms of May are gone, the seeds of the elm and soft maple are already ripening, and from that time on the fruits of trees and shrubs add to the interest generally felt in the summer and autumn foliage. Not only do the flowers, leaves, and fruits please us with their thousand shapes and colors, their surfaces sometimes smooth and glossy, sometimes dull and soft, but the trees and shrubs

From *Second Report of the American Park and Outdoor Art Association* (Boston: Rockwell and Churchill, 1898), 75–80.

themselves, by the manner in which their foliage is massed, by their effect when seen close at hand or in the distance, when seen in sunshine or mist, in a still atmosphere or in a breeze, by daylight which brings out every detail, or silhouetted against the night sky, help to make up that wonderful variety and beauty which must surely be appreciated by all who expect to feel at home in the next world. There is time merely to allude to the humbler forms of vegetation, the grasses and herbaceous plants that cover the earth so attractively, to the clouds that should be admired by each of us as much as they were by the poet Shelley, and which should be given a place in every design, to the varying shapes of ground surface, to the far-reaching seas, and to the running brooks and placid lakes with their rocky or leafy margins.

Probably each of us could give illustrations showing how people fail to get the most out of life through inability to see such things as I have mentioned. Someone who attended our meeting last year, and who lived in Kentucky, where the tuliptree grows to perfection, had never before seen its blossoms. An enthusiastic Board of Park Commissioners commenced their operations by clearing away all the undergrowth, denuding the steep hillside as well as the valley. A glance at the adjoining land showed dozens of groups of magnificent specimens of the prairie rose. The commissioners acknowledged the beauty of this growth when it was pointed out to them, and also their own mistake in having destroyed similar bushes, and they were quite willing to let the steep bank become recovered with the wild grapes and roses, lindens and thorns, which were already sprouting from the surface after having

been cut away by the caretaker's scythe. This effort of Nature to clothe herself in an attractive garb had also been unnoticed till attention was called to it. The practice of cutting away the undergrowth on the part of those who start out to make improvements is one of the most common sins committed against outdoor art. Many have not learned that children, whether of men or trees, do as much as their parents to make the world attractive and fit to live in. The young growth of vegetation is not only beautiful with its large leaves and vigorous shoots, but it is a protection to the older trees by checking the drying winds and holding the natural mulching of leaves. A farmer in a district of Michigan, where there is plenty of land, had near the roadside perhaps an acre that was low and wet. It supported a rank, beautiful growth. For a background, there were many young, white pines—trees about twenty feet high, covered to the ground with dark bluish-green needles. A few native larches interspersed here and there lightened up the autumn picture with their old-gold leaves. Flanking the group on either side were most perfect specimens of red maples, while in front along the fence and almost hiding it were masses of Carolina roses with their shining red fruits and, brighter still, groups of winterberry bushes with their holly-like berries. These were mostly scarlet, so intense as to attract at once one's attention from the brow of the hill on either side, but there were also a few of the orange-colored variety. You can imagine my disappointment when, on looking for this place one spring, I found that all the trees and bushes had been cut down. Later in the season a fire destroyed every vestige of green that was left, and the area has remained a barren, blackened waste ever since. If the farmer who owned this bit of roadside beauty, and who could see it nearly every day, had derived half as much pleasure from it during the year as I did during the half dozen times I passed by it, he would have taken his winter exercise in some other way. Often a desire for physical exercise during the long months of winter is the only excuse I can think of for the mischief that is done, since, as in the case just given, no use is afterward made of the denuded land. Near a large Eastern city lived a well-to-do citizen who had, along the front of his land, a belt of native growth, including sumach, witch-hazel, redbud, dog-wood, viburnum, wild grape, and rose, virgin's bower, golden-rod, and aster. A landscape gardener who lived still farther from the business centre told me that it gave him the greatest pleasure to see this graceful, irregular, natural growth, and that he felt it a personal loss when he found one day that the owner had just had it all cut down. Strange as it may seem this owner applied to the landscape gardener for advice as to what shrubbery he should plant along the roadside. He was told by the latter that it would take at least ten years to produce an effect as good as that which had just been destroyed. A man in the suburb of another city built a house costing seven thousand dollars, and then decided he would spend twenty-five dollars on his grounds. A man will often spend several hundred dollars for a painting, and then be quite indifferent to the views from his windows.

Such cases and many more that might be given show a failure on the part of many to appreciate natural beauty; a failure to get that keen enjoyment that comes from seeing clearly and truly the things that an artist would like to paint. The ability to see in this way is not wholly born with one. The blindness, if I may call it such, is due as much to lack of proper surroundings and suitable training as to heredity. This is shown by the fact that many learn, after reaching maturity, to see new beauties in things with which they had been surrounded all their lives, but had never truly seen. They gradually learn to admire a landscape even in winter, when they had supposed all outdoors was dreary. We need more men like Mr. Strauch, who used to go about with his mirror to show the exquisite landscapes he had helped to create; more men like Mr. Stiles whose death during the past year seems like a personal loss to many of us, since he was one of the best of teachers; more men like Mr. Olmsted to help add to our enjoyment by making us sensitive to landscape; more men like Mr. Cleveland to tell us how to make our parks and cities; and we also need more women like Mrs. Van Rensselaer, Mrs. Robbins, and Mrs. Seavey to help with their criticisms and suggestions.

Professor McBride told us that a beautiful country made people patriotic. A man, he said, would love his country if it was attractive, and he gave examples to prove his statement. I believe that to love trees and shrubs, and open fields, birds and flowers, rivers, lakes, and skies makes a man unselfish. He wishes others to enjoy that which he values so highly. It makes him have at heart the true welfare of his country, the happiness and contentment of its citizens. He looks forward, perhaps for generations, to the time when some of the trees he has planted will reach maturity. He wishes the land to remain fertile and the climate suitable for the welfare of his friends—the trees, shrubs, and flowers. He does not like to see the forests disappear, the rivers dry up, and the vegetation suffer from drought.

If people could see and appreciate the beautiful things about them the world would grow better looking, because they would seek to have these things around their homes—to make them a part of their homes in fact. They would try to secure the broad lawns or meadows, the water view, the distant skies, and those landscapes which they might not have room for at their city homes, by establishing generous parks. They would gradually obliterate the scars which the railways have made with their cuts and fills by covering the bare spaces with verdure. They would reduce the amount of smoke that pollutes the air. They would make our roadsides one continual source of delight. Farmers would learn that bits of woodland are not the least profitable part of their farms. The hideous signs that now mar or obstruct many a charming vista would disappear.

People even in the United States would in time learn to take as much pride in the appearance of their country as the Englishman takes in his.

While we are often grieved by the destruction of trees, shrubs, and scenes that have gladdened our hearts, there is ground for encouragement in the fact that every year more parks are established, and every year more people seek the country to get its scenery, its pure air, its strength, and its vitality. Much good is being done by the camera, the quantities of well-illustrated books and newspapers, and especially by the study of art to which increasing numbers every year devote themselves. Let us hope that our Association may aid in this movement for better things, that it may lead people in their efforts to secure more beautiful homes and surroundings, that it may open our eyes until, by and by, we shall have a heaven on earth, and that it will teach men not to wait until they are ready to die before they begin to really live.

HORACE WILLIAM SHALER CLEVELAND

Influence of Parks on the Character of Children

(1898)

The following paper was read by Mr. C. M. Loring, of Minneapolis, who gave the following interesting incidents in Mr. Cleveland's Life:

Eighty-six years ago a child was born in the old town of Salem, Mass. This child was reared under the grand old trees of that city until his twentieth year, when he started out on a mission to make beautiful everything he touched. He was one of the very first of the "park gardeners," as he called himself, that we had in this country. He was associated with Copeland, one of the first writers on horticulture and floriculture. Some of his work began near his own home. He did work in Boston; he laid out the Roger Williams Park in Providence. He continued his work westward until he reached Minneapolis. He did a great deal of work in Chicago. He was the friend and associate of that greatest landscape architect this country has ever produced, Frederick Law Olmsted, and they are still very warm friends. A short time since I called upon him at Chicago, and I found him, in his eighty-sixth year, the same genial, pleasant, unselfish character that I had known for so many years, and I said to him, "The Park and Outdoor Art Association are to have a convention at Minneapolis; now I think you had better write a paper."—"Oh," said he, "I have been dead too long for that."—"No," I said, "they all remember you. Thousands and thousands of children will remember you long after you are gone."—"Well," said he, "at least your suggestion has given me something to think about." A short time ago I received a paper written in the trembling hand of age, and this is what he says:

Whatever new devices may have been contrived to increase the attractive interest of the parks of any city, the grand principle remains unchanged, that they must

From *Second Report of the American Park and Outdoor Art Association* (Boston: Rockwell and Churchill, 1898), 105–8.

be founded on a love of Nature, and their object is weakened or defeated by the introduction of artificial decorations which conflict with natural laws. Do not understand me as saying that I would exclude works of art in scenes where they are appropriate to the adjacent surroundings. On boulevards, for instance, which are lined with residences whose architectural elegance is enhanced by the presence of trees and shrubs, and flowers and grass, the introduction of statues and artistic fountains is appropriate, and it is equally so in those portions of the park which are expressly intended to afford entertainment to crowds of visitors. But the primary object of all parks is to give to the citizens, whose lives of necessity are passed in the din and throng of the streets, the occasional relief of the quiet seclusion of rural scenes from which artificial decoration is excluded. And this demand becomes the more onerous from the modern tendency towards city life, and the excitement attendant upon the pursuit of wealth.

It seems to me that few people fully realize the value of parks for children, and above all for the children of the poorer classes. The rich man may have his country seat, or his summer residence by the seashore or in the mountains, but think of the great mass of the laboring population whose children are growing up to fill the places of the present population, and many of whom may be the rich men and the rulers of the future. We claim it as the chief blessing of our country that its highest offices are open to all classes alike, but does not that fact carry with it a responsibility we have no right to shirk? It is a sufficient answer to my question to point to our free schools and the obligation of every

parent to send his children to them unless his means enable him to educate them by a more costly method. But it is needless to cite examples our own history furnishes to prove that the most important part of every man's education is acquired out of school, and the inequality of the advantages of the different classes in the opportunities afforded them is too obvious to need pointing out. Can anyone doubt the value of parks in the education of children who are born and bred in the crowded tenement-houses which are the (so called) homes of thousands of the inhabitants of every city? I do not, of course, presume to say that the evil influences to which they are exposed can be wholly counteracted by the contrast afforded by scenes of natural beauty, but long and careful observation has served to convince me that the effect upon the mind of a child is such as can hardly be imagined by anyone who has not carefully observed it. I was first led to reflect on the subject many years ago by observing a man who was leading a cow in the streets of New York. He had brought her by steamboat from some point on the North River and, as he told me, was taking her across the city to ship her on one of the Sound boats. She was a beast of rare blood and beauty, and the attention she excited led me to follow her. As she passed that classic locality known as Five Points, a shout was raised by the host of little gutter-snipes who swarmed the street and trooped after her with wonder and delight. A casual observer would probably only have laughed at the spectacle, but it seemed to me to have a deep significance. "Here," said I to myself, "are thousands of children whose lives are passed amid the scenes of squalor and vice. They have never seen anything more attractive, and the sight of a cow being led quietly through the streets is to them an amazing novelty." What would be their emotions if taken into the country and allowed to compare the beauties of nature with their daily surroundings? How few of us realize that every one of those wretched little rag-a-muffins is growing up either to be a blessing or a curse to the community. He may prove a benefactor to his race, or he may become a thief or a murderer.

Much depends upon the impressions he receives in the years of his childhood, and is it not a peremptory duty devolving upon us to let him see that life has something better to offer him than such misery as is his daily lot?

Need I say more? Is it not obvious that the parks of a city are as essential to its moral health and vigor as the vital organs of its inhabitants are to every individual?

LIBERTY HYDE BAILEY

The Outlook to Nature

(1911)

THE REALM OF THE COMMONPLACE

I sat at the window of a hotel chamber, musing at the panorama that comes and goes in a thousand cities. There were human beings pouring in and out, up and down, as if moved by some restless and relentless machinery. Most of them were silent and serious and went quickly on. Some sauntered, and returned again and again as if looking for something that they did not expect to find. Carriages went up and down in endless pageant. Trolley-cars rushed by, clanging and grinding as they headlonged into the side streets. Meretricious automobiles with gorgon-eyed drivers whirred into the crowds, scattering the street crossers. Men passed with banners and advertising placards. Women paraded with streaming headgear and tempestuous gowns. A resplendent trumpeter rolled by in a tallyho. A hundred other devices to at-

From *The Outlook to Nature* (New York: Macmillan, 1911), 1–49.

tract the eye and distract the ear came out and vanished; and yet no one stopped and no one seemed to care. Now and then a knot of men would form, as someone fell or as wagons collided; but the knots as quickly dissolved, and I knew that they were made up of the idle, who were amused for the moment and then floated on hoping for fresh entertainment. A hurdy-gurdy attracted only a bevy of scurrying children. A little girl with armful of newspapers moved in and out unnoticed.

Suddenly a dog leaped down a flight of steps and was followed by two little children laughing and screaming. The dog felt his freedom and the children were in pursuit. The crowd stopped; the stern-faced men with high hats stopped; the well-dressed women stopped. Even a cabby pulled up his horse as the children dashed on the pavement after the escaping dog. Back and forth the children ran. On the far side of the street the people halted and took their hands out of their pockets. The children caught the dog and bundled it lovingly into the house; the crowd applauded, and dispersed.

Every person seemed to be surprised that he had stopped. From my height I thought I could discern the reason for such curious phenomenon: in all the blare and blazonry of that tumultuous thoroughfare, this was the only episode of real spontaneous and exuberant human nature. All else was a kind of acting, and every person unconsciously recognized that it was so. I thought how rare must common naturalness be, and how much has it been driven from our lives!

THE SPONTANEOUS

If a person has given any serious thought to public questions, he has his own contribution to make as to the causes of present conditions and the means of bettering them; so I make mine: what is now much needed in the public temper is such a change of attitude as will make us to see and appreciate the commonplace and the spontaneous, and to have the desire to maintain and express our youthful enthusiasms. And it is my special part to try, so far as possible, to open the eyes and the heart to nature and the common-day condition. My point of view is, of course, that of the countryman, and no doubt it has the countryman's bias.

So great has been the extension of knowledge, and so many the physical appliances that multiply our capabilities, that we are verily burdened with riches. We are so eager to enter all the strange and ambitious avenues that we overlook the soil at our feet.

We live in an age of superlatives, I had almost said of super-superlatives, so much so that even the superlatives now begin to pall. The reach for something new has

become so much a part of our lives that we cease to recognize the fact, and accept novelty as a matter of course. If we shall fail to satisfy ourselves with the new, the strange, and the eccentric, perhaps we shall find ourselves returning to the old commonplace and the familiar, and perhaps we shall be able to extract new delights from them because of the flights we have taken. Perhaps in their turn the commonplaces will be again the superlatives, and we shall be content with the things that come naturally and in due order. Certain it is that every sensitive soul feels this longing for something that is elemental in the midst of the voluminous and intricate, something free and natural that shall lie close to the heart and really satisfy his best desires.

THE RETURN TO NATURE

It is not likely that we shall greatly simplify our outward physical and business affairs. Probably it is not desirable that we should do so, for we must maintain our executive efficiency. We have seen a marvelous development of affairs, expressed in the renovation of a hundred old occupations and the creation of a thousand new ones. Most of these occupations are clear gain to the world, and we may expect them to endure.

This rise of affairs has emphasized the contrasts of business and of home. Machinery and intricacy belong to affairs; but a plainer and director mental attitude should belong to our personal and private hours. The effective simplicity is not the lessening of physical conveniences and aids, but the absence of complex desires in eating and dress and entertainment and accessories, and in a native attitude toward life.

Perhaps our greatest specific need is a wholesome return to nature in our moments of leisure, —all the more important now that the moments of leisure are so few. This return to nature is by no means a cure-all for the ills of civilization, but it is one of the means of restoring the proper balance and proportion in our lives. It stands for the antithesis of acting and imitation, for a certain pause and repose, for a kind of spiritual temper, for the development of the inner life as contrasted with the externals.

IT IS NOT EMPTY RESIGNATION

Some persons have supposed that the "contentment" of the nature-lover implies unvexed indifference to the human affairs of the time, and that therefore it makes for a kind of serene and weak utopianism; but to my mind, the outlook to nature makes for just the reverse of all this. If nature is the norm, then the necessity for challenging and amending the abuses that accompany civilization becomes baldly apparent by very contrast. The repose of the nature-lover and the assiduous exertion of the man of affairs are complementary, not antithetical, states of mind.

The recourse to nature affords the very means of acquiring the incentive and energy for constructive work of a high order; it enforces the great truth that, in the affairs of men, continued progress is conditioned upon a generous discontent and diligent unrest.

The outlook to nature is the outlook to optimism, for nature is our governing condition. Men look upward and outward to nature.

THE OUT-OF-DOORS

By nature, I mean the natural out-of-doors, —the snow and the rain, the sky, the plants, the animals, the garden and the orchard, the running brooks, and every landscape that is easy of access and undefiled.

Every person desires these things in greater or lesser degree: this is indicated by the rapidly spreading suburban movement, by the vacationing in the country, and by the astonishing multiplication of books about nature. Yet there are comparatively very few persons who have any intimate contact with nature, or any concrete enjoyment from it, because they lack the information that enables them to understand the objects and phenomena.

THE YOUTHFUL LIFE

Our eager civilization prematurely makes us mentally old. It may be true that the span of man's life is increasing, but at twenty we have the knowledge and the perplexities that our grandfathers had only at forty. Our children may now be older when they are graduated from school, but the high-school course of today is more complex than was the college course of fifty years ago. All this has a tendency to lessen the years of free and joyous youth.

You have only to see the faces of boys and girls on your city streets, to discover how old the young have grown to be. In home and school our methods have been largely those of repression: this is why the natural buoyant outburst that I described for a city thoroughfare challenged such instant attention and surprise. We need to emphasize the youthful life; and a man or woman may have a youthful mind in an old body.

Therefore, I preach the things that we ourselves did not make; for we are all idolaters, —the things of our hands we worship. I preach the near-at-hand, however plain and ordinary, —the cloud and the sunshine; the green pastures; the bird on its nest and the nest on its bough; the rough bark of trees; the frost on bare thin twigs; the mouse skittering to its burrow; the insect seeking its crevice; the smell of the ground; the sweet wind; the silent stars; the leaf that clings to its twig or that falls when its work is done.

Wisdom flows from these as it can never flow from libraries and laboratories. "There be four things," say the Proverbs, "which are little upon the earth, but they are exceeding wise:

"The ants are a people not strong, yet they prepare their meat in the summer;

"The conies are but a feeble folk, yet make they their houses in the rocks;

"The locusts have no king, yet go they forth all of them by bands;

"The spider taketh hold with her hands, and is in kings' palaces."

WHAT LITERATURE CAN DO FOR US

Some of us do not enjoy nature because there is not enough sheer excitement in it. It has not enough dash and go for this electric age; and this is the very reason why we need the solace and resource of nature so much.

I am led to these remarks on looking over the lists of Christmas books, and finding myself challenged with the recurrence of the word "sensation." In the announcement of the forthcoming number of a magazine, I find twenty articles, of which at least nineteen are to be "tragic," "thrilling," "mystery-laden," or otherwise worth buying. The twentieth one I hope to read.

One would think that a piece of writing is valuable in proportion as it is racy, exciting, startling, astounding, striking, sensational. In these days of sensational sales, to have a book sell phenomenally well is almost a condemnation of it. An article or book that merely tells a plain story directly and well is too tame; so even when we write of nature we must pick out the unusual, then magnify and galvanize it. From this literature the reader goes out to nature and finds it slow and uninteresting; he must have a faster pace and a giddier whirl of events. He has little power to entertain himself; and, his eyes never having been trained to see what he looks at, he discovers nothing and the world is void. He may find temporary relief in some entertainment provided for him out of hand, as the so-called news of the newspapers or some witless frippery on the stage.

Yet, unless the poets and philosophers have misled us, the keenest delights that men have found have been the still small voices of the open fields.

THE NATURE WRITING

This is a real objection to much of the nature writing, —the fact that it is unrepresentative of nature. It exploits the exceptional, and therefore does not give the reader a truthful picture of common and average conditions. This has been true to some extent even of textbooks, —they choose so-called "typical" forms and structures, forgetting that typical examples exist only in books for purposes of definition.

The good nature writing, as I conceive of it, is that which portrays the commonplace so truthfully and so clearly that the reader forthwith goes out to see for himself. Some day we shall care less for the marvelous beasts of some far-off country than for the mice and squirrels and birds and woodchucks of our own fields and for the cattle on our hills.

If I were a naturalist, I should go forthwith to study the mice and then write of them for all children; for, of all untamed animals, what ones are known to a greater number of children? —and yet what do the children know except that they have been early taught by their elders to dislike or even to fear these entertaining animals? The embodiment of all agility, of all quick dispatch, of all neat habits and of comeliness, of unseen and devious ways, is the mouse. What other object was ever so swift and silent and graceful as it slides along the corners of your room as intangible as a shadow! What explorer was ever so successful as it peers into drawers and sniffs in cupboards!

In my boyhood the field mice were a constant source of entertainment and mystery. I found them scuddled in the corn shocks, burrowed in the dry grass, nesting in the corn-crib. I saw their faint narrow trails on new-fallen snow, leading into strange pygmy caverns.

THE NEWSPAPER

Just now I said something of the "news." It is important that we recur to this subject, since we are a people of news readers, and continuous reading strongly, though silently, influences our outlook to nature and affairs.

Much of what is called news is so unimportant that it is not worth the while of a person whose time is of value; but my chief objection to it, as to some of the nature writing, is that it is no way representative of human affairs, —if it were, I suppose it would not be new and therefore would not be news. It is made up to a large extent of exceptional and meaningless episodes and extravagancies.

Yesterday I saw hundreds of persons on cars and ferries eagerly reading the "news." I bought a paper resplendent with photography and colored ink. The first page had eight articles, seven of which were devoted to cases of divorce, common rascality and crime, and unimportant local accidents, all displayed as if it would advantage a man to read them. Only one article dealt with public affairs, and this was hidden underneath small headlines. The newspaper had no sense of proportion. All the detail of a divorce case was given with as much circumstantial minuteness as if it were of equal importance with a debate in Congress or the deliberations of the international peace conference.

As I was about to write these sentences, I chanced to pick up the following editorial paragraph from a country newspaper (The Seneca Falls, N. Y., *Reveille*):

The sound and wholesome qualities which make for all that is most prized in life are to be found in the great masses of the people, and are scarcely touched by the currents of the time which make for evil, and with which the news of the day is necessarily so largely concerned. It is not the doings or the ways of the great bulk of the people—those who quietly earn a modest living by ordinary industry—that furnish much material either for news or for comment. We take all that for granted, and when we think of the tendencies of the time, we almost forget its existence. When a touch of nature happens to bring into unaccustomed relief the existence of the homely but sturdy and sterling virtues of the great American people, their right-mindedness and true-heartedness, it is well to draw from the event the lesson that manhood and merit are after all the things which create the very best character for our country and government.

REAL PROGRESS MOVES QUIETLY

We gather from this extract the opinion that what we call the "slow" and "dull" may, after all, be the saving strength of a people. In the hamlets and villages and small country cities, great problems are working themselves out just as effectively as in the mighty cities; and although slowly, or even because slowly, they may be working out more fundamentally than elsewhere. The great mass of mankind is unrecorded and practically unknown. A few of us are actors, and we pass with some noise and flourish across the stage; but the sources of events are behind and beyond. I have heard the saying attributed to a statesman that if the discussions either at the country four-corners or in the President's Cabinet were to cease, it were better to do away with the Cabinet. Public opinion does not seem to originate to any extent with the leaders: the leaders are more likely to catch and voice the crystallizing sentiments of the commonplace, originating slowly and perhaps unconsciously with those who work first-handed with the forces that make for prosperity.

It is too bad that all this may not be reflected in our common literature.

THE FARM IS FUNDAMENTAL

We might go even farther than the hamlet or the town, —to the family unit on the remotest farm. This unit is considered by most of the other members of the race to be the commonplace of the commonplace; yet, along with the farming, human problems are being worked out. There boys and girls are being reared and even trained, who some day may come to your cities and distance your own sons and daughters; for it is a discouraging fact that, with all we are doing for schooling, merit and efficiency do not seem to increase in proportion, and those whom we are in the habit of calling uneducated may take the highest prizes that the world has to give.

The farm, in its turn, is being exploited in our current literature; and, significantly enough, much of this literature is of the sensational order. Of all things to be sensationalized, the farm should be the last. The farm need not be prosaic nor devoid of good intellectual interest; but its very spirit is that of constancy.

We should stimulate the ideals in every occupation; but the ideal should follow closely the facts and the spirit of the real. We need to idealize the commonplace, for then we show its possibilities. When we develop the ideals in farming, we shall add a great resource to our people.

NATURE PICTURES IN LITERARY FORM

We need a new literature of nature and the open country, a literature that shall not be lifelessly descriptive. We need short, sharp, quick, direct word-pictures that shall place the object before us as vividly as the painter would outline some strong simple figure with a few bold strokes of his brush; and it is not essential to the truth of the picture that a rhetorical climax be added. It may not be necessary even to make a "point," but only to bring the picture before the mind.

Every object and every common labor awaken some response beyond themselves, and this response can be set to words. The man employed at useful and spontaneous work is a poetic figure, full of prophecy and of hope. The cow in the field, the tree against the sky, the lands newly plowed, the crows flapping home at night, the man at his work, the woman at her work, the child at its play—these all are worth the stroke of the artist.

I saw a man walking across the fields, with spade on his shoulder and dog at his side; I saw his firm long stride; I saw his left arm swing; I saw the weeds fall beneath his feet; I saw the broad straight path that he left in the grass. There were brown fields and woods in the first tint of autumn. I saw birds; and in the distance was the rim of the sky. And beyond him, I saw the open ditch to which he was returning.

THE GREAT WRITERS

With the nature writers I like to include some of the authors who do not write specific natural history topics. If they write from the out-of-doors, with a keen love of it and a knowledge of what it comprises, adding to it touches of good human nature, then they lead men to the open as effectively as those to whom we customarily apply the term "nature writer." The landscape is as important as any object that it contains, and the human sentiment is more important than either.

These writers invariably write the commonplace, and touch it into life and meaning. One of the greatest of these writers, to my thinking, is Stevenson, —simple, direct, youthful, tender, and heartsome. His life was with nature; his work touches the elemental.

O Stevenson! On far Samoa's tropic shore
You moored your slender bark,
And there in calm secludedness did live
To write the spirit of your gentle soul
And over all the world to pour
The fragrance from the tropic of your heart.

And thence you passed beyond, —
Passed not with the proud acclaim
Of pageant and tempestuous bells
That drown themselves in blank
*   forgetfulness—*
But fell away as falls the wind at eventide;
And all the trees on all the isles and shores
Bowed their heads in solitude.

NATURE POETRY

I like to think that some of our poetry is also leading us nature-ward in a very practical way, since it is becoming more personal and definite, and brings us into closer touch with specific objects and demands greater knowledge of them. It has been the progress of our attitude toward nature to add the concrete to the abstract; and this may be expected to proceed so far that every object of the environment and every detail of our lives will be touched with inspiration. If I cannot catch a note of inspiration from the plainest thing that I touch, then to that extent my life is empty and devoid of outlook.

The great voices appealed to the early Greeks, —the thunder, the roaring wind, the roll of the waves, the noise of war; but we do not know that the shape of the leaf, and the call of the young bird, and the soft gray rain appealed much to them. The Greek lyrics are mostly personal or personifying, and lack any intimate touch with the phases of natural phenomena. As men have come more and more to know the near-at-hand and the real in nature, this knowledge has been interpreted in the poetry; for poetry always reflects the spirit of the time. All English poetry illustrates this general tendency; but what we are in the habit of calling "nature poetry" is of comparatively recent growth. It is to be hoped that we shall never have less nature poetry that expresses the larger moods; but we must have more that is specific as to natural history facts, and which will still be poetry.

The individual seems sometimes to recapitulate the development of the race: as each of us grows old and conventionalities lose their meaning and the small voices make a stronger appeal, we are conscious that we have had Wordsworth's experience:

In youth from rock to rock I went,
From hill to hill in discontent,
Of pleasure high and turbulent,
Most pleased when most uneasy;
But now my own delights I make, —
My thirst from every rill can slake,
And gladly Nature's love partake
Of thee, sweet Daisy!

INDUSTRY IS POETIC

It is often said that as this is a practical age, with industrialism extending everywhere, therefore poetry must die away. Nothing could be farther from the truth.

It is true that industrialism is developing at great pace; this, in fact, is the glory of our time, for civilization has entered on a new epoch. Men's minds are concerned with things that never concerned them before; yet, the resources of the old earth have merely been touched here and there, and the wealth of mankind will increase. But all this does not mean that sentiment is to be crushed or that the horizon of imagination is to be contracted, but rather the reverse. It is only by the exercise of vast imagination that the great conquests of our time are being won. The flights of science and of truth are, after all, the flights of fancy.

WE NEED NEW STANDARDS

We need the poetry of the new kind. Perhaps the day of the formal "sustained" poem has passed, —with its ambitious disquisitions, long periods, heavy rhetoric, labored metaphors. It is a question, also, whether even the sonnet, although highly artistic, is free and strong enough to express the nature-feeling of our time; for this feeling seems to be more and more impatient of historical forms. The new nature poetry must be crystal clear, for we have no time for riddles, even though they are set in meter and rhyme. It must be definite, and it must apply.

The best nature poetry will be hopeful, joyous, and modern. At least some of it will deal with objects, phenomena, and emotions that are common to common men that it may become a part of men's lives. Perhaps this more vital song will relieve poetry writing of much that is too theoretical and fine-spun; and I hope that it may also divert the current from the petty lovelorn type of verse-making which exploits personal love affairs that ought to be too private and sacred, as they are also too small, for publication.

This poetry, whether its flight is small or great, must be born of experience, and must be intrinsic; it must be the expression of a full heart, not the sentiment of a looker-on. The nature poem of wide reach must be the poem of the man who is free. Such poetry must spring from the open air; perhaps it must be set to words there, —at least outside the city. The city will have its great poems, but they will rise out of the city as Venus rose out of the sea.

It seems to me that we have really very little genuine nature poetry (a subject to which I shall refer again in my fourth lecture). Our poets, in spirit or in fact, now write largely from the city and the study outward, and their work is bookish. The product is too often the "cultured" poetry of the literary cult, under the influence of tradition. It continues to be burdened with useless metaphor, and it follows conventional forms of verse and line, as if verse and line were more than essence. Literary criticism still looks backward rather than forward, and much of its criterion is not applicable to present-day conditions. We must face toward the future. Walt Whitman—poet of the commonplace—has most completely freed himself from the bondage of literary form; and he is only an earnest of what shall come.

It is doubtful whether the great nature poet will be taught in the formal curricula of the schools. His spirit and his method will be as unconfined as the farm lands, the inaccessible mountains, the great plains, or the open sea.

The old-time short nature poem was wont only to point a moral, —usually dubious and far-fetched and factitious, —having little vitality of its own. It really was not a nature poem, for the real nature poem is its own moral. The poems and stories of the Old Testament are always interesting because they have something to say, they are direct, not heavy with adjectives or with rhetoric, and they are moral because they tell the truth.

PERSONS STILL LIKE POETRY

I am constantly surprised at the poems that busy and practical men know; and also at the poetry that many busy men can write. There is reason to believe that there were never so many poets in the world as now. Poetry-making is not an occupation, but the incidental spark that strikes off from useful labor; it is the result of full and serious lives. The roll of machinery is rhythm and rhyme; the blowing of the wind is music.

It has been my good fortune to have had many years' experience in the teaching of farm boys. They are interesting boys, — strong, virile, courageous. They have had the tremendous advantage of having been let alone, and of having developed naturally. They hold their youth. It is my habit to call these agricultural students together frequently, and, amongst other exercises, to read them poetry. Usually at first they are surprised; they had not thought of it before; or they thought poetry is for girls:

but they come again. They may hide it, but these farm boys are as full of sentiment as an egg of meat. There was one fellow who had to support himself and help members of his family. He was a good student, but the lines of his life had been hard. Whenever he called at my office it was to ask advice about money affairs or to tell me of difficulties that he feared he could not overcome. Apparently there was no sentiment in his life, and no room for it. One evening I read to the students Matthew Arnold's "Buried Life." The next day, Jenkins came to my office, entered hesitatingly as if requesting something that he might not have, and asked whether I would loan him the poem till he could learn it, for he could not afford to buy.

If sentiment is necessarily eliminated from business transactions, it is all the more important that it be added to the recreation and the leisure. The world never needed poetry so much as now. This thought is forcibly expressed in Charles Eliot Norton's advice, that has now been so effectively used by the press: "Whatever your occupation may be, and however crowded your hours with affairs, do not fail to secure at least a few minutes every day for refreshment of your inner life with a bit of poetry."

THE RESOURCE OF THE SILENCES

We need now and then to take ourselves away from men and the crowd and conventionalities, and go into the silence, for the silence is the greatest of teachers. Walt Whitman expresses this well:

When I heard the learn'd astronomer,
When the proofs, the figures, were ranged
in columns before me,

When I was shown the charts and
*   diagrams,*
to add, divide, and measure them,
When I sitting heard the astronomer where
he lectured with much applause in the
*   lecture-room,*
How soon unaccountable I became tired
*   and sick,*
Till rising and gliding out I wander'd
off by myself,
In the mystical moist night-air, and
from time to time
Look'd up in perfect silence at the stars.

THE WAYS OF APPROACH TO NATURE

It will be gleaned from what has been said that we are to consider literature, including poetry, to be one of the means of the enjoyment of nature. It is fundamentally important, however, that we regard literature only as a means: it is not nature.

One can never be fully appreciative of this natural world unless he has technical knowledge of some special part of it. One assuredly cannot be zoölogist, geologist, botanist, and meteorologist; but if he has intimate personal knowledge of one limited part, he has the key to the whole. The person must have pursued some branch of natural history for a time with serious purpose, —the purpose to discover and to know the subject-matter for himself. This gives him point of view; tells him what to look for; enables him to look beneath the surface; trains his judgment as to causes and effects; guides him in distinguishing the essential; saves him from error.

But before one takes up any serious bit of study for himself, he must have the wish to take it up. In every person there is a latent desire to know something of the enclosing world, but it is usually ironed out in the laundering processes of the schools and the misdirections of the home. In some persons this native desire is so strong that nothing extinguishes it: these persons become professional investigators and widen the boundaries of knowledge. Most of us, however, must give our main thought to other matters, and let the outlook to nature be chiefly a well-guided affection.

THE NATURE COMPANION

The best possible introduction to nature is that afforded by a sympathetic person who knows some aspect of nature well. You imbibe your friend's enthusiasm at the same time that you learn birds, or plants, or fishes, or the sculpturing of the fields. By enthusiasm I mean never exclamation, but that quiet and persistent zeal that follows a subject to the end for the love of it, even though it take a month. This person need not be a professed "scientist," unless he is also a good teacher and knows what is most important in the subject and most relevant to you. The earlier the child has such a guide—if arrived at the age of reason—the more vital and lasting the effect: even one or two excursions afield may change the point of view and open the way for new experiences, although neither the guide nor the child may be aware of it at the time. The ideal guide was "Gramp," as James Buckham knew him (Country Life in America):

What a man to fish and camp,
What a hand to hunt and tramp
Up and down the woods, was Gramp!

How he led me, high and low,
Plunging through the brush and snow!
Boy-like, how I loved to go!

Oh, the sweet days that we spent
In the forest's pure content!
Oh, the long, still miles we went!

Keen-eyed Gramp! How well he knew
Where the biggest berries grew,
Where the witch-like woodcock flew!

Learned was he in all the lore
Of the wood-wise men of yore—
Subtle knowledge, taught no more.

Ah, a happy boy was I,
Loving God's free woods and sky,
With dear Gramp to teach me why!

THE WEATHER

That which is first worth knowing is that which is nearest at hand. The nearest at hand, in the natural surroundings, is the weather. Every day of our lives, on land or sea, whether we will or no, the air and the clouds and the sky environ us. So variable is this environment, from morning till evening and from evening till morning and from season to season, that we are always conscious of it. It is to the changes in this environment that we apply the folk-word "weather,"—weather, that is akin to wind.

No man is efficient who is at cross-purposes with the main currents of his life; no man is content and happy who is out of sympathy with the environment in which he is born to live: so the habit of grumbling at the weather is the most senseless and futile of all expenditures of human effort. Day by day we complain and fret at the weather, and when we are done with it we have—the weather. The same amount of energy put into wholesome work would have set civilization far in advance of its present state. Weather is not a human institution, and therefore it cannot be "bad." I have seen bad men, have read bad books, have made bad lectures, have lived two years about Boston, —but I have never seen bad weather!

"Bad weather" is mainly the fear of spoiling one's clothes. Fancy clothing is one of the greatest obstacles to a knowledge of nature: in this regard, the farm boy has an immense advantage. It is a misfortune not to have gone barefoot in one's youth. A man cannot be a naturalist in patent-leather shoes. The perfecting of the manufacture of elaborate and fragile fabrics correlates well with our growing habit of living indoors. Our clothing is made chiefly for fair weather; when it becomes worn we use it for stormy weather, although it may be in no respect stormy weather clothing. I am always interested, when abroad with persons, in noting the various mental attitudes toward wind; and it is apparent that most of the displeasure from the wind arises from fear of disarranging the coiffure or from the difficulty of controlling a garment.

If our clothes are not made for the weather, then we have failed to adapt ourselves to our conditions, and we are in worse state than the beasts of the field. Much of our clothing serves neither art nor utility. Nothing can be more prohibitive of an interest in nature than a millinery "hat," even though it be distinguished for its floriculture, landscape gardening, and natural history.

Our estimate of weather is perhaps the best criterion of our outlook on nature and the world. The first fault that I would correct in mankind is that of finding fault with the weather. We should put the child right toward the world in which he is to live. What would you think of the mariner who goes to sea only in fair weather? What have not the weather and the climate done for the steadiness and virility of the people of New England? And is this influence working as strongly today as in the times when we had learned less how to escape the weather? We must believe in all good physical comfort, —it contributes to the amount of work that we can accomplish; but we have forgotten that it is possible to bear an open storm with equanimity and comfort. The person who has never been caught in rain and enjoyed it has missed a privilege and a blessing.

Give us the rain and the hail and the snow, the mist, the crashing thunder, and the cold biting wind! Let us be men enough to face it, and poets enough to enjoy it. In "bad" weather is the time to go abroad in field and wood. You are fellow then with bird and stream and tree; and you are escaped from the crowd that is forever crying and clanging at your heels.

THE COMMON NATURAL HISTORY

The first consideration of special study should be the inhabitants of your yard and garden: they are yours; or if they are not yours, you are not living a right life. Do you wish to study botany? There are weeds in your dooryard or trees on your lawn. You say that they are not interesting: that is not their fault.

We have made the mistake all along of studying only special cases. We seem to have made up our minds that certain features are interesting and that all other features are not. It is no mere accident that many persons like plants and animals but dislike botany and zoology. It is more important to study plants than special subjects as exemplified in plants. Why does the weed grow just there? Answer this, and you have put yourself in pertinent relation with the world out-of-doors.

If one is a farmer, he has the basis for his natural history in his own possessions, —animals domestic and wild, plants domestic and wild, free soil, pastures and lowlands and woodlands, crops growing and ripening, the daily expression of the moving pageant of nature. Zoölogical garden and botanical garden are here at his hand and lying under his title-deed, to have and to hold as he will. No other man has such opportunity.

I would also call the attention of the townsman to his opportunity. If the range of nature is not his, he still has the wind and rain, the street trees, the grass of lawns, the weed in its crevice, the town-loving birds, the insects, and I hope that he has his garden. Even the city has its touch of natural history—for all things in the end are natural, and we recognize them if we have had the training of a wholesome outlook to the commonplace. Timrod's sonnet on the factory smoke is a nature-note:

I scarcely grieve, O Nature! at the lot
That pent my life within a city's bounds,
And shut me from thy sweetest sights and
* sounds.*
Perhaps I had not learned, if some lone cot
Had nursed a dreamy childhood, what the
* mart*
Taught me amid its turmoil; so my youth
Had missed full many a stern but whole-
* some truth.*
Here, too, O Nature! in this haunt of Art,
Thy power is on me, and I own thy thrall.
There is no unimpressive spot on earth!
The beauty of the stars is over all,
And Day and Darkness visit every hearth.
Clouds do not scorn us: yonder factory's
* smoke*
Looked like a golden mist when morning
* broke.*

THE GROUND

I would preach the surface of the earth, because we walk on it.

When a youth, I was told that it was impossible for me to study geology to any purpose, because there were no outcroppings of rocks in my region. So I grew up in ignorance of the fact that every little part of the earth's surface has a history, that there are reasons for sandbanks and for bogs as well as for stratified rocks. This is but another illustration of the old book-slavery, whereby we are confined to certain formal problems, whether or not these problems have any relation to our conditions. I well remember what a great surprise it was to learn that the sculpturing of the fields can be understood, and that the reasons for every bank and swamp and knoll and mud-hole can be worked out.

There was a field back of the barn that contained hundreds of narrow knolls, averaging three to four feet high. At one side of every hummock was a narrow deep pocket that until midsummer was filled with water. The field was so rough that it could not be plowed, and so it was continuously used as a pasture. It was an Elysian field for a boy. Every pool was a world of life, with strange creatures and mysterious depths, and every knoll was a point of vantage. Near one edge of the field ran a rivulet, and beyond the rivulet were great woods. What was beyond the woods, I could only surmise. I recall how year by year I wondered at this field, until it became a sort of perpetual and compelling mystery, and somehow it came to be woven as a natural part of the fabric of my life. To this day I try once each year to visit this dear old field, even though it is long since leveled. All the sweep of my childhood comes back to me unbidden. The field is still a pasture, and generations of cows have passed on since then. Yet, as much as this field meant to me, I do not remember to have had any distinct feeling that there was any cause for the pools and knolls. My father cut the field from the forest, yet I do not remember that I ever asked him why this field was so; and I never heard any person express any curiosity about it. We all seemed to have accepted it, just as we accept the air. As I think of it now, this field must have been the path of a tornado that turned over the trees; and long before the settlers came, the prostrate trunks had decayed and a second forest had grown. Would that I could have known that simple explanation! One sentence would have given me the clew. How the mystery of the ancient tornado and the rise of another forest would have conjured a new world of marvel and discovery!

When I had written this sketch of my pasture field, I called in a little school girl and read it to her. I wanted to hear her estimate of it.

"That's a nice story," she said; "but I don't want to study such things in school."

"And why not?" I asked.

"Because they are hard and dry," she said.

Poor child! She was thinking of her books and I remembered that I also had written books!

THE HEAVENS

I would preach the sky; for the sky compels one to look upward.

When in the open country we are impressed most with the sense of room and with the sky. City persons have no sky, but only fragments of a leaky roof; for the city is one structure and needs only a cover to make it a single building. They have no free horizon line, no including circle laid on the earth, no welkin. There are no clouds, —only an undefined something that portends rain or hides the sun.

One must have free vision if he is to know the sky. He must see the clouds sweep across the firmament, changing and dissolving as they go. He must look deep into the zenith, beyond the highest cirrus. We have almost lost the habit of looking up:

Look unto the heavens, and see;
And behold the skies, which are higher than
   thou.
Lie on your back in some quiet spot, and
   let yourself go out into the endless
   distances.

Or, if we note the sky, it is chiefly a midday or sunset recognition. Our literature is rich in sunsets, but relatively poor in sunrises. Civilization has led us away from the morning, and at the same time it has led us away from youthfulness. We have telescoped the day far into the night, and morning is becoming obsolete. I know that this cannot be helped; but it can be mentioned.

I have asked person after person whether he ever saw the sun rise. The large number have said no; and most of those who had seen the sun rise had seen it against their will and remembered it with a sense of weariness. Here, again, our farm boy has the advantage: he leads something like a natural life. I doubt whether a man can be a poet if he has not known the sunrise.

The sky is the one part of the environment that is beyond our reach. We cannot change it; we cannot despoil it; we cannot paint signs on it. The sky is forever new and young; the seasons come out of it; the winds blow out of it; the weather is born from it:

Hast thou entered the treasuries of the
    snow,
Or hast thou seen the treasuries of the hail?

THE HIGH PLACES

I preach the mountains, and everything that is taller than a man.

Yet it is to be feared that many persons see too many mountains and too many great landscapes, and that the "seeing" of nature becomes a business as redundant and wearisome as other affairs. One who lives on the mountains does not know how high they are. Let us have one inspiration that lifts us clear of ourselves: this is better than to see so many mountains that we remember only their names.

The best objects that you can see are those in your own realm; but your own realm becomes larger and means more for the sight of something beyond.

It is worthwhile to cherish the few objects and phenomena that have impressed us greatly, and it is well to recount them often, until they become part of us. One such phenomenon is idealized in my own memory. It was the sight of sunrise on Mt. Shasta, seen from the southeastern side from a point that was then untouched by travelers. From this point only the main dome of the mountain is seen. I had left the railway train at Upton's and had ridden on a flat-car over a lumber railroad some eighteen miles to the southeast. From this destination, I drove far into the great forest, over volcano dust that floated through the woods like smoke as it was stirred up by our horses and wagon-wheels. I was a guest for the night in one of those luxurious lodges which true nature-lovers, wishing wholly to escape the affairs of cities, build in remote and inaccessible places. The lodge stood on a low promontory, around three sides of which a deep swift mountain stream ran in wild tumult. Giant shafts of trees, such shafts as one sees only in the stupendous forests of the far West, shot straight into the sky from the very cornices of the house. It is always a marvel to the easterner how shafts of such extraordinary height could have been nourished by the very thin and narrow crowns that they bear. One always wonders, also, at the great distance the sap-water must carry its freight of mineral from root to leaf and its heavier freight from leaf to root.

We were up before the dawn. We made a pot of coffee, and the horses were ready, —fine mounts, accustomed to woods trails and hard slopes. It was hardly light enough to enable us to pick our way. We were as two pygmies, so titanic was the forest. The trails led us up and up, under pitchy boughs becoming fragrant, over needle-strewn floors still heavy with darkness, disclosing glimpses now and then of gray light showing eastward between the boles. Suddenly the forest stopped, and we found ourselves on the crest of a great ridge: and sheer before us stood the great cone of Shasta, cold and gray and silent, floating on a sea of darkness from which even the highest tree crowns did not emerge. Scarcely had we spoken in the course of our ascent, and now words would be sacrilege. Almost automatically we dismounted, letting the reins fall over the horses' necks, and removed our hats. The horses stood, and dropped their heads. Uncovered, we sat ourselves on the dry leaves and waited.

It was the morning of the creation. Out of the pure stuff of nebulae the cone had just been shaped and flung adrift until a world should be created on which it might rest. The gray light grew into white. Wrinkles and features grew into the mountain. Gradually a ruddy light appeared in the east. Then a flash of red shot out of the horizon, struck on a point of the summit, and caught from crag to crag and snow to snow until the great mass was streaked and splashed with fire. Slowly the darkness settled away from its base; a tree emerged; a bird chirped; and the morning was born!

Now a great nether world began to rise up out of Chaos. Far hills rose first through rolling billows of mist. Then came wide forests of conifer. As the panorama arose, the mountain changed from red to gold. The stars had faded out and left the great mass to itself on the bosom of the rising world, —the mountain fully created now and stablished. Spriggy bushes and little leaves—little green-brown leaves and tender tufts of herbs—trembled out of the woods. The illimitable circle of the world stretched away and away, its edges still hung in the stuff from which it had just been fashioned. Then the forest awoke with calls of birds and the penetrating light, and the creation was complete.

THE CONCLUSION OF THE WHOLE MATTER

I have now reviewed some of the elements of the sympathetic attitude toward nature, and have tried to show how this outlook means greater efficiency, hopefulness, and repose.

I have no mind to be iconoclast, to try to tear down what has been built, or to advise any man to change his occupation or his walk in life. That would be impossible to accomplish, even were it desirable to advise. But even in the midst of all our eagerness and involvedness, it is still possible to open the mind toward nature, and it will sweeten and strengthen our lives. Nature is our environment, and we cannot escape it if we would. The problem of our life is not yonder: it is here.

The seeking of truth in fresh fields and for the love of it is akin to the enthusiasm of youth. Men keep young by knowing nature. They also keep close to the essentials. One of the New Sayings of Jesus is this: "Raise the stone, and there thou shalt find me; cleave the wood, and there am I."

SELDEN LINCOLN WHITCOMB

The Value of Natural Areas to Literature and Art

(1926)

Some few early American poets wrote of the skylark and the nightingale. They followed the easy path of inherited literary tradition, and did not seem to realize the wealth of new natural material at their very doors. Other poets, however, very soon discovered the poetic values of the whippoorwill, the passenger pigeon, and the ruby-throated humming-bird. Freneau, poet of the American Revolution, has a well known poem on the honeysuckle. A little later Bryant's poem on the yellow violet almost marks an epoch in the poetic treatment of American flowers. Alexander Wilson may be considered, in a sense, as the last of the pioneers among the American writers on American nature. In his poetry, as well as in his letters and his *American Ornithology*, he has left wonderful records of his personal observations of birds, plants, and landscapes over a very large section of the region east of the Mississippi River.*

From the days of Wilson to the present time, there has been, on the part of American writers, an alert and continuous interest in the varied aspects of American nature. Perhaps no literature is richer than ours in the literary presentation of local nature. The "nature essay" is a very characteristic and practically indigenous literary type in this country. As American territory expanded, our writers accompanied or soon followed the pioneers of the new regions. Our literature now offers us entire volumes of nature lore from the region *Where Rolls the Oregon* (Dallas Lore Sharp) to that of *A Florida Sketch-Book* (Bradford Torrey), and from *The Maine Woods* (Thoreau) to *The Land of Little Rain* (Mary Austin). Dr. Neil E. Stevens has an interesting article in *The Scientific Monthly* for February, 1921, on "The Botany of the New England Poets." There is abundance of material for analogous articles—on the botany or the zoology of writers—for every section, yes, for every state of the Union.

*For a fairly extended treatment of "Nature in Early American Literature," see the writer's article in *The Sewanee Review,* 1894.

From *Naturalist's Guide to the Americas,* edited by Victor E. Shelford (Baltimore: Williams and Wilkins, 1926), 7–8.

The student of American literature welcomes any reasonable movement to preserve, in as nearly the original state as possible, as many as possible of the regions which have been observed, loved, and described by our authors. The present writer has visited the site of Thoreau's famous cabin at Walden Pond, and has followed the path of Thoreau, with *Cape Cod* in his hand, for miles and miles along the Cape. (Incidentally, as the writer lay on high land tracing the route from the book, an unsuspicious fox came trotting to within two yards or so of him.) Mankato, Minnesota, is a typical and beautiful prairie town and it was the western limit of Thoreau's only western trip. Mankato has a wonderful system of natural parks. The student of literature hopes that a section of prairie or woodland, known to have been visited by Thoreau, may yet be located and preserved.

Among other places of somewhat similar interest in American literary biography, in the Middle West, these may be suggested: haunts in Wisconsin, which inspired James Gates Percival (poet as well as geologist); places in or near Fort Gibson, Oklahoma, which stimulated the pen of Washington Irving; certain environs of Osage and Clear Lake, Iowa, which were of notable significance in the development of Hamlin Garland, etc.

Here and there in the prairie country, one finds small areas of open ground still in their natural state. This is sometimes the case with the railroad right-of-way. Here may be found plants, and, to a lesser extent, animals which seem to have passed from the neighboring regions. Such areas are especially welcome to the lover of literature. If their natural phenomena are not yet known to our literature proper, let us not destroy the opportunity for the writ-

Upper Buttermilk Falls, Ithaca, N.Y. (Photograph by Carol Betsch.)

ers of the future. The natural forest edge also—let us preserve as many sections of it as possible. Here, where the prairie meets the woods, were the original haunts of many of our familiar herbs and shrubs and birds—spring migrants: white-throated sparrow, hermit thrush, etc.; summer residents: thrasher, catbird, Bell's vireo, etc.; winter visitants: juncoes, tree sparrows, the great northern shrike, etc.

We have already destroyed much which cannot be replaced. No sane student of literature will deny the national importance of the lumber industry or of the greatest possible extension of grain producing land. But the same student is anxious to prove to himself and to the world that America is not entirely commercial in spirit. He hopes for and believes in the American artist—painters, musicians, and writers—of the near and of the distant future. For these artists and for those thousands if not millions of citizens whose lives are to be enriched by these works of pen and brush, we should preserve, all over the country, carefully selected, representative areas, as nearly in the primitive condition as is now possible.

STANLEY WHITE

The Value of Natural Preserves
to the Landscape Architect

(1926)

Inasmuch as one of the chief interests of landscape architecture is the preservation of beautiful landscapes, nothing can be more evident than the importance to the profession and to those deriving benefits from its works of this movement to save various natural regions from possible injury or destruction. Landscape architects have always maintained a keen interest in such movements: as private practitioners in urging the development of organizations interested in natural preserves, and through their national professional society in formally supporting the movements in defence of our great national reservations against improper exploitation.

Frederick Law Olmsted, in speaking of our national parks, says:

The National Parks are set apart primarily in order to preserve to the people for all time the opportunity of a peculiar kind of enjoyment and recreation, not measurable in economic terms and to be obtained only from the remarkable scenery which they contain—scenery of these primeval types which are in most parts of the world rapidly vanishing for all eternity before the increased thoroughness of the economic use of land. In the National Parks direct economic returns, if any, are wholly secondary to the one dominant purpose of preserving essential esthetic qualities of their scenery unimpaired as a heritage to the infinite numbers of the generations to come.

One of the most notable achievements in this direction was the creation of the Boston Park system, with its rich natural and semi-natural preserves largely through the original idea and subsequently the active work of Mr. Charles Eliot, Landscape Architect, concerning which there is an excellent account in his biography.* Many other instances could be cited, as

From *Naturalist's Guide to the Americas,* edited by Victor E. Shelford (Baltimore: Williams and Wilkins, 1926), 8–9.

*Charles Eliot, Landscape Architect, by C. W. Eliot.

the design of public areas is a considerable part of the regular work of the profession.

President Emeritus Charles W. Eliot of Harvard University, at the meeting of the American Society of Landscape Architects, Boston, 1911, made the following remarks:

> If I were asked to mention the most important public movement of the last twenty years, I should say it was the movement to obtain for all classes of society—indeed, for the entire population—better means of health, rational enjoyment, and real happiness. Much sympathy has been expressed in these later years for the unhappy condition of large elements of the population. Something more than economic remedies must be found for the great evils which beset modern society, and particularly for the diseases, physical and moral, which are caused by congestion of population. This profession is called upon to deal with all these problems of congestion. You must take account of the desires and hopes, tastes and purposes of the population to be relieved; and these sentiments and emotions will all be found to be closely related to that pursuit of happiness in which a free people is always engaged in accordance with their tastes and inclinations. . . . The Declaration of Independence declares that all men have a right to life, liberty, and the pursuit of happiness. Now it is the pursuit of public happiness which, I think, should be the main standby of this profession in urging the public to use the landscape art, to seek its benefits, and to employ its artists.

But the preservation of natural beauty is not the only object sought in saving the untouched tracts. Not that their beauty is not a sufficient object in itself, but other factors, not less important but simply less apparent, can be justly ascribed. The training of the landscape architect begins not only with pictorial composition and practical design, but also with the study of plants, of soils, of bodies of water and of all the great natural forces and influences that have shaped and given character to the physiognomy of the land and its vegetation. Now the original sources of the literature in all these vast fields of special sciences have come from the many investigators who have utilized the *natural areas* not as an accessory to their mode of study but as the supreme fundamental basis of all determinations. Unlike the investigators in other than the so-called "Natural Sciences" whose laboratories are often merely specially equipped ordinary buildings, these workers must depend on all outdoors for their laboratories and particularly on the few portions of the earth's surface still remaining as an original record of the earth's history. The plea of this work is that these original tracts are so rapidly becoming modified that steps should be taken to save their destruction before too late. From the standpoint of the landscape profession their loss would be not a mere sentimental misfortune, but a real catastrophe reaching into every branch of science which contributes to the development of landscape study.

From these great sources of natural beauty comes all our inspiration; from them comes the unlimited store of fine examples teaching us the arrangement of our materials; from them comes the lesson of growth, development and natural strife that shows the way to a permanent landscape; and finally, from them comes the suggestion to the layman of the value of beauty and the desire for it in the surroundings of human habitations. It is not enough that we grow fine floral displays, well-clipped hedges and smooth lawns. We must bring to the most humble cottage in all parts of the land at least a suggestion of nature's charm, power and delicacy, the inspiration for which, unless these natural preserves are secured, will disappear for all times in spirit and in fact.

WILLIAM WILLARD ASHE

The Value to Silviculture of Reserved Areas of Natural Forest Types

(1926)

The setting aside of vestigial units of the various forest types has three important objects in view: First, to supply the means for studying the laws which control the distribution of different species of trees. Second, to ascertain the factors which determine forest types. Third, to note the changes in such types induced by the artificial conditions which result from exploitation and silvicultural practice.

The practical silviculturist is principally concerned with the last named of these objects. It is his function to modify natural conditions, often to a profound degree, in the interest of increased yields of commercially desirable species. In this, however, he is constantly taking a chance, since his crop is a slow growing one and he is unable to wait for the results of the painstaking research, extended through the life of a stand of timber, needed to supply the accurate results under which he could proceed with complete confidence.

By determining these factors of distribution and using these vestigial units as check plots, however, it may be possible for him to prevent mistakes or to rectify errors which may be made through deviating too far from the normal.

It is reasonable to suppose that each site, the biotic corollary[*] of which is the forest type, bears in its natural condition (unless modified by fires) the heaviest stand which the native species are capable of producing on that site. That is, nature has already established that species or association of species which is best suited for growing under the limiting edaphic and meteorological conditions which are termed site, among the most important of such conditions being soil acidity, rate of nitrification, maximum moisture content, number and length of critically dry periods, depth of soil, and available heat units and their distribution. The species forming the type reproduce themselves, not invari-

From *Naturalist's Guide to the Americas*, edited by Victor E. Shelford (Baltimore: Williams and Wilkins, 1926), 10–11.

*W. W. Ashe, "Forest Types of the Appalachians and White Mountains," *Journal of the Elisha Mitchell Scientific Society* 37 (1922): 183–98.

ably in a definite proportion, but definite within a certain latitude, the oscillation of the type,[*] and utilize the full resources of the site, which is capable of producing annually (or on an average) a fixed amount of wood material (cellulose). Silviculture seeks to modify or increase this natural yield by cultural methods. There may be an attempt to concentrate increment in a few select individuals or to simplify the composition of the natural stand by eliminating from it certain of the components which are economically or silviculturally less desirable; or to replace the native species in whole or in part with other species or by a single species which is regarded as more desirable economically or silviculturally.

The problems which arise in connection with such changes can be met in two ways. They can be solved empirically for each site, as in connection with the introduction of foreign species, by experimental planting with a view to determining what species or combination of species is more advantageous than those in the original type. The establishment of final conclusions by this method may require many decades, during which time a portion of the land might not be producing to its full capacity or many irreparable and costly errors may have been made. This was the method employed in testing the adaptability of certain species in the plantations on the Biltmore Estate at Asheville, N.C. For example, wild black cherry (*Prunus serotina*) was planted with a view to its possibly becoming a timber tree. We now know from a careful study of the forest types within which this tree attains commercial proportions that there is no site on the Biltmore Estate on which this species can be expected to attain first size or to be more, in fact, than a straggling slow growing tree.

The other method of meeting these problems is by a study of the fundamental factors which control each forest type within the type itself. Some, if not all, of these factors should be determined on sites on which the type is unmodified or least modified, for whenever it has been materially modified, especially for a long period, there has been an accompanying, though possibly slight and temporary, modification of the site.

When types formed of mixed stands are cut over it is difficult and at times impossible to determine their original composition. For these reasons it is urgently desirable that such unmodified units of the different forest types be located before the silvical conditions are altered by repeated fellings and that they be reserved for the study of their controlling factors. In a few years such vestigial units purposely reserved will be the only unmodified remnants of many of the forest types. It will be only by the setting aside now of such unmodified areas that there can be any assurance of having these plots of the various forest types available for conducting such studies.

As has been stated in a previous paper on this subject[†] it is eminently undesirable that there should be a possibility of the development of American silviculture being hampered by the failure to reserve such vestigial units of the important forest types as fields for research, and as check plots by

[*]Ashe, "Forest Types of the Appalachians and White Mountains."

[†]W. W. Ashe, "Reserved Areas of Principal Forest Types as a Guide in Developing an American Silviculture," *Journal of Forestry* 20 (1922): 279–83.

means of which it will be possible to note the changes which take place in the same types under the stress of exploitation and silvical development. As a prerequisite for making the highest use of such reserved units and the studies which may be made in them, the areas of the different forests' types should be carefully mapped after the types have been standardized. Only this procedure will establish similarity of conditions and will permit the extension to them of the laws which are found to control on the vestigial units.

The study of the unmodified areas, in connection with those which are modified, will indicate the extent to which it will be possible to deviate from the normal and yet retain the equilibrium necessary for maintaining the factors of the locality. Such studies will determine whether it will be possible economically to replace one species by another; whether it will be advantageous to substitute a pure coniferous stand for one of mixed hardwoods, or if not, as to what proportion of the stand the conifers can occupy. The natural areas must in large measure serve as the means of developing our silviculture; their elimination from exploitation and their preservation is essential to that end.

ARTHUR SPERRY PEARSE

The Value of Aquatic Preserves to Fisheries

(1926)

There are few "natural" environments for freshwater fishes in the United States. Artificially stocked streams, lakes, and ponds seldom produce such desirable fishes as are found in localities where the wilderness has not been disturbed by man. Great natural preserves like the Great Lakes and the Mississippi River should be kept as near their original condition as possible.

In general the larger a fish preserve is, the better. It is highly desirable to keep the environmental complexes furnished by great rivers and lakes as complete as possible. Variety of habitats is necessary because many species do not carry on their cycles of activities in the same habitat. The bass feed largely among plants, but require bare bottom for spawning. The cisco lives in the deep cool waters of lakes, but comes into shallow water on stony bottoms to breed. Many young fishes frequent shoals, even though they live elsewhere as adults.

Attempts to rear fishes in small bod-

From *Naturalist's Guide to the Americas*, edited by Victor E. Shelford (Baltimore: Williams and Wilkins, 1926), 11–12.

ies of water are often without success. In general the ecological succession in ponds eliminates the species most desirable for man. A pond left to "run" according to "nature" chokes with aquatic vegetation and becomes a swamp, populated by mud minnows, sticklebacks, and bullheads. If game fishes are desired, bare bottom is essential. Fishes confined year after year in a restricted area may be overrun by parasites. One of the trout hatcheries of the Wisconsin Conservation Commission is situated in an excellent locality and has an adequate supply of fine spring water, but is of little value because the trout are heavily infected with a parasitic copepod.

Pollution may easily destroy the value of a fish preserve. Poisons may be introduced from natural sources or from the byproducts of the industries of man. Substances which use up oxygen or produce other injurious gases may be present. Minerals may be precipitated from or dissolved in the water by substances not in themselves injurious to fishes.

If fishing is permitted in a preserve, it

should not be so restricted as to catch certain fishes and allow others to increase unduly. If angling only is practised in a lake the game fishes are most often caught and undesirable species, like the carp, sucker, and dog fish, which seldom take a hook, become too numerous. The restricted use of fyke nets or seins for the capture of the latter fishes is desirable in such a locality.

It is doubtful if the suitability of a body of water as a fish preserve can ever be judged by any single criterion. Two lakes may be of the same size and depth. The one may be "plankton poor," have a scanty bottom fauna, contain undesirable mineral constituents, lack oxygen, and have barren shores, while the other furnishes a favorable environment in all these essentials.

A river may change its whole character as a habitat for fishes on account of the introduction of factory wastes, the building of a dam, or some other apparently unimportant change in a locality. Rush Lake, Wisconsin, has abundant food and shelter and furnishes excellent breeding grounds, but is so shallow that its oxygen is used up when it is covered by ice in winter, hence it contains no large fishes.

The important features for a fish preserve are: (1) sufficient *size* to permit variety in habitats and to lessen the dangers from contamination and rapid fluctuations in temperature, (2) adequate resources in the way of *food, shelter,* and *breeding grounds* to maintain a sufficient number of fishes to make the preserve profitable.

STEPHEN SARGENT VISHER

The Importance to Geography
of the Preservation of Natural Areas

(1926)

At least four of Geography's several sub-divisions will be aided by the preservation of natural areas. These are (1) Descriptive Geography, (2) Historical Geography, (3) Ecological Geography, and (4) Economic Geography.

Descriptive geography is concerned not alone with describing relief features and the cultural additions. It considers likewise the vegetation and the characteristic animals. Preserved areas, where natural conditions can be studied readily facilitate good geographic descriptions in *two ways*. First they afford examples of natural conditions. Only after type areas have been studied can a really good description of a region be written. Second, the setting aside of definite areas for preservation results indirectly in increased information about the location of typical areas, the methods of reaching them, and other significant facts concerning them. Fairly full information is gathered and made available concerning very few privately owned tracts partly because the work and expense entailed may soon have been in vain. The owner may decide to keep out even the most worthy scientists, or else the natural biota may be largely destroyed as by the cutting of the timber or otherwise altering the conditions. Thus although many nearly natural areas still remain, few geographers know just where to go, how to get there, and what they will find when they arrive.

Teachers of descriptive geography will benefit, also, from the presence of preserved areas especially near cities, for in such areas their students can learn much in a short time about natural conditions, the conditions the pioneers encountered.

This leads to the advantage to historical geography of the preservation of natural areas. The specialists who interpret the historical development of any region must have a full appreciation of conditions as they were in earlier times. Carefully preserved natural areas will aid greatly in understanding primeval conditions.

From *Naturalist's Guide to the Americas*, edited by Victor E. Shelford (Baltimore: Williams and Wilkins, 1926), 12–13.

Ecological geography differs from plant and animal ecology chiefly in being more comprehensive, including both, and as the advantages to each have been discussed at length elsewhere, it is not necessary to consider the numerous advantages to this phase of geography which would result from the preservation of numerous typical natural areas. However, there are many problems which special students of either plants or animals have not adequately investigated but which the geographer, with his more inclusive view wishes to study. For example, the influence of geographic factors which because of their rareness, have not been considered significant, such as the "free-air foehn," or the hurricane, need to be investigated. The native flora and fauna may show far plainer adjustments to such influences than do the recently introduced forms. Since it is probable that in the future there will be a great increase in the number of ecological studies carried on by geographers, it is advantageous to geography that many areas be preserved now before it is too late.

Economic geography with its interest in all products of commercial importance is interested in the preservation of natural areas especially because of the probability that in the future new uses will be found for native plants and animals not now very useful. If many are exterminated, as will surely result unless numerous natural areas are preserved promptly, all possibility of their ever being of economic importance will have disappeared. After a form is extinct, or practically extinct, it will be very distressing to learn that it had potentialities of great value had they been taken advantage of. Until every living form is well known, none should be allowed to become extinct. Economic geographers join with agriculturists, physicians and students of many other sorts, therefore, in advocating the setting aside of areas where the native forms can continue to live and can be advantageously studied.

VICTOR E. SHELFORD

The Importance of Natural Areas
to Biology and Agriculture

(1926)

Some biological subjects are of course only remotely related to habitat questions; others can hardly proceed to certain conclusions without reference to habitat relations. An adequate interpretation of evolutionary relations can hardly be made without knowledge of environment. This is true even if natural selection operating on characters which arise from internal causes, is assumed to be the only cause of the origin of new forms. The geneticists have rarely separated environmental effects from purely hereditary phenomena. It is safe to assume that a considerable part of the phenomena described as hereditary is some form of environmental effect. The results of genetical study can hardly have important evolutionary bearing until relations to environment have been brought into it.

The relations of physiology to ecology are more intimate under present conditions; the general physiologists are interested in and are appreciative of ecological

From *Naturalist's Guide to the Americas*, edited by Victor E. Shelford (Baltimore: Williams and Wilkins, 1926), 13–14.

work. The interpretation of physiological characters in connection with environmental relations is a growing field. Medical physiology is less intimately related to environmental subjects but is far from as remote as the present status of various other biological subjects.

The purpose of pointing out the relations of the various branches of biology to ecology and the study of natural habitats, and of calling attention to neglected relations is merely to indicate that present interest in the preservation of natural habitats for scientific purposes is far less than it may be expected to be in the near future. It is safe to predict that when the neglected field of habitat relations comes to attention a little more, not merely ecologists, but all biologists will require *preserves of natural conditions* in connection with their various scientific interests. The relations of the pure science of biology to natural conditions are believed to be much more important to future research than is generally recognized.

Agricultural problems include the development of new kinds of cultivated plants and domestic animals, and the destruction of pests of all kinds. In understanding conditions which most favor pests, a knowledge of their original habitat is often very important and will save years of work on the part of investigators. For example the chinch bug was originally found on grasses in waste places along the coast of the Carolinas. Rainy, hot seasons similar to those found in the original area are favorable to the chinch bug. Knowledge of the climate and other conditions in the original habitat would have saved much useless speculation and misinterpretation. Knowledge of the original conditions under which a pest lives is usually important. Accordingly *preserves of natural conditions* are important from the standpoint of insect pests and equally important for other plant and animal pests.

Domestic animals, especially sheep, have been studied in relation to climate. After thousands of years of domestication sheep still require conditions similar to those in which they are said to have originally occurred—mountain grassland—and failure to supply these conditions is one of the causes of difficulty in the sheep industry. A reservation with sheep of the wild sort in their natural conditions would have facilitated this study greatly. There are many species now in a wild state which may be utilized in the near future for domestication or crossing with domestic species and they should be preserved in their native haunts for this purpose.

PART II

OUR AMERICAN FLORA

This section chronicles the discovery of the value of our native flora which evolved through the nineteenth and early twentieth centuries. Many of these authors advocate for increased use of native species in American horticulture. It seems appropriate to open the section with "The Neglected American Plants," published in 1851, Andrew Jackson Downing's observations on why native plants were so frequently overlooked in the early nineteenth century.

A series of essays from *Garden and Forest* by Charles Sprague Sargent and William Augustus Stiles, Henry Nehrling, Charles H. Shinn, and E. J. Hill explores groups of native plants, ranging from trees to grasses and geographically from Florida to the midwestern prairie to the Sierra Nevada in California. Each of these articles expresses a growing fascination with the wide variety of plants available across North America which had at that time been little used in gardens. Nehrling had purchased forty acres of land in Orange County, Florida, where he created an experimental garden for testing native and ornamental plants

for the U.S. Department of Agriculture. He was highly instrumental in popularizing many plants indigenous to Florida and the southeastern United States within the nursery trade.

In "The American Hawthorns," Sargent and Stiles explore the value of these small trees, which had until then been largely neglected, as garden ornamentals. Sargent explains the often confusing genera of *Crataegus* and points out hawthorn species he considers of particular worth. The hawthorn would become a potent symbol for the so-called prairie style of landscape gardening practiced by O. C. Simonds and Jens Jensen and described in Wilhelm Miller's essay in Part III. Jensen considered the hawthorn to be the icon of the great midwestern prairie and included a hawthorn motif in his professional letterhead (Grese, *Jens Jensen*, 156–58). Jensen's article "I Like Our Prairie Landscape" records the special attraction the prairie expanses and woodlands held for him, which were the inspiration for so many of his parks and gardens.

ANDREW JACKSON DOWNING

The Neglected American Plants

(1851)

It is an old and familiar saying that a prophet is not without honor except in his own country, and as we were making our way this spring through a dense forest in the State of New Jersey, we were tempted to apply this saying to things as well as people. How many grand and stately trees there are in our woodlands that are never heeded by the arboriculturist in planting his lawns and pleasure grounds; how many rich and beautiful shrubs that might embellish our walks and add variety to our shrubberies that are left to wave on the mountain crag or overhang the steep side of some forest valley; how many rare and curious flowers that bloom unseen amid the depths of silent woods or along the margin of wild water-courses! Yes, our hothouses are full of the heaths of New Holland and the Cape, our parterres are gay with the verbenas and fuchsias of South America, our pleasure grounds are studded with the trees of Europe and Northern Asia, while the rarest spectacle in an American coun-

From *The Horticulturist*, May 1851, 201–3.

try place is to see above three or four native trees, rarer still to find any but foreign shrubs, and rarest of all to find any of our native wild flowers.

Nothing strikes foreign horticulturists and amateurs so much, as this apathy and indifference of Americans to the beautiful sylvan and floral products of their own country. An enthusiastic collector in Belgium first made us keenly sensible of this condition of our countrymen, last summer, in describing the difficulty he had in procuring from any of his correspondents here American seeds or plants, even of well known and tolerably abundant, species, by telling us that amateurs and nurserymen who annually import from him every new and rare exotic that the richest collections of Europe possessed, could scarcely be prevailed upon to make a search for native American plants, far more beautiful, which grow in the woods not ten miles from their own doors. Some of them were wholly ignorant of such plants except so far as a familiarity with their names in the books may be called an acquaintance. Others knew them but considered them "wild plants," and therefore too little deserving of attention to be worth the trouble of collecting even for curious foreigners. "And so," he continued, "in a country of azaleas, kalmias, rhododendrons, cypripediums, magnolias and nyssas, —the loveliest flowers, shrubs, and trees of temperate climates, —you never put them in your gardens, but send over the water every year for thousands of dollars worth of English larches and Dutch hyacinths. *Voila le goût Republicain!*"

In truth, we felt that we quite deserved the sweeping sarcasm of our Belgian friend. We had always, indeed, excused ourselves for the well known neglect of the riches of our native flora by saying that what we can see any day in the woods is not the thing by which to make a garden distinguished, and that since all mankind have a passion for novelty, where, as in a fine foreign tree or shrub, both beauty and novelty are combined, so much the greater is the pleasure experienced. But, indeed, one has only to go to England, where "American plants" are the fashion (not undeservedly, too), to learn that he knows very little about the beauty of American plants. The difference between a grand oak or magnolia, or tulip-tree, grown with all its graceful and majestic development of head, in a park where it has nothing to interfere with its expansion but sky and air, and the same tree shut up in a forest, a quarter of a mile high, with only a tall gigantic mast of a stem, and a tuft of foliage at the top, is the difference between the best bred and highly cultivated man of the day, and the best buffalo hunter of the Rocky Mountains, with his sinewy body tattooed and tanned till you scarcely know what is the natural color of

the skin. A person accustomed to the wild Indian only, might think he knew perfectly well what a man is, and so indeed he does, if you mean a red man. But the "civilizee" is not more different from the aboriginal man of the forest than the cultivated and perfect garden tree or shrub (granting always that it takes to civilization, which some trees, like Indians, do not), than a tree of the pleasure grounds differs from a tree of the woods.

Perhaps the finest revelation of this sort in England is the clumps and masses of our mountain laurel and our azaleas and rhododendrons, which embellish the English pleasure grounds. In some of the great country seats, whole acres of lawn, kept like velvet, are made the groundwork upon which these masses of the richest foliaged and the gayest flowering shrubs are embroidered. Each mass is planted in a round or oval bed of deep, rich sandy mould, in which it attains a luxuriance and perfection of form and foliage almost as new to an American as to a Sandwich Islander. The Germans make avenues of our tulip-trees, and in the South of France, one finds more planted magnolias in the gardens than there are, out of the woods, in all the United States. It is thus, by seeing them away from home where their merits are better appreciated and more highly developed, that one learns for the first time what our gardens have lost, by our having none of these "American plants" in them.

The subject is one which should be pursued to much greater length than we are able to follow it in the present article. Our woods and swamps are full of the most exquisite plants, some of which would greatly embellish even the smallest garden. But it is rather to one single feature in the pleasure grounds that we would at this moment direct the attention, and that is the introduction of two broad-leaved evergreen shrubs that are abundant in every part of the middle states, and that are, nevertheless, seldom to be seen in any of our gardens or nurseries from one end of the country to the other. The defect is the more to be deplored, because our ornamental plantations, so far as they are evergreen, consist almost entirely of pines and firs—all narrow-leaved evergreens—far inferior in richness of foliage to those we have mentioned.

The native holly grows from Long Island to Florida, and is quite abundant in the woods of New Jersey, Maryland, and Virginia. It forms a shrub or small tree, varying from four to forty feet in height, clothed with foliage and berries of the same ornamental character as the European holly, except that the leaf is a shade lighter in its green. The plant, too, is perfectly hardy, even in the climate of Boston, while the European holly is quite too tender for open air culture in the middle states, notwithstanding that peaches ripen here in orchards, and in England only on walls.

The American laurel, or Kalmia, is too well known in all parts of the country to need any description. And what new shrub, we would ask, is there, whether from the Himalayas or the Andes, whether hardy or tender, which surpasses the American laurel when in perfection as to the richness of its dark green foliage or the exquisite delicacy and beauty of its gay masses of flowers? If it came from the highlands of Chili and were recently introduced it would bring a guinea a plant, and no grumbling!

Granting all this, let our readers who wish to decorate their grounds with something new and beautiful undertake now, in this month of May (for these plants are best transplanted after they have commenced a new growth), to plant some laurels and hollies. If they would do this quite successfully they must not stick them here and there among other shrubs in the common border, but prepare a bed or clump in some cool, rather shaded aspect—a north slope is better than a southern one—where the subsoil is rather damp than dry. The soil should be sandy or gravelly, with a mixture of black earth well decomposed, or a cartload or two of rotten leaves from an old wood, and it should be at least eighteen or twenty inches deep to retain the moisture in a long drought. A bed of these fine evergreens made in this way will be a feature in the grounds, which after it has been well established for a few years will convince you far better than any words of ours of the neglected beauty of our American plants.

CHARLES SPRAGUE SARGENT
AND WILLIAM AUGUSTUS STILES

American Trees for America

(1897)

Looking at the matter broadly, comparatively little, in northern countries at least, has been accomplished toward beautifying the earth's surface by transferring trees from one region to another, although a great deal of time, energy and money has been expended during the last two hundred years in the attempt to do it. It has given to Europe from America the Locust, the great southern Magnolia, the Negundo, the White Pine, several California conifers, the Arbor Vitae, one or two Thorns, and the Staghorn Sumach, as truly permanent and valuable additions to the native silva; China has really enriched Europe, as it has eastern North America, with the Ginkgo, the Ailanthus, the Paulownia, the Yulan Magnolias, the Weeping Willow and the flowering Apples; western Asia has sent to Europe the Cedar of Lebanon, the Oriental Plane, the Oriental Spruce and the Cypress, while experiment has shown that of the trees of Europe and western Asia only the White Willows, the

Beech, the Elm, the Norway Maple, the Oriental Plane, the Larch, the Box, the Hawthorn and the Mountain Ash can really be depended on in the eastern states to live out their lives in health and beauty. These results may appear small to economists, but certainly all the effort that has been expended in testing exotic trees in Europe and America has been well repaid in the stimulus it has given to the study of botany, in the increase of knowledge and in its few really important practical results. Still, the lesson to be drawn from these two centuries of effort is clearly that the best trees to plant in any particular region are those that grow and thrive naturally in that region. No teacher in such matters is so wise, experienced and unprejudiced as Nature herself, and when her teachings have been followed the best results from tree-planting have always been obtained. The Elms and Maples taken from adjacent swamps and hillsides, which grace the streets of many New England country towns and adorn many New England homesteads, and the Magnolias, Live Oaks

From *Garden and Forest*, December 29, 1897, 509.

and Water Oaks in the streets and gardens of the south testify to the value of native trees; and in England, too, it is the native Oaks, Elms and Beeches which give its distinctive aspect to the land and make its parks the most dignified in the world. Fortunately, in this country it is not difficult to apply this rule, for no other land is blessed with such a rich, varied and splendid silva. In the southern United States the great evergreen Magnolia, the most beautiful of the broad-leaved evergreen trees of the northern hemisphere, the Live Oak, the Water Oak, the Laurel Oak, the Pecan and noble Bay trees, are available for the planter. In the Pacific coast states the conditions are somewhat different; the number of native trees is smaller than it is in the east, and many of the finest of these are found naturally only at high elevations and cannot be successfully cultivated in the warm, dry valleys in which the people of these states have principally established their homes. Some of the trees which grow in the valleys spontaneously are not ornamental, and are often difficult to cultivate, but some of the noble California Valley Oaks surpass in stately beauty any exotic trees which are likely to flourish in that peculiar climate, and two California conifers, the Monterey Cypress and the Monterey Pine, are generally and successfully grown from Vancouver Island to San Diego. These are both beautiful trees, but California will doubtless always be obliged to depend on other parts of the world for many of her ornamental plants. The trees of the eastern states do not flourish west of the Rocky Mountains; it is not probable that those of Europe or Asia will ever gain much foothold in the soil of California, and it is to Australia, Mexico and other dry countries that California planters will continue probably to derive much of the material needed for the decoration of their parks and gardens.

Hawthorn. From Liberty Hyde Bailey, *Cyclopedia of Horticulture* (1914), 884.

It is in the eastern and middle states, however, where there is a greater interest in ornamental planting than in other parts of the country, that most is to be obtained from the native silva. That of no other part of the world is richer in handsome trees. From its Magnolias, Oaks, Hickories, Walnuts, Elms and Ashes, its Tupelo and stately Tulip-tree, its Rhododendrons and Mountain Laurels, its Birches and Lindens, its Coffee-tree and Honey Locust, its Sourwood and Sassafras, its Beech, Chestnut, Yellow-wood and Wild Cherry, its Catalpas, its Persimmon and Silver-bell tree, its Flowering Dogwood and Fringe-tree, its Liquidambar and Hackberry, its Sumachs, its Wild Crab and its Hawthorns, planters of deciduous-leaved trees can choose material enough to satisfy every taste and fill every requirement. And among coniferous trees none is more picturesque in youth or more stately at maturity than the northern White Pine, more graceful than the Hemlock, or more symmetrical and enduring than the Red Cedar.

In the past our gardens have suffered from the general ignorance with regard to the true beauty and value of native trees, which appears to have been peculiar to us as a nation. Too often the planter, unable to obtain American trees, has had to rely on the Spruces, Oaks, Ashes, Maples, Pines and other trees of Europe, and these are still too largely used in this country, although it is now known that they are entirely unsuited to our climate and that where they have been used in public parks they must soon be replaced by native species. The lesson has been a costly one, but the experience has not been dearly purchased if we have finally come to realize that Nature has placed for us in America a greater number of beautiful trees, large and small, than is found in any other part of the world, and that American trees are the best for America.

HENRY NEHRLING

Native Plants for Florida Gardens

(1894)

The hummock woods and swamps of Florida are rich in ornamental trees and shrubs, and the sandy Pinelands and flat-woods are rich in perennial and herbaceous plants. The beauty of the evergreen leaves and large flowers of the Magnolias, the delicious perfume of the Carolina Jessamine, the penetrating odor of the Spider Lily, all growing in the rich black soil on the edges of the lakes; the singular beauty of Holly, *Icacorca paniculata, Myrsine floridana* and Cherry Laurel, the stateliness of the Loblolly Bay, the grandeur of the Live Oaks, the tropical picturesqueness of the Palmettos, always bring delight to any visitor here who loves nature. All of these and many other plants grow easily on dry Pine-land in Florida if transplanted from the hummock woods; but, as a rule, we see nothing but Orange-trees and white sand around the houses of the settlers. Nobody seems to think that there is abundant material for ornamental planting so close at hand. Now and then we see an Oleander,

From *Garden and Forest,* January 10, 1894, 13.

a Gardenia or a Hibiscus, or a few clumps of Crinums, which are invariably called Lilies, but very few native trees, shrubs or herbaceous plants, Settlers from the north often attempt to grow their old garden favorites, but the Snowballs and Lilacs, Bush Honeysuckles and Spiraeas, the Hollyhock and Paeonies generally fail, although the ordinary Philadelphus usually grows well.

Such native trees as the Magnolia, Gordonia, Live Oak and Red Bay, Holly and many others which love rich moist soil will grow well on the sterile Pine-land when care is taken to plant them properly and fertilize and water them afterward for a time when necessary. The instructions which I can give on this point I received originally from Mr. Walter N. Pike, who has derived them from actual experience, and since then I have proved their value by personal trial. The earlier the plants are obtained in winter the better, and some commercial fertilizer will always be beneficial in helping them to start. Even a few shovelfuls of hummock-soil, mixed with the ordinary sand and placed about the roots, will be found very useful, since a great deal depends on their first growth. Heavy mulching should never be neglected in Florida about newly transplanted plants, not only for immediate effect, but for carrying them through the drought, since the mulch not only arrests the escape of moisture, but keeps the soil cool. Of course, newly set trees and shrubs should be watered well and the soil should be trodden firmly about the roots. It is always best to have a rim of soil raised about the trees with a hoe, so that they set in a saucer-like depression from four to six feet in diameter, and this circle should be at once covered with mulch, and the mulch should be weighted down. The roots are then in damp, cool soil, beyond the baking power of the sun's rays when the dry season comes. If the tree then droops, two or three pails of water must be poured into this depression, and each pailful should be allowed to soak away before another is added. Some exotics, like *Michelia fuscata* and *Thea bohea,* are benefited if a little clay is mixed with the soil about the roots, and perhaps the same would be true of many native plants, but *Magnolia foetida* grows like a weed when transplanted to high Pine-land, and so does the Holly, *Ilex opaca,* when lifted from the hummock to a hungry soil of sand.

It is small trouble to collect these trees, and with a single companion I once collected in one day in the latter part of October most of the trees and shrubs which I shall now name as desirable ones. *Andromeda nitida* is a singularly elegant shrub, found in peaty soil near the water. It grows five or six feet high, has thick, shining fragrant leaves, and in April is covered with pendulous clusters of white and fragrant blossoms hanging from the axils of the leaves. The nearly allied *Leucothoë racemosa* is found in similar locations and grows to a height of ten feet. Its dense racemes of twenty to thirty white bell-like flowers appear early on the naked branches. These plants were removed with balls of soil about the roots and transplanted to the edge of a small lake. Native Ferns were planted among them and other species of *Andromeda.* I had not yet learned the necessity of mulching, and every one died, although I have since had success with these and other plants of the Heath family. Trees of *Magnolia foetida,* owing to their lack of fibrous roots, are difficult to transplant, but I obtained a few of these and they are now all growing well. All the Magnolias are easily raised from seeds and make a rapid growth on high, poor Pine-land if a little fertilizer is worked about them. Four years from the seed they will be specimens ten feet high, making a solid mass of lustrous foliage to the ground, and I have seen trees of that size which flowered freely. The Loblolly Bay needs the same treatment. *Myrsine floridana* is a small broad-leaved evergreen tree, which, like the Holly, Loblolly Bay and Magnolias, never shows its full beauty in the woods where it lives in a constant struggle with coarser trees. When planted alone, however, it makes a conspicuously beautiful object, having a perfect form and very dense foliage. *Magnolia glauca,* which is almost as desirable as the Big Bay, will thrive under the same treatment. The Silver Bush, *Leucophyllum texanum* (see *Garden and Forest,* vol. iii. p. 488), is one of the most conspicuous objects on my grounds. I have seen this shrub growing abundantly in western Texas on dry and barren soil as a spreading shrub five to ten feet high and flowering at intervals from May to October after every heavy shower. These thimble-shaped, rosy flowers, when seen among the woolly leaves of an ashy-gray color, are exceptionally beautiful. It transplants readily and can be cut to any desired form.

Many other native trees should find a place in every Florida garden. The sweet-leaved *Symplocos tinctoria* is one of the prettiest small evergreen trees of the south. *Ilex dahoon* is a beautiful evergreen shrub. The Wax Myrtle, *Myrica cerifera*, here is another evergreen which is very pretty and interesting. The American Olive, *Osmanthus americanus*, a beautiful southern forest tree, which attains a fine form, and is densely covered with foliage when planted in the garden. The Sea Grapes, the common name for two species of *Coccoloba*, are also desirable broad-leaved evergreens, while the Virginia Fringetree, the Flowering Dogwood, *Itea virginica*, *Calycanthus floridus*, the Palmetto and many more could be used to make a garden of native plants in Florida a most interesting and delightful spot.

CHARLES H. SHINN

The Wild Gardens of the Sierra

(1896)

Our California Sierra is five hundred miles long and seventy miles wide. The elevation is from 6,000 to nearly 15,000 feet. No great mountain range is more easy of access or better adapted to outdoor life. John Muir calls it not the Snowy Range, but the Range of Light, so marvelous are its sunbursts of morning, its clear noonday radiance from glacier-polished rocks and gleaming snows, its golden rivers of sunset, its alpine moonlights and starlights, its glories of blossoms of every hue, but chiefly white, blue, scarlet, golden, and all sorts of clear, vivid colors.

Wonderful are the peaceful mountain lakelets that find places on no maps—pellucid, transparent, hidden in sheltered hollows of glacial valley-basins, at the lips of ancient moraines, or strung like beads on mountain streams, as in Lake Hollow in Tolumne Cañon, where ten such lakes lie close together. These snow-fed pools begin to throw off the chains of winter in May, June or July, according to the altitude, and

From *Garden and Forest*, August 26, 1896, 343–44.

then their margins suddenly run riot with a most bewildering variety and multitude of plants. Thousands of attractive lakelets exist in the Sierras; in the Merced district alone, Muir notes 131 of not less than five hundred yards in circuit; other thousands of hollows, once occupied by lakes, have now become green and blossoming meadows, while some are in the transition state—cold swamps where the *Droseras* grow, and one may look for *Darlingtonia,* or find in deeper channels the *Nuphar polysepalum.*

The margins of these countless lakelets are soft with Mosses, pale green *Hypnums,* silky and lustrous *Dicranums,* dark *Polytrichums* and other *Musci;* green and purple *Sphagnums,* slender, flat-branched *Selaginellas,* and a multitude of as delicate plant-carpetings. In such wet places rise the tall stems and graceful white perianths of *Spiranthes romanzoffiana,* the Sierra Ladies' Tresses, with white and greenish *Habenarias.* Sometimes one finds the white-racemed *Hastingsia, Sagittaria variabilis,* or the *Damasonium californicum* of Torrey, with many species of *Juncus* in the water edges. In a few cases, the ripe, salmon-colored capsules of the Bog Asphodel, *Narthecium,* gleam over the lesser water plants; and along the moister levels, whole acres of tall *Veratrums,* or False Hellebore, uplift their broad leaves and heavy spikes of dull cream-colored and greenish flowers. Mingled with the Rushes are bright green Quillworts, *Isoetes,* and the cordate-leaved *Caltha leptosepala.* Every inch of ground is occupied with overflowing plant-life.

Bright-hued Mountain Grasses, *Stipas, Festucas, Trisetums, Bromi, Calamagrostes* and many more give soft hues of brown, purple and gold as they bloom and ripen on the sunny slopes or beside the blue lakelets. Beetles, ants, dragonflies, *Vanessas, Papilios* and many other species of butterflies in busy armies crawl and flutter through the warm summer land; mountain quail and grouse are in the thickets of dwarf Pines, Oaks, Poplars and Willows. Robins, swallows, grosbeaks and goldfinches are nesting or singing in tree-tops by rushing rivers and waterfalls; while the water ousel, swift bird-wonder, flashes through the spray, and the saucy Douglas squirrel, *Sciurus douglasi,* makes a lively part of every scene.

But I have hardly begun to describe the variety of plant-life upon the shores of the laklets in the alpine meadows and on the descending rock slopes. Around such lakes are vivid golden *Ranunculi* in many shades, *Ranunculus andersonii, R. oxynotus, R. alismaefolius* and others; purple-beaked *Dodecatheons,* dwarf *Mimuli,* yellow or pink, with crimson-spotted or copper-red hoods; bee-haunted *Limnanthes,* white and pale yellow; rose-tinted *Claytonias;* tall, fragrant *Trifoliums,* red, white or purple-flowered, massed by drip-ping springs against still statelier *Aralias, Ferulas* and *Heracleums,* or grouped with white and yellow *Hosackias* by the edges of splintered granite rocks, while underfoot are nodding Pearlworts, modest little *Stellarias* and *Cerastiums* and the water-loving *Lobelia carnosula.* Creeping *Violas,* white, yellow and blue, are blossoming by thousands in the warm half-shade; under the trees one may at rare times find the delicate *Anemone multifida;* the *Aconitum fischeri* lifts its pale blue flowers and pubescent stems through acres of orange-yellow and red-spotted Lilies, *L. pardalinum,* and near it is the pale lilac of *Clarkia rhomboidea.* By some of these alpine lakes the dwarf Willows are mingled with purple-flowering *Kalmias,* fringes of *Cassiope* and fragrant *Vacciniums, Symphoricarpi* and *Loniceras,* which by September add their glowing white and orange-red berries to the reds and rose-purples of the dwarf Mountain *Ribes.*

If a mountain torrent falls into the lake hollow you shall find many Saxifrages, white, creamy brown or purple, hanging to the damp rocks. *Primula suffrutescens* will be there also, and where the spray dashes are white-blossoming *Rubus leucodermis.* On almost every sheltered, soil-covered shelf of rock millions of creamy yellow and purple-shaded *Erythroniums* begin to blossom as the snow melts and linger until the lake-shores fairly waken. Hidden at the bases of the crags are multitudes of *Asters* and *Aquilegias* (*A. truncata*), and if one climbs far enough he can find the large-flowered blue and white *A. coerulea.*

The blossoms of the hill-sides, ravines and rocks are so many and so varied that every cañon and lake-basin has its distinctive features, and a complete list would be merely a catalogue. Rose or flesh-colored *Dicentras* hide among the grasses; *Silenes,* pink, white, scarlet or purple, cluster about rock points; *Castilleias,* yellow-red and fire-tipped, deepening to almost crimson; vivid scarlet *Zauschnerias* and crowded glowing masses of blue Lupines illuminate the landscape; white and rose-colored Phloxes; *Pentstemons* of pink, violet and blue; close-knit corymbs of rose-hued *Spiraeas;* the almost prostrate, dense-clustered scorpioid spikes of *Spragueas;* silky, glistening cups of *Lewisia rediviva*—these, with an enormous number of wonderfully glowing *Compositae,* clothe the dry, granite dust and furrows of the dark rocks. *Helianthi, Wyethias, Erigerons,* Golden-rods, *Heleniums,* and many others great and small, by lake-shores and streams and to the limits of alpine vegetation, mark the sway of the *Compositae* in the Sierras. Often the color-scheme is strongly blue and gold for miles, for the tall Forget-me-nots, the lovely Gentians, such as *Gentiana amarella, G. simplex* and *G. calycosa,* the fine alpine Linums, Lupines, Larkspurs and other vividly blue flowers quite hold their own with the rich *Compositae.*

Especially brilliant, also, are some of the alpine *Ericaceae,* such as *Bryanthus breweri,* that dwarf evergreen with thick, obtuse, Heath-like leaves and saucer-shaped rose-purple blossoms gleaming upon high and rocky peaks of the Sierras. Another lovely Heath is the white or rose-colored *Cassiope,* a suffrutescent evergreen, with finely imbricated foliage. These grow far above the Oaks and the dwarf, trailing *Manzanitas,* where Hemlock Spruces, *Tsuga pattoniana,* and mountain Pines, *Pinus albicaulis* and *P. monticola,* are the outposts of the great Sierra forests. Still one finds golden *Compositae,* brighter and more luminous than ever, in great congregations close to the edges of the glaciers. Again, as far down by the lake hollows, the Mosses and other forms of lesser plant-life take the place of the glowing hosts of the mid-Sierra. The *Woodsias* and larger Ferns disappear, but *Pellaeas, Allosori, Cheilanthes* and *Cystopteris* have grown in the shadows of granite crags and in crevices of the giant mountains all the way from the land of Lilies, of wild Sierra Roses and of thickets of white-flowered *Prunus emarginata.* On the gray pinnacles, among sky-blue Flaxes, silvery *Astragali,* with cream-white and purple flowers and mottled pods, rattle sharply in the winds. Alpine Sages creep up from the Nevada desert plateau and make the eastern horizon gray. The blue and white Polemoniums, the hoary *Lithospermum pilosum* and other flowers of the highest peaks are found here in gardens of their own.

E. J. HILL

Prairie Woodlands

(1894)

When pioneers began to settle in our primeval forests, the natural impulse to plot in right lines led to the clearing of rectangular spaces, so that the surviving pieces of woodland are mostly bounded by straight lines. Time has, however, modified and beautified the abrupt and naked forest-borders that skirted the newly cleared fields. The taller trees along the margins have been overturned by the wind, lower ones have grown up with rounded tops and limbs which spread out to reach more light; an undergrowth of shrubs and herbs has sprung up by the enclosing fences, so that an unbroken bank of foliage stretches from the ground to the tree-tops.

In the woodlands of a prairie region these sloping borders are characteristic, and the bounding lines naturally curve with the windings of streams and valleys and the outlines of timber-clad hills. These masses of timber are often surrounded by treeless prairie or cultivated fields, the woods being left to supply the adjoining

From *Garden and Forest,* October 17, 1894, 412–13.

country with forest-products. The large trees have been cut off, but the ground is left to grow up with timber again, and under the stimulus of self-interest a kind of rude forestry is practiced. If the wooded areas are too large to be embraced with profit in adjacent farms, they may be divided into portions of a few acres, and be owned by several farmers living within easy distance. These small holdings in the groves are bought and sold with the main estate, and this also tends to their preservation and keeps them in larger tracts, so that one may sometimes follow belts of unbroken woodland for miles along a stream. Fed by springs which issue from the bases of the bordering slopes, even the small streams become perennial in the shade of the woods, though when followed away from the forest a dry bed may mark their course through the prairie in summer. The farmer thus becomes a conservator of the woodlands which help to preserve moisture for the soil, as well as to form one of the most pleasing elements of the landscape; for this region is monotonous as a whole—a plain with no striking features in the way of hills and mountains.

These wooded areas are generally used for pasture, frequently to their injury; but cattle and horses being chiefly kept, the undergrowth is not as closely cropped as when sheep have their range. Portions of the adjoining prairie are often included in the pasture, especially on the hills or along swampy lands. Points of timber jut out from the main body into the prairie, running down the hillsides or along ravines and watercourses, or out into swamps into which drier land projects. An occasional tree or small group of trees stands apart from the rest, still further varying the outline of the border, while larger groups, like islands in a sea of prairie, lie apart from the main body. The use of the tree-covered ground and the adjacent prairie for grazing often saves these isolated trees and groups; for where land is devoted to the plow they are apt to be cut down, as may be observed where the rich soil of the prairie comes close up to the woods. If in wettish grounds the trees may be spared, because they do not encumber a meadow from which hay is taken, and which may be pastured only a part of the year. The limbs of these detached trees or groups come down low about the trunks, the tops are round and spreading, and a sturdy and symmetrical habit has been developed by the free play of light and air on every side.

A pleasing feature of these woods is the way in which the border merges into the green of the prairie. Belts of trees lining low and swampy prairies, or the sloughs with which they are interspersed, become attractive, or even beautiful, notwithstanding many of their unpleasant surroundings. A continuous mass of foliage joins the green below with that at the tops of the tallest trees. Willows and Alders, the Swamp Rose, Button-bush and Osiers of various kinds are followed by Viburnums, Sumachs and Sassafras. These and other tall shrubs or low trees furnish a gradual or undulatory slope from the rank Grass, Reeds and Rushes of the swamp to taller Elms and Swamp Maples, and the Oaks and Hickories of the drier background. The wide variety in the tints of green foliage makes these borders attractive in summer, and when autumn kindles its fiery colors in the leaves they are fairly radiant with beauty. Various shrubs connect the dry upland woods with pasture and meadow. The leaves and glandular twigs of the Hazel are not agreeable to browsing animals, and it becomes common along the margins of woods and fields, or forms outlying masses between the field grasses and the foliage of Oaks and Hickories. In lower and richer ground the Hazel is replaced by the Crab Apple, the Wild Plum and different species of Thorn.

The prevalence of Oaks with smooth and glossy leaves gives to many of these woodlands a peculiar distinctness under the glow of the summer sun. A shimmering light plays upon them, as well defined, although not as bright, as that which glances from a water-surface, and these bright areas catch the eye from a distance, and in the broad sweep of the green landscape these forest-masses rise out of the general level as sources of clear mellow light.

CHARLES SPRAGUE SARGENT
AND WILLIAM AUGUSTUS STILES

The American Hawthorns

(1892)

Our American forests are rich in Haw-thorns, nearly one-third of the forty species which are now known being found within the territory of the United States. They are scattered from Newfoundland to Vancouver Island and to Florida and Texas, and every state and territory, with the exception of Arizona, contains its representative of the genus. They are more common, however, in the east than in the west, and in the number of species and individuals the south is richer than the north. They abound in the country between the Red River and the Trinity, which must be considered the head-quarters of the genus, as more species occur there than in any other region of similar extent, while individuals of several species grow in greater abundance and luxuriance there than in any other part of the country.

The American Hawthorns have long puzzled students of trees, and botanists have regarded them as difficult subjects. But it is the botanists themselves, rather

From *Garden and Forest*, May 11, 1892, 217–18.

than the peculiarities of these trees, which have made them hard to understand, and the chief difficulties in elucidating the different species are literary, and not morphological. For many of the species having been early introduced into the gardens of Europe, there developed under cultivation, numerous more or less distinct forms which were described as species, and often as genera, different names being sometimes given to the same cultivated form. This making of species went on for a century in nearly every country of Europe, while in America botanists were hardly less active in burying these unfortunate plants under a load of almost inextricable synonyms. It is, nevertheless, possible to obtain a correct idea of the species if the student will remember that two Hawthorn-plants raised from seeds taken from the same tree may be and probably will look very unlike one another and their parent; that individuals of most of the species vary in the form of the leaves, in the amount and character of the hairs which cover them, in the presence and absence and in the size and character of the glands which are often found on their leaves and calyx-lobes, in the size and shape of the stipules, which vary on different parts of the same individual, in the number of styles and of the nutlets of the fruit, which is sometimes round and sometimes pear-shaped, and red or yellow in the same species. The student of trees must remember, too, that climate and environment modify individuals, and that when a species has a north and south range of two thousand miles an individual at the north may look very different from one which has grown in the extreme south. If all these facts are remembered, a patient observer able to keep his mind clear of the pitfalls in synonymy dug by Moench and Willdenow, by Aiton and Du Mont de Courset, and by Roemer, Wenzig and Kaleniczenko, and with abundant opportunities for studying in their native forests the different species in all parts of the territory which they inhabit may be able at the end of twenty years, perhaps, to recognize the different species and find characters for separating them, although botanists will probably never agree whether certain forms shall be called species or varieties.

The American Hawthorns fall naturally into two groups; the first contains those species which produce large many-flowered compound corymbs, and the second those species with simple few-flowered corymbs. The species of the first of these principal divisions may be divided into three groups; the first with black or blue fruit, the second with large scarlet or yellow fruit, and the third with minute scarlet fruit, while the species of the second of the principal divisions fall naturally into two groups, the first with red or greenish yellow fruit, and the second with large globose red fruit.

These divisions being established, there is nothing better than the shape of the leaves, in these plants a variable and therefore unsatisfactory character, by which to distinguish the species.

It is not our purpose to describe here all the American Hawthorns in detail, but rather to call attention to the value of the genus as a good subject for study, promising our readers that they will find in it much interest and excellent opportunities for intellectual development, and to remind cultivators that some of the species are beautiful and desirable garden-plants still too little known or appreciated in their native land.

From a gardener's standpoint the most desirable of our Hawthorns is *Crataegus crus-galli,* the Cockspur Thorn, which is perhaps better known in cultivation than any of the other species. Its hardiness, the beauty of its lustrous foliage, the lateness of its flowering-time, all recommend it. The head of this tree, which is sometimes round, with pendulous branches, and sometimes flat-topped, with spreading horizontal branches, is always handsome and interesting. The autumn color of the leaves is not surpassed by that of any of the species, and the abundant fruit hangs on the branches without changing color throughout the winter. The Cockspur Thorn is little subject to fungal diseases, which disfigure many Hawthorns, and it is usually long-lived in cultivation. The long thorns which arm its rigid branches make it a good hedge-plant, and early in this century it was much used for this purpose in some of the eastern states. In the form of its leaves the Cockspur Thorn is one of the most variable of our species, and in addition to the varieties which are found growing wild in different parts of the country others have appeared in European gardens, where this species has been cultivated for nearly two centuries, and where it is now more often seen than any other American Hawthorn.

Of the broad-corymbed large-fruited species the White Thorn is, next to the Cockspur, the best garden-plant. This tree has been considered a variety of the Scarlet Thorn and also as a species. Perhaps the latter view is the most sensible, as the two plants differ in size and habit, in the size of their flowers and the time of their appearance, in the size of the fruit and the length of time this remains on the branches, as well as in the pubescence which covers the under surface of the leaves and the young branchlets. *Crataegus mollis* is the name the White Thorn must bear if it is considered worthy of specific distinction. It is the largest of the Hawthorns of the northern states, and one of the most widely distributed of the American species growing from the shores of Massachusetts Bay to Missouri and through Arkansas to Texas and the mountains of northern Mexico. It is one of the common species in the states west of the Mississippi River, growing to its greatest size in Texas. In cultivation the White Thorn is a beautiful plant, of rapid growth and good habit, conspicuous in winter for the whiteness of its branches and for the number of its large chestnut-brown shining spires. The flowers, with the exception of those of one species of the southern states, are the largest produced by any member of the genus. The leaves are large and of a lively green, and the fruit, which is as large as that of a small crab-apple, is brilliant scarlet with a conspicuous bloom; unfortunately, it falls as soon as it ripens.

The Washington Thorn of the small-fruited species is the best known in gardens; it is the *Crataegus cordata* of botanists, an inhabitant of the southern Appalachian region, and rather a rare plant in its native wilds. It is, however, better known in gardens than any of the other species of the southern states, and its vernacular name is due to the fact that early in the century it was introduced into eastern Pennsylvania as a hedge-plant from the neighborhood of the city of Washington. It is a handsome small tree with an oblong round top, bright triangular leaves brilliant in autumn, and small flowers which open later than those of any of the other species, and bright scarlet fruit the size of peas, which hang on the branches until the leaves appear the following spring. The Washington Thorn is free from serious fungal diseases and is always a satisfactory tree in cultivation. Fifty years ago it was more often planted than it is at present.

An interesting garden-plant, also, is *Crataegus douglasii,* the only representative of the genus in the coast-region of the north-west and in California. In the warm climate of Washington and Oregon this tree often attains the height of forty feet and forms a trunk a foot and a half in diameter. The leaves are large and lustrous, the flowers are small but very abundant, and the fruit, which is black, falls in early autumn as soon as it ripens. It is one of the few trees of western America which are absolutely hardy and satisfactory on the eastern edge of the continent, where it thrives as far north as Nova Scotia.

Some of the most beautiful of our Hawthorns were once cultivated, but have long been lost from gardens, and a few have never been cultivated at all. *Crataegus flava,* a native of the maritime regions of the south Atlantic and Gulf states, where it grows in the arid sandy soil of the Pine-barrens, was first described a century ago from plants cultivated in England at that time and the source of endless confusion in the literature of the genus, probably long ago disappeared from gardens, although the name still appears in most garden lists. It is a beautiful small tree, with a narrow round-topped head of graceful pendulous branches, large flowers in two or three-flowered corymbs, and pear-shaped greenish yellow fruit. The Parsley Haw, another inhabitant of the southern states, and beautiful from the shape of its finely divided leaves, was once cultivated in English gardens, from which it has, however, long ago disappeared. But the most beautiful of the southern Hawthorns are still unknown in gardens; these are the Pomette Bleue, of the Acadians of Louisiana, and the Summer Haw, of South Carolina and the Gulf states. The first of these, *Crataegus brachyacantha,* although it is one of the largest and most distinct of the whole genus, strangely escaped the knowledge of botanists until very recently, although it was collected long ago without flowers and fruit. It is the most local of all our species, growing only in the extreme western part of Louisiana, where it borders in broad groves, small low prairies, and in the adjacent portions of Texas. It is perhaps the largest of the genus, sometimes rising to the height of fifty feet, with a tall straight trunk and slender branches, which form a beautiful compact round head. The leaves are not large, but they are bright and shining, and the flowers, which are comparatively small, are produced in many-flowered clusters, which completely cover the branches. The fruit is large and abundant and is bright blue—a color otherwise unknown in the fruit of Crataegus. Unfortunately, it falls in early autumn. There is not a more beautiful small tree in the southern states than this, and it is to be hoped that the attempts made a few years ago by the authorities of the Arnold Arboretum to introduce it into the temperate countries of Europe will prove successful. In the Arboretum itself the seedling-plants have not proved hardy.

That no recorded attempt has been made to cultivate *Crataegus aestivalis,* the May Haw, and that no figure of this beautiful plant his ever been published, are remarkable facts, although botanists have known of its existence for more than a century. Unlike our other Hawthorns, it flowers before the leaves appear, in February or March; the flowers are larger than those of any other species, and the fruit is larger and of better flavor and quality than that produced by any other Crataegus. It is as large as a medium-sized crab-apple, bright red with pale spots, and ripens in May. Pomologists might well devote some attention to this tree, for excellent jellies can be made from the fruit, which is gathered in large quantities for this purpose and is sometimes sold in the markets of the towns of western Louisiana, where this tree is most abundant and best known.

We have only briefly mentioned a few of the species which seem best deserving the attention of gardeners, although among the others are several handsome plants which are hardly known to the cultivators of this generation.

JENS JENSEN

I Like Our Prairie Landscape

(1920)

My first impression of the prairie country was of its richness in flowers. It was one grand carpet of exquisite colors such as is fit for a Forest Cathedral, and such as nature only knows how to weave. Some of the color expressions were as dramatic as the afterglow of the setting sun. And above this carpet, like a flare of trumpets, rose the hawthorn and the western crabapple— the hawthorn garlanded with myriads of white roses, and the crabapple painting the edge of the prairie with its delicate virgin pink. Only on a flat, level plain is it possible to notice the character and beauty of these small trees. Strong and daring, with a feeling of freedom and nobility, they lift their heads above the surface of the land. They are always the first to greet us, and they are interesting and beautiful at all seasons of the year, whether in flower, in leaf or in fruit. In winter, the bare, gray outstretched branches of the hawthorn, that symbolizes the horizontal lines of the prairie, light up the purple borders of the forest, and the

From *The Park International* 1, no. 1 (July 1920): 63–65.

violet branches of the crabapple, playing in the different lights of the day, add a poetic charm to the woodlands, and especially to the purple ridges of oaks—those centuries old monarchs of noble birth.

These were my first impressions. As years have passed by, they have grown both in number and depth. There is no season of the year that this Illinois landscape does not possess its charm for me. At times it has intimate notes of great delicacy. One early spring, strolling through a bit of woods that were but a ruin of their former grandeur, I met a group of gray dogwood showing the first signs of life. The delicate rose of their spreading buds put a refinement into these scarred and despoiled woods that brought back some of their primitive wealth. Nearby a gray haw, with lace-like branches wove itself into the dark timber of the decaying trees. It was refreshing to find these slender notes here where all was tragedy, and what a promise they gave for the future. There is a tenderness in the deciduous forest that the conifer forest does not possess. One realizes this when

Prairie and oak savanna, Dexter, Mich. (Photograph by Robert E. Grese.)

one passes through the dividing line of the Wisconsin woods and the Illinois woods.

I used to wonder why our parks and gardens were so poor in their fall colors, but gradually I came to understand that it was because they were in discord with the native landscape. With their foreign plants, they were nothing but out-of-doors museums; they represented a conglomeration of things purchased over the counter. Except for a few plants, their growing things had no coloring, or were not ripe for the change of foliage when the first frost threw it withered to the ground. They were an importation, unfitted to meet the struggle for life here, and hence doomed to destruction. Their expression was material, not spiritual; one of possession rather than of art. They did not belong. They were not what the Great Master had meant for this place.

If America shall ever pride itself for any art of its own, that art must grow out of the native soil. We shall never receive credit for things that we steal or copy from others. Landscape gardening is the one art that is dependent upon soil and climatic conditions. How can it ever become native and thrive if we have utter disregard for the materials of which it is composed? Those gardens that have survived in ancient Europe grew out of materials that gave that particular section of the country its character and its charm. So must ours, if we are ever to build parks and gardens which express the best that our country can give.

However, there will never be only one type of American landscape gardening, but there will be as many types as there are differences in climate and differences in topographical character of the various sections. How wonderfully rich then will this country become, when the noble art of landscape gardening has been fully understood and appreciated by our people; when each section of our great land has developed the thing that fits it best! For each section has a soul of its own, a beauty of its own. Eventually there will be eyes born to see the truth.

For me, I like our Illinois landscape best. Deep down through its rich prairie land, during countless ages, the river has cut its winding path in water-worn canyons, bordered by woody bluffs and lofty cliffs. This is the garden of the prairie country, a motive for landscape art, full of imagination, mystery and poetic charm— a hidden garden, as it were, in the broad expanse of the prairie landscape. Interesting by contrast with each other, both have a spiritual value and give a wonderful vision. The one is romantic, lovely and intimate in its finer expressions, while the other breathes breadth and freedom. There is nothing in the out-of-doors that excels this landscape. Here are shadowy nooks and sunlit fields, singing waters and rustling leaves. In the streams fish play hide-and-seek with the rushes and water nymphs, and one hears the splash of a leaping bass. Over the meadows, butterflies flit from flower to flower to the song of the meadow lark. It is a sanctuary, a cathedral in the out-of-doors.

From the towering hills one gets the full significance of the free and spreading prairies. Just now they are dotted with great bouquets of apple blossoms. There are shady lanes where the birds may nest and thrill the wanderer with their lovely song, and there are broad stretches of flowers, a symbol of the prairie that has passed. Here is a grove of western crabapple, carpeted with violets, and there a knoll of birch and Juneberries, carpeted with hepaticas. There are colonies of native plum, bride of early spring, amongst the lovely bluebells. There are secret groves of white oaks in their spring dress of silver and rose, and with their golden tassels shining in the sun.

I am looking into this landscape now. The spring is in its making—a shimmering green like a mysterious mist is visible. Nowhere in the world is the meaning of the returning sun so forceful as in this deciduous forest of the north. No landscape is richer in poetic expression, none more tender and refined in color and form. To desecrate such a shrine is vandalism. On its purity and nobility will eventually be founded a great American art.

PART III

THE NATIVE LANDSCAPE AS A SOURCE OF INSPIRATION

Reconciling landscape design with the forms and patterns of nature is clearly one of the central challenges of creating "native gardens." The essays in this section reveal how various designers drew inspiration from the native landscape. Their approaches range from a general study of nature for its aesthetics to the structured analysis of ecological conditions and patterns that might be applied to design situations.

The first article is also the earliest, published by Andrew Jackson Downing in 1851. Speaking to an audience who believed there to be a strong separation between nature and garden, Downing argues the value of native trees and the lessons to be learned from our native woods and fields. His exhortation to "study landscape in nature more, and the gardens and their catalogues less" is perhaps equally valid to us today, more than a century and a half later.

In the second article of this section, Jens Jensen articulates his design philosophy as he was developing the "prairie

style" in the early years of his career. He speaks of approaching nature with reverence, using the art of design to preserve and refine nature's essential qualities. Themes evoked in his work throughout his life are highlighted here: attention to the interplay of light and shadow, of land forms and sky, and the idea that a garden is most successful when it reflects both cultural tradition and the inspiration of the regional landscape. Wilhelm Miller summarizes the basic tenets of the prairie style in his article "The Prairie Spirit in Landscape Gardening," a condensed version of an agricultural extension circular of the same title he published originally in 1915. Miller describes landscape designs by O. C. Simonds, Jens Jensen, and Walter Burley Griffin, explaining the relationship of the design approach they reflect to the plants and patterns found in the midwestern prairie landscape.

The next selection is a chapter from Frank Waugh's *The Natural Style in Landscape Gardening*. Waugh's book was one of the earliest attempts to describe the "natural" style that was emerging in the early twentieth century. As a professor of landscape architecture at the University of Massachusetts in Amherst, Waugh wrote much as he would have lectured to his students, exploring ideas beyond the conventional debates over formal vs. informal landscape design. Waugh explains the "natural style" as an approach to plant arrangement and landscape form which evokes the *spirit* of a natural landscape, though not necessarily by using a palette solely of local native plants. Waugh acknowledges Wilhelm Miller's argument for using exclusively native Illinois plants in landscape designs for that region, but he describes Miller's "Illinois Way" as more restrictive than he would advocate for the natural style. Instead, he suggests that designers in the natural style can incorporate a mix of native and non-native plants in their compositions.

The two other articles by Waugh included here, "A Juniper Landscape" and "Natural Plant Groups," illustrate the type of analytical processes he was exploring with his students in the late 1920s and early 1930s for mapping the compositional patterns and plant forms found in natural habitats in western Massachusetts which could be adapted to planting design. The article by Howard Caparn, who practiced and taught landscape architecture in New York City and Pittsburgh, originally published in *Landscape Architecture,* presents a similar approach, laying out a thoughtful process for studying the masses and forms of plants in the wild and applying the lessons in landscape composition.

Simonds continues with "Nature as the Great Teacher in Landscape Gardening." He advocates a model of design based on close direct study of nature. Plant materials and associations, landforms, compositional patterns, and processes of nutrient recycling are all lessons from nature that a designer might learn and apply. A strong advocate of design inspired by specific regional nature, Simonds is considered one of the originators of the prairie style. This essay, originally a lecture given at University of Illinois, was published posthumously in *Landscape Architecture* and is one of the most eloquent summaries of Simonds's design philosophy.

Finally, in "An Ecological Approach" Elsa Rehmann presents a summary of her ideas on ecologically based design after the publication in 1929 of *American Plants for American Gardens,* which she co-wrote with Edith Roberts. Rehmann, too, urges designers to study the patterns and processes of natural systems as models for a new ecological approach to landscape design.

ANDREW JACKSON DOWNING

A Few Hints on Landscape Gardening

(1851)

November is, above all others, the tree-planting month over the wide Union. Accordingly, everyone who has a rood of land looks about him at this season to see what can be done to improve and embellish it. Some have bought new places where they have to build and create everything in the way of home scenery, and they, of course, will have their heads full of shade trees and fruit trees, ornamental shrubs and evergreens, lawns and walks, and will tax their imagination to the utmost to see in the future all the varied beauty which they mean to work out of the present blank fields that they have taken in hand. These look for the most rapid-growing and effective materials, with which to hide their nakedness, and spread something of the drapery of beauty over their premises, in the shortest possible time. Others have already a goodly stock of foliage and shade, but the trees have been planted without taste, and by thinning out somewhat here, making an opening there, and planting a

From *The Horticulturist*, November 1851, 490–91.

little yonder, they hope to break up the stiff boundaries, and thus magically to convert awkward angles into graceful curves, and harmonious outlines. Whilst others, again, whose gardens and pleasure grounds have long had their earnest devotion, are busy turning over the catalogues of the nurseries in search of rare and curious trees and shrubs to add still more novelty and interest to their favorite lawns and walks. As the pleasure of creation may be supposed to be the highest pleasure, and as the creation of scenery in landscape gardening is the nearest approach to the matter that we can realize in a practical way, it is not difficult to see that November, dreary as it may seem to the cockneys who have rushed back to gas-lights and the paved streets of the city, is full of interest and even excitement to the real lover of the country.

It is, however, one of the characteristics of the human mind to overlook that which is immediately about us, however admirable, and to attach the greatest importance to whatever is rare, and difficult to be obtained. A remarkable illustration of the truth of this, may be found in the ornamental gardening of this country, which is noted for the strongly marked features made in its artificial scenery by certain poorer sorts of foreign trees, as well as the almost total neglect of finer native materials, that are indigenous to the soil. We will undertake to say, for example, that almost one-half of all the deciduous trees that have been set in ornamental plantations for the last ten years, have been composed, for the most part, of two very indifferent foreign trees—the ailantus and the silver poplar. When we say indifferent, we do not mean to say that such trees as the ailantus and the silver poplar, are not valuable trees in their way—that is, that they are rapid growing, will thrive in all soils, and are transplanted with the greatest facility—suiting at once both the money-making grower and the ignorant planter; but we do say, that when such trees as the American elms, maples and oaks, can be raised with so little trouble—trees as full of grace, dignity, and beauty, as any that grow in any part of the world—trees, too, that go on gathering new beauty with age, instead of throwing up suckers that utterly spoil lawns, or that become, after the first few years, only a more intolerable nuisance every day—it is time to protest against the indiscriminate use of such sylvan materials—no matter how much of "heavenly origin," or "silvery" foliage, they may have in their well sounding names.

It is by no means the fault of the nurserymen that their nurseries abound in ailantuses and poplars while so many of our fine forest trees are hardly to be found. The nurserymen are bound to pursue their business so as to make it profitable, and if people ignore oaks and ashes, and adore poplars and ailantuses, nurserymen cannot be expected to starve because the planting public generally are destitute of taste.

What the planting public need is to have their attention called to the study of nature—to be made to understand that it is in our beautiful woodland slopes, with their undulating outlines, our broad river meadows studded with single trees and groups allowed to grow and expand quite in a state of free and graceful development, our steep hills, sprinkled with picturesque pines and firs, and our deep valleys, dark with hemlocks and cedars, that the real lessons in the beautiful and picturesque are to be taken, which will lead us to the appreciation of the finest elements of beauty in the embellishment of our country places instead of this miserable rage for "trees of heaven" and other fashionable tastes of the like nature. There are, for example, to be found along side of almost every sequestered lawn by the roadside in the northern states, three trees that are strikingly remarkable for beauty of foliage, growth or flower, viz.: the tulip tree, the sassafras, and the pepperidge. The first is, for stately elegance, almost unrivalled among forest trees: the second, when planted in cultivated soil and allowed a fair chance, is more beautiful in its diversified laurel-like foliage than almost any foreign tree in our pleasure grounds: and the last is not surpassed by the orange or the bay in its glossy leaves, deep green as an emerald in summer, and rich red as a ruby in autumn—and all of them freer from the attacks of insects than either larches, lindens, or elms, or a dozen other favorite foreign trees, —besides being unaffected by the summer sun where horse chestnuts are burned brown, and holding their foliage through all the season like native born Americans, when foreigners shrivel and die; and yet we could name a dozen nurseries where there is a large collection of ornamental trees of foreign growth, but neither a sassafras, nor a pepperidge, nor perhaps a tulip tree could be had for love or money.

There is a large spirit of inquiry and a lively interest in rural taste, awakened on every side of us, at the present time, from Maine to the valley of the Mississippi; but the great mistake made by most novices is that they study gardens too much, and nature too little. Now gardens, in general, are stiff and graceless, except just so far as nature, ever free and flowing, reasserts her rights in spite of man's want of taste, or helps him when he has endeavored to work in her own spirit. But the fields and woods are full of instruction, and in such features of our richest and most smiling and diversified country must the best hints for the embellishment of rural homes always be derived. And yet it is not any portion of the woods and fields that we wish our finest pleasure ground scenery precisely to resemble. We rather wish to select from the finest sylvan features of nature, and to recompose the materials in a choicer manner, by rejecting any thing foreign to the spirit of elegance and refinement which should characterize the landscape of the most tasteful country residence—a landscape in which all that is graceful and beautiful in nature is preserved—all her most perfect forms and most harmonious lines—but with that added refinement which high keeping and continual care confer on natural beauty, without impairing its innate spirit of freedom, or the truth and freshness of its intrinsic character. A planted elm of fifty years, which stands in the midst of the smooth lawn before yonder mansion, its long graceful branches towering upwards like an antique classical vase, and then sweeping to the ground with a curve as beautiful as the falling spray of a fountain, has all the freedom of character of its best prototypes in the wild woods, with a refinement and a perfection of symmetry which it would be next to impossible to find in a wild tree. Let us take it then as the type of all true art in landscape gardening, which selects from natural materials that abound in any country, its best sylvan features, and by giving them a better opportunity than they could otherwise obtain, brings about a higher beauty of development and a more perfect expression than nature itself offers. Study landscape in nature more, and the gardens and their catalogues less, is our advice to the rising generation of planters, who wish to embellish their places in the best and purest taste.

JENS JENSEN

Landscape Art—An Inspiration from the Western Plains

(1906)

Broadly speaking this is the beginning of the American Renaissance, the constructive period in more than one art. From a western view it is pioneer life. The composer tries to form his composition from real life as he sees it on our plains. His material is more than interesting, but as his art is in the developing stage, false notes appear constantly to his mind; his compositions are subject to them. He, himself, is a part of the existing conglomeration. Pitched to the highest key, such real life of the West may at times fall into a chaos of uncertainty not unlike the blending together of a dozen races in chorus. His markings may be few but they count nevertheless, and are destined to become part of a great and beautiful composition, national in product but international in character.

Landscape art is subject to such influences as religion and climatic conditions. These direct the habits and customs of the people. Harmony in composition is as essential in landscape art as in music. It

From *The Sketch Book* 6, no. 1 (July 1906): 21–28.

must talk to us and inspire the soul with good. It must be lovely, fascinating and sublime, yet quiet, restful and dignified in its make-up, awakening the finer senses to the noblest of impulses.

Landscape art is seen at its best in the home and its surroundings. More thought has, perhaps, been bestowed upon the garden. Our gardens should reflect our lives; they should be a part of us, a part of our material and spiritual life. They should be a part of the landscape expressing those things which we admire and worship. Unpretentious, free from arrogant and vulgar expression, simple, charming, lovely, full of poetry and music, the composition must be perfect.

Harmony in colors is essential. There is delight and joy in a perfect color contrast against a green background. There is purity in the quiet pool of crystal water and in the snow white lilies. There is music in the dripping water supplying the pool. There is poetry in the virgin bower safely hanging over the rocky ledge where tall lilies vie with the waters of the hur-

Lincoln Council Ring, Lincoln Memorial Gardens, Springfield, Ill. (Photograph by Robert E. Grese.)

rying brook beneath for a place behind dark, secluded cedars. There is inspiration in it all! And above all, the garden walk, which has been remembered in song and story and picture from time immemorial. A happy medium of distinct character and fascination, expressing well the old adage that there is nothing in this world worth having that does not cost some trouble.

To preserve and *refine* that which nature has so generously given us and to which we should show our reverence, that which no human hand can duplicate and only the higher intelligence appreciate, that is our duty.

The meadow landscape must be beautiful in spring like the song of the bird, quiet during the hot summer days and full of splendor when bidding us goodbye for winter rest. The parting tone, the grand encore, assisted, as it were, by the afterglow of the setting sun, produces one of the grandest panoramas of our prairie landscape.

The meadow is the bright spot of the North, reflecting light and sunshine. It has forever become an indispensable part of the home of the North—the only place in the world where real home sentiment exists. The home is sacred to those so fortunate as to have it; it is their own, the most precious and beautiful possession any mortal being can claim. This sentiment must be reflected by the artist, the desire of seclusion and privacy, but without destroying the beauty from without.

The material at the disposal of the artist is wonderful—land, sea, sky, with ever-changing colors and varied sky-lines, reflecting light and shade in endless variety. A beautiful picture must excel in good forms and color. Nothing is so fascinating as the light behind the immediate shade: the lining to the cloud; to some, the hope beyond, which may be the greatest part of life itself; with its allurement of mystery, its enticement for reaching the goal beyond, yet withal, the futility of the effort, the inborn, onward striving of the soul toward the unattainable.

Every nation develops its own art. We are young as a nation and still in the process of crystallization. Every race or nationality brings to us some of its customs and habits which are gradually but surely being molded together, ultimately to form one national character. The environs amongst which the immigrants settle lend their great influence—sung by the poet, painted by the painter and idealized by the gardener.

The West is full of great possibilities, great, strong, fertile, with the right zest and thrill in its make-up. The atmosphere is pure and penetrating. There is no sleeping zephyr, but wide-awake blizzards and health-bringing summer breezes. Life, health and energy everywhere abound. What a glorious country from which to draw inspiration! This great prairie landscape, with the wonderful Rocky Mountains as its setting to the West and the Father of Rivers flowing through its fertile valleys. Its destiny is great—yes! and from this grand landscape we draw our inspiration.

WILHELM MILLER

The Prairie Spirit in Landscape Gardening

(1916)

In matters of Art our country has borrowed prodigiously from the Old World. Coming from across the seas our ancestors brought with them ideals foreign to the new continent. These ideals have been cherished and renewed as time passed until in many instances they have come to be hampering rather than inspiring. In architecture we have witnessed the transplanting of the Classic temple, the Gothic church, the French chateau, the Italian villa, the English manor house and even the Queen Anne anomaly. In landscape gardening we have repetitions of French, English and Italian designs. In painting and sculpture we can trace the influence of the great European School. All of this influence has not been detrimental, but it is time now that we were becoming a full grown nation with definite characteristics and hence an art of our own. That such is indeed coming to pass is

From *The American Magazine of Art* 7, no. 11 (September 1916): 448–50.

witnessed by much of the work of contemporary architects, sculptors and painters. Further testimony to this effect is found in an extremely engaging article on "The Prairie Spirit in Landscape Gardening," by Prof. Wilhelm Miller, published recently in pamphlet form as Circular 184 by the Illinois Agricultural Experiment Station and reprinted in part herewith by special permission. —The Editor.

The Middle West is evolving a new style of architecture, interior decoration, and landscape gardening, in an effort to create the perfect home amid the prairie states. This movement is founded on the fact that one of the greatest assets that any country or natural part of it can have, is a strong national or regional character, especially in the homes of the common people. Its westernism grows out of the most striking peculiarity of middle-western scenery, which is the prairie, i.e., flat or gently rolling land that was treeless when the white man came to southern Minnesota. On the prairie you can see the whole horizon, just as if you were on top of a mountain. The line of the horizon has been called "the strongest line in the western hemisphere."

This horizontal line is the fundamental thing in the prairie style of architecture, as the vertical line is in the Gothic style. The founder of the middle-western school of architects is Louis H. Sullivan of Chicago, who first jumped into fame in 1893, when he designed the Transportation Building at the World's Columbian Exposition. Sullivan's work, however, has been chiefly devoted to skyscrapers. His pupil, Wright, was the first to develop what is now called the prairie style of architecture. Naturally neither of these men is willing to accept this or any other title for work which they consider unique, but Wright acknowledges the influence of the prairie. There are now about twenty architects in this middle-

western school, and several of them are willing to accept the name of prairie style until some better name can be found for this wonderful new method of expression, which they hope will become dominant in all the states from Michigan and Ohio to South Dakota and Kansas.

The prairie style of interior decoration is too new to be represented by "best sellers" in every department store. But the old styles do not look at home in these new houses, and the architects generally design special furniture to fit each case. In general straight lines are followed, but these are modified as much as necessary for comfort and convenience. Mr. and Mrs. Sherman Booth who had much to do with getting woman suffrage for Illinois, declare that they will never live with anything but the new style furniture. They spent many years in collecting genuine antique Colo-

Hawthorns in meadow, Edsel and Eleanor Ford House, Grosse Pointe Shores, Mich. (Photograph by Robert E. Grese.)

nial furniture and then sold a houseful of it at auction to make way for something which they believe expresses the genius of the Middle West, instead of being a slavish copy of the East. In the famous Dana house at Springfield, Illinois, now owned by Mrs. German, is a window decoration, inspired by the common sumach, which was formerly despised by farmers, but is now much planted about middle-western homes because of its gorgeous autumnal colors. The sumach is a "red badge of courage" which is often considered a symbol of the indomitable western spirit.

The prairie style of landscape gardening is likewise a new mode of designing and planting, which aims to fit the peculiar scenery, climate, soil, labor, and other conditions of the prairies, instead of copying literally the manners and materials of other regions. It is not all theory, for one landscape gardener has submitted an itemized list of $6,000,000 worth of work done in the prairie style since 1901.

The principles of design on which the "prairie men" lay most stress are conservation, restoration, and repetition. They believe in saving or restoring as much of the local color or native vegetation as is practical. They believe in repeating by means of "stratified plants," i.e. plants with strongly marked horizontal branches or flat flower clusters. There are eighty-seven trees, shrubs, vines and perennials answering this description which are commonly advertised by nurserymen. There is little danger of monotony, because of the great variety in height, season of bloom and color of flower.

The origin of the "middle-western movement" in landscape gardening, if it may be so called, can be traced back to 1878 when Mr. Bryan Lathrop "discovered" Mr. O. C. Simonds and persuaded him to become a landscape gardener. The latter then began to lay out the new part of Graceland Cemetery, which, during the next quarter of a century, was perhaps the most famous example of landscape gardening designed by a western man. It is more than a mere cemetery, for it is full of spiritual suggestion and its wonderful effects produced by trees and shrubs native to Illinois have profoundly influenced the planting of home grounds. In 1880 Mr. Simonds began to transplant from the wilds the common Illinois species of oak, maple, ash, hornbeam, pepperidge, thorn apple, witch hazel, panicled dogwood, sheepberry, elder, and the like. Many of these plants have achieved great size and beauty. All the species named are nowadays called "stratified plants," but there was no talk then of "repetition," or even of "restoration." The guiding spirit was that respect for the quieter beauties of native vegetation which comes to every cultured person after he has lived a few years among the showiest plants from all foreign lands as assembled in ordinary nurseries and in the front yards of beginners. Graceland was to be a place of rest and peace, not a museum or a gaudy show. Should not the same ideal prevail in our home grounds? The first piece of work done by Mr. Simonds that suggests what is now called "restoration," was begun in 1895 at Quincy, Ill., when its famous park system overlooking the Mississippi was projected under the leadership of the late Edward J. Parker. Some of the best known work of Mr. Simonds is in Lincoln Park, Chicago, but the whole "North Shore" shows his influence in home planting.

Probably the first designer who consciously took the prairie as a leading motive is Mr. Jens Jensen, who was trained in Denmark and came to America in 1883. In 1885 he settled in Chicago and was at once impressed by the surrounding prairie, which was then a sea of grasses and flowers. Acres of phlox and blazing star, and thousands of compass plants were a familiar sight. The first design in which prairie flowers were used in a large, impressive way, was made in 1901 for Mr. Chalmers of Lake Geneva. Here were planted hundreds of the wild *Phlox paniculata,* parent of more than 400 garden varieties; hundreds of purple flags (*Iris versicolor*) collected from the banks of the Desplaines River, and hundreds of swamp rose mallows which glorify the rivers of Illinois in August with their pink flowers five inches in diameter. The first attempt to epitomize the beauty of Illinois rivers was made in 1901 for Mr. Harry Rubens at Glencoe, where there are a miniature spring, brook, waterfall, and lake. Practically all the surrounding trees, shrubs and flowers were planted, and more than ninety per cent of the species grow wild within a mile of the spot. From 1905 to 1907 he designed and planted the Prairie River and Prairie Rose-garden in Humboldt Park, and the Conservatories in Garfield Park, Chicago.

A third landscape architect who has been greatly influenced by the prairie is Walter Burley Griffin. He received his training in landscape gardening at the University of Illinois, and supplemented it by work in the offices of several architects of the western school. He planned many houses in the prairie style. His chief American work in landscape architecture has been done at DeKalb, Decatur, Oak Park, Hubbard's Woods and Edwardsville, Ill., and Veedersburg, Ind. The planting list for DeKalb shows that as early as 1906 he was using a high percentage of plants native to Illinois—especially the stratified materials. In 1912 he won a world-competition for a city plan for Canberra, the new capital of Australia. Mr. Griffin must be regarded as a middle-western landscape architect since he maintains an office in Chicago and undertakes new work in the Middle West.

There are many other good landscape gardeners now practicing in the Middle West. Those who acknowledge the prairie as a leading motive in their work are, however, not numerous at the time this paper is prepared. There are several young men whose work is promising, but not mature or extensive enough to show their feeling for the prairie style.

FRANK A. WAUGH

The Natural Style in Landscape Gardening

(1917)

WHAT IS MEANT

All the older men and women now living whose recollections of garden matters run back, say into the seventies, will remember the violent controversy then raging between the advocates of the formal garden on the one side and of the natural style on the other. Those were days of violent partisanship in all matters. In politics and religion people were habitually intolerant. In certain families it was held that to vote the democratic ticket was prima facie evidence of murder, arson, and embezzlement of funds. In other circles it was fully agreed that unless one were immersed into a particular church he would surely land in the eternal fires. Amongst people trained in this temper the ardent disagreements over garden style were perfectly natural and necessary.

And, we ought to add, altogether bad. Though some theorists may argue that the

From *The Natural Style in Landscape Gardening*, by Frank A. Waugh (Boston: Richard G. Badger, 1917) 11–42.

modern man's lack of strong convictions is a weakness, it is perfectly plain that the growth of tolerance, the broadening of view, the greater catholicity of taste in all matters, mark a very genuine advance. It is a great and genuine gain for the spirit of humanity.

This change, which has marked all realms of thought, has been as effective in the field of landscape gardening as anywhere else. To those of us who remember it, it has been equally agreeable.

We may fairly claim to have achieved a full freedom in these matters. Every well-trained landscape architect in America designs freely in either the formal or the natural style, frequently using both styles in different parts of the same project. The ill-natured polemics of the seventies have disappeared altogether from the garden literature of the present day.

This change has been wholly for good. I rejoice in every thought of it; and as I take up now a discussion of the natural style, my unwavering allegiance to the modern catholicism must be most emphatically declared. Thus when I find it necessary to praise the natural style, to allege some neglect of it, and to make some comparisons in its favor, these statements must not be taken to reflect adversely on any other style nor to indicate a partizan opinion.

To trace fully the development of the idea of a natural style in gardening would be exceedingly interesting, but it would require a great deal of time and space. Fortunately a complete historical review is not necessary to our present purposes. It is essential to observe, however, that the natural style has meant very different things at different times. Nearly every reformer has advertised his own work as more natural than his predecessors, or as a "return to nature." The garden of Eden is described as designed in the natural style.

Batty Langley was one of the most interesting of these reformers, and it is worth while now to note what was his idea of the natural style.

Another curious episode was the career of Lancelot Brown—"Old Capability Brown," as his jealous critics dubbed him. His contribution to the natural style was the discovery that "Nature abhors a straight line." Therefore away with straight lines. With a strong start in this direction it is easy to conclude that the further we get away from the straight line the nearer we get to Nature. So Brown made walks and drives and artificial watercourses so crooked that they lost their way. It was said that his walks tied themselves in true lovers' knots and that his made rivers often doubled and crossed their own courses. Brown made himself thoroughly ridiculous, but he illustrated one idea of the natural style, and an idea which has more recently and in a milder form had a distinguished hearing in America.

After Brown arose a small group of doctrinaires who theorized that the only way to make a truly natural composition was to copy it in detail from nature. The neglected moraine, the common stone heap and the untutored wayside copse became their patterns to be slavishly reproduced in their "gardens." Because broken, dead and blasted trees were found in the native woods these enthusiasts transplanted dead trees to their private parks. These extravagances, however, soon followed Lancelot Brown's crooked line theory into the limbo of discarded jokes.

The idea of making literal transcriptions from Nature has had a much greater and more interesting development elsewhere. What we know (and very vaguely understand) as the Japanese style of landscape gardening—a style which it appears originated in China—is founded precisely on this theory. The original idea was to copy certain classic landscapes or landscape arrangements; and as these first oriental landscape gardeners were priests, and as their gardening was primarily for the embellishment of the temple grounds, their prime models were certain sacred landscapes, made sacred by association with other shrines.

These sacred landscape arrangements were then reproduced in other localities, but, as in a drawing, to a scale considerably smaller than the originals. It was considered obligatory to preserve this reduced scale throughout the copy. Thus, if the copy was at one-tenth the size of the original, each lull and each tree must be reduced in the same proportion. While obviously this theory has not been rigidly adhered to in all examples of Japanese gardening, it has been carried far enough to make most gardens seem very curious to occidental eyes. But the Japanese gardener sometimes asserts that his is the only natural style, and from his point of view he is just as nearly right as anybody else.

In America there have been less radical but very plain differences of opinion as to what really constitutes a natural style. The idea which has had the widest vogue has certainly been the native flora cult. A very respectable number of very respectable gardening persons (with perhaps the tender sex predominating) have made themselves quite delightful grounds with plants selected strictly from the local flora. Of course there have been some differences. One gardener would accept any species native to America; another insists on plants from his own state; the garden maker of real convictions accepts nothing but what grows naturally on his own farm.

My friend Dr. Wilhelm Miller in his recent crusade for "the Illinois way" represents a temperate recrudescence of this native plant propaganda. For it is a part of "the Illinois way" to use Illinois plants. The arguments for this way are largely the arguments for a natural style of gardening.

Probably the majority of trained landscape architects when designing in the natural style employ a good many non-indigenous species. Their test is simply that a plant shall be effectively naturalized. Their compositions are pictorial—made to appeal to the eye rather than to a botanical education. If a plant looks perfectly at home it is to all reasonable requirements natural.

This seems to be a safe middle-ground. Certainly he would be a hard theorist and an intolerable puritan who would exclude the common lilac and the homely apple tree from his grounds simply because they are not native to America. It wouldn't be good democratic Americanism, either, for the great bulk of our citizens are derived from foreign stocks.

The anti-straight-line theory as a fundamental element of the natural style seems to have been held by Downing and by Olmsted, Senior. It has been much emphasized by some of their followers; but careful designers have learned that simply to avoid straight lines and radial curves gets one nowhere. It certainly does not lead to naturalness. Indeed, it seems philosophically impossible to found any positive or constructive method on any purely negative dictum.

In order to arrive at a perfectly clear conception of what we now mean when we talk among ourselves about the natural style, it seems best to consider more carefully what is meant by style in landscape gardening. It is one of the unfortunate vagaries of language that this term has assumed a special meaning in landscape gardening distinctly different from what it carries in other arts. In literature, where this other meaning is clearest, style signifies the personal peculiarities of the author. Mr. William Dean Howells has his style by which his work can be recognized, and David Grayson has his.

In landscape gardening, on the other hand, styles are national—perhaps, more strictly speaking, racial. The Japanese style embodies the garden characteristics of a whole race. The Italian style does the same. Every style which ever had a name was called by the name of the race or nation which practiced it; and one of the questions now before the house is whether we shall ever have an American style.

Field study of the landscape. (Photograph by Frank A. Waugh. Date unknown. Glass lantern slide, Frank A. Waugh Collection, W.E.B. Du Bois Library, University of Massachusetts Amherst.)

We may therefore define style, as used in this particular art, as being the expression of the national, racial or ethnic quality in landscape gardening.

But what of the natural and the formal styles of gardening? They do not bear national names, though they have been often and inaptly called the English and the Italian styles. The fact is that these are not styles at all in any strict use of language, but great garden forms. The formal form may be closely compared to poetry and the informal form to prose. Each is a structural method of composition—a form. Poetry is one literary form; prose is another. National or personal styles may be expressed through either of these forms.

Up to this point, therefore, and subject to a very important addition later to be made, we may say that the so-called

natural style is really a fundamental garden form. It is a structural form characterized by certain resemblances to the natural landscape. These points of resemblance are sometimes quite arbitrarily chosen by the garden designer, and sometimes quite artificially developed; but it is always the logical aim of the artist to discover and to follow the principles of composition followed by nature.

This structural form is distinguished further, in a purely negative manner, by contrast with the formal garden form, which is symmetrical, balanced, enclosed and determinate, whereas the informal form is unsymmetrical, not obviously balanced, not apparently enclosed and not marked by visible boundaries.

(Our terminology here, where we speak of the formal form and the informal form, is execrable, but it is unavoidable, and the ideas are perfectly definite and logical.)

Our partial definition of the so-called natural style of landscape gardening speaks of it in terms of form. But any vital style must have something more than form. It must also have a living, breathing spirit. Any form without spirit is dead and fit only for the crematory.

What then is the informing spirit of the natural style? Is it not the spirit of the natural landscape? We speak of the spirit of the woods, or the spirit of the mountains; and, quite as precisely as common language can ever convey spiritual ideas, we know what we mean. We do actually have a perfectly clear idea in mind when we speak of these things.

The idea is not only clear, but valuable in the highest degree. Our spiritual ideas are always more important than our thoughts about materials; and it is more important to any man—much more important—to know the spirit of the woods or the spirit of the plains or the spirit of the mountains, than to know the properties of benzine or the names of golf clubs or the uses of gunpowder.

It is not difficult to see that this spirit of the landscape is different from the spirit of architecture. Thus anyone who is capable of a spiritual conception of any sort can readily accept the principle that, while the formal garden should be animated by the architectural spirit, the informal garden should live by the spirit of the landscape.

We are all so much unaccustomed to thinking in spiritual terms, and the significance of this idea is so essential, that it will be well to spend a little more time upon it. For purposes of illustration let us imagine ourselves sitting on the pasture fence in the friendly sunshine of a warm June afternoon. Before us there spreads, let us say, the rolling green pasture lands, interspersed with scattered oaks, and in the midst a dimpling deliberate river. In the shade of the trees the well-fed cows rest and ruminate. Over all stretches the quiet blue sky, deepening to a purpling haze along the distant horizon as the afternoon wanes. It is a landscape which appeals to every physical sense. We rejoice to be alive in it.

But does it not appeal to other than our physical senses? Does it not touch some spiritual sense? As we, civilized human beings, sit there amidst the glory of that June landscape, do we apprehend nothing but the physical landscape? What do we really see? Only the trees and the grass and the river? Only these? If that is really all we see then the good Jersey cow ruminating under the tree has a very substantial advantage over us. She sees the tree and the grass and the river; and besides that she sees a square meal. She crops the grass, drinks the water, retires to the shade of the tree and ruminates.

Do we bring back from that fair landscape anything which we may ruminate? If we really do succeed in capturing something more than what the cow gets, that harvest must be a spiritual product. It is the spirit of the landscape.

There may be men and women who get less from the landscape than the cow does. If there are, I am sure they will not admit it. So perhaps we may let the case rest there for the present. In a subsequent chapter we shall give more extended discussion to the meaning of the native landscape. This is in reality an endeavor to understand the landscape in spiritual terms, and thus to make more clear our full definition which is that *the natural style of landscape gardening endeavors to present its pictures in forms typical of the natural landscape and made vital by the landscape spirit.*

In this connection it is essential to remember that a good deal of landscape art, and especially that which adopts the natural style, is not required to make every picture out of whole cloth. It might be more accurately described as intelligently letting alone a natural landscape. What does the wise landscape gardener do when called upon to treat a stretch of attractive natural scenery? He must, first and foremost, endeavor to understand the spirit of his landscapes. Then his work will be to simplify and accentuate the characteristic natural forms (chiefly topography and flora), and to clarify and interpret the spirit of the place. This clarification and interpretation of spiritual values is the real work of the real artist.

THE NATIVE LANDSCAPE

Whether our foregoing definition of the natural style is adequate or defective, it must be plain that any naturalistic style of landscape gardening is largely dependent on the native landscape. The ideas, motives, and methods must come mainly from nature. Indeed, it would seem certain that any landscape architect of any school must know and love the landscape. Such knowledge and such sympathy would be fundamentally and absolutely necessary.

Whenever the designer professes, however, to do his landscape gardening in the natural style, it would seem doubly incumbent on him to bring to his work a critical understanding of nature's landscape and a love of the native landscape at once ardent, sane, discriminating and balanced. A mere boyish enthusiasm will not answer. It must be the true, tried and fixed love of maturity.

Thus it becomes the first and perhaps the most important step in landscape gardening, especially naturalistic landscape gardening, to know and to love the native landscape. Both knowledge and love are required. Can we, now, point out any practical approach to the landscape? any way of understanding it better? especially any means of loving it more? Assuredly we can.

At the outset we may gain some respect for the landscape by observing its power. It does exert a truly marvelous power upon the intelligence of men; and their feelings, which lie deeper, are even more profoundly affected. Common men love the landscape passionately. The attachment to home is largely the love of landscape. When the army of Cyrus, defeated and disheartened, came back from their long campaign in Persia, they fell down and wept when, from the top of a hill, they caught the first view of the sea. It was to them the landscape of home. They were not especially susceptible or responsive men—certainly not artists trained to the love of beauty. Human nature is still the same. Any man, no matter how dull, who has grown up amongst the hills of Vermont has, necessarily and positively, a deep love of that particular landscape in his heart. Let him be exiled for a few years in Texas or France or Chicago and then let him revisit the Green Mountains. His heart will leap up like a mother to her child. His emotions will be stirred to their profoundest depths. There is hardly a human experience anywhere of greater reach or power.

This particular experience, while universal and known of all men, is somewhat provincial. Cultivated men learn to love other landscapes than those to which they were born. A part of the value of landscape lies in its universality. The landscape is everywhere. The lover of books cannot always live in a library; the lover of music cannot find anywhere a perpetual concert; the lover of painting cannot shut himself up in an art gallery; but the lover of the landscape has his joy always with him. Even the hater of the landscape, if there could be such a man, could not escape from it.

Now since art is after all primarily the love and enjoyment of the beautiful, and since the landscape is physically present to all people, and since it appeals powerfully to practically all people, we must regard it as the principal source in the world of esthetic joy. It is the world's principal reservoir of beauty. It does more for the esthetic life of mankind than all the painting, sculpture, poetry and architecture in all the world taken together. This is a large claim, but it is a simple and obvious truth.

For this reason we should all greatly reverence the native landscape, should seek to conserve it for human use and enjoyment, should endeavor to make it physically accessible to all, should try to make it intelligible to all, should work to open up for it the way to men's hearts.

Let us take the case of the young man who proposes to become a landscape architect and who hopes to do some of his work in the natural style—or the informal form, if we prefer an exacter nomenclature. In his earnest desire to know and love the native landscape his first plain step will be to associate with it. He will go out with the landscape. He will spend hours, days and weeks with it. Instead of going to the bowling alleys, the billiard rooms, the dances and the movies, he will go to the hills, he will visit the lakes, he will follow the brooks, he will camp on the plains. All this is so simple, so obvious, so easy, that it needs only to be mentioned to be established as a fruitful means of landscape study.

Of course the student will visit the landscape—no, he will live with it—with an open mind and heart. He will be trying to see what the landscape has to offer, trying to hear what it has to tell. He will look long, quietly, silently, intently at the horizon, or at the distant valley, or at the mountains. And most of all he will consciously seek their spiritual message. He will know that as a man it is absolutely obligatory upon him to see something in that landscape more than the cow sees. Whatever he gets beyond what the cow gets is the spiritual harvest of the landscape. It is the only part which is of any human use.

In another place I have tried to extend the definition of the landscape to include such items as the sky, and the weather. The man who is thus conscientiously seeking the spiritual message of the landscape will look long and often at the sky. My own students are directed to spend frequent hours of solitude lying on their backs looking up into the depths of the heavens.

This exercise should be practiced nights as well as days. The deep infinities of the sky are more visible when pricked out by the twinkling stars than when illuminated by the sun. The exercise should be used also in all weathers—when the sky is full of fresh falling snow or of pearly raindrops. For the landscape lover must love all aspects of the sky and all moods of the weather.

While the fundamental psychological appeal of the landscape is universal, reaching to all men's hearts, there are differences in minor manifestations. The landscape does not mean the same to everybody. The landscape, like religion or any other great experience, is "all things to all men."

To the farmer the landscape is a part of the day's work. He plows and sows and harvests the landscape. If he is a true farmer his fields become inestimably dear to him. The sun, the wind, and the rain are his friends. He knows and loves them.

The forester lives in the woods. To him the landscape is full of trees. These are spread over rocky mountain sides and interspersed with friendly brooks. So the landscape takes on for the forester a very special color and character.

In America the pioneer has played a deeply significant role. There have been generations of pioneers, from those who landed at Plymouth and Jamestown to those who settled the plains and captured the Oregon. This body of pioneers has moved forward across the continent from one ocean to the other with a slow, steady, indefeasible march. For more than 200 years their campfires lighted the way. Generation after generation of hardy men and women lived roughly in the open or sheltered by log huts or sod shanties. They lived very near to the landscape. They loved it profoundly. Many of them loved it so deeply that they could not bear to share it with neighbors. As soon as the settlements arrived and the landscape was invaded and despoiled, the pioneers moved on.

To understand anything of American history it is necessary to understand these pioneers, and to understand them at all we must understand their love of the land-scape. This element has had a wide-reaching influence in American life.

This feeling, perhaps in a form of genuine heredity, shows itself frequently in the best established citizens in the midst of our most complicated modern civilization. Men break away from big cities year by year and seek the wilderness. They go to the farthest solitudes. They spend the longest vacations they can capture in hunting, fishing, tramping. They find a fierce joy in the wilderness. The landscape to them means freedom. It means release from a strenuous civilization which at best they find only partly good.

All outdoor sports constitute more or less temporary release from civilization and a return to the landscape. Fox chasing, automobiling, fly fishing, and the entire list of outdoor recreations belong in this category. They are merely so many different ways of reaching the landscape.

Even the more socialized competitive outdoor sports, such as baseball and football, are still outdoor sports. The baseball game would be worthless if it were not played under the open sky. The spectators on the bleachers must still look up and see the blue heavens even if the horizon is damned with a circle of painted signs advertising the worst brands of beer and tobacco.

A more refined and lady-like approach to the landscape is found in gardening. Gardening as a polite domestic art is perhaps the most complete combination of civilization and the landscape which has yet been devised. If we press this on to the point where it becomes really landscape gardening it would surely deserve this description, for what could landscape gardening be except such a full and final fusion of the landscape with the social human artificial domestic garden?

One who undertakes to study the native landscape with any thoroughness should properly approach the subject by studying the principal types of native landscape. It will not do simply to study the landscape in general. One must be more analytic and specific.

As a matter of fact most persons in their primary love of home found their love of landscape upon acquaintance with a particular type. The citizen of Cape Cod loves the sea and the dunes. The native of Nebraska loves the plains. The habitant of Quebec loves the woods, and the men bred amongst the mountains of Colorado must love the white-peaked Rockies.

The man who really sets out to know and love the landscape, however, whether he be a student of landscape architecture or a mere citizen of the universe, will try to know different types of landscape. He will seek to make the acquaintance of as many distinct types as possible. For this reason it is desirable to consider what are the principal landscape types.

It is reasonably accurate to say, though there is nothing scientific in the classification, that the four great types of landscape are the sea, the mountains, the plains, and the forests. These great types everyone should know. Certainly every man who professes to be a landscape architect should assimilate into his own life these fundamental landscape forms.

The sea has always been a power in human thought. Its wide and infinite reaches, its constant motion, its vivid expression of power, its versatile changes, its human and super-human moods, its delicate colorings, even its salty smell, make it so vivid that no human consciousness could possibly escape it. A mere glimpse of the sea must profoundly impress the most unsympathetic stranger. How deeply it affects those who live with it all history can tell.

Likewise the mountains in their sublime altitudes are capable of moving men's hearts and minds to the utmost. They have a character of their own as much as the sea. Whole nations have lived with the mountains and drawn their character from them.

To the man from a different environment the plains seem monotonous. Their wide expanse, their level horizon, do not make an instant impression. Yet the men and women who live there know that this wide unbroken circle of horizon which the eye can barely reach, speaks to the mind always of infinity. Nothing could be wider and nothing could appeal more to the imagination. Nothing could assist more in the enlargement of humanity. When these wide plains are beautifully spangled with native flowers, when they are swept into billows by summer winds, when they are capped by rolling mountains of cloud, when they are ablaze with great prairie fires, when they take on any of their other native aspects they become tremendous, they present magnificent and tragic spectacles which leave the human mind as profoundly moved as it can ever be by the sea or mountains. Yes, the plains must always be reckoned as one of the great types of landscape.

The forests are more friendly and familiar. There is more of the feeling of domesticity about them. It is a strange fact that in the early settlement of America pioneers who had their choice avoided the prairies and settled first among the forests, even though they were there compelled to clear away the trees with infinite labor to make fields for farming. The natural human love for the forest landscape needs nothing more than mention. It is worthwhile to recall, however, how this has been put to special use in such enterprises as the "forest cure." It is well known that many sanatoria have been established in the forests and that thousands of men and women have found life and health simply in being exposed to the healing influence of the crowded trees.

Besides these four main types of landscape, there are minor types of considerable importance. There are great rivers which throughout their entire courses completely dominate the landscape. They establish its character. Anyone who is to know the landscape should know some of the great rivers and should have felt their spell.

The little brooks too are well worthy of acquaintance. As they sing and gurgle down through the forests or roar down the mountainside, they too have a story to tell. It is a story to which every man and woman ought to listen.

There are many sections of country which could not be called mountainous, but which are characterized by their rolling hills. Such hilly country, whether found in central New York, Missouri, or Bohemia, has a character of its own. It is neither plains nor mountains, but a kind of human compromise. These hills are good to live with. They support large populations. They are mild and pleasant without being so tragic as the sea or mountains. For this reason they are psychologically better for daily human association. If one is a real lover of the landscape he will not seek always for the extreme and spectacular types. One of the greatest qualities in all art is restraint and the willingness to accept a moderate expression of feeling. This quality of moderation is expressed in the rolling hill country characteristic of wide sections on every continent. It is a type of landscape which has been too much neglected,—that is, there has been little attempt to understand its spiritual significance.

In some districts the character of the landscape is taken from its lakes. One whole section of England is called the Lake County. The magnificent territory bordering on Lake Champlain, whatever its topography and its other beauties, must render chief homage to the incomparable lake. The lover of the landscape ought also to know some lakes.

Everywhere where men live the landscape has been more or less changed. Where considerable populations have become established the landscape is much subdued. The most fertile countries are fully developed in farming lands. In some places the forests have been cut away. In others the prairies have been obliterated. In place of forests and prairies there are now checkered fields of corn and wheat interspersed with orchards and pastures. This agricultural landscape, however, has an effective appeal of its own. It is not unfair to say that it is quite as beautiful as the native landscape which it has supplanted. This type of landscape also has been widely overlooked. The American people especially have not felt its beauty nor understood its significance. In the old country civilization has done better. In England there is a lively and conscious love of the cultivated landscape, for practically all England is cultivated. In the German language the same feeling is recognized in the settled term *Kultur-Land-schaft*. Doubtless, we in America will presently come to a similar understanding of the beauty of well farmed country, and will learn to love the farm landscape and to realize its deeper spiritual significance.

The student and lover of the landscape must not only cultivate its acquaintance, he must especially seek what is beautiful in this outdoor world. He must discriminate. He must find the best and give his chiefest homage to that.

It is one of the first requirements in art, though often overlooked, that one must find the best and associate with it chiefly. The beginner spends too much time criticizing what is bad or trying to improve what is indifferent. The artist will find beauty in many places where thoughtless or untrained persons overlook it; but wherever he may have to search, he will look only for what is good, dismissing from his attention as quickly as possible everything squalid or disorderly or ugly.

Now this exercise of seeking out whatever is best in the landscape and fixing the attention on that is a perfectly simple undertaking and can be practiced by children. For some years I have experimented with this method of instruction in the public schools. The method is of enough importance to bear restatement.* A set of landscape exercises is made up, each one of which calls direct attention to some beautiful feature.

Here are sample exercises:

No. 1. Trees. Where is the finest tree in town? What kind of a tree is it? How old? What is its history?
No. 2. Views. Where is the best view or outlook in town? What can you see from this point? How might this view be improved?

And so on. The characteristic feature of each exercise is that it sends the pupil to seek something beautiful, it leads him to consider carefully the relationships which influence its effect, it helps him to make comparisons, while appealing frankly to his personal preference (and this is fundamentally important), it urges on his thought some reasons for his opinion.

When a series of such exercises, carefully planned and fairly superintended, are carried out in school, they lead to a pretty thorough acquaintance with the local landscape, always with emphasis on the features of greatest beauty. This constitutes genuine art education, and also it exemplifies the kind of acquaintanceship with the landscape which is fundamentally necessary to the man or woman who would know what the natural style of landscape gardening means.

*This plan of school instruction is more fully stated in my book *The Landscape Beautiful*.

HAROLD A. CAPARN

Thoughts on Planting Composition

(1929)

The frame of mind that is prone to classify things, that is, to group them in their proper relationship, is constructive and helpful so long as this is done to promote thought, but not if it is done to evade thought, to pigeonhole things that should not be pigeonholed, so that places for them can be settled without further consideration. If it is done to simplify a general subject by resolving it into its component parts in their due relation so that it may be viewed and better understood as a whole, the classification is plainly a good thing. It is hoped that the analysis of planting design here attempted may be of the latter kind.

Planting Composition, by which is meant the combining of planting material to produce pleasing effects, may be divided into two classes: (1) architectural or formal, and (2) other.

By "architectural" planting is meant the use of the material much as the architect uses his bricks or stone. He translates

From *Landscape Architecture* 19, no. 3 (April 1929): 141–56.

walls, arches, columns, obelisks, pylons, and even sculpture into terms of vegetation. But as soon as we leave the architectural manner we reach a different set of conditions. Nothing is on axis, though everything should be subtly balanced. Symmetry is disagreeable, though that stability of composition which gives a sense of equilibrium, and which alone satisfies, must govern. Irregularity and a certain unexpectedness are pervading, though repose is essential. Variety is orthodox; restlessness and confusion are tabooed. Simplicity must prevail, though elaboration be everywhere.

These generalities will hardly be denied, but they are not of very much use, either to the planting designer or his critics, without more specific application to examples. Fortunately, these may be found in all good works of landscape design in an informal manner, and in the works of nature wherever man has not interfered with them.

Planting designers have obtained their ideas and their inspiration primarily from two sources, (1) the works of Nature, and Nature modified by man, and (2) the works of painters. Inasmuch as the painters got their inspiration originally from the works of Nature, selecting from them such subjects as seemed paintable and worth recording, it might appear that their works may be neglected in the present discussion; but second thought will show that they may be of value as indicating interpretations of natural conditions by trained and gifted brains and hands.

We live in a mathematical Universe. The stars and planets move in calculable orbits at calculable distances, and in calculable periods of time. All have mathematical forms. All are interdependent, and obey the laws of periodicity, and perhaps of recurrence.

As above, so below. Our earth revolves on an axis, and every part of it, from a grain of sand to a mountain, contains a line which, if supported, would maintain it in equilibrium. This earth and all its parts depend for existence and progress on a vast series of balances under the law of compensation. Everything, from a cloud to a butterfly, has a middle and two sides. All things tend to compensation and mutual adjustment, if not in one form, then in another, from the forces that control the weather to those which influence human action.

The whole vegetable world exemplifies this. From a round trunk of generally symmetrical structure are suspended branches arranged to keep it in equilibrium considering the weight of leaves, the wind pressure and the other forces that we do not understand. Every branch and twig is a replica of the trunk, but rooted in the trunk instead of in the soil. Leaves are constructed on either side of a central rib, and the sepals, petals and stamens of a flower are disposed

round the axis of the stem, not in perfect symmetry, but so as to produce a mental impression of symmetry. This impression, far more vital and interesting than if the symmetry were "perfect" is produced by perfect balance, not by duplication of size.

When man emerged from his caves and began to construct things for himself for which there was no original to copy and no precedent in Nature to follow, it was inevitable that he should be impressed, or rather controlled, by the universal law of symmetry and balance. So he built his structures with four sides and made their doors and windows of the same general shape. In fact, he made his buildings on axis. As time went on, he became so fascinated by the practical and visual effects of compositions on axis that he produced such structures as the Karnak temple and the Parthenon, where the axis pervades all the parts and is felt in the smallest of them. In this case, man was not copying anything that he saw in Nature; he was introducing and utilizing without limit a thing that does not exist in Nature, except as a mathematical abstraction, namely, the right angle: but as an abstraction, the right angle is everywhere, of infinite pervasion: and, for the prototype of a material thing, may be the soundest of bases. So every time man built a room he assembled his right angles and created axes, and it turned out to be one of the best and most important discoveries he had made, one of the greatest works he has accomplished; for ever since that high and far-off time, the structure on axis has housed and protected civilization after civilization. It is a sign and symbol of the community instinct, for it makes possible the living together of numbers of people in a small space.

All this has evolved because the composition balanced on axis is based on natural law. All things are in equilibrium, and if a void is created the forces of compensation hasten to fill it. If there is an upheaval, these forces begin to work for repose. Every real work of art (whether its prototype or original is in Nature or not) is balanced on axis, is in a state of equilibrium. If it is not visibly on axis like a building, it is invisibly on axis like a statue or picture. If it is a building, the axis is likely to be manifest with equal weights on both sides. If it is not a building, the axis will not be manifest and the sense of balance will be obtained by other means than by equality of masses, by different distances of the parts from the center of gravity. Thus we have a distinction between the "formal" and the "informal" manner of design, and are tempted to give way to a distinction and a definition to this effect: "A formal design is one that is visibly on axis. An informal design is one that is invisibly on axis."

Nearly all the things that man makes for his use, from a rivet to an ocean steamer, from a pie to a platitude are visibly on axis. They must be, to fit into the mechanical world that he has created. But he usually assembles them in an informal manner. Nature creates everything living on visible axes, but when it comes to assembling them, whether in relation to each other or to her other works, she uses the invisible axis and the informal manner.

Man, being unable to create anything with life, follows Nature's example as faithfully as he can and constructs almost everything on visible axes, but when it comes to assembling them, either with each other or with the works of Nature, he usually does it without any axis, visible or invisible. Thus it is that they so often lack equilibrium, and appear aimless and dislocate, banal,

Tree masses based on natural patterns by Jens Jensen, Columbus Park, Chicago. (Photograph by Robert E. Grese.)

wasteful, and inconvenient. That is why they are always changing. Man is naturally discontented with the things he has made, yearns for improvement and toward perfection, yet is unable to attain it and mostly unwilling to take the means that would enable him to approach it. Nature changes continually also, but her changes are along lines of evolution, not of haphazard and whimsical experiment. In every stage her works are in equilibrium, whereas man's seldom are, excepting in spots.

A careless glance at the plantings of Nature might give the impression that, as far as anything that artists would term "design" goes, they are purposeless and confused. Forests may consist of one kind of tree, or they may be mixtures of many, broadleaf and conifers seemingly jumbled together without discrimination. So with a meadow or prairie or the forest floor: they seem to show an unrestrained scramble for existence. Yet more deliberate observation will show in them certain important characteristics of a work of art. They are generally beautiful: they are usually "in the picture," and when and to the extent that they are not, it is because of something that man has injected into it. And they all have unity and repose, by which is meant that their constituent parts produce an impression of being the right thing in the right place.

If we try to analyze the makeup of, say, a mountain forest of the Catskills or Appalachians (a mountainside being easy to see), two things will be apparent: (1) that the broadleaf trees are so mixed that they produce an expression of continuity not less than if they were all of the same kind, but more varied; (2) that the several kinds, and especially conifers if any there

be (conifers being more easily discerned), though they may appear at first to be dotted at random, yet they are quite likely to be arranged in some kind of grouping or sequence through which one could draw lines, curved or straight, which would fit into the imaginary frame of the picture. There is quite likely to be one or more main groups from which stragglers or outposts at varying distances extend in more or less orderly progress. In the meadow, if it be in flower time when daisies and black-eyed-susans or Queen Anne's lace or asters or goldenrod display their planting scheme in gay colors, the general effect to the casual beholder will be that of a continuous expanse of white or yellow or blue as the case may be. But if one looks more carefully and analytically, a certain kind of grouping will probably appear. Masses are thicker in one place than in another: they get thinner as they get further from the center, and seen in perspective, are likely to produce the effect of long horizontal or sloping more or less even or very irregular lines of a kind that a painter likes to use if he is deft enough, and has gone to school to Nature as his teacher often enough. These lines, which of course are really masses, merge into one another, retreat behind each other, or come to the front much in the way of the islands of an archipelago or the clouds in a summer sky which break away from a main mass and are driven apart by the wind, but which float or lie in the sky in a certain relation to each other, producing an effect not of purposeless spotting but of sequence and interrelation. Light breezes on the surface of a river or lake produce local disturbances which cause quite analogous effects. This is the same kind of thing that we observed in the conifers on the mountainside forest, and proceeds from a similar set of causes. So does the veining in a wood or marble panel. Even though one walks around the whole meadow, similar variety of coloring and texture of the fabric of flower and leafage will appear, though changing, of course, with every step we take. Such composition is always consistent, uniform and beyond cavil of its kind. Perhaps one kind of plant has become so established that it has crowded out the others, and developed a uniform growth over the whole surface; in this case, the groups will be hardly detectable; they will have grown together into an expanse homogeneous like the ocean; the only variety will depend on the summer zephyrs, or the shadows of passing clouds.

Similar characteristics may be found in every tree, bush or weed. Anyone who will take the trouble to block out the lights and shadows, the foliage or flower masses with the spaces between them, the solids and voids of one of them will find the same kind of subtle relation of form and proportion that appears in forest, meadow or drift of clouds.

By this time it will be easy to see that all these natural effects are produced by repetition and sequence, by continuity and movement, all being phases of the same thing. Repetition is exemplified by the trees in the forest, the flowers in a meadow, or the waves of the sea as producing a primary appearance not of individuality and separation, but of unity, —of one thing, not many. When from any cause and from any aspect these become divided into perceptible parts, we get also sequence; they seem to follow or merge into each other by easy gradations, not to fly asunder and remain disparate and at variance. Thus, for instance, the lights and shadows on a plain or mountain have often been described as "chasing each other," an effect of sequence which is, in turn, produced by the clouds and cloudlets following each other in the intercepted sunlight. If one looks up at the clouds, they are apt to appear broken, but never disorderly: their separation always appears seemly and rational: they follow their leaders like the waves on the ocean or the wavelets on a brook, or falling leaves, or drifting sand, or any other numerous thing set in motion by wind or water. And if one looks down again at the meadow, one can see, nearly always, that it too divides its surface into parts, and that they have such a sequential relation to each other as waves or the cloudlets. These parts are the groups or masses of whatever weed happens to be in flower. No matter where one stands, they show a kind of succession that looks so simple on the ground but is so difficult for the unskilled to imitate with pencil or brush or arrangements in planting. These sequential masses, appearing in perspective like horizontal or inclined bands (and so represented by the painter) would look more nearly circular if seen from an airplane. It is surprising how many cloud or wave or sand drifts, and groupings of flowers and foliage in meadow or forest could be represented in general direction by lines, curved or straight, either parallel or running to a point usually outside of the picture (the picture being what can be taken in by the lens of the camera or the unmoving eye.)

This sending forth of subordinate masses and individuals from a main mass, either by fission as in clouds or by increase as in the forest or meadow, is a manifestation of economic laws; in the case of the

Cloud masses and prairie, Alex Dow Field, Nichols Arboretum, Ann Arbor, Mich. (Photograph by Robert E. Grese.)

cloud, of response to the forces of dispersal; in the case of the trees or weeds, of the impulse of reproduction. A single tree or weed drops seeds or extends underground suckers, establishes a colony or main mass around itself, and this continually tends to send out more colonies and individuals until stopped by competing growth or other causes.

Thus we are easily led to the one general purpose behind Nature's works, one might almost venture to say, spiritual as well as material. That purpose is economic. It is geared to the production of phenomena which the mysterious scheme of things requires. Take, for instance, the forest or the meadow. Back in the very far-off times some long succession of geologic processes upheaved the land on which it stands from the sea or lowered it from the mountains and covered it with the kind of soil that it has, whether sandy or clayey, sweet or sour, sterile or rich. Gradually the surface was modeled so that the soil in the low places is not just the same as in the high ones. Thus the growth is somewhat different, corresponding exactly to the differences in soil and elevation. What this tract produced when it was first raised high and dry as it is, no one knows. After a greater or less length of time it was probably covered with forest, which perhaps persisted until it was cleared for farming. At that period we may assume that Nature's purpose was the production of forest; now that the forest is gone, her purpose, for the present, is the production of weeds, just as important in balancing the scale of things as timber trees. Or perhaps the wild animals, which are an inseparable part of the vegetable scheme of things, browsed on the early growth and prevented trees from growing, so that a natural meadow or prairie came into being and persisted to support the grazing creatures. Whether trees and "brush" were produced or grass and weeds, the immutable law of the survival of the fittest controlled. The trees or the weeds that, for one reason or another, soil, stamina or proximity to others, could not hold their own, perished. The survivors were regulated with inevitable precision by natural law in variety, size, form, color, position, and length of life. In other words, Nature's design was to produce the maximum crop of trees or weeds on a given area under the conditions provided for them. The quality and quantity of these crops were the result of all the interdependent play of subtle causes that were a stage in the sequence of other subtle causes extending back into infinity. All their processes and effects were entirely logical and scientific, mathematically correct, perfectly balanced, without waste or deficiency, all responding to the law of compensation. They demonstrate an economic system of entire perfection, a product adapted exactly to soil, climate, water and food supply and total environment, and one of their innumerable results was to provide scenes made up of forms, colors, textures and arrangements which poets have so often sung, and to which painters and the rest of us desiring suggestion and inspiration must always finally resort in the hope of catching the spirit of their form and relationship. If Nature can be accused of producing by-products not provided for in her broad scheme, this must be among them. But there may be no such things as by-products excepting of man's manufacture, the rewards of what he

did not foresee mid provide for. There is no evidence that the Cosmic Thought fails to foresee anything, and it is quite likely that It considers the inspiration of the poet and the painter as important as any part of Its program.

The more we observe the phenomena of Nature, so familiar that few pay real attention to them, the more we are struck by their similarity in the midst of immense variety, the same idea running through them, as though they were all inseparable phases of one plan, different manifestations of the same great purpose. Are clouds to be dispersed, still waters to be troubled, or myriads of flowers or trees to be assembled? One thought will set them all in motion, will put them all in place, and each with the qualities that belong to its capacities and functions.

Inasmuch as, in the last analysis, the plantsman's informal compositions must be based on those of Nature, and as he depends upon her for his materials, it follows that he too will be greatly influenced by the economic law, though applied to different purposes, and that his work will not be convincing and stable unless he is so influenced. In an artificial planting this will take the form of adaptation of species to soil, climate, and exposure, to room allowed for growth, to proximity to other species. The not uncommon refusal of plants* in a garden to thrive if set next

*Dr. C. Stuart Gager, Director of the Brooklyn Botanic Garden, states this, and further that this refusal may depend "also on the fact that one kind of plant may absorb water from the soil more rapidly than another, and thus interfere with the healthy growth of the latter. It has also been suggested that the roots of certain plants secrete substances in the soil which are toxic to the roots of other plants, but investigators of equal competence are not agreed as to whether this is true beyond question."

to certain other plants may depend, not merely on unsuitability of soil or climate, but on toxic conditions set up by neighbor plants. In the present state of knowledge of this subject, we have little to rely on but observation of the species that get on well together in wild or cultivated plantations. When we can think of no precedent and guessing becomes necessary as to what will grow in company with which, the cultivation of the instinct for divining such things will be about all we have to rely on, and if the instinctive perception of that obscure subject, what kinds of planting material look well together, has been well developed, we shall probably be appreciably helped along the economic line also.

An attempt to analyze the principles of natural planting where nothing is visibly on axis will not lead us very far in formal design where everything is visibly on axis. An axis connotes a pair, two similar things, whereas when one leaves the individual vegetable or animal, even though everything is balanced, there are no pairs, no twos of a kind, and consequently no visible axes. But endless suggestion for one member of a formal pair may be found in natural groupings. Once in a while one runs across some conjunction of wild trees or bushes, or both, which could be repeated on both sides of an axis (as, for instance, at one or both ends of an avenue, or at an entrance) with admirable effect. Accents, single objects that attract the attention, from a lichen-painted boulder to a Shasta, from a lone pine to a single plant of startling floral display in a meadow, are everywhere. Eyetraps abound, but it remains for man to put his own punch into them by putting some screen of his own on either side so that the object really becomes an eyetrap because the eye cannot escape it. The

Wetland flora, Waterloo State Recreation Area, Washtenaw County, Mich. (Photograph by Robert E. Grese.)

axis was discovered and utilized when a man first concentrated his gaze on some object to the exclusion of others. When he put up his hands on either side of his face to exclude other objects, he created an axis. It was but a step further to substitute for his hands a screen of trees, walls, or other barriers to an inclusive view. In fact, all the visual devices discovered and employed by designers have their prototypes somewhere in Nature, put there perhaps, amongst other reasons, for him to see and employ in his own way and for his own needs.

The writer is not trying to prove that we should attempt to copy or imitate the works of Nature in arranging planting compositions. The designer of planting seldom does that, and probably even less often than he thinks he does. Consciously or unconsciously he follows a convention, and it is right that he should, for landscape design is not a reproduction of nature any more than any other art. Nevertheless, the forms, proportions, and sequence of flowers in a meadow, trees in a forest, or clouds in the sky, the foliage or flower masses and the intervening voids of individual plants, the repetition and irregular yet purposeful grouping of all these may suggest motifs on which we may surely rely when we arrange our trees, shrubs and perennials, our lawns and plantations, foliage masses and open spaces. No one would wish to arrange a herbaceous border to look like a meadow or prairie or processions of clouds, yet to these one could safely resort for precedents to apply to the problem on hand. No rules can be formulated for the proportions of these subordinate masses or broken-off pieces, nor can any precise instructions be given for imitating them. But any time spent on copying them with pencil or brush (the only real way to become acquainted with their forms) will be so much pure gain, and will react in originality, vigor, and sureness in one's own compositions. The difference between what we find in Nature and what we produce lies in the nature suggestion having passed through a human brain, and having been molded to its personality and its needs. It might be said that our creations are just as subject to Nature's inscrutable laws as her own works, and that what we do badly is due to our ignorant transgression of those laws.

To summarize: —*First,* as to what we can learn:

The parts of natural phenomena are all in equilibrium in obedience to law, and that equilibrium or the balance of parts is an essential of design.

Natural compositions have main and subordinate masses and motifs: they depend on repetition and sequence.

The parts have the exact relationship to the whole and to each other that proceeds from the interrelation of causes and the law of compensation. Perhaps this is where we have most to learn from our model.

Nature has one great motif behind all her works, which is economic, —that is, the production of the things we see and those by which we live.

Second, as to what we can do to make this knowledge of value to design.

Though we cannot control natural laws, we can to a limited extent summon them to our aid and avoid transgression of them as far as we are able.

Though we are unable, or would not desire, to imitate the processes and consequences of creating a wild forest or swamp or meadow: though we cannot reproduce the perfect proportions, distances, and adjustment of the members of a group or sequence of clouds, or waves, or trees or bushes, or the conformation of individual plants, we can observe and store them in memory to guide, influence, and restrain our own layout and planting designs.

In short, we can find all around us the prototypes of the dominating purpose, unity, consistency, proportion and subordination of parts that we seek for our own creations.

FRANK A. WAUGH

A Juniper Landscape

(1931)

Anyone with an eye for landscape beauty has sometime, perhaps frequently, been arrested by a hillside covered with old junipers. Such striking pictures are most abundant in the eastern seaboard states, from Maine to North Carolina, but they are also to be seen, with variations, in Michigan and the north-central states as far south as Tennessee. Altered to the famous juniper-pinyon association, they are also widely prevalent in New Mexico and Arizona. In brief, the juniper landscape is an unusually familiar one, as it is always arresting and often beautiful.

The critical analysis of such a landscape type always presents important lessons to the landscape architect, for which reason we may now consider a few field notes.

The practical purpose may as well be avowed at the outset. It is to discover whether this natural plant association offers any guide in the formation or modification of landscape pictures as practiced by the active landscape architect. One theory of landscape composition is that the designer shall select a "motive" and follow it throughout any given area, developing it in successive paragraphs or episodes.[*] There are, of course, several types of motives available to the landscape, but one of the most eligible lies in the thematic development of the native flora in its original associations. For purposes of clearer statement I have ventured to call these "ecological motives."

Just who first began to preach the use of ecological motives in landscape architecture it would be hard to say. Mr. Jens Jensen, of Chicago, certainly early had the idea and pled for it with fervor. Wilhelm Miller,[†] who made a good statement in print of the method, possibly derived his notions from Mr. Jensen. The most recent

---

[*]This method has been expounded by the present writer in *The Natural Style in Landscape Gardening* (Boston, 1917), 63; also in *The Book of Landscape Gardening*, 3rd ed. (New York, 1926), 44; and in *Everybody's Garden* (New York, 1930), 39.

[†]Miller, *The Prairie Spirit in Landscape Gardening* (Urbana: University of Illinois, Circular 184, 1915).

From *American Landscape Architect*, November 1931, 16–20.

and highly practical publication has been that of Misses Roberts and Rehmann.[*] To complete this review one must not fail to cite Willy Lange,[†] who, very early and with characteristic German thoroughness, made an extended exposition of the theory and the practice of landscape design founded on principles of ecology.

Briefly stated, this particular tenet of this doctrine teaches that the landscape architect in developing a given area of landscape, especially when a definitely natural result is desired, should select a motive composed of the floral complex (or association) native to that area, or at least clearly adapted to the area. This complex will nearly always consist of ten to twenty species, of which two or three may conveniently be designated as dominants, since they are the most conspicuous and generally important. There will then be six or eight secondary species, of considerable importance, but clearly subsidiary to the dominants. Often there follow in turn several tertiary species, inconspicuous or incidental, but worth planting in a small way. Last, there may even be other species more completely negligible, of no importance whatever, but not so inimical to the picture as to require exclusion.

Such a complex of dominant, secondary, and tertiary species is obviously capable of infinite development in ever changing compositions, the typical character of the association being clearly retained in each new variation. These successive combinations may be spoken of as paragraphs or episodes in the development of the leading motive. The methods by which each paragraph is to be developed to its climax, how the transitions from paragraph to paragraph are to be made, how the most effective order of paragraphs is to be determined—these are technical problems of great interest and importance, but aside from the main point in the present study.

The examination of concrete details in which we are here engaged was made on two adjoining low hills in Amherst, Massachusetts. These hills support a quite remarkable stand of junipers, both the red cedar (*Juniperus virginiana*) and the common juniper (*J. communis*). The soil is built upon granite bedrock, heavily glaciated and covered with glacial till mixed with gravel and large coarse stones. It is well drained and dry. The hill which we shall designate as "A" slopes to the southeast; hill "B" slopes to the southwest. On "A," the common juniper predominates; on "B," the red cedar. Both areas are in fenced pasture, heavily grazed by cattle, occasionally by horses. This grazing has had an obvious influence in modifying the flora. The steady and heavy trespass of the junipers on these pastures has been a local wonder for years. In both places, especially on hill "A" with its common junipers, vigorous and repeated efforts have been made to stay their encroachments. Trees have been cut and burned and many of the junipers have been soaked with kerosene and burned in place. In spite of all measures and heavy pasturing, the junipers have spread and are now on the point of driving the cattle from their pastures.

The ecological significance of these facts cannot be mistaken. Obviously we have here two species adapted to their environment in a remarkable degree.

[*]Roberts and Rehmann, *American Plants for American Gardens* (New York, 1929), 24.
[†]Lange, *Die Gartengestaltung der Neuzeit*, 1st ed. (Leipzig, 1907).

Neither should the artistic significance of the results be overlooked. Perhaps it is always true, at least nearly always, that plants are most beautiful and best adapted to the requirements of the landscape architect when they grow normally, lustily and with evident joy in their conditions of life. Certainly these two juniper hillsides supply an almost endless series of interesting plant forms and of delightful pictorial compositions. No landscape architect nor any painter could be satisfied here with a mere casual glance.

Notable variations occur in both dominant species. The common juniper, in particular, shows so many and such diverse forms that one begins to doubt whether we are dealing with a single species or a miscellaneous hybrid progeny. There are low, prostrate forms, sturdy, upright forms, and everything in between. Many of the individual specimens are of striking beauty.

Even in this remarkably pure stand of junipers, where the two dominant species so completely fill the picture, there are still other species present which are far from negligible. In the particular area studied, these secondary species are less conspicuous than usual, possibly on account of the heavy pasturing; but perhaps these conditions give a special test of their persistence and so mark them as belonging with considerable certainty to the juniper association.

Below are listed those plants of sufficient size and importance to interest the

JUNIPER ASSOCIATION

A, B and C in all cases indicate degrees, e.g., in the first column,

A=abundant. B=moderately abundant. C=rare.

SCIENTIFIC NAME	COMMON NAME	ABUNDANCE	ECOLOGICAL VALUE	DECORATIVE VALUE
DOMINANT SPECIES				
Juniperus communis	Common juniper	AAA	AA	AA
Juniperus virginiana	Red cedar	AA	AA	AAA
SECONDARY SPECIES				
Betula populifolia	Gray birch	A	A	C
Comptonia asplenifolia	Sweetfern	A	A	AA
Crataegus	Hawthorn	B	A	AA
Gaylussacia baccata	Huckleberry	C	A	A
Rhus copallina	Shining sumac	A	A	AA
Spiraea tomentosa	Hardhack	A	A	B
TERTIARY SPECIES				
Gnaphalium decurrens	Everlasting	B	B	nil
Pinus rigida	Pitch pine	B	A	A
Rosa rubiginosa	Sweetbrier	C	C	C
Verbascum thapsus	Common mullein	C	B	C

Red cedars at Ivy Creek Natural Area, Charlottesville, Va. (Photograph by Robert E. Grese.)

Old field juniper in prairie, Ann Arbor, Mich. (Photograph by Robert E. Grese.)

landscape architect. It is more than probable that a study of other juniper areas would discover other species of equal importance. To this suggestion it must be replied that, while more generalized studies are certainly desirable, it is deemed of first importance to make critical examination of particular cases. It will generally be accepted as a sound principle that an exhaustive study of details should precede any generalization. It is the opinion of the present writer, moreover, that this critical and intimate study of Nature in its manifold details is an exercise peculiarly useful to the landscape architect.

It will be remarked that for some of the species listed the association with the junipers is judged to be more or less accidental and of little ecological significance. Such species are marked "C" in the column headed "Ecological Value."

It will be seen further that certain of these species seem to have a much greater decorative value than others. The sweet-fern, hawthorn, and shining sumac are most in be prized for ornamental planting.

Red cedars, Cedars of Lebanon State Park, Lebanon, Tenn. (Photograph by Robert E. Grese.)

Red cedars, Edsel and Eleanor Ford Estate, Detroit, Mich. (Jensen Archives, Sterling Morton Library, Morton Arboretum, Lisle, Ill.)

They seem to harmonize admirably with the junipers.

This last observation, of course, is a matter of personal opinion. It also must be confessed that all the ratings in the table are subject to the same qualification. However, it may be hoped that this fact will not wholly destroy their value.

With this material before us we cannot resist the temptation to savor its pictorial value and to speculate as to the compositions which the landscape architect might adopt or create upon this interesting site.

Anyone who ponders on this thematic treatment of the juniper landscape will quickly understand that the shift from summer to winter changes the whole picture and changes it radically. Quite definitely, therefore, we should have one series of episodes (paragraphs) for each season.

FRANK A. WAUGH

Natural Plant Groups

(1931)

If we will look about on an open hillside or upland pasture until we find an undisturbed group of sumac (Rhus typhina, R. glabra, or R. copallina), we shall be able to make some interesting observations. A few measurements will show the group to have approximately the form shown in Diagram A; i.e., the plan will be generally circular, anywhere from ten to a hundred feet in diameter, and a central cross section will be a segment of an oval. This form is capable of easy biological interpretation: it is a clonal group starting from a seedling plant at the center and spreading radially by suckers. The plants toward the circumference are successively younger and shorter.

Having grasped this simple idea one would expect, of course, to find a similar group form in every other species having the same habits of reproduction, —an expectation quite likely to be fulfilled. A few other examples may be mentioned. The common lilac, sprouting from the roots and

slowly spreading from a center, gives the same form. The sweetfern (*Comptonia*), which inhabits the same upland pastures with the sumacs, has the same habit of group formation, though in this species the result is less conspicuous to casual observation because the upward growth of the sweetfern is very slow and the oldest plants never become very tall. Very fine and frequent examples of this type of grouping are found in the plum thickets of the South and Middle West. Practically all the native plums have the suckering habit. The one most commonly seen is *Prunus angustifolia,* abundant throughout South Carolina, Georgia, Mississippi, Alabama, Louisiana, and well known in neighboring states.

It will be convenient to designate this form as the lenticular group in description of its generally lens-like outline.

A similar though essentially different group form is found in those species which spread by suckers or stolons but which do not have woody stems to extend their upward growth year after year. The Gnaphaliums are good examples. Though

From *Landscape Architecture* 21, no. 3 (April 1931): 169–79.

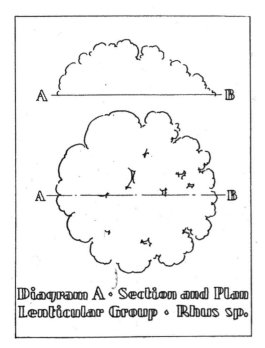

Diagram A

the outline of the groups as seen in dry pastures at flowering time (August and September) is clearly lenticular, the explanation is soon found in the habit of the marginal plants to droop and spread outwards. The plants throughout each group are really all of the same height, quite different from the sumacs and lilacs. Other examples may be named such as the perennial sunflowers, many of the native asters, some goldenrods, many stoloniferous grasses, etc. We may reasonably call this the disk type of group.

But there is another circular group form sufficiently different from the last to warrant distinction. The best example which may be cited is supplied by the fairy-ring mushroom. This pleasant and delectable fungus parades its crop of mushrooms during late summer in circles on the lawn, whence the name "fairy-ring." There are, indeed, many kinds of fairy-ring mush-

rooms belonging to several genera (*Agaricus, Marasmius, Lycoperdon, Lepiota,* and *Catastoma*) which occur widely in the open fields and on the prairies and which show the characteristic annular formation.[*] Certain ferns develop colonies in the same form, though less marked by the careless eye. Numerous other plants form these annular groups, more or less distinctly, such as *Petasites niveus* and *P. officinalis, Arnica mollis, Stachys grandiflora, Mentha alpigena, Iris flavissima, I. ensata (pallasii),* and to some extent the common garden forms of German iris, *Juncus trifidus,* etc.[†] This group form would have to be called the annular-clonal type.

Very similar biologically but different to the eye are the linear groups springing up along aerial or subterranean rootstocks. Species which form recognizable colonies of this form are the European aspen (*Populus tremula*) and, less distinctly, the American aspen (*P. tremuloides*); *Lycium barbarum;* and *Asclepias syriaca.*[‡] These are interesting but somewhat rare and have only theoretical value to the landscape architect.

Groups of this type may be called linear-clonal.

The four forms already described are all clonal groups determined by peculiarities of vegetation, propagation, and growth. Obviously those species which propagate freely from seed will present a very different aspect. Good examples may be cited from the common annual farm and garden weeds, —the sunflower, pigweeds, purslane, etc. These, wherever conditions of

*Shintz and Piemeisel, "Fungus Fairy-rings in Eastern Colorado," *Journal of Agricultural Research* 11 (1917), 191.
†Kerner and Oliver, *Natural History of Plants* (London, 1902), 700.
‡Kerner and Oliver, *Natural History of Plants,* 795.

germination are favorable, tend to spread evenly and thickly over the whole available area, —i.e., to form what the ecologists call a "free association" or "consociation."* The distribution of individuals in these groups, often covering considerable areas, tends to be notably even with a spacing determined by the size, spread, and especially by the tolerance of the mutual competitors.

For our purposes we may regard this type of group as belonging only to species generously propagated from seed—a conception near enough to the scientific fact to miss any serious criticism—and for a convenient terminology we may refer to such groupings as "seedling consociations."

If we are looking about the fields, however, for first-hand observation of natural plant groups, we shall soon discover that many of the most conspicuously grouped species are controlled by quite different considerations. Their group forms will be the resultants of external or environmental forces rather than of reproductive or vegetative habits. One of the simplest examples of this sort is to be found in the ordinary roadside groupings of species, a subject more fully treated in another paper.[†] Here will be seen a long narrow strip of dog fennel; yonder a thin ribbon of plantain; elsewhere a zone of dirty ragweed shedding hay fever by the mile; in the woods a delightful roadside border of *Aster cordifolius*.[§] These long, linear roadside zones, strictly determined by conditions of light, heat, and moisture, constitute one of the most positive, obvious, and frequently recurring groupings in the whole landscape vegetation.

Similar to these roadside groups are others along fences. In every part of the country where agricultural occupation has ever occurred, are the marks of existing fences, and even of those long extinct. The stone fence and the old "worm fence" of rails were especially influential because each one sets up a well protected zone and, particularly in the case of the stone fence, one of highly modified ecological conditions. Here all sorts of plants gather and thrive until the "fence-row" becomes the ready vernacular for such a brushy strip of weeds and woods. For even the largest and hardiest trees do not disdain the protection of the fence-row. Here grow maples and elms galore, with ample representation of pin cherry, chokecherry, blackcherry, birches, oak, even butternut and hickory. And for half a century or longer, after the fence has been removed and two fields consolidated, the row of elms or maples persists. Such tree rows, planted by no hand of man, but originating in a quite competent ecology, may be traced in hundreds of localities by any discerning eye.

Just in passing, the landscape architect may be permitted to remark that these fence-rows of trees and shrubbery often present highly pleasing units in the landscape picture. They have often been painted by artists (Tryon had a special penchant for them), and a few experiments with the camera will convince anyone of their compositional possibilities. Perhaps here is a grouping which the landscape architect might sometimes imitate.

Before leaving this topic, however, we may remark that the most meager fence, even a strand or two of wire, will give

---

*Clements calls this grouping a *consocies*. See his *Plant Indicators* (Washington: Carnegie Institution, 1920), 72.
†Waugh, "Ecology of the Roadside," *Landscape Architecture* 21, no. 2 (January 1931): 81–92.
§A good example of *Euphorbia marginata* is shown by Clements, *Plant Indicators* (Washington, 1920), opp. p. 96.

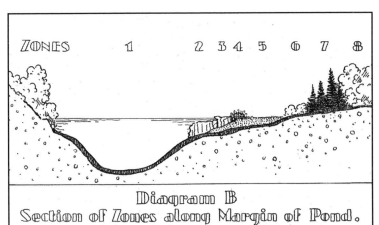

Diagram B

ZONES   1   2 3 4 5   6   7   8

Diagram B
Section of Zones along Margin of Pond.

sometimes enough protection to establish an interesting plant grouping. Indeed if one will glance along the division line between two farms where no fence is maintained and where the adjoining fields are perhaps both under efficient tillage, he will be sure to discover a ribbon of weeds marking this accidental ecological zone.

In the Middle Western states, and often elsewhere, the small watercourses are marked to the eye by fringes of tree and shrub growth. In moister regions farther east every line of seepage and every ancient meadow ditch has its own flora, a linear zone of moisture-loving species. The swamp aster, *Aster puniceus,* is strikingly typical of this group form.

Of course the margins of streams everywhere are characterized by plant groupings in lateral and parallel zones, very much like the lateral zones along roadsides. There is hardly space here for an analysis of these zones, interesting as the subject is.

Another somewhat different group formation is found along the margins of lakes and ponds and other still water. Here there is a definite and usually rapid succession from the open water at the center of the pond to the surrounding forest, rocks, or prairie (typically forest), the whole constituting a hydrosere or complete succession of zones, some of them quite narrow, but for that reason all the more clearly recognized by their characteristic dominants. In a good typical example eight zones may be distinguished, as follows, proceeding centrifugally* (See Diagram B):

1. Floating plants—microscopic forms, larger algae, duckweeds, etc.
2. Wholly submerged vegetation—pond weeds, etc.
3. Floating leaved plants—water lilies, etc.
4. Marsh plants—sedges, bulrushes, cattails, etc.
5. Marsh meadow—grasses, sedges, many annuals.
6. Marsh shrub or swamp shrub—willows, alders, etc.
7. Swamp forest—red maple, black ash, elm, etc.
8. Climax forest—maple, beech, birch, hemlock, and white pine.

*Bray, *Development of the Vegetation of New York State* (Syracuse: New York State College of Forestry, Technical Publication no. 29, 1930), 87.

Similar zoning of species is a familiar phenomenon at successive altitudes on mountain sides, but under these circumstances the several plant societies are more widespread, rarely forming groups small enough and definable enough to the eye to serve as a model for the groupings made by the landscape architect.

This study of natural plant groups could easily be carried much further, but enough material has now been adduced for our present purpose, which is merely to direct the attention of the landscape architect to the desirability of this line of observation and reflection. Abundant instances will come to every landscape architect's mind, quite possibly from his own practice, in which the natural laws of plant grouping have been seriously, needlessly, and unintentionally contravened. The man who plants a "natu-

ralistic" border of sumac patterned in plan like a Chinese dragon and filled, of course, with plants of equal size, realizes a group which is no more "natural" than a straight row of plants spaced ten feet apart. And the desire to have some "old-fashioned lilacs" for a country place is by no means fulfilled by planting a truck-load of even-aged suckers in a kidney-shaped group on the side lawn. Perhaps the most unnatural naturalism of all is to be seen when the landscape architect builds a winding road through a country club grounds and plants the adjoining lands, including the road margins, with quasi-circular masses of trees, shrubs, and perennial herbs, fondly imagining that his duty to nature has been discharged in the choice of indigenous species for his planting list. The contrast of this quite usual type of planting plan (I have made many myself) with the group forms developed by untouched nature, is set forth in Diagrams C and D.

The fact is, nature has a good many lessons still to teach us.

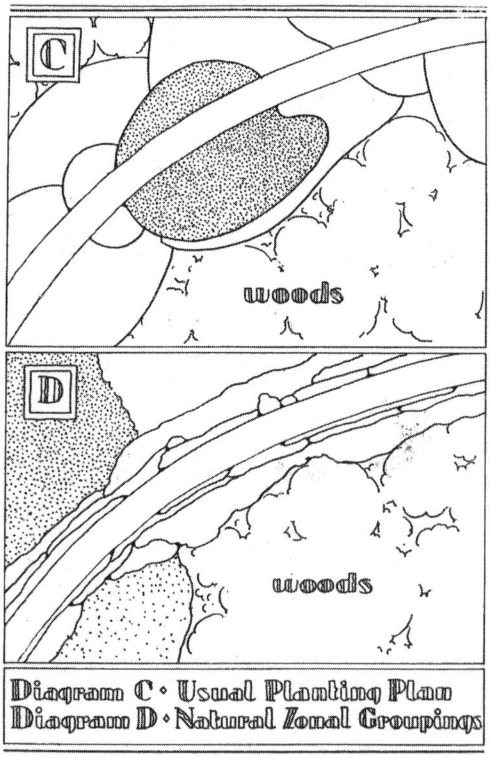

Diagram C · Usual Planting Plan
Diagram D · Natural Zonal Groupings

Diagrams C and D

OSSIAN COLE SIMONDS

Nature as the Great Teacher in Landscape Gardening

(1932)

There is a saying which you have no doubt read or heard many times and yet you may not have taken it to heart and made it a part of your lives as you should. It is often applied to other arts as well as to landscape gardening, but seems especially adapted to the latter. It contains only five words which are: "Nature is the best teacher." As I have grown older in years and experience, the importance of this saying has impressed me more and more until now the teaching of Nature seems almost to cover the whole subject that we are studying. No matter how much one may study, Nature always keeps ahead of her most devoted pupils.

Why is Nature the best teacher? One reason is that she has had several million years' experience in making landscapes. She makes all her own materials, —rocks, earth, water, plants from the largest trees to the microscopic bacteria, and animals from whales and mammoths to the smallest of Infusoria. Her long and wide experience in arranging trees, shrubs, and flowers has produced many effects which give a designer his best inspiration. It is true that trees are often too close together. Valleys often lose their importance by being filled with trees. Nature often shows what not to do as well as furnishing us with the best examples, but the variety of her effects is so great that man can always find combinations of growth and open spaces, or associations of trees, shrubs, and herbaceous plants with their many-colored flowers and fruits that will stimulate his imagination and help him to produce the result he desires.

From *Landscape Architecture* 23, no. 2 (January 1932): 100–108. Original note: Through the courtesy of Professor Karl B. Lohmann, the Editors are privileged to present here an unpublished address given before the students in the Department of Landscape Architecture of the University of Illinois on January 12, 1922, by the late O. C. Simonds whose very recent death makes particularly appropriate the publication of these words of his on a subject most dear to his heart. The reader should remember that Mr. Simonds was talking to young students about one phase of his art, a phase which is of the greatest help to landscape designers and too often neglected in the exigencies of drafting-room study. He is not talking about all possible kinds of design, but of problems where the natural inspiration is dominant. He shows how the observation of natural forms is a stimulation to the designer's sense of beauty, and how the observation of natural processes is essential to the stability and success of the landscape architect's work.

In developing landscapes, Nature has first shaped the ground, sometimes moving rocks and earth for hundreds of miles. By the action of wind and water in its various states she has given form to the land, carving out valleys, leaving mountains and hills, and making an endless variety of interesting and intricate shapes. In creating and shaping the land, she has often made use of animal life, and after the ground is formed she has gradually covered most of it with verdure. In doing her work, she has usually followed the same order of procedure that a landscaper would adopt.

What does Nature teach? First, she teaches grades. Look at the hills and fields as you pass them in a railway train, or see them from an automobile, or observe them during your walks about the country. Their contours are nearly always strong, yet graceful and pleasing. As a rule, the outlines are convex at the tops of hills and change gradually to concave surfaces at the lowest levels. Such outlines come naturally from the action of water. At the top the water coming from rains and melting snows has very little power, but, as it seeks a lower level, its increasing volume and rapidity of motion give it great erosive force until its velocity is gradually reduced by the comparatively level ground upon which the hill rests. Most of our hills and valleys were produced ages ago, but work on some of them is still going on, and the action of Nature in shaping surfaces is often illustrated in piles of sand or earth left by builders, or in the ridges along drainage canals or ditches. In shaping hills and valleys Nature always seems to have just enough material. There is never too much or too little. The surfaces flow into each other, the valleys winding around between hills in a way that just uses up the material at hand. I have recently taken a ride through southern Michigan and parts of Illinois and have derived the greatest pleasure from the beauty of natural surfaces. A study of these should enable one to create pleasant artificial surfaces. Nature also teaches how to use rocks, boulders, and ledges with good effect, and how to shape land about bodies of water.

In grading yards about our homes, after studying Nature's example in grading, one will naturally wish to make a gentle flowing outline, perhaps almost level at the house, gradually changing to a slope which may become level at the sidewalk or may even drop before reaching it to form a valley. If there seems to be a surplus of material, it can often be used to advantage in creating a very gentle eminence, upon which there may be placed a tree or a group of planting. The flowing lines of natural grades give one an opportunity to produce a most varied and pleasing effect of surface which will be far more beautiful and interesting than a flat or terraced grade.

Through the decay of fallen leaves and other vegetation Nature has produced a layer of plant food of varying thickness at the surface of land where it will receive rain and sunshine and serve most effectually the needs of trees and other growth. We should learn from this to place a similar layer of good earth over any grades that are made from the material excavated from the deeper portions of cellars and basements. A knowledge of grades and of the importance of furnishing plant food would be the first lessons which Nature has to teach.

After learning how to shape the ground and supply near its surface an abundance of good earth full of plant food, we can next learn from Nature something about the arrangement of plants. Perhaps the first lesson is to avoid planting trees, shrubs, and herbs in rows. There are exceptions to this rule where space is limited to long, narrow strips and where it is necessary to cultivate trees as in an orchard; but where there is ample space and freedom of choice, the rule to avoid rows should be almost as universal as it is in natural woods. Another lesson to learn from Nature is how to form pleasing skylines and, in studying these lines, to note a great number of examples and follow only the best. Often Nature's own lines can be greatly improved by cutting a few trees. *In advocating Nature as a teacher,* I wish to emphasize the caution *that you should make a proper selection of material and arrangements which she offers.* Again, by inspecting the margins of open fields bounded by woods and the margins of marshes, lakes, and rivers, and by observing the growth on hills and hillsides, many useful lessons can be learned about how, what, and where to plant.

When a farmer clears a field in a forest, the boundary of his field has a rather raw and forbidding appearance. Many of the trees have tall and ungainly-looking trunks. The cutting of the trees to provide an open field has made a scar in the forest when considered as a whole. What does Nature do to heal this scar? Perhaps some of the trees put out new branches along their trunks while their branches at the top grow longer and take a graceful droop. The undergrowth at the edge of the opening, on account of receiving more light, grows rapidly. Young trees, shrubs, and herbaceous plants find a congenial home at the edge of the forest. Before many years the

scar is healed. The boundary of the field is then largely made up of foliage, perhaps varied in spring by masses of flowers and in autumn by scattered fruits, with here and there a trunk or branch showing. In the winter there will be a network of branches in place of the foliage, snow occasionally taking the place of leaves. If the field opens into other fields it may be seen from some distance, perhaps from the farmer's house. As thus seen, the details of leaf and flower will be merged into a general effect of color, and their beauty will sometimes be heightened by having certain parts lighted up with bright sunshine which will contrast pleasingly with the shaded portions. In the field just mentioned, the boundaries may be too straight, but if we will examine the wooded banks of rivers and lakes we will find this defect corrected. If we wish to give a park-like effect to our open field, we can do so by cutting bays here and there.

It we think of the field just described and reduce it in imagination to the size of one's front yard, the tall forest trees being reduced to those of medium size like hawthorns or crabs, and the tall shrubs, like viburnums, to still smaller ones like aromatic sumacs or wild roses, we shall have a pleasant boundary of foliage for the home grounds. In this case the outline can be varied as much as is that of a lake or river by carrying out points perhaps toward the angle of the house and leaving deep bays opposite the main windows. By studying the margins I have mentioned, Nature will help us greatly in designing the planting for any ornamental grounds whether these be parks or home grounds.

I have said that Nature will teach us how to plant. Often I see trees planted that look like posts set in the ground. They have no appreciable enlargement at the base, and upon digging in to find the roots they may be discovered six inches or a foot below the surface.

Such trees often die, and if they live they do not flourish. Note the trees of Nature's planting. They have started from seeds at the surface of the ground. The tree roots have penetrated the ground, but, as they have grown, their enlargement has raised the ground about the base of the tree so that usually a tree that has grown naturally stands on a slight elevation. This gives a good appearance and serves, as well, a useful purpose by shedding surface water to the area where it is most needed, namely, at the end of the feeding roots. We should learn from this to plant trees and shrubs so that when the ground in which they are planted has settled, they will occupy the positions they would have occupied if grown from seeds in the places where we plant them.

Nature teaches what to plant. By going to neighboring woods and seeing what trees and shrubs they contain, one can tell pretty accurately what trees will do well in any given locality. For instance, if I went to a piece of woods and found tuliptrees, I would assume that it would be safe to designate sassafras for planting in the neighborhood, because I have seen tuliptrees and sassafras growing together in so many places. I should also be hopeful regarding redbuds, flowering dogwoods, spicebushes, and possibly beeches. I should feel quite safe regarding many of the oaks, lindens, witch-hazels, elders, and a host of other plants. If I found in the woods mountain-laurels, I should feel hopeful regarding rhododendrons and other ericaceous plants.

In going to any new locality, before designating the species for planting, it is well to examine the native forest or any other native growth. In Montana I found an indigenous *Philadelphus,* snowberry, and wild rose. These species should undoubtedly fill a prominent place in a planting design for the neighborhood examined. In southern Georgia there were acres of open pine forest with a ground covering of ink-berry. There were also oaks of many species. These guide one as to what plants to use. In making a planting design for any given territory, one should seek to retain the local character, and this he can do very largely by using indigenous plants. To be sure, a designer will wish to use some plants that come from other countries such as lilacs, barberries, mockoranges, azaleas, and so on, but he can usually judge the best plants to use when he knows that they have done well in the neighborhood of certain American plants with which he should be familiar.

What to plant includes not only the species that should be used, but also the number, and here Nature can be of the greatest assistance. The number will depend upon the available space. If there is a large area, notice how Nature treats such areas. Look at the distant hillside. It is covered with scattering oaks and great areas of sumac. One would hesitate about planting with shrubs a bed which was more than fifty or sixty feet in length, but Nature does not hesitate to cover an entire hillside, perhaps several hundred feet in length, with one species.

A landscape designer must be continually on the lookout for effects that are pleasing, note why they are attractive, and put away in his mind a record of the information gained so that he can use it whenever the right occasion arises. By taking long walks and observing the indigenous growth, he will learn the proper plants for different locations. Birches and hemlocks, for instance, will be found to do better on a north slope than on a south slope. Wild crabs and hawthorns do well in almost any location. Sugar maples and some of the oaks seem to thrive best on well-drained, high land, and sometimes thrive even in clear sand. Nature teaches where to plant because, naturally, the different species are found in situations best adapted to them. The most useful information will be a knowledge of how to arrange the open spaces with reference to the planted spaces. Here the lakes, rivers, and marshes that have been mentioned will be of the greatest assistance. Hillsides that can be seen across a valley will give valuable suggestions.

I have often compared painting and landscape gardening, claiming that the two were more nearly related than any other of the fine arts. This conviction grows the more I consider the matter. A painter likes to do most of his work in the open. He goes about studying hills, valleys, foliage, arrangement of branches, water, and buildings, and when he finds a location which he says will make a picture, he plants his easel and records the main features on his canvas. He may complete the picture in his studio, but he gets his main facts, his inspiration, his design, out in the open.

A landscape designer should follow the same course. Let him go out and walk over the land he is to treat. Let him go to neighboring woods, and, after he has familiarized himself with the hills and valleys, the level areas, the location of buildings, the distant views, the existing growth, the surrounding property, the ponds, lakes or rivers if such exist, and all the facts that will have a bearing on his problems, he can go to work on his design. Often he can judge of the effect of any planting he has in mind by reaching out and using his thumb, his hand, or a pencil in place of the shrubs or trees he contemplates planting. For instance, let him stand where a house is to be built, or if the house is already built let him stand on a veranda or sit in front of a window. A pencil held horizontally a little distance in front of the eye will shut out a roadway, thus connecting the two sides of the street. A thumb may take the place of a tree and shut out a telephone pole. A hand may take the place of a group of trees and shrubs. Often some such device will not only help to confirm the advisability of a given design in one's own mind but it will also help to convince a client. To study Nature and impart the knowledge gained to those whom we desire to help, to open their eyes so that they will see the beauty around them, is often the most important service that we can render. Such service need not necessarily be confined to one's clients. A landscape designer is in many ways a missionary: that is, he might consider himself as having a mission to investigate, study, and acquire knowledge regarding the beauty of Nature and to impart this knowledge to those with whom he comes in contact. Sometimes clients will become so interested that they will go ahead making independent investigations and perhaps far outstrip the designer in certain special directions. A certain class, family, or group of plants may make a special appeal to a man who is developing his home grounds, and then in addition to creating beautiful grounds he may produce results of real scientific or educational value.

It is not for our clients alone that we should study landscape gardening. It is for ourselves fully as much. In fact, I doubt if any study undertaken at the University will have a more important bearing on general culture than that study which has primarily to do with the growing objects all about us, and their arrangement in such a way as to produce beautiful pictures. The ability to see and receive pleasure from the natural pictures which we pass almost daily will broaden and enrich our whole lives.

In advocating the study of Nature I would not for a moment deprecate the work you are doing here at the University. Your study of books, your practice in drawing, and your study of botany, geology, history, English, and all the other subjects that contribute to a liberal education must supplement the study of Nature. Such study and practice help to give one a written and spoken language as well as ideas to express. Sketching is perhaps the most expeditious and convenient way of conveying ideas. Although some clients would understand models better, it takes longer to express ideas with models.

The study of books, drawings, and Nature should go on together as a general rule, but the study of the latter might commence very early, even before the age for attending school, and continue through life.

In his book called *Under the Maples*, John Burroughs, after speaking of the study of rocks, chipmunks, ants, spiders, and other natural objects, expresses his thought: "Thus the naturalist finds his pleasures everywhere. Every solitude to him is peopled. Every morning or evening walk yields him a harvest to eye or ear." — "The born naturalist is one of the most lucky men in the world. Winter or summer, rain or shine, at home or abroad, walking or riding, his pleasures are always near at hand. The great book of nature is open before him and he has only to turn the leaves."

Similar remarks might be made regarding the man who sees and appreciates beautiful landscapes. He, too, is one of the luckiest of men, and it he can combine with his love of scenery an acquaintance with the earth's crust and the life upon it, he should be one of the happiest.

In another place Burroughs writes: "The secondary men go to books and creeds and institutions for their religion, but the original men, having the divine chlorophyll, go to Nature herself. The stars in their courses teach them. The earth inspires them."

ELSA REHMANN

An Ecological Approach

(1933)

Plant ecology is a comparatively new science. It had its origin at the turn of the century.[*] Scientists seemed no longer satisfied with the taxonomic study of plants nor even with a wider segregation in accordance with geographic and climatic differentiations. They found that vegetation was divided into distinct groupings through the inherent adaptation of plants to the environment in which they grew. These groups they called "plant associations." The observations made as to what plants grow together and what they have in common as to soil, light, moisture, and temperature (all of which are the factors which make up what is called the plant's "environment") became the basis of the study of plant ecology. This study has been kept almost entirely of a scientific turn. It needs, therefore, to be translated into a form that will make it available, in nomenclature and substance, to all those who are doing work in which the landscape and the vegetation which forms so vital a part of it come into consideration. In this list we can include not only landscape architects, owners and gardeners of private estates, and all those interested in national, state, and county parks, parkways, and reservations for the preservation of natural scenery, but those working on watersheds, reservoirs, and other public lands, and as real estate subdividers, city and town foresters, and engineers on roadway construction, including those in charge of roadside planting and maintenance as well as telephone and telegraph linemen. All in these several groups

[*]In answer to an inquiry as to the origin of Plant Ecology, Professor Henry C. Cowles of the Department of Botany at the University of Chicago writes: "We generally figure that ecology was organized as a definite science in 1895 through the publication of *Oecology of Plants: An Introduction to the Study of Plant Communities*, by Professor Warming of the University of Copenhagen. This book stimulated efforts and research all over the world. However, there were special papers on the subject long before that. The word 'ecology' itself dates back to 1866, when it was coined by Haeckel; and as far back as 1836 an important work was published by Unger on the relation of soil to vegetation." Professor Cowles adds that "plant geography is an older science than ecology, being generally dated back to the time of Humboldt, who wrote a very important treatise on the subject in 1804. Books on the subject were written in the twenties and thirties of the last century."

From *Landscape Architecture* 23, no. 4 (July 1933): 239–45.

ought to be instructed in elementary ecology at least, if only to stimulate a respect for the native vegetation and the landscape of which the plants are so integral a part.

In *American Plants for American Gardens** an attempt has been made to bring to popular attention the subject of ecology in its relation to landscape architecture. This book had its origin in a pamphlet prepared for the Conservation Committee of the Garden Club of America by Edith A. Roberts, Professor of Botany at Vassar College, with the assistance of Margaret F. Shaw of the same department, who listed the plants native to Dutchess County, New York, and arranged them according to ecological associations. With the idea of unlocking the treasure that, except for the initiated, lay hidden in these lists and of making it available to the general reader, a series of magazine articles was written;[†] these were later gathered into book form. The lists were reorganized to fit a wider geographic scope as well as a nonscientific audience, and a descriptive and explanatory text was developed in connection with the most significant associations. Important plants were mentioned, the fundamentals that underlie each association were indicated, the natural compositions that they make were suggested, and the way they can be used about the house and in relation to it were outlined.

For a book of its kind and size, the authors had to content themselves with a rather set plan and with suggestions which were limited to the private estate. But, with a little ingenuity on the part of the reader,

the book can be adapted for wider use. It can, for instance, be used as a field book since it is really a primer to a more comprehensive understanding of native plants as well as to a keener appreciation of the relationship inherent between native vegetation and the landscape. It is this inherent relationship that many a landscape architect seems to forget in his eagerness to organize land and landscape for human use and to show his creative ability as an artist.

It must be remembered that, despite its inclusive title, the book deals with but a small section of the United States, primarily the northeastern states, and that it discusses only the plant associations to be found in this section: namely, the open field, the juniper hillside, the gray birches, the pines, the oak woods, the beech-maple-hemlock woods, the hemlock ravine, the stream-side, the pond, the bog, and the seaside. Even a slight knowledge of these plant associations is tremendously worthwhile because it increases our enjoyment and understanding of the natural landscape. There is great need for studies of other sections of the country that would be available to the landscape architect and to the general reader, remembering that a plant is no longer native if it is transferred to a locality in which it is not really indigenous or, in a real ecological sense, to a location not environmentally correct. The study of ecology stimulates, too, a whole series of earnest questionings. It draws attention, for instance, to the artistic waste of uprooting blueberry bushes to replace them with flower beds, and of making lawns on uneven rocky fields that, if not destroyed, are so fascinating in their natural contours and in their native grasses and

*American Plants for American Gardens, by Edith A. Roberts and Elsa Rehmann (New York: Macmillan, 1929).
†"Plant Ecology," by Edith A. Roberts and Elsa Rehmann, in *House Beautiful* (June 1917–May 1918).

flowers. It strengthens an ever-increasing dissatisfaction with the general run of hedgings, miscellaneous shrubberies, and so-called naturalistic plantings. It quickens a sensitiveness to the loss to native vegetation when extraneous material is added, no matter how sparingly. It emphasizes the shortcomings of the English landscape school when its ideas are imposed upon the wilder and more rugged topography of the American landscape, and lays stress upon the fallacy of using European plant material in the English park manner instead of using our native vegetation in its own characterful distribution. It stresses the growing realization that the overactive clearing away of natural growth along the roadside is destroying the foreground which is so important to the beauty of landscape views. It stirs up an ever keener distress at the manner in which the too vigorous leveling and straightening of roads and highways disturb the natural undulations of the whole landscape. And moreover, it starts increasing misgivings as to the necessity of wiping out whole sections of native growth, whole ridges of oak woodlands, for instance, by suburban colonies where owners, who have come for the purpose of living in the country, allow the destruction of indigenous material and natural contours for artificial slopes and exotic vegetation.

But the study of ecology is also of constructive value. It holds an important clue to planting that is based not upon any man-made rules of composition but upon natural groupings. The cataloguing of plants that grow together under given conditions, as they are listed in *American Plants for American Gardens,* is of assistance in the use of these natural groups. But this is not enough. The varying quantities of the plants and the manner in which we find them assembled are also of primary importance. It will be necessary, therefore, to make a quantitative analysis and an accurate charting of actual areas. As far as I know, this has not been done in any comprehensive or systematic manner, if at all, from the point of view of the landscape architect. The scientist has an entirely different objective. The plotting of small areas, sometimes of only a few feet, is often sufficient for his use. And he often uses plants of little or no landscape value for his investigation. But the work scientists have done along this line illustrates the method which we shall be able to follow and adapt in plotting larger areas of distinctive landscape beauty. Such scholarly works as John W. Harshberger's *Vegetation of the New Jersey Pine Barrens* and Fred E. Clement's *Plant Physiology and Ecology* have many suggestions for our investigations. And the work done by Frank A. Waugh with his students at Amherst, as shown in recent numbers of *Landscape Architecture,* is significant.

Student investigation in the field can be supplemented by design problems in the drafting room in which native groupings are reconstructed to fit special situations. The problem might be an actual hillside within sight of the drafting room to be transformed into a cedar garden. Here we might concentrate upon the characteristic groupings of *Juniperus virginiana* and the more important members of the juniper association, with a suggestion of a gray birch and an occasional white pine to show that these would be present in the natural evolution when the cedars were reaching maturity. A second problem might be an imaginary spot in a woods with a hemlock as the dominant tree, for the purpose of studying the manner in which the herbaceous plants native to a woods of beech, maple, and hemlock are distributed.

Intensive observation of the landscape, observation ecologically attuned, is of course the best schooling. Scenes of great beauty are to be found everywhere, —laurel-filled oak woods; hemlock woods where yews spread their needled branches under the trees; hillsides where cedars stand in monumental arrangements or group themselves in a seemingly more spontaneous manner with ground junipers, wild roses, and sometimes bayberries, sweetferns, and huckleberries; tumbling brooks between fern-encrusted ledges; streams flowing slowly through luxuriant water-loving vegetation. Here are some of the scenes that are ready with many a suggestion for garden use. To be naturalistic, in the very truest sense, the plants have to be assembled in compositions that are true reproductions or sympathetic interpretations of the landscape scene.

From such beginnings we reach out to larger, more comprehensive problems. Once such a program fixes itself, these scenes are not considered singly but in their relation to the entire estate. Such an undertaking has seldom, if ever, been consistently developed throughout. Many a house, even where it might have been, is not adapted to the surroundings. It is, moreover, difficult to overcome usual landscape procedure and to prohibit foreign plant material. But how logical it seems that the style of a country house, the shape, root lines, plan, and material should be controlled by the "lay" of the land and by the character of the landscape, and that the rocky slopes and woods, meadows, ponds, and streams should compose a natural setting that is kept intact and re-created in its minutest details. Such an undertaking is not easy, but it becomes more and more significant as the inherent beauty of the natural vegetation becomes manifest to us. And while such a program grows in vision, it is not visionary.

The rural scene is not to be forced upon an urban setting. There is no possibility of retaining the native vegetation intact where houses are placed close together and where streets are laid out in a set manner. The very building of houses and streets, with the enforced changes of contour which such work entails, creates more violent changes of environment than plants will endure. In the leveling of fields, the flowers are destroyed; in the filling of streams, the characteristic water-loving vegetation disappears; and when forest trees are left isolated without their accustomed undergrowth and canopies of interwoven branches, they sicken and die.

But there are still suburbs and rural communities where houses are sufficiently isolated. In such places it would still be possible to build roads that would adapt themselves to the natural contours of the land, to select appropriate house sites, to keep hedgerows and surrounding woodlands intact, and to outline a program for the preservation of vegetation and for the re-creation of such scenes as may have been unavoidably destroyed. The possibilities of such a community are excitingly enticing though they are dependent upon a well-nigh unprecedented cooperation of neighbors based upon a far-sighted policy of subdivider and engineer.

It is not bad to consider such idealistic programs. They are naturally and artistically possible. But there are other programs that may be more easily realized and put into effect. One is the preserving of roadside vegetation and the replanting of vegetation that is not only native but in keeping with the specific environmental conditions. This is all the more possible as people are awake to the destruction that has taken place and are eager to avoid further lessening of whatever beauty is left. Another problem is the creation of parks and parkways in a truly naturalistic spirit. The urban park must become more and more formal to conform to city conditions. Playgrounds can no longer be consistently welded into the informal park. But once the park approaches country environments, it becomes, to all intents and purposes, a reservation in which the characteristic landscape should be emphasized and retained without a single exotic note.

The work that is being done in the forests of reservations and in the woodlands of private estates is suggestive. It draws attention to the esthetic value of the landscape forest—that is, the forest in its natural state—in distinction from the more obvious commercial value of the stands of trees started in many places as town forests. It has created the profession of landscape forestry in distinction to pure or commercial forestry. The program reduced to its simplest outline consists of clearing out dead wood, thinning overcrowded areas, and rejuvenating and replanting burnt-over tracts. Much work of this kind is being done in entire disregard or ignorance of natural laws. The work demands an understanding not only of ecological groupings but of the manner in which these groups follow one another and interweave in the natural evolution from the open field to the beech-maple-hemlock forest which is termed the climax association.

The most important phase of any work along these lines depends upon the intelligent preservation not only of the vegetation but of the environmental factors that control it. The re-creation of natural scenes is much more difficult. It cannot be done as yet, except in a fragmentary way or, in exceptional cases, by actual replanting. It must be accomplished by means through which the native vegetation can reestablish itself. This is a slow process, and yet sometimes it is not as slow as it would seem. A ten-year-long observation of a field after it has been abandoned as pasturage will illustrate the rapidity with which fresh growth appears. A ten- or fifteen-year term, in which a not too seriously burnt-over oak woods is helped in reestablishing itself by fostering the young growth, produces unexpected results. And while an age-old beech-and-hemlock woods cannot be re-created, even so, if there are any trees of fair size left at all, the natural habit which young beeches and hemlocks have of growing up in such a woods produces effects of rare beauty and promise.

PART IV

NATURAL PARKS AND GARDENS

The authors in this section believed in the importance of educating people about native landscape design and wrote essays for both popular magazines and professional and scientific journals. Their subjects here range from private gardens to county parks, botanical gardens, and arboreta.

The author of the first selection, J. Horace McFarland, was an important civic leader in Harrisburg, Pennsylvania, and ardent conservationist. Together with John Muir he fought for the protection of the Hetch Hetchy Valley in Yosemite National Park. He also advocated for the establishment of the National Park Service to manage the newly founded national parks and served as a member of the National Park Trust Fund. In this article, he celebrates Warren H. Manning's design for Dolobron, the country home of Clement A. Griscom near Philadelphia, which featured a great range of native plants.

Manning wrote the second article, which describes his experiments in creating a garden out of remnant bog habitats on his property in Billerica, Massachu-

setts. An influential pioneer in American landscape architecture, Manning wrote widely on landscape design, civic improvement, and landscape planning during the early twentieth century. The son of a nurseryman, he began work in Frederick Law Olmsted's office in 1888, specializing in horticulture and planting design. During his tenure with Olmsted, Manning was responsible for several significant planting projects, including Biltmore, the George Vanderbilt estate in the mountains of Asheville, North Carolina, and the 1893 World's Columbian Exposition in Chicago. He was a founder of the American Park and Outdoor Art Association as well as of the American Society of Landscape Architects, for which he served as president in 1914. Manning's diverse Boston-based practice spanned private estates, parks and park systems, college campuses, and town plans across the country. One of his most extensive and longest-lasting client relationships was with the industrialist William G. Mather of Cleveland. His commissions included the planting design for Gwinn, Mather's home on Lake Erie, as well as many projects for the Cleveland-Cliffs Mining Company, including the company town plan for Gwinn, on the Upper Peninsula. Manning was not averse to using non-native plants in his work, but his true interest lay in creating native-based gardens, such as the twenty-one-acre wild garden at the Gwinn estate and the bog garden he describes here.

Wilhelm Miller wrote "What Is the Matter with Our Water Gardens?" while he was serving as editor for *Country Life in America*. Miller was a strong supporter of the work of O. C. Simonds and Jens Jensen and here discusses one of Jensen's projects in the Chicago area, a commission for Henry Rubens. The pool on the Rubens estate, relatively small in size, was among Jensen's first experiments in wetland gardens which led to the celebrated "prairie river" gardens he created at Chicago's Humboldt and Columbus parks just a few years later.

Arthur G. Eldridge's article "Making a Small Garden Look Large" features an O. C. Simonds design for the Howell family in Dixon, Illinois. On their relatively small (100 x 300 foot) parcel along the Rock River, Simonds worked closely with the Howells to reclaim the severely disturbed site as a wildlife refuge and low-maintenance garden. The resurgence today of interest in using native plants for sustainable and low-maintenance gardens and in creating backyard wildlife habitats reveals how prescient Simonds and others were in their work.

In "Natural Parks and Gardens," written with Ragna B. Eskil for the *Saturday Evening Post,* Jensen offers a clear summary of his design philosophy as he neared the end of his career. By this time, Jensen had become one of the leading proponents of design based in an aesthetic and ecological understanding of the native landscape. Here he traces his evolution, from his earliest gardens, in which he used an eclectic plant palette, to his mature work, clearly focused on native flora of the region. Jensen also discusses the aesthetic features of the native landscape that inspired him—the expanse of the prairie, specific plant forms and arrangements, patterns of sunlight, and experiential qualities.

The naturalist and teacher May Theilgaard Watts concludes the section with a short account and a poem describing the loss that occurs when a native landscape of rich complexity and subtle beauty is replaced with a suburban lawn and few select trees. "A Story for Ravinians" was published in 1936 as part of a booklet, *Ravinia—Her Charms and Destiny,* written by Watts and Hazel Crow Ewell. Printed by the Ravinia Garden Club and distributed to residents of Highland Park, Illinois, as well as to local schools and area libraries, the booklet was intended to build interest in the native landscape of Ravinia and Highland Park. In 1980 it was reprinted by the Park District of Highland Park and the Highland Park Historical Society with the additions of information about Watts and her previously unpublished poem "On Improving the Property," again to foster appreciation and conservation of Highland Park's unique beauty.

J. HORACE MCFARLAND

An American Garden

(1899)

What else is a garden in America? Yet there are in our broad land not many real American gardens. Few realize that the trend of rural decoration and lawn adornment in our country has been, for the most part, distinctly imitative of European forms. It was natural that our forefathers, when they began, as Bacon puts it, to "garden wisely," should look for models to their old homes across the Atlantic. In England and on the Continent the adornment of public and private grounds summed up generally as gardening is the growth of centuries of living beyond the struggle for mere existence. It has its distinctive and ripened character, and its materials are quite naturally those of the Eastern hemisphere. True, American plants were introduced in Europe long before the Revolutionary War, and such gentle souls as John Bartram sent to the home lands many members of the distinctively American flora in the last century; but the home gardening sought mainly to introduce the plant life of the older coun-

From *The Outlook*, October 7, 1899, 327–33.

tries. Thus there were brought in and cultivated many familiar plants which are hardly now recognized as foreigners—the geraniums, heliotropes, tulips, fuchsias, of the flower garden, the Norway maples, lindens, and European ashes of the parks.

This growing gardening art became more and more formal, and some quaint old examples of that extreme cultivated barbarism called "Italian gardening," with its clipped and sheared yews and box-trees, yet survive among us. The free, open, hearty plant life of America was practically unknown to us a century ago, in a decorative sense. The pioneers saw little beauty in the wild tangle of the woodlands they had to cut off for home sites, and the rich flora of the meadows and marshes must be subdued to make pastures. The pets of the housewife in her dooryard, when she came to have time for flowers, were exotic strangers, tenderly nourished, and she exchanged with her neighbors "slips" of the rarer foreign treasures.

But our European cousins have helped to show us the glory of our own woods and hills, and discovered for us the gems of our meadows and roadsides. Many an estate in England exhibits as its chief glory a planting of American laurel and rhododendron; and the ubiquitous American tourist learns with astonishment that the common bushes and weeds of his generous home land are esteemed as rarely beautiful abroad.

Our greater landscape artists have begun to realize the possibilities of America's wealth of distinctive plant life. The Wooded Island at the World's Fair and the great Vanderbilt estate in North Carolina have furnished notable object-lessons. It is a smaller but most interesting example that I ask the reader to visit with me.

Dolobran, near Philadelphia, is the country home of Mr. Clement A. Griscom. Differing little, as approached by the Haverford road, from other well-kept suburban residences, its broad lawns and fine effects in massed foliage show merely the correct taste of the landscape architect. It is not until one passes the gateway of the chestnuts that the distinctively American garden is entered, and the free beauty of native woodland, marsh, and copse presents itself.

What a change! Here is no tailor-made lawn! No geranium-beds or coleus borders of monotonously continuous coloring meet the eye; no "carpet gardening" of mosaic plants offends the taste. Just the natural beauty of American plants, located cunningly where they love to grow, unrestrained, untrimmed. True, the plants are cared for—fed, if need be, watered on occasion—but no attempt is made to guide them into preconceived forms.

It was said of Thoreau—he who loved and lived with American flora and fauna far ahead of his generation—that he could hardly keep away from him the usually shy denizens of the forest about Walden Pond. In a measure, this seems to be the feeling of the plants in this American garden which Mr. Griscom's liberality has created—the plants fairly outdo themselves in repayment of the love lavished upon them. See the richness of this great white boneset—it is actually the same herb of bitter memory to the youth of a passing generation, and it is a despised roadside weed elsewhere. Here its majestic spread of bloom in September excites our wonder and admiration. A sister eupatorium, the "Joe-pye-weed," throws up its purple richness in company.

In this garden the changes are quick. We visit it on a spring morning, and greet, freshly bloomed, a dozen friends of last year. We come back in the afternoon, and the curtain has risen on a new scene. One of the charms of the native plants is their evanescence. You look for their first appearance, you watch the growth of the tender shoots, and you greet the shy blossoms on a notable day. The processes of Nature go on; the seed-making follows, the plant may pass into its seasonal retirement. The garden is never two days alike, never tiresome—who wants strawberries every day in the year? Would these white trilliums be esteemed if with us continually?

The time of the moss-pink is eagerly awaited at Dolobran. Great beds of it border a rocky walk in the "quarry"—its carmine-pink blaze seems to absorb and store away the sunshine in which it luxuriates. While it is at its height, in a rocky, shady corner we find the lovely columbines lifting jeweled blossoms of red and yellow, white and purple, to sway in every passing breath. But we must not overlook the springing of the ferns. See these white "croziers" of the energetic cinnamon fern; how they push up from the black mold, and fairly revel in the early warmth! Look at them later, when the splendid foliage has developed, and the odd fruiting fronds are dressed in cinnamon brown—can any exotic pet present more of interest and life?

In kindly nooks a great fern-cluster nestles away from the sunshine, close by a noble American rhododendron. This latter aristocrat of our hills and mountains has not yet attained the majestic size of its nature at Dolobran, but its vigor proves its satisfaction with the environment. A colony of laurel is established in happy conditions in a chestnut grove, and is already a wealth of white and delicate pink in the blooming season.

The dogwoods cannot be overlooked, for the native trees in the Dolobran groves have responded to the impulse of kindly care, and their snow-drifts of blossoms enrich the tender greens of the spring foliage along the roadsides, while their soft whiteness showing across the quarry takes the eye even from the glow of moss-pinks. These splendid trees have even invaded the formal lawn, to its great distinction.

East of the quarry a wood road has been named the "Pansy Path." Just as the dogwood blossoms are falling to carpet the ground, we may see here, gleaming out from the tangle of green things, a tree whose branches are thickly hung with the silver bells which give it name—and, for once, a sensible "common" name!

When Mr. Warren H. Manning, the landscape artist whose love for and acquaintance with American plants has accomplished this notable result, began the work at Dolobran, he found a succession of excavations from which building-stone had been taken. These quarries, right in the woodland of chestnut, oak, maple, and dogwood which is the happy possession of the estate, were selected as caskets for the floral jewelry to be naturalized. No tilling up was attempted, save as rich soil had to be introduced in the borders and fern-pockets. Between the two principal quarries rough stone steps were placed at several points, and appropriate plant life encouraged around and over these steps. The various paths of the garden are named, and unobtrusive but permanent labels give both common and botanical names to the inquiring visitor. There is a constant increase in the number of species, the test being only American origin and adaptability—the rich orange carpet of California poppies is hard by the bright scarlet of the Virginian silene, while on a lovely path in the woods, passing by a group of the delicate and exquisite maidenhair ferns native to the neighborhood, we find a flourishing colony of the rare shortia from North Carolina—not yet common enough to have a common name! If we search carefully among the leaves and undergrowth, we may look upon the rare flowers of the ginger-plant, produced almost underground. All about are shade-loving plants, fern-clusters, trilliums, and the like.

One of these stairways leading directly to the "old quarry" is itself a thing of beauty, covered with a delicate ivy, bordered by masses of ferns and rhododendrons, and giving upon tall forest trees. Down another rocky stairway, past nodding ferns and a pert plant of the Solomon's-seal, just about the time of the early rhododendrons, one looks across to a notable cluster of the

American columbine to the left, while the steep slope to the right is a sheet of exquisite green fern fronds. Clear into the shady depths of this "old quarry" is the home of the *Tiarella,* or foam-flower, with its delicate white spikes. A little later these grayish-green plants close by give us a burst of forget-me-nots. Almost under our feet are colonies of the primrose-eyed quaker ladies, dressed in lavender. Deeper yet, where the sun never lights, we step reluctantly upon a wonderful moss carpet, softer to the tread than any handiwork of man, until in a bit of a cavern the peculiarly delicate fern-fronds of the phegopteris are before our admiring eyes.

Step where we will, new beauties are seen. This old quarry is a treasure-house of shade-loving plants, and its cool breath is always refreshing. Here the plants which last week were delighting us in the larger or main quarry are just peeping out now—the shade and the "coolth" have provided a second edition of bloom for us.

Let us return again to the main quarry, along the rich border of the west quarry path, with its changing hues from day to day. Clamber down into the lower walks at evening, amused by the hoarse croak of the frog who has made himself at home in the "gold pond," and we come upon a rare sight—the blooming of the yellow pitcher-plants. Their oddly formed flowers, to be followed later by the curious pitchers, gleam among the rushes and cattails as little lamps with amber globes. To the left, a little later, the light purple spikes of pontederia will be open. A step aside, and against the rock face shows a rank of the now fading flower spikes of the pink helonias, close to a beautiful natural bouquet, made up of the wild geranium, the giant

chickweed, and the feathery seed-heads of the dandelion.

The plant-world is not lavish in blue flowers—perhaps Nature has balanced the azure skies against the masses of white and pink, red and yellow, which are most familiar. Hence the additional interest felt in the blue flowers we have. At Dolobran, in a shady roadside nook, one is fairly startled at the springtime loveliness which the drooping blossoms of the bluet, or mertensia, afford. The shy flowers almost hide beneath the whitish-green foliage, until closer looking discloses their shading from pale pink to richest sky-blue. Back of the blue, the clustered umbrellas of the May-apple are seen, the waxy white and almost concealed flowers just ready to open; and beyond, the wood vista of bursting leaf and bud is a fitting background.

Along the shady "Engagement Glen" Mr. Manning has encouraged the well-known spring-beauty to locate, and its delicate, starry white blossoms fairly carpet the slopes. No one will deny the appropriateness of the common name who sees this claytonia here. The violets at Dolobran are a revelation. White as well as blue, the delicate yellow, the bird's foot with its two-colored form—all are here, and happy they are!

While springtime seems to hurry and crowd its profusion of flowers to make up for the bleak days of winter, the American garden has its glories of early summer as well as its rich autumn blossoms. In late June comes the wild-rose time—and what a time of beauty! The fragrant sweetbrier clambers over the north quarry bank in perfect abandon. I saw it first near the sunset of a warm June day, and the great sheet of delicate pink, with the upspringing buds and twigs, gave a new cause to thank God for eyes. The encouragement of food and care has brought this rose into a wonderful richness here, and not even the masses of the prairie-rose, the white loveliness of the multiflora, still less the rich hues and primp bushes of the French-grown June roses in the formal "rose garden," cause one to waver in his admiration for this wild beauty.

Just about rose time comes into bloom a handsome shrub, the oak-leaved hydrangea. Its flat white heads border the quarry path, and on a rocky little promontory nearby one sees an interesting result of Mr. Manning's desire to have growing things everywhere—the gray sedum has fairly covered the rock-face, dotted only here and there with associate plants. It is charming to see here, on another bold rock full in the sun, fine little colonies of the quaker-lady which does also so well in the shade and coolness of the old quarry.

In the bright August days we find a succession of warm yellow blooms. The soft sunflower presents its handsome flowers in a picturesque confusion, giving a sharp contrast to the accepted idea that all sunflowers are large and stiff and coarse. Not far away the delicate blossoms of the gaura hang along graceful branches, and a simply gorgeous cluster of rudbeckia, our common "black-eyed Susan," stops you with its bold beauty. Contrasting sharply, we catch the scarlet-hued bloom-heads of the bergamot. To add grace and delicacy to the picture, here are six-foot plants of the ragged-sailor (a most unaccountable "common name"), with lightly hung spikes of bright carmine. You have probably kicked aside the same "weed" on many a road-path!

Dolobran is a repository for our lovely native asters and goldenrods, which in late summer give so much beauty, the great

New England aster, and starry smaller ones, flank successive bits of the various goldenrods all through the September days, when the rich and mature greens of the tree foliage give place to occasional flashes of scarlet as a maple throws out its brilliant signal of the summer's end.

There is much enjoyment in watching the gamut of greens struck by Dame Nature in any varied woodside, if only the scales have fallen from one's eyes. With the very hint of warmth in the March air the willows show silvery green, and for three months the color harmony is changing and forming, until mid-July finds the established hues of maturity, with less of delicacy than strength and depth. If my reader has never seen the magic spring procession of greens, let him make a sharp note of it for the early months of next year, and count lost the opportunities he has missed! Here in this American garden I have intensely enjoyed Nature's growth of the leaves which breathe for the tree fraternity, and seen the whole range from delicate pinks, greens, and brighter red-purples of earliest spring to the robust and solid hues of August, giving place to the browns, yellows, and reds of autumn. In the main quarry a rare American poplar has sometimes shaken its spring foliage of silver and sea-green right in front of the moss-pink garland, until one's eyes were almost surfeited with the color joy of it all!

Do I give the impression that Dolobran's American garden is a great park in extent? I do not want to, for its richest setting covers a few acres only, and the variety and beauty are the result of Mr. Manning's careful planning, artistic conception, and sheer love for the work. The miles of Biltmore are but yards here and well so, for in a happy spring morning one may grasp nearly the whole range of America's rich flora, less than an hour's trip from the shadow of William Penn's statue in Philadelphia.

If the slight hint here given of the delights of this purely wild garden—for there have been mentioned but a chance few of the twelve hundred odd species growing at Dolobran—shall give an impetus to someone who needs to see the beauty and glory of our home plants, I shall be happy. The more friends one has in the appreciation of Nature, the greater the enjoyment.

Dolobran is becoming an epitome of America's plant wealth: but Dolobran can have no monopoly of our native flower jewels. A shady city back yard will give kindly place to ferns and trilliums from the woods, and a suburban place of limited extent may become a thing of unique beauty if we dress it in the inexpensive, easily procured plants of America. These plants need not the coddling of the hotbed, nor do they require renewal (from gorgeous catalogues) every year; they lived here before you were born, and they are suited to the climate!

WARREN H. MANNING

The Two Kinds of Bog Garden

The muck swamp that can be made glorious with cardinal flower and gentian, and the sphagnum bog that rejoices in orchids and pitcher plants—how to have a unique garden, instead of mosquitoes and unhealthful conditions, or a big bill for grading

(1908)

I was greatly rejoiced when buying my summer home in Massachusetts, to find that the old farm included part of a sphagnum bog, and after maneuvering for several months I was able to buy enough land to control the whole of this precious little spot. For you must know that a sphagnum bog is a very much choicer thing than an ordinary plebeian swamp. Orchids will grow in it, and insectivorous plants, and the shyest members of the heath family.

Sphagnum is that peculiar moss which is much used by florists, especially in orchid baskets. It is also the chief factor in the formation of peat bogs. It makes a wonderfully dense, soft, springy turf, and trembles under foot, so as to suggest the name "quaking bog." Sphagnum is always dying below and branching above, so that the lower parts are pale, while the tips are green.

The sphagnum bog is the cleanest and healthiest kind of wet place there is, for it is a singular fact that its waters contain

From *Country Life in America*, August 1908, 379–80.

no bacteria! Not only is there a complete absence of the ordinary organisms of decay, but the waters are strongly antiseptic. This explains why oak and other trees that have fallen into such bogs have been preserved for many centuries. It also explains why sphagnum bogs furnish the best peat for burning and for horticultural purposes, because the best peat—true peat—is soil in which the plant forms are still clearly visible, whereas in muck the germs of decay have destroyed all trace of vegetable structure. (Unluckily, most people do not understand this obvious and all-important distinction. Muck is cheap; good fibrous peat costs money.) Swamp peat, when burned, yields a great deal of ash; sphagnum peat, very little.

Another astonishing fact about a sphagnum bog is that it is poor in plant food, while the common swamp is rich. Both kinds have luxuriant vegetation, and the ordinary muck swamp, when drained and sweetened by the use of lime, becomes good land for leafy crops, such as celery and lettuce, which need plenty of nitrogen. But the sphagnum bog is very poor in nitrogen, and that is why the pitcher plants, Venus's flytrap, sundew, and butterwort have to get their nitrogen in the form of proteids, by capturing insects and minute animals.

This poverty in nitrogen also explains why nobody ever succeeds in growing most of our hardy native orchids. The bog-loving members of the orchid and heath families are now known to be "partial saprophytes." They are not downright parasites, like the mistletoe and dodder, which get all their nourishment from living organisms and often cause the death of their hosts, but they are more nearly comparable to mushrooms and the Indian pipe, which feed on decaying organic matter. (Coulter and Barnes, "Plant Life.")

This, then, is the secret of growing hardy orchids and pitcher plants, a group which fascinates everybody sooner or later. You cannot reproduce the conditions of a sphagnum bog. The ordinary swamp is wet enough, but presumably has too much nitrogen. And even if you move plants with a liberal amount of their native soil, you cannot be sure that you have transplanted the conditions associated with their saprophytism.

Consequently, it is nothing short of vandalism to move native orchids to the garden or woodlot, even if the act is performed by loving hands. Also it is vandalism to fill or drain a sphagnum bog. There are thousands of such bogs in America, but not one to spare. Every one of them should be a botanical garden for these ineffably precious flowers that will perish from the face of the earth if these bogs are drained for farm lands, or filled in to make building lots.

The easy, simple, natural, tasteful, economical thing to do is to buy one of these sphagnum swamps which are of no earthly use to a farmer. Anyone who can afford a summer farm home in New England at ten dollars an acre can get one. Then your cultural problem is solved. There is nothing to do but root out the poison oak, if you are afraid of it. Your plants are already there and will grow forever.

How the man with a real bog garden made in nature's way pities the fellow who spends his money on an artificial back yard mud puddle, where a few bog-plant samples struggle for a brief period, then give way for a new set. The pity of it all is that so few persons now appreciate the beauty that is in, or that may be developed from, existing conditions. They will buy a place having much diversity of natural conditions, then begin to "improve" it by clearing out the woodland undergrowth with its wealth of shrub and herb flowers, plowing up the pasture, with its exquisite carpet of fern, moss, and lichen, and drain or fill every "unhealthful" wet place.

In the light of modern investigation it is established that mere wetness is not unhealthful. It is only wetness so disposed as to provide a breeding-place for certain species of mosquitoes; conditions that can be corrected by a drainage that will not impair the value of your bog garden conditions. They say you do have to "watch out" for the wiggler's retreat in pitcher plants, the special pets of certain boggists.

The few treasures that are wanting you can get from nurserymen who make a specialty of bog plants, and after you have planted them, there is nothing to do but wait. They will either grow, or not grow, and all the fussing and coddling in the world may have no effect. It is a happy kind of gardening.

Let me now contrast for you my two bog gardens.

The Swamp is fringed with:
A common upland flora, e.g.,
Maple,
Birch,
Bunchberry,
Spiraea,
Viburnum,
Seedling apple,
White pine,
Pitch pine,
Trailing blackberry,
Sweet ferns.
In the swamp are:
Cassandra,
Winterberry,
Sweet gale,
Wild rose,
Hardhack,
Dogberry.
It is carpeted with:
A common wet meadow flora, e.g.,
Ludwigia,
Dwarf evening primrose,
Burr reed,
Elodea.
Of showier plants the following would doubtless thrive:
Cardinal flower,
Fringed gentian,
Lythrum salicaria,
Marsh marigold,
Tall blue lobelia,
Lysimachia thyrsiflora.

The Sphagnum Bog is fringed with:
Plants that like wet feet, e.g.,
Spruce,
Tamarack,
Red maple,
Mountain holly,
Huckleberry,
Swamp huckleberry,
High blueberry,
Black alder,
Poison dogwood,
Alder.
In the bog are:
Sphagnum,
Pitcher plants,
Orchids,
Cotton grass,
Chain fern.
It is carpeted with:
Heaths, etc., e.g.,
Kalmia angustifolia,
Kalmia glauca,
Marsh rosemary,
Smilacina trifolia,
Sarracenia purpurea.
Other fit treasures:
Twin flower,
Creeping snowberry,
Sarracena rubra,
Sarracena flava,
Scheuchzeria,
Wild calla.

My swamp is long and rather narrow, has a sand or shallow mud bottom, and is sometimes well filled with water, sometimes partly dry, but accessible at all times and places with high rubber boots. Conditions favor pretty solid freezing in winter that will do injury to all but the hardiest bog plants. Nevertheless, such showy plants as cardinal flower, and others named above, would doubtless thrive and make gorgeous masses of color in their season, and they are the very things that will not thrive as well in the other bog.

My sphagnum bog is a deep, round

Bog behind the Manning Manse, Billerica, Mass. (Photograph by Carol Betsch.)

bowl, more than three hundred feet across, surrounded on one side by steep wooded slopes leading down from a plateau with great patches of lupines, carpets of mosses, lichens, club mosses, thickets of pine, birch, and oak, and on the other side by low-lying dry fields and moist meadows. This bowl is filled with soft, oozy black mud, so deep that a twenty-foot pole will not touch bottom. Around its edge is a fifty-foot zone of tamarack and the other trees and shrubs named above that like wet feet.

In the open within this zone is a deep and most exquisitely colored mat of sphagnum mosses, out of which grow low herbs and shrubs. All this low growth in the open is floating so lightly on soft mud that to walk over it is like treading on soft air cushions. The nucleus of this zone of vegetation is a round, black pool of water with almost never a ripple, so well is it protected. It is

a very tragedy in pools, so weirdly black and still it lies, and indeed it may even now cover a tragedy, for a more treacherous spot than where the plants thin out at the edge, but look thick, would be hard to find. A friend with a long pole, who undertook to sound the depth of mud through the ice of this pool, stepping incautiously from its edge to the carpet of shrubs, plunged through without an instant's warning, and it was only the long pole which he held to firmly that prevented him from disappearing forever from view, for he was alone.

It is this deep, soft mud, and warm, thick comforter of sphagnum and shrubs, covering the feet of the plants so well that rarely, if ever, are they nipped by frost, that present the ideal conditions for growing rare bog plants. How rare is indicated by the plants now growing there. First are the sphagnums, beautifully colored in winter and summer in shades of cream, straw, brown and red. Near the tall shrubs that face down the spruces and tamarack zone, grows in great numbers the rare *Smilacina trifolia,* with its glossy green leaves, starry flowers, and red fruits. Broad, loosely cushion-shaped masses of marsh rosemary, thinly interwoven with *Kalmia glauca* and alternating with Cassandra masses, give a beautiful toning of gray-green, with sparkles of white merging with the brownish-green of the Cassandra. The Kalmia is so thin that its dark, glossy, green leaves count for little, but its shallow rose bells, each swinging on slender hair-like stems, are a charming foil to the regimental rows of narrow, deep Cassandra bells, and the waxy white groups of marsh rosemary globules.

And now comes another joyful item, for some of the choicest plants of Southern bogs are quite hardy in my Massachusetts bog garden. Two of the southern *Sarracenas, flava* and *rubra,* have seemed for three years to be quite as much at home here as in the wet "branches" of Pinehurst, N.C., from which they came. The plants are increasing in size, and *S.˙ flava* has trumpets as large as any I have ever seen in the South. It has also formed flowers and fruit. Nearby an old log is a patch of the twin flower (*Linnaea borealis*) from a friend's woods in Deer Isle, Maine, and in the drier edge, under an old pine, is *Delibarda repens,* from western Massachusetts, with hepaticas from a friend in central New York, not far away, and snowy lady's slippers from Camden, Maine.

WILHELM MILLER

What Is the Matter with Our Water Gardens?

How most people ruin the waterside by showy planting—the pictorial style
illustrated by a prairie river landscape reproduced in miniature

(1912)

What a pity it is that Americans, who have such good taste in many other matters, have such low standards of beauty in gardening! Take the treatment of water, for instance. I presume that a hundred owners of brooks, ponds, lakes, river banks, and seaside places have showed me water gardens which seem to them perfectly beautiful, but to me are perfectly disgusting. They point with pride to flawless Colorado spruces reflected in the water, grand old purple beeches, superb specimens of cut-leaved Japanese maples, weeping pink-flowered dogwood, and everything that is rare, costly, and brilliant. Every detail is faultless of its kind, yet the effect on the landscape is murderous. There is not one breath of nature in it; the whole thing is as artificial as rouge and powder. For these plants are not nature's varieties, but the nurseryman's, and they are scattered so as to produce the greatest brilliancy, instead of being grouped so as to make a nature-like picture. There are perhaps 10,000 wa-

From *Country Life in America*, June 15, 1912, 23–26, 54.

ter gardens, big and little, in the world, that answer the above description and there must be 1,000 quack "landscape gardeners" who make gardens of variegated, cut-leaved, and weeping plants. Any beginner can have that sort of garden with the help of any gardener or nurseryman. And there is no question that it will be showy and will delight most visitors, simply because our standards of beauty in gardening are low.

The pity of it is that nearly all this wasted money is spent in lamb-like innocence. Of course, there are a few benighted souls who deliberately plant showy things in showy ways, honestly wishing their places to suggest money. But most of the people who have showed me their water gardens would consider it shocking taste to mention, even casually, that a certain tree had cost $250. It never occurs to them that there is such a thing as loudness and vulgarity in gardening. Men who would never think of wearing clothes with conspicuous stripes or checks will have lines of scarlet sage crossing the lawn or big squares of cannas by the waterside. They simply have failed to perceive that the essence of all this badness is the spirit of the show. In houses, books, automobiles, plays, friends, etc., they want the best, not the showiest. Yet in gardening, they do what the "mucker" does (and always will do until the crack of doom), because it is the cheapest and most obvious way of getting gorgeous color. How else can you explain this phenomenon? It is simply that people don't know what is the best in gardening. We need higher standards.

Now the highest standard of gardening beauty is the pictorial, or artistic, which aims at nature-like pictures, and grows right out of the climate, soil, and practical needs of the family—comfort, utility, privacy. We can never make pictures with gaudy plants; we can only ruin them. And the world is in great danger of looking too much alike everywhere, because the home grounds of every beginner are planted with gaudy and abnormal varieties, like golden elder, purple-leaved barberry, and shredded foliage plants. The right way to get variety in this world is to restore and intensify the native beauty of each locality upon which nature has set a peculiar stamp. When you wake up from a night's ride on a train you are most refreshed if you can see a new and different landscape. If you wake up and see grand old white pines growing out of granite hills you may know you are in New Hampshire. If your waking vision is one of sand dunes covered with marram grass, you can almost taste the salt of the seashore. If you see live oaks hung with long gray moss you know you are in the Carolinas or somewhere in the coastal plain. If you wake amid endless cornfields, you know you are in one of the prairie states. It goes straight to the heart—this local color. And it builds up patriotism like beef, wine, and iron.

I have met a man who knows what is best in gardening, and he has cut and burned out of his heart every trace of the cancerous spirit of show, pretense, display. He is a rough diamond in Chicago, by the name of Jensen. He has the aspect of a Danish Viking and the soul of an artist. He is a real landscape gardener—not a quack. I was prejudiced against the man until I saw his work. Then I spent with him three days to be marked with a white stone. I saw how he had spent $3,000,000 in two years on the west side parks. I saw the water garden—which is a sample of the new native art of every kind that is growing right out of the prairie soil, full of local color, absolutely sincere, and tingling with Americanism. The point about this garden is that it reproduces the spirit of a prairie river. It restores and intensities a sacred type of beauty which dozens of cities and thousands of villages on the prairie are thoughtlessly allowing to fall into ruin. The garden is not far from Lake Forest, the fashionable suburban section of Lake Michigan. The sheet of water is only 100 feet long and about 30 feet wide at most. But there is a complete water system— spring, brook, cascade, and lake. The rocks are not meaningless piles of brightly colored stones; they are stratified, like the St. Peter's sandstone which is the characteristic rock of the prairie rivers. The water lilies are not the kind you see in every tub and marble basin the world over; they are the wild white lily of the prairie lakes. And the flowers that fringe the margins of the water are not the bedding plants of every public park, but the flowers that actually grow beside the prairie rivers.

All that Mr. Jensen had to begin with was a little brook and a mud hole. But that is enough for any one. That is the way every one of those lovely ravines began. So Mr. Jensen resolved to epitomize the whole of this ravine country in a picture only 220 feet long. Then he studied the bluffs of Lake Michigan for miles. The most inspiring native plant on the steep banks was the red cedar. This gave him the clue. He resolved to make a garden of inspiration—a place for communion with nature.

The main feature is the lakelet, and below it the miniature valley leading to the bluffs of Lake Michigan. Therefore the main vista is made from the seat by the spring over the miniature lake toward the infinite blue of the great one.

The next thought was to give seclusion to this sanctuary. Therefore it is hidden from the house by irregular belts of trees and tall shrubs, and planted, not formally, but in a dense, impenetrable thicket, so that they will grow fast and high, tower above the lake, and become a note of aspiration in the landscape. Vegetable exclamation points, like red cedar, Lombardy poplar, and Roman cypress, are dangerous materials. Beginners spoil landscapes by planting them in avenues, where their monotony is deadly. But see how this landscape painter has avoided monotony. The groups are so irregular that the ground line is full of variety. He has animated the skyline by using cedars of different heights. And to prevent dead, somber reflections in the water he has selected cedars with a great variety of color, form, and texture.

Next consider the outline of that lake. There is a broad and simple part and there is a narrow and complicated part. The broad and simple part is right below the seat near the spring from which you get a vista of Lake Michigan. Now, in a vista nothing should distract the attention, for the mind cannot, with pleasure, attend to more than one thing at a time. Amateurs spoil many a fine vista by putting flowers in the foreground. But below this seat you find no gorgeous water lilies, no complicated shore line. The place where the varied shore line and brilliant color are needed is where you have to cross the lake by stepping stones. There the stratified rocks crop out and the tiny bays and promontories glow with little stonecrops. There the great pink five-inch blossom of the marshmallow rises in stately dignity. Nearby sail the starry white chalices of the prairie water lily. Even the wildlings of the woods seem to feel the spirit of the master, for the red columbine sows itself amid the stepping stones.

The climax of all this beauty is, or was, the campfire. For the finest thing in life is the companionship of cultivated people living in harmony with nature. Fancy yourself in this garden on a moonlight night. The colony of cedars casts a sable shadow. The waterfall alone breaks the silence. The breeze moves the prairie reeds. The spectral water lilies shimmer in the moonlight. A few old cronies gather by the fire. The blaze leaps up and the shadows of the cedars answer. You know the rest. Isn't this what we all want, my friends? Is there anything about the showy garden that moves the heart?

It was the campfire, not books, that taught Mr. Jensen to be a great artist. Half a dozen times a year he goes with his artist friends to the dramatic points of the prairie country, such as the sand dunes of Lake Michigan and the Rock River of Illinois.

By the campfire the painter, the poet, the sculptor, the geologist, the botanist, and the landscape gardener fight it out. Each tells how nature really is and how it ought to be. And between camps these daring innovators meet one another at a club in Chicago called "The Cliff Dwellers." What a revolution they represent! Our early literature is full of fear and hatred of the prairie. For the pioneers dreaded the blizzards, the winter winds, the hot summer winds that licked up the crops, the wolves, the prairie fires, the loneliness, the monotony, the grinding toil. But how these new Western artists love the prairie! The wonderful fecundity of it is now a joy to all—the infinite cornfields and countless droves. All the marvelous wealth of Chicago has sprung out of those prairies and that lake. But these artists glory in the very flatness of the prairie—the horizontal lines of land,

crops, woods, and sky, for even the fleecy clouds have level bottoms. The architects repeat these lines in their great buildings and they decorate them with the conventionalized flowers of the great plains.

Can't you see these men hunting beauty along the tree-lined rivers of the prairie just as Daniel Boone stalked his deer in Kentucky? Consider how Mr. Jensen uses the prairie material in this water garden. To frame the vista of Lake Michigan he uses wild hawthorns and crab apples, so that their horizontal branches will repeat on a smaller scale, like a distant and broken echo, the majestic horizon of the lake. To obscure the ugly line where land and water meet he plants beside his water garden sweet flag, native rushes, strong colonies of the narrow-leaved cattail, and soft waves of colorful blue iris and white-flowered arrowheads. Notice the restraint

Wetland garden by Jens Jensen, Harry Rubens estate, Glencoe, Ill. (Glass lantern slide, Frank A. Waugh Collection, W.E.B. Du Bois Library, University of Massachusetts Amherst. Original photograph by Henry Fuerman.)

in all this. He knows well enough that variegated sweet flag and double Japanese iris are showier, but he uses the wilder, native plants. He collects "spike rush" and "water grasses," careless of their scientific names, and ignoring improved varieties, but seizing upon their peculiar beauty along the prairie streams. Prairie shrubs—black elder, western gooseberry, sumac, and *Viburnum americanum*—make billowy masses on the banks and double their beauty by reflection. The only great mass of color he allows is a sheet of phlox—a prairie flower.

What an appreciation of water this nature-lover has. Who else would place wild clematis beside a waterfall so that its misty veil of white may blend with the falling spray? Who else would discover the watery feeling in tamarisk and use it to connect his stiff cedars with the lake by a drooping spray of feathery foliage? And now consider the valley between the lakelet and the bluff. There was not water enough to let a brook wind through the valley and plunge over the cliffs to Lake Michigan, but as you sit beside the spring you have a feeling that the water must sink into the ground and run away through the valley. Else how account for the lush grass, and the water-loving plants that margin the valley—the robust colonies of native iris and swamp rose mallow? As I paced up and down this enchanting little valley, flanked by luxuriant masses of high-bush cranberry and nine-bark, I could hardly believe that there was a house only 150 feet away.

Nothing is more interesting than an artist's account of his own motives, ideals, soul life. "Money cannot tempt me to make a vaudeville show," said Mr. Jensen. "I aimed to make a garden of inspiration. The whole effect is rather quiet, almost solemn, possessing in the moonlight a mystic feeling of wonderful charm. Peace reigns over the garden. It is a place in which to meditate, in which to be alone. Add song and music vibrating through the deep mystic green of the cedars, and this garden exalts life beyond belief. In a different mood, shared with others, it is equally charming. With the sun setting in the western sky and the blue smoke of the camp fire rolling up leisurely between the dark forms of cedars reflected in the twilight of the pool, with the air filled by the merry voices of happy youth, the garden gives one that feeling of keenest pleasure which the great out-of-doors alone is able to inspire."

My quarrels with Mr. Jensen are of a petty nature and chiefly about the foreign plants he employs. He uses Japanese barberry beside the lake, which seems to me to gardenesque; I would use the common barberry, because it has more flowing lines and blends better with water. I concede that he uses eulalia and *Rosa rubrifolia* with restraint and in the pictorial spirit, but these variegated and purple-leaved plants belong to the dangerously showy class. Florists and gardeners have spoiled so many lawns with them that I would rather not use them at all in a composition that is designed to symbolize a prairie landscape. But the big fact is that ninety-nine per cent of the plants Mr. Jensen uses are absolutely consistent. I have never seen a plan which reveals so clearly the purpose of every plant and how all the conflicting interests are blended. You may remember how Ruskin declared that the great landscape painters obeyed the ten laws of composition in every stroke. And that a master is like a general commanding an army, while a beginner is like an old woman swept off her feet by a mob.

The only serious criticism I have to offer is against the manner in which this garden has been treated. A later owner has ripped out the campfire and replaced it by grass. He has put beside the stepping stones four vases filled with hydrangeas. And he has penetrated to the shady spring where the ground was carpeted with daintiest ferns, mosses, and shyest flowers of the deep woods, and introduced a bit of classical statuary, such as the Greeks used to put beside their sacred springs to personify the nymphs that haunted these mystic shrines of beauty. Mind you, there is not one particle of the show spirit in all this. Evidently we are dealing with a person of refinement who knows his classics and acts on principle. But the consistency of the whole art work is, in my opinion, spoiled. It is just as if you were to take an American landscape by Inness, and introduce into it some of those conventional sylph-like figures clad in white which were usually thought necessary as late as the time of Corot. Indeed the spirit of formalism, though subtler than the spirit of show, is a deadlier foe to landscape beauty. The formalism innate in us all makes day laborers plant daffodils in straight lines; it makes country gentlemen bisect lawns with avenues: it is responsible for dozens of stiff, hard, cold "Italian gardens" in America. I yield to no man in love of formal beauty where it belongs. But you cannot mix the two styles. Compromises I abhor. Let us have one thing or the other. Therefore I lay down a good-natured challenge to my adversary. So far I have respected his privacy. I hope he will come forth, and if I am wrong, correct me publicly.

If my reader likes this idea of restoring and intensifying disappearing landscapes I beg him to go to Humboldt Park, Chicago, and see a prairie river landscape that is perhaps a quarter of a mile long. See the exquisite brook emptying into it, and the pictorial rock work. See the lush colonies of sweet flag, reeds, eupatorium, swamp milkweed. Go, if possible, in larkspur time, to see how Mr. Jensen has lengthened his picture by putting at the end of it blue flowers to melt into the sky. Then turn the corner and see that isolated wild garden in yellow—all characteristic prairie flowers such as the compass plants, cone flowers, gaillardias, and perennial sunflowers.

Of course this garden does not attempt to reproduce literally the broad, treeless prairie. No garden can do that, because it would require too great a scale. It merely symbolizes. The open part or lawn suggests the freedom and flatness of the prairie; the irregular border of trees suggests the woods that line every river. This garden does not aim to portray the cottonwood-lined rivers of Nebraska, or any other type of prairie. The case is analogous to program music. Beethoven in his "Pastoral Symphony" did not try to imitate a storm. Music cannot do that, but music can arouse in us the emotions we have during a storm. These red cedars do not suggest any prairie I have ever seen, but they grow wild on the lake shore, and they arouse feelings such as the first white man may have had on gazing from these bluffs upon the infinite expanse of Lake Michigan.

If you have seen so many showy gardens that you have come to hate them worse than poison, if you believe that the goal of our effort should be an American style of gardening, if your heart burns to restore and intensify every bit of local color, look about you and see if your land does not represent a disappearing type of landscape—some portion of meadow, hillside, mountain, seashore, valley, brook, pond, lake, rocks, or bog. Then try to find out what it was like when the first white man came. Consult the local and state historical societies about the oldest descriptions and pictures of your locality. Ask the nearest botanist to help you evolve a consistent plant society. Go to the art galleries and see all the paintings that deal with your type of landscape. Or engage a landscape designer of Mr. Jensen's type and you will have a garden that is really unique, a garden that will mean something in the history of art, a garden that will become more precious to you every year, and in centuries to come will be preserved as religiously as any work of the old masters. Finally, if you live on the prairie but cannot see the beauty of it and do not understand what I am driving at, read "The Prairie and the Sea," by William A. Quayle. Then the scales will drop from your eyes and you will enter into a new wonderland of beauty.

ARTHUR G. ELDREDGE

Making a Small Garden Look Large

Where many types of wild beauty find themselves at home
on a 100 x 300 ft. lot only five minutes by trolley
from the business center of an Illinois city

(1924)

This is the story of how an unpromising city lot was developed into a unique garden and landscape. The property is 100 x 300 ft. extending from the city street to the Rock River. The contours are what many people would call undesirable. Sometime after Mr. Howell purchased the land someone said to him: "I always gave you credit for having sense, but now I know you have none. It will cost more to fill than the lot is worth." The new owner proceeded to make a "bad" lot "worse," by digging the ravine deeper. In the workings of his imagination he decided that the types of wild beauty that he had found and loved on camping and fishing trips should be brought home to his dooryard. Here in hours of respite from business cares he could gain recreation and the enjoyment of intimate acquaintance with flowers, plants, and wild scenery which may come only from daily contact through the seasons.

By going to a competent landscape

architect (Mr. O. C. Simonds) with his general ideas, a working plan was obtained. Mr. Howell says: "After going over the place we were so well agreed that practically no changes were made in the preliminary sketch. I then proceeded to carry out this plan to the letter with my own hands." He feels that most of the credit for success belongs to the architect while some is due himself for having the good sense to follow his advisor's plans and principles.

The first ideas called for a ravine with water, a White Pine grove, a sunny bank and a shady one and development of the river view. The location and plan of the house were decided with great care, particularly its relation to the river and a large Elm already on the property.

A little nursery was started on the lot, using seeds, cuttings, and nurseryman's transplants to supply the plant material. This required a considerable digging into methods of plant propagation which in itself became a recreation, the by-products of which passed to neighbors' gardens. Mr. Howell says: "This has been of the very

From *Garden Magazine* 28, no. 6 (February 1924): 332–35.

greatest benefit to me in acquiring knowledge of plants, their cultivation, their place in a landscape, and as a healthy interesting occupation."

There were six years of work on the landscape before the house was started. This gave time for careful consideration of all the problems. The result is a very successful one—from every aspect the house seems to be an intimate part of the landscape. The entrance door is inconspicuous, but your mind is so occupied with the thing as a whole that lack of entrance display is not felt.

Intrusion of the garden on the river views is prevented by the contours supported by shrubs. Views of the river are well framed by trees and, although only five minutes by trolley from the business center of the city, too much of the city is shut off by friendly branches. You may sit on the ground-level porch at night enjoying the dancing reflections of the bridge lights yet most of the bridge is hidden. Looking up stream, a well framed portion of the river reflects the rising moon with an almost wilderness setting. The brow and side of the twenty foot bank is clothed with shrubs and vines while below a canoe waits in the Willows by the river path.

The garden is one that attracts the casual visitor and is doubly attractive to those who are fond of our native plants whose quiet beauty does not flaunt itself, yet speaks loudly to some. Here there is a subtle charm due to compositions loose in texture, flowing lines, quiet colors. Without the irregular shaped pool, much would be lost. It makes a perfect scale of plant material from aquatics to that of woodland shade and to dry rocks, with the intermediate plants which we usually think of as growing in watered regions. The pool also brings by reflection that blue of the sky for which there is no substitute, it also brings life, water life, with the song and flutter of bathing birds. There is a satisfaction in seeing wild birds confidently bathe within a few feet of you: catbirds with their varied song, the domestic robin, flashes of the blue jay with his mischievous ways, thrashers with pied breasts, and the wood-thrush, owner of those matchless liquid notes.

The Rock River flows here in a limestone region where flat faced and eroded cliffs record the water action of ages past. It was therefore fitting that a miniature cliff and water edge of limestone appear by the pool on one side of the ravine. I confess it deceived me the first day into thinking it had merely been uncovered in an original setting. Limestone steps of the moss-gathering kind lead out of the garden in two places. The soil here is, of course, hostile to ericaceous plants. In the region of Dixon there are areas where soft sandstone is dominant but the greater part of the region is limestone soil. There is a marked difference in the flora of these two soils. You will find, for instance, lupine in the sandstone outcrops but they are scarce elsewhere; Campanulas, too, are always found in the crevices of sandstone cliffs, likewise ferns such as *Pellea atropurpurea*, but not elsewhere.

A portion of the lot is used for vegetables without much disturbance to the landscape. Another portion, well hidden by shrubs, permits the small boy to experiment with things which concern only boys.

There is a circle of White Pines about fifteen feet high which have developed a good forest floor. You may sit within the dense shade and be reminded of the wonderful grove nearby in Ogle County, the most southern Pines in this region. On one side of these pines is a bank of Prairie Roses nearly ten feet high for which the evergreens are a good foil.

For a small place Mr. Howell's is extraordinary in its variety of contours and aspects, in the blending of the house with its setting, in the use of native stone and plant material and the introduction of water. The fact that its care—except for grass cutting—is well within the spare hours of a business man, affording recreation and healthful exercise, marks it as an example which many might profitably follow.

Natural Parks and Gardens

(1930)

It will probably be news to most people who have driven over the extensive park system of Chicago that as late as 1885 little seventeen-acre Union Park that lies over on the West Side not far from the scene of the Haymarket Riot was the important park of the city. It had the zoölogical garden, and people came from far and far to see the bears and the eagles and the monkeys. Lincoln Park had just gone through its transformation from a cemetery to a park. Columbus Park was waste land; Douglas, Garfield and Humboldt parks were only partly developed, as were the two big South Side parks, Jackson and Washington. That year, however, the animal house in Lincoln Park was finished and the animals were moved there, and after that Union Park was not such an attraction as it had been.

It was still in its heyday, though, when I applied for a job and was taken on as day laborer. I had had my technical training in Copenhagen and had spent three years

From *The Saturday Evening Post*, March 8, 1930, 18–19, 169–70.

sketching parks in Germany, but the day I came they needed a laborer and not a trained landscapist, and I needed money. In a year, however, I was foreman, and in 1894 I was made superintendent of Humboldt Park, and then superintendent of the whole west park system, and then consultant landscape architect. In 1920 I severed my connection with the west parks—or, more truly, politics severed it for me—and since that year I have been laying out private estates and parks in other cities. So much for biographical data. This is an article on gardens.

FORMAL BEDS AND FOREIGN PLANTS

Perhaps it might not be amiss to make just a brief statement of the history of the park system in Chicago. Chicago, for all its faults, is famous the world over for the vision of the men who have tried to give it beauty. First of these were those giants who in 1869 planned the present large park areas, with their continuous system of connecting boulevards. In no other city in the world can you ride for so many miles through parks and boulevards. Then there were those who planned the World's Fair; those who made the famous City Beautiful plan; those who in the beginning of the twentieth century established the playground system, and a few years later secured the enabling act for the forest preserves—that stretch of natural wooded and cut-over lands that lies like a great green belt around the city proper and its suburbs.

Lately the emphasis has been all on the lake front. I don't begrudge the beautifying of this, but I wish some group would undertake to establish numerous small parks through the congested West Side district. They need breathing spots there. To my notion, there should be a park area within walking distance of every city resident.

When, as foreman, I had my chance to design a garden, I laid out just as formal a plantation as was ever made, and was quite proud of it. If any of the members of garden clubs or university landscape classes who have heard me lecture on natural gardens read this, they will probably smile. But at that time there was nothing else done. Every garden I had seen was formal. I still have some photographs of these early geometric designs in my office files, and occasionally a superintendent or draftsman will bring me one of them and inquire innocently, "Who laid this out, Mr. Jensen?" and I'll say, "Put it away. That's the folly of youth." And I know that before it is put away there is a good deal of snickering at my expense. However, I can say for myself that I never did commit the crime of clipping trees into sculptural forms.

There were two reasons why I turned away from the formal design that employed foreign plants. The first reason was an increasing dissatisfaction with both the plants and the unyielding design—I suppose dissatisfaction with things as they are is always the fundamental cause of revolt— and the second was that I was becoming more and more appreciative of the beauty and decorative quality of the native flora of this country.

NATIVE BEAUTY

In these formal beds, the foreign plants didn't take kindly to our Chicago soil. They would die out no matter how carefully we tended them, and our propagating beds were kept busy growing replacements. And after a while I began to think, "There's something wrong here. We are trying to force plants to grow where they don't want to grow." And then I took less and less pleasure in looking at these formal designs. They were always the same. There was no swaying of leaves in the wind, no mysterious play of light and shade. And a garden should give more delight the more you look at it.

Then, too, as I said, I was becoming acquainted with the native trees and shrubs and flowers. One of the most vivid memories I have is my first view of a native crab-apple tree. It was on the train coming into Chicago, and through the car windows I saw silhouetted against the sky the delicate rose of a wild crab apple in early bloom. And when I was told it was a native tree, I said to myself, "That tree is a symbol of the beauty of this prairie landscape we have been passing through." And it still is to me today—it and the native hawthorn, whose gray horizontal branches are typical of the rolling lands of this mid-country. Nearly every Sunday and holiday, summer and winter, spring and fall, through those early years, I spent botanizing, studying and learning to know every plant that was native to this region. You see, in those days the city limits weren't so far out as they are now, and by riding to the end of a street-car line and then walking, one could see quite a number of plants in a day; and by taking the steam cars, one had a radius of thirty miles or so. And I was amazed at the richness of color in every season of the year, particularly in the fall. Northern Europe has some color in the autumn, but nothing to compare with this country. Some Japanese shrubs turn red—for instance, the barberry—but otherwise most of the imported shrubs have a dull dead look that is decidedly uninteresting. And there were some lovely American shrubs that nature has adapted to the soil, completely neglected in any park planting. Again I said something was wrong.

So I thought I would experiment by moving a number of those plants in and seeing how they looked and fared, and in 1888, in a corner of Union Park, I planted what I called the American Garden. As I remember, I had a great collection of perennial wild flowers. We couldn't get the stock from nurserymen, as there had never been any requests for it, and we went out into the woods with a team and wagon, and carted it in ourselves. Each plant was given room to grow as it wanted to. People enjoyed seeing the garden. They exclaimed excitedly when they saw flowers they recognized; they welcomed them as they would a friend from home. This was the first natural garden in Chicago, and as far as I know, the first natural garden in any large park in the country. To my delight the transplantings flourished and after a while I did away with the formal beds. There was now a period of expansion in the west park system, and the new areas, in Humboldt Park first, and then in Garfield and Douglas parks, were given over to me to design. A part of these parks had been laid out, and beautifully laid out, by Major Jenny, that picturesque figure whose name will go down in history as the designer of the first skyscraper. In the early days park design was done by gardeners, engineers, or architects. The famous gardens of Versailles were laid out by Le Nôtre, a gardener; the landscaping of our capital in Washington by the French engineer, L'Enfant; and when the west park system in Chicago was planned in the early '70s, the design was, as a matter of course, given over to a leading architect. Of late years the work has become specialized, and a number of universities now give training in landscape architecture—Harvard was the first in this country.

The new areas gave me an opportunity of trying out on a large scale this idea of employing indigenous stock, and all the new shrubbery and trees that we planted were native, and wherever replacements were needed in the older areas, these were largely made with indigenous material. Smoke is hard on green things, and parks that are situated in commercial and factory districts, such as Douglas and Garfield are, require a great deal of replanting, and consequently are expensive to maintain. It isn't only humans that suffer from breathing smoke.

A PIECE OF THE TROPICS
IN CHICAGO

In these two parks there is quite a large area in lagoons—as much as we could have without interfering with the play space for the children; for in a congested district the children must have plenty of ground for recreation purposes. I believe that an inland park should have a great deal of waterscape. Water helps cool the air, it is beautiful to look at, and it provides facilities for boating, swimming, fishing and skating. In the flower garden in Garfield Park we installed a fountain device that made a mist of the spray, so that on sunny days a rainbow played continuously across the top of it. There would always be a crowd of people watching this. Then one dry summer the residents in the neighborhood had difficulty in getting the water to run from their third-floor faucets, and they complained that the fountain was using too much water. So the city ordered it turned off. I wanted the park board to install pumps that would permit us to use the same water over and over again, but they didn't see fit to make the appropriation, and the fountain has never played since, although the pipes are still there.

Speaking of Garfield Park brings to mind the Garfield Park conservatory. There had been small conservatories both in this park and in Douglas and Humboldt parks, and it required a lot of money to maintain and keep them in repair; also there was necessarily a great deal of duplication in the plant life they contained. I conceived the notion of putting all three conservatories under one roof, and since this was Chicago, and Chicago is accustomed to doing things on a big scale, I thought while we were about it, we might as well build the largest publicly owned conservatory under one roof in the world. The park board appropriated $275,000—I had wanted a larger sum for larger building, but didn't get it—and in 1907 the conservatory was completed. Many persons called it Jensen's Folly; they predicted that the glass wouldn't hold up in a building of such size, that a windstorm would smash it, that it couldn't be heated. But the conservatory is still there; it is still the largest in the world under one roof; last year more than half a million people visited it—there were more than 27,000 on one day—and the value of the plants in it was estimated in the annual report at nearly $1,000,000. And it is still one of the sights of Chicago.

Perhaps it might be interesting to tell an incident in connection with the designing of the palm and fern rooms, which face the main entrance. My idea in the first room was to show an idealized tropical landscape, and in the second room an idealized swamp scene. The first room was not so hard to arrange, but in the fern room we encountered difficulties. Since Chicago is in prairie country, I wanted this to have the feeling of the prairie, and we employed stratified rock for the ferns to grow in. For the end of the room I designed a prairie rapids and a prairie waterfall. When the workman who was to build the waterfall had finished it, he expected me to praise him, but I shook my head. I said he was thinking of an abrupt mountain cascade, but here on the prairie we must have a fall that tinkled gently as it made its descent.

He tried again and again, but every day I said, "No, you haven't it yet."

Finally he said, "I can't do it any better."

I made no comment, but asked him if

Waterfall by Jens Jensen, Columbus Park, Chicago. (Photograph by Robert E. Grese.)

he could play Mendelssohn's Spring Song.

He looked at me in a startled way and answered, "No."

I asked, "Can your wife play it?"

"No."

"Do you know anyone who can play it for you?"

He thought a moment and then said they had a friend who was a good pianist.

"Well," I said, "you go to her house tonight and ask her to play the Spring Song over and over for you."

HOW TO BUILD WATERFALLS

This is what I heard later. He had gone home that evening, and the first thing he said to his wife was, "Jensen's gone cracked. He has so much work to do that it has at last affected his head." She asked what made him talk so, and he repeated the conversation. She considered a while, and then she said, "Maybe he meant something by it. Anyway, we'll go over to Minna tonight, and ask her to play." So they did, and the friend played the Spring Song for him four times. Then he jumped up, exclaiming "Now I know what Jensen meant." And the next time I came, he stood to one side, smiling proudly. "Ah," I said, "you have heard the Spring Song." And the water tinkled gently from ledge to ledge, as it should in a prairie country.

Those who have been in the conservatory may remember the plain green slope of moss that lies between the brook and the waterfall. The contour of that slope was the most difficult small thing that I have ever done. I wanted it to give the feeling of greater depth to the room. It took me six months before I got it so that it satisfied me, but there isn't a line of it that has been changed since.

But this is indoor landscaping. Going back to the out-of-doors again, I want to tell you about the prairie river in Humboldt Park. As I made my Sunday excursions to the woods for the purpose of studying the native flora, I came to love the native landscape for its contours and physical aspects as well as for its plant life. It was God's out-of-doors—His own workmanship, as yet untouched by the hands of man. It seemed to me we all needed contact with this for our own spiritual development. Yet everyone from the city couldn't go to the out-of-doors, and the thought grew stronger and stronger with me that it was my obligation as a park man to bring this out-of-doors to the city. I do not mean by this that I was to try to copy Nature. A landscape architect, like a landscape painter, can't photograph; he must idealize the thing he sees. In other words, he must try to portray its soul.

So, in the new land in Humboldt Park, I designed the prairie river. It started in a little pool that seemed to well from some hidden source in the ground, then it trickled down as a brook in singing rapids over stratified rock, and then grew wider and wider until it made the stream that winds lazily, as a natural river does in prairie country. Along the edges we planted reeds and marsh plants, and the whole gave the feeling of a prairie landscape, and yet it is a city park. I put a prairie river in Columbus Park also when this was laid out in 1917. In fact, this whole park is a typical bit of native landscape idealized, as it appears near Chicago. The prairie bluff of stratified rock along the river has been symbolized with plant life. To the west extend the great lawns that symbolize the prairie meadow. These lawn areas are used for golf, but the greens are laid out in such fashion as not to destroy the horizontal aspect of the scene. Limestone rock from our native bluffs, with a backing of native forests, has been used in natural walls for the swimming pool and the wading pool for children.

IDEALIZING NATURE

This pool, when it was built, was the largest in any public park in the country—Chicago, again, you see, doing things on a big scale. The pool, or rather the swimming hole, as we have named it, is 450 feet long and will take care of 7000 a day. The deep pool has a depth of nine feet, and there is a wall between it and the shallow pool, so that the nonswimmers can't get into too deep water. The entrance to the pool is from the street. I always have a street entrance to every public swimming pool I have designed, for various reasons. For one thing, when boys come to a park to swim, they seem to have a single-minded notion that nothing else in the park matters, and they are apt to hit at branches of trees and to behave otherwise in a destructive way that they do not do when they come to a park for a walk or to play. And for another thing, it is disturbing to nonswimmers to have all these swimmers trooping past them. So everybody is made happy and at the same time the park is saved from thoughtless vandalism by this arrangement.

Columbus Park has special interest, too, because it is situated above and below one of the ancient Chicago beaches. The prairie river lies below the beach. The natural topography suggested such a layout.

Not only in parks but in private gardens as well, it has become my creed that a garden, to be a work of art, must have the soul of the native landscape in it. You cannot put a French garden or an English garden or a German or an Italian garden in America and have it express America any more than you can put an American garden in Europe and have it express France or England or Germany or Italy. Nor can you transpose a Florida or Iowa garden to California and have it feel true, or a New England garden to Illinois, or an Illinois garden to Maine. Each type of landscape must have its individual expression.

But in trying to make a garden natural, we must not make the mistake of copying Nature, as I said before. Copying Nature is only one step removed from copying another garden. Art idealizes; it is creative, and a reproduction is only a reproduction, no matter how fine and noble the model is. The landscape garden must have a dominant thought or feeling in it, just as a great painting must have a dominant thought in it. To me, that feeling should be spiritual; it should be love for the great out-of-doors, for the world that God made. Such a garden will be a shrine to which one may come for rest from the strife and noise of the man-built city. It will have in it the mystery of the forest, the joy and peace of a sunlit meadow, the music of a laughing brook, the perfume of flowers, the songs of birds, the symphony of color in tree and shrub.

A SPOT OF SUNLIGHT

And the elements one works with are the contours of the earth, the vegetation that covers it, the changing seasons, the rays of the setting sun and the afterglow, and the light of the moon.

When I plan a garden, I do not make a single pencil mark on paper until I have the complete picture of the whole composition in my mind. And the composition is never a matter of many things, but of a few things that will blend harmoniously every season of the year, and that will also suit the temperament of the client.

Sometimes I start with the setting of the house. If the home is not already built, I choose the location and, together with the house architect, decide on the material out of which the house is to be built, and on the color, so that it will blend into the surrounding landscape. Always the house should have a setting of trees. I am fond of quoting the Norwegian poet Björnstjerne Björnson's lovely poem, "Hidden by trees you find my home." The home should be a retreat away from the public eye. Sometimes I start with the road that curves away from the public highway to the house. I say "curves," for in the composition of an important road I never use a straight line—Nature's lines are curves, and I believe, with the ancient Greeks, that the curve is the line of beauty. But the road should never be serpentine; there should always be a reason for the curve, and the road should always be in shadow, emerging upon the lawn in full sunlight. Sometimes I start with the open meadow as my keynote. I always have a clearing in every garden I design—a clearing that lets in the smiling and healing rays of the sun. A sunlit clearing invites hope. George Inness, whom I consider the greatest landscape painter this country has produced, always has a ray of light in every picture he painted. No matter how storm-tossed the clouds are, there is this ray of hope promising a better day. I am never in the Art Institute of Chicago without making a visit, if only for a few minutes, to the splendid Inness collection there. And every time I come away refreshed. Inness was a great master.

Perhaps I will make this matter of design more clear if I give specific examples of what various problems have been and how they have been solved.

One of the first private estates I laid out was for a big corporation attorney who was of a very nervous temperament. He had been offered a number of places and he gave me the responsibility of making the choice. I selected the site that had a meadow over which the sun set both winter and summer; for, with his office in the city, my client could be home to enjoy his garden only during the late afternoon and evening. Toward the south was a low depression where water stood most of the year. It was in the line of the moon, so I placed an informal pool at that point, and backed it with red cedars in order to get the reflection of the moon and the dark mystery of the cedars' shadows in the water.

To the east was Lake Michigan; part of the open exposure here was planted out to keep the cool winds away from the porch during the early morning and evening. At one corner we planted sugar maples and sumac. Here the afterglow of the setting sun in autumn would illuminate their gay plumage, and against the purple background of water and dusky eastern heavens would give a note not unlike that of Wagner's Tannhäuser.

The kitchen garden was planted to the north, and, as the space was small, we built a wall to protect the cut flowers and veg-etables from the north winds. Where more space is available, I use hedges for protection to the kitchen garden. This is the only spot in a garden plan where I think hedges are allowable.

Several years after the garden was finished, I was invited to dinner by the owner, and, as we sat smoking on the porch, with the full moon playing on the pool and the dark cedars making black shadows, he said to me, "When I've had a hard day downtown, there are only two things that can rest me—the sunlight on the meadow I when come home, and then, later, the pool of water." So you see this garden had suited the temperament of the client.

On another estate the house was built facing a depression that was too wet for trees, with the east front on Lake Michigan. Part of this depression ran into a forest of oaks on the west side of the estate. The whole depression was cleared of its small shrubs and made into a lawn. The thought back of this was that through this long opening during the fall the setting sun could be seen from the house enlivening the oaks in their autumn red, thereby giving the whole landscape a more brilliant color than would otherwise be possible. We named this the Path of the Setting Sun. Another interesting problem on this estate was the fact that the entrance gate was on ground that was higher than the site of the house.

Now, the house, to be commanding, should seem to be the higher. You want to go up to a house, not down to it. This is how we solved that difficulty. To the left was a bit of natural woodland, which we augmented with some planting, and a little farther on was a ravine. The road was made to go through this woodland and planting, and then to skirt the ravine, and so, when the house emerged quite suddenly to view over the lawn, you had no thought of its being lower. It seemed higher, and yet the road was not long.

REVEALING THE HOUSE

On the Edsel Ford place near Detroit, we had the problem of making the house seem higher than the road in an absolutely level country. Lake St. Clair, a rather shallow lake, lies to the west of the house. By making the road follow the margin of this lake and planting out the view of the house until the right point was reached, and then letting the house emerge suddenly, it was possible to give the effect of a greater rise than the few feet there actually are.

An entirely different situation was offered at Mr. Ford's summer home on the coast of Maine. Here is a mountainous country consisting largely of granite rocks. There was no difficulty in getting a commanding site for the house; the problem was to anchor earth for plants to grow in. So we had to confine ourselves to a small garden, and this was accomplished by building walls and filling in so as to secure a level surface. The garden was constructed out of native rocks and plants, with native evergreens for a background, and with an informal pool under a bit of cliff. In place of grass, we used carpets of dwarf mountain plants. The entrance to the garden was treated in a similar fashion, and as the home is built out of the same stone as the garden, quarried right on the grounds, the whole represents an expression of what can be done with the material at hand of that region. I have had as much

pleasure in making this garden as I have had in any garden I have designed.

Down in the blue-grass region of Kentucky, where limestone is everywhere, I was asked to remodel an estate that had been landscaped some years before in the formal manner. Not far from the house was a natural sink hole, so common in Kentucky, and it was the formal garden that had been laid out in the bottom of this that was the particular eyesore of the owner. My thought was that this sink hole would make a lovely rock garden, with rocks set on the edge of the bowl and interspersed with cedars, flowering dogwood and other characteristic trees of the region. So it was developed. There was a pool with water lilies that reflected also the plants growing above it, and then there were shady nooks for ferns and sunny ledges for sun-loving rock plants. This garden was entered from a lane that connected up with a vegetable garden and orchard. I had not visited this garden for many years until a year ago last spring, and then I found it full of mystery, and the owner said it was a retreat he liked to go to. This, you see, was a bit of old Kentucky idealized.

GARDENS FOR SMALL HOMES

On a hillside place in Tennessee, facing the Smokies, the problem was to see both the beauty of the valley below and to bring the mountains, so to speak, to the door. In other words, to arrange the contours of the land near the house in such a way that you felt the mountains coming to you. This was done by making the slope from the porch concave, so that the eye could follow the whole slope down into the valley. Toward

Wetland garden, Henry Ford Estate, Fair Lane, Dearborn, Mich. (Photograph by Robert E. Grese.)

the right the concave line was terminated abruptly by coming forward with the slope and planting it with trees native to the hillside, thus producing the effect of rolling lands beyond, while the forest-covered hill close by seemed united with the planted trees. A little path edged with ferns led through the grove and helped give the feeling of going into a forest. The effect of this whole arrangement was that the character of the surrounding territory seemed to terminate right at the door.

At the home of Mr. Julius Rosenwald on the north shore of Chicago there were numerous difficulties on account of the narrow width of land, between Lake Michigan and a ravine running almost parallel to it, on which the house was built. A spur of a smaller ravine, however, entered the large ravine almost opposite the house to the west. This made possible a lawn that extended itself into this small ravine, revealing the high land on the opposite side in a way that made it look like a high hill. Incidentally this view was in the path of the setting sun. Hawthorns, crab apples and prairie roses planted along the edge of the ravine prevented anyone being conscious of a deep ravine directly on the edge of the lawn, and also gave color and light to the meadow in the spring. The setting sun illuminates this planting, too, in a most charming way in the fall. The ravines were utilized by putting in tanbark trails and by planting native flowers on the slopes, so that these became beautiful gardens. The main entrance drive was made to come down another spur of the ravine, and is entirely unseen from the residence or the lawn. The idea of this estate is to give the feeling of a country made beautiful by deep ravines.

At the south of the house is a pool for the reflection of the moon, with a background of native woodlands, whose floor is covered with wild flowers. I have used wild flowers on an extensive scale in other places also. For instance, on a hill slope of an estate in Freeport, Illinois, we planted thousands and thousands of black-eyed Susan and goldenrod, and you can imagine how refreshingly yellow this slope was through the summer and early fall. And on another estate we planted the purple coneflower. The flat-topped purple seed pod of this stays on during the winter, too, and when the snow is on the ground the pods reflect a lavender tint on its surface—a very lovely effect. Aside from its beauty, a field of wild flowers is practical, too, for it obviates a great deal of lawn cutting.

Just one other example—a small estate of scarcely an acre. But this was large enough to have woods so dense that they hid the street. And there are two sun openings, one at the front of the house, and the other spreads out from a sun room that connects the house and garage. In the latter we put a bird pool, because the owners are great bird lovers, and whatever shrubs and plants we brought into this place are the kind the birds like. A little lane, planted with violets, led to a council ring with a fire in the center, in the southwest corner of the property. Around the council ring were planted Western crab apples and violets, so, you see, in the spring there is a rose bloom overhead and a blue carpet underneath. To the north was a grove of native crab apples and hawthorn that we left untouched, except for a path leading through them from the council ring to the kitchen garden. This garden contains apple trees, blackberries, gooseberries, currants and grapes, besides beds for vegetables and cut flowers nearest the house, and it has much sunlight. Economically, the garden is a success, and viewing it from the house, it has an air of domesticity that is essential.

As a minor note, I often bring into my compositions a council ring, which consists of a ring built of stone, of a diameter of nineteen to twenty feet, and with a fireplace in the center, with an elevation of eight to ten inches above ground. The idea of the ring is partly Indian and partly old Nordic, though the construction is modern. Practically the ring brings people close together, and the fire chases away the mosquitoes, so often an annoying hindrance to our enjoyment of the out-of-doors. From a spiritual standpoint, there is something within us that loves the fire, and gathering about it has a social leveling effect that puts us all on a par with one another. A council-fire gathering is the most democratic institution we have. We are, after all, children of the primitive, and we like to go back to it.

Very often I make a combination of outdoor swimming pool and stage. I always elevate the stage, and I call it "players' hill," for I believe the stage should be looked up to rather than depressed as the Greek stage was. The swimming pool usually has a background of rock—here on the plains, of lime or sandstone, for besides being native, their horizontal strata typify the prairies—and in granite country, granite. On top of the elevation is the actual stage, backed by cedars or groups of deciduous planting, depending on the environs and the composition of the rest of the landscape. The stage is lighted by natural fires from one or two depressed fire pits. This natural firelight gives a wavering, mysterious appearance to the faces of the actors that no artificial lighting can do, and the movements of the actors are reflected in the pool below in a most poetic way. The pool serves also to separate the audience from the players, and as a carrier for the voices. Where there is no pool, I make a players' hill by slightly elevating a corner of the garden. The players' hill should always face the moon, so that on moonlight nights plays can be produced with no other lighting. Perhaps it might interest you that in the latest pool we built we also incorporated a sun bath; keeping up with the times, you see.

NO FENCES OR HEDGES

The large estates, of course, are only for a few people. I am asked every once in a while, as other landscape architects are asked, what suggestions I would make for the designing of a small garden that must be laid out and tended by the owner himself. Naturally, I believe that this, like the public park or the large private estate, should be planted with the trees and shrubs and flowers that are native to the surrounding landscape, with the addition, of course, of old-fashioned garden flowers and shrubs, such as the lilac, hollyhock, oleander, geraniums—plants that the white man has carried with him wherever he has gone and that have become through the centuries household pets, just as the dog and the cat are. In a desert section, there should be desert plants, in a mountainous section, mountain plants, and in a prairie section, prairie shrubs and flowers. Then one will at least be certain that, given a little care, the garden will grow.

To my mind, the ideal location for the small house on a small lot is about forty feet back from the walk. There should be a lawn in front with a few trees, and if the ordinances of the town permit, some shrubbery should be planted in the parkway. This gives a feeling of privacy to the entrance. There should never be any shrubbery planted against the walls of the house, unless there is some uninteresting space that had best be covered. The architecture of the house should be allowed to reveal its full beauty, and this it cannot do if it seems sunk in a mass of shrubbery, as if it were in a swamp. If the house is covered with vines, then the source of the vine should show—it has its own beauty.

Fences destroy the peacefulness of the scene. If used, they are least objectionable if not more than three feet high. And no clipped hedges! Hedges are useful only when they serve as a windbreak, and a windbreak is not needed next to the street. However, I am not much concerned that the clipped hedge will become a permanent feature of the American town scene. Clipped hedges require a great deal of work, and the American home owner is too fond of golfing and motoring to put in many hours with the clipping shears.

The flower garden should be in the back, and the vegetable beds can be separated from the rest of the garden by beds of flowers that are frankly meant for cutting. Flowers for cutting should be planted in rows the same way that carrots are. The ornamental flowers can be planted along the paths or spaces against the house, but they shouldn't be crowded or packed like sardines. Compression is against the rules

of art. A plant should be given all the room it needs, and then its individual beauty will stand out and we grow to love it for itself, and our enjoyment of the garden is greatly enhanced. A garden without love has no story. There should be a festival of color in the flowers that bloom in the spring, and a glory of color in the foliage of the plants that are at their best in the fall of the year. And there should be some flowers for perfume, for there should always be perfume in a garden. Trees can be associated rather closely together, but not any closer than will permit the ground floor to grow plants that like the shade. If possible, the garage should be hidden with planting.

There should be few paths, and they should not be of cement or brick. For a formal path raked gravel is best. Paths of stone with grass in between are much softer to the eye. But stone in a garden must always be used with care. Too much stone is cold and makes a garden lose its friendliness.

Sometimes it is interesting to introduce a rock garden, because then one may have plants that cannot express their full beauty otherwise. Rock plants become flat in a border, but crawling over rocks for sun, their struggle is a picture worth having. Associated with the rock garden may be a pool where the birds may drink, and where fish may make one contemplate their manner of life. The pool should be in the background, so it can have a setting of shrubs whose shadows will bring the mystery of the forest and at the same time give shade to the plants that want it.

But above all, a garden should be individual. It should not be like one's neighbor's, for then it is monotonous; it should express the personality of the owner. If one likes birds, one should plant shrubs the birds like; if one likes Shasta daisies, they should be the prominent feature. But a garden that is fitted for a hillside should not be put on a plain, or vice versa.

It is not size that makes a garden beautiful. It is the love that you give it and the spirit of the out-of-doors—of God's out-of-doors—that is in it.

MAY THEILGAARD WATTS

A Story for Ravinians

(1936)

West of Chicago lies a bungalow and cottonwood suburb with a catalpa tree, or a distorted mulberry, or a round bed of cannas, in the exact center of each front lawn. Not long ago these streets were cut through rich woods. There were red oaks, white oaks, sugar maples, and lindens above, and yellow violets, ironwood, elderberries, wood anemones below.

A certain family bought a lot out there. They enjoyed the beauty of texture in the varied foliage of the forest undergrowth.

"We are tired of the neat smug scenery of Rogers Park," they said. "Here is a different beauty, —a tangled richer loveliness."

When their house was being completed they sent out laborers to clear the property. It was March. No one knew when a clump of trembling aspens followed hawthorns and viburnums and crabs on to the roaring bon-fire. These were all "underbrush"

From *Ravinia: Her Charms and Destiny*, by May Theilgaard Watts and Hazel Crow Ewell (Highland Park, Ill: Ravinia Garden Club, 1936; repr., Park District of Highland Park and the Highland Park Historical Society, 1980).

to the laborers, and they had been ordered to "Clear out the underbrush".

When this job was finished, they took the heaped-up soil excavated for the basement, and spread it neatly and firmly to the four exact corners of the property. No one knew when a lush bed of white trilliums and sweet wild phlox was forever buried alive under a blanket of stiff wet clay. Nor did anyone realize that the levelled surface raised the soil several inches around the trunks of those white oaks and hickories that had been marked for preservation, and that this soil was cutting off the air supply of the feeding root tips, so that even these trees must soon die.

Abundant rich forest still lay all around the subdued lot, and birds sang. It was a beautiful place to live.

Others thought so too. They came, and each one firmly corseted and manicured his own lot, before settling down to enjoy the gypsy-like charm of his surroundings.

The dying forest trees were gradually replaced, mostly with cottonwoods. Presently there was no undisciplined charm left to distract the inhabitants from a comparative contemplation of each other's lawns and privet hedges. So they settled down to planting red geraniums on these rectangular graves where they had buried beauty.

But last Spring the same family that had so appreciatively bought the first lot in that suburb west of Chicago—discovered Ravinia. They saw the gray rain of aspen catkins. They saw crab apples in bloom above yellow violets, and they saw new white oak leaves above white trilliums. They bought a beautiful wooded lot.

Will they send laborers out to clear and level it?

This little book seeks to point out to such new neighbors the things that are probably on their property, and to talk to our old neighbors about the charms of Ravinia, so that we may enjoy them together, and perhaps lend a hand toward preserving them, and even reinstating some of them.

MAY THEILGAARD WATTS

On Improving the Property

(1980)

They laid the trilliums low,
and where drifted anemones and wild
    sweet phlox
were wont to follow April's hepaticas—
    they planted grass.

There was a corner that held a tangled
    copse
of hawthorne and young wild crabs,
bridal in May above yellow violets,
purple-twigged in November.
They needed that place for Lombardy
    poplars—and grass.

Last June the elderberry was fragrant
    here,
and in October the viburnum poured its
    wine
beneath the moon-yellow wisps of the
    witch-hazel blossoms.

They piled them in the alley and made a
    burnt offering—to grass.
There was a slope that a wild grapevine
    had captured long ago.
At its brink a colony, of mandrakes held
    green umbrellas close,
like a crowd along the path of a parade.
This job almost baffled them; showers
    washed off the seed
and made gullies in the naked clay.
They gritted their teeth—and planted
    grass.

At the base of the slope there was a
    hollow
so lush with hundreds of years of fallen
    leaves
that maiden-hair swirled above the
    trout-lilies,
and even a few blood-roots lifted frosty
    blossoms there.
Clay from the ravaged slope washed down
and filled the hollow with a yellow hump.
They noticed the hump—and planted
    grass.

From the reprint edition of *Ravinia: Her Charms and Destiny*, by May Theilgaard Watts and Hazel Crow Ewell (Highland Park, Ill.: Park District of Highland Park and the Highland Park Historical Society, 1980). This poem seems to have been inspired by "A Story for Ravinians" and in the 1980 reprint was listed as previously unpublished.

There was a linden that the bees loved.
A smug catalpa has taken its place,
but the wood ashes were used to fertilize
    the grass.
People pass by and say: "Just *look* at that
    grass—

not a weed in it. It's like velvet!"
(One could say as much for any other
    grave.)

PART V

RESTORATION AND MANAGEMENT OF THE NATIVE LANDSCAPE

In recent years, we have recognized the need for greater attention to ongoing management as well as restoration in our efforts to preserve the ecological integrity of nature. Yet the idea of management is not new. Discussions about restoration and management as parts of an overall conservation strategy can be traced to the late nineteenth and early twentieth centuries, when ideas about forestry, nature preserves, arboreta, and public parks were emerging. In this section, issues of landscape management are treated as they relate to forestry, to parks as preserves, and to both wilderness and recreational resource policy.

H. W. S. Cleveland's 1882 booklet *Culture and Management of Our Native Forests* is one of the earliest discourses on managing forest areas in North America for timber, horticultural, and recreational purposes. Cleveland developed a lifelong friendship with George Barrell Emerson (1797–1881), author of *A Report on the Trees and Shrubs Growing Naturally in the Forests of Massachusetts* (1846), and designed

a tract of land for him in Winthrop, Massachusetts. Their wide-ranging discussions and correspondence throughout Cleveland's career certainly had an impact on the landscape architect's approach to forest management. (A letter from Cleveland describing his relationship with Emerson is included in Waterston, *Memoir of George Barrell Emerson,* 21–23.) Cleveland traveled throughout the East, Southeast, and Midwest, and to Cuba, observing different forestry practices in these places. His article here compiles practical advice based on those varied experiences. Cleveland's work predates the scientific forestry methods developed by Frederick Law Olmsted, Warrren H. Manning, and Gifford Pinchot for George W. Vanderbilt's forest lands at Biltmore.

Olmsted wrote "The Use of the Axe" for the park commissioners of New York to provide guidelines for managing the native and planted forest preserves in the city's parks, including the need for careful thinning of stands of timber. Olmsted's practice typically included collaborations with foresters and horticulturists, and he was also involved in many pioneer conservation efforts, including Yosemite Valley and the Mariposa Big Tree Grove in California (see Beveridge, "Frederick Law Olmsted, Sr.").

Charles Eliot was visionary in his ambitious plans for establishing a system of land reservations in the Boston metropolitan region. Critical for the long-term care of these varied landscapes was the development of appropriate management strategies for each of the types of vegetation included within the preserves. The young Eliot apprenticed with Olmsted for two years, during which he assisted with the plans for the Boston Park System. At Olmsted's suggestion, in 1885 Eliot traveled to England and Europe, meeting with leading landscape gardeners and visiting private parks and estates, including Prince Pückler-Muskau's in Germany. Eliot became a regular contributor to *Garden and Forest,* and in February 1890 wrote a letter urging the protection of the Waverly Oaks, a stand of virgin trees in Belmont, outside Boston. In the article, he proposed a regional plan for saving lands around the city in a system of nature preserves. Just fifteen months later, the governor of Massachusetts signed a bill establishing the Trustees of Public Reservations, the first conservation organization in the world, a tribute to Eliot's remarkable vision and tireless dedication to the project. His article is a classic among writings in the early history of landscape architecture and a model for combining both practical and aesthetic strategies for landscape management based on its natural character.

The two pieces by Jens Jensen provide a glimpse of his early conservation efforts. The first is a report prepared for the Chicago Special Park Commission, which was charged with documenting the needs for park expansion in and around the city. The commission's landmark work called for the establishment of a network of small neighborhood parks as well as the creation of a regional system of conserved lands. The resulting Cook County Forest Preserves were later replicated in the other counties of the Chicago metropolitan area. Jensen's report details an on-the-ground assessment of the ecological conditions of the lands being considered for protection.

The second piece is a letter Jensen submitted in support of efforts to set aside a portion of the Indiana Dunes on Lake Michigan as a national park. Jensen was instrumental, working through his friend Stephen Mather, recently appointed director of the National Park Service, in getting a series of hearings held on the protection of the dunes. The conservation organizations in which Jensen was a force—including the Prairie Club and the Friends of Our Native Landscape—were a significant presence during the hearings.

Henry Cowles's testimony, also included here, demonstrates his ease in communicating ecological issues to a broad public audience. Cowles had earned a PhD at the University of Chicago in 1898 with his dissertation, "The Ecological Relations of the Vegetation on the Sand Dunes of Lake Michigan," considered to be a landmark study in ecology. At the time of his testimony, Cowles was a popular professor at the University of Chicago and active in a number of conservation organizations, including the Friends of Our Native Landscape.

The horticulturist Lars Peter Jensen, who was manager of the Missouri Botanical Garden Arboretum in Gray Summit from 1926 until his death in 1941 and a member of the St. Louis Naturalists' Club, explores the notion that city parks can be important preserves for the native flora of a region. Lamenting the destruction of native flora in parks to make way for brightly colored gardens of annual flowers arranged in the style known as carpet bedding, Jensen argues that citizens have a moral duty to preserve and protect local flora.

By the early 1920s, Aldo Leopold's work with the U.S. Forest Service had convinced him of the need to protect lands in the American West from development. Leopold went on to become a critical national force in preservation, cofounding the Wilderness Society in 1935. His eloquent 1926 essay included here was used extensively by the American Civic Association and other organizations in their efforts to build support for setting aside wilderness lands. Paul Riis was a writer and editor for the "Conservation of Wildlife" section of *Parks and Recreation* magazine. His article details plans for the University of Wisconsin Arboretum, a pioneering effort in the restoration of native ecosystems led by Aldo Leopold (then a professor of wildlife management at the university), together with other professors, such as John Curtis, G. William Longenecker, and Henry Greene (see Jordan, *Our First 50 Years*).

HORACE WILLIAM SHALER CLEVELAND

The Culture and Management of Our Native Forests, for Development as Timber or Ornamental Wood

(1882)

Man's progress from barbarism to civilization is indicated by the degree of skill he has attained in the cultivation of those products of the earth which minister to his necessities and comfort. As long as the natural resources are sufficient to supply his primary wants of food and clothing, he will make no effort to increase them, and it is only as he is driven by the necessities of increasing demand and diminishing supply that he exerts himself to secure relief by artificial means.

The first efforts of the savage at cultivation are of the rudest description, and just in proportion as tribes and nations advance in numbers, power and intelligence, do they also gain in improved methods of tillage, in greater knowledge of the science of culture, and in better implements and machinery for its performance.

These are simple truths, which everyone will recognize. Their application to the

From *The Culture and Management of Our Native Forests, for Development as Timber or Ornamental Wood*, by H. W. S. Cleveland (Springfield, Mass.: H. W. Rokker, 1882), iii–xvi.

subject of forest culture, lies in the obvious fact that it is not until a nation has reached mature age, and an advanced stage of civilization, that the native growth of wild forest proves insufficient for the increasing demand for timber, and the necessity of providing, by artificial culture, for an additional supply, begins to be felt.

We could hardly have a more striking illustration than is here afforded, of the adaptation of the provisions of nature, first, to the immediate necessities of existence, and subsequently to the development of the latent powers of the human race. The cereals and vegetables which are essential to man's daily support are of annual growth. Their culture is comparatively simple, and he soon learns that his very existence is dependent upon their renewed production with each recurring summer. The forests are equally essential to his further development, by furnishing material for the construction of houses and ships, and the countless implements by whose aid he attains to almost superhuman power. But the forest requires the lifetime of two or three generations for the full attainment of maturity. In the infancy of the race, the necessity of providing for such distant wants could not be foreseen.

Nature, therefore, as if she had been conscious that forest culture was too arduous an undertaking for primitive man, has furnished so abundant a supply, that no deficiency or necessity of economy is felt till the nation has acquired such a degree of intelligence as to be competent to the solution of the problem. And this is the point at which we now stand, and which the older nations of Europe have long since passed, seeing plainly that our natural sources are well-nigh exhausted, yet shrinking from the unfamiliar task of seeking to supply the deficiency by artificial means.

Many once powerful nations have dwindled into insignificance in consequence of their neglect of this lesson which nature imperatively demands that we should learn. Their fate should be to us a warning, as the efforts of the most intelligent nations of today should be to us an example, to save us from a like fate. The necessity for action is imminent, and can not be averted. The subject of the increasing demand and rapidly diminishing supply of timber throughout the country has been so thoroughly discussed by legislative committees, both State and National, by agricultural societies and by able individual writers, that it would seem but a waste of time to bring forward the oft-repeated statistics in evidence of the danger that threatens us, and the urgent need of adopting measures of protection and relief.

Assuming, therefore, that my readers are familiar with the data which prove the necessity, I pass at once to the consideration of the means of averting the danger.

The only measure of relief thus far suggested with any definite prospect of success, is the planting of new forests. Much has been said, it is true, about the preservation of those that remain; but the words seem meaningless, in view of the fact that private property is beyond the control of the Government, and Congress declines even to grant means to prevent the destruction of that which still pertains to the public domain.

The planting of new forests is indeed an all-important work, which can not be too strongly urged, but we have not yet reached the period when it is likely to be successfully inaugurated, except perhaps, in occasional instances by railroad or manufacturing companies, with a view to their own future wants. Individuals will not engage to any great extent, in a work which demands the investment not only of a large amount of money, and the continuous expenditure of a great deal of labor, but also of a long period of time, which is the one form of capital of which we never have a surplus. It behooves us, therefore, to study rather more closely than we have heretofore done, the possibility of improving the condition of that which remains. The woods still standing contain a vast amount of available material, which is susceptible of development in far less time than would be required for the planting and growth of new forests, our utter neglect of which furnishes one of the most striking proofs of our ignorance of forest culture.

No one can travel through any portion of the States east of the prairie regions without being impressed by the fact that he is never out of sight of woodland. In fact the chief cause of the prevailing apathy on the subject of forest planting arises from the fact of the great abundance of groves and extended forests, which convey the impression, in spite of the assertions of staticians, that there is still enough wood growing to supply the place of that which is removed.

The Duke of Argyle, in the interesting sketch of his trip through the States, published after his return to England, says emphatically that nothing in the aspect of the country surprised and impressed him so much as the great amount of wood still remaining, and everywhere giving beauty and variety to the landscape; but he added that it was everywhere that beauty of the wild wood, which never bore any evidence of culture or effort to increase its value by artificial development.

"I saw nothing (he says) that could be called fine timber, and no woods which showed any care in thinning, with a view to the production of such timber in the future."

Such a criticism is not surprising from one who, like most country gentlemen of England, is familiar with the process of forest culture, but it certainly is surprising that, with all our boasted intelligence, we still remain practically insensible to the fact that, while almost every tract of woodland contains a large percentage of such trees as are most valuable for timber, already well advanced in growth, and susceptible, by judicious management, of being developed into proper form and size for use in far less time and at far less cost than would be required for the planting and growth of new forest; yet, if left to themselves, not one tree in a thousand will ever be fit for anything better than fencing stuff or fuel. Vast resources of wealth are lying latent and running to waste in our woodlands, and we

stand stupidly unconscious of the fact that its development requires simply the application of the intelligent culture we bestow on all other crops. In many instances, it is true, the native woods have been so long neglected, that they are past redemption, but there are, nevertheless, large areas of continuous forest, and smaller groves and woodlots in every section of the country, now yielding no revenue, which might, by proper annual thinning, pruning and culture, be developed into timber forests of very great value, while yielding an annual crop of firewood in the process.

Where shall we find, or how shall we create, the men who are competent to the work? To judge from invariable practice, our people seem not only to be ignorant of the first principles of forest culture, but unconscious even of the possibility of its application to the development of our native woods. The fact of such prevailing ignorance rests not alone upon negative evidence. We have positive proof in abundance in the attempts which we often see at the "improvement" of a piece of woodland when it is appropriated as the site of a residence. It is hard to conceive of anything more dismal and forlorn than the average result of the effort to impart a homelike aspect to such a place; the dwelling, with its "span new" expression, standing in the midst of a multitude of tall poles, with tufts of leaves upon their tops, looking like fowls stripped of their feathers, and the bare ground fretted everywhere with freshly upturned roots, the sole remnants of the wild shrubbery which has been ruthlessly exterminated.

In order to a comprehension of the principles of healthy forest growth, let us consider some of the processes of nature, and learn from them her requirements.

If we plant the seed of a maple, chestnut, linden, oak or ash tree by itself in the open ground in suitable soil, and suffer it to grow without molestation, simply guarding it from injury, we shall find that the first act of the young plant is to send out broad leaves, which serve among other purposes to shade completely the stem, and the ground immediately around it in which the roots are growing. As the tree grows, it preserves a symmetrical shape, the limbs spreading and the trunk increasing in size, in proportion to its height, but always preserving the condition of keeping the trunk and the ground for a considerable distance around it, in the shadow of the foliage till mature age, when the roots have penetrated to such a depth as to be safe from injury, and the trunk is protected by thick layers of cork like bark, which safely guards alike from heat and cold the inner layers and young wood in which the sap is performing its functions.

Such are the conditions to which nature adheres, if not interfered with by accident or design, and such, therefore, we may be sure, are those best adapted to healthy and vigorous growth. The fact that they are continually violated with apparent impunity, serves only to show the wonderful power of nature to supply deficiencies, and adapt herself to circumstances, but in artificial culture, we should aim as nearly as possible to imitate the course she would pursue if unimpeded.

The requirements of nature are of course the same when trees are growing together in a forest, as when they stand singly, but the conditions of growth are so changed that the end is attained by entirely different means.

If we enter a tract of wood land, covered with a hard wood growth of an average height of thirty or forty feet we find it composed almost exclusively of trees which have run up to a great height in proportion to the spread of their limbs. The largest and oldest of them may have had some lateral branches which are now dead, but the younger growth will consist only of tall, slender stems, without a branch or leaf except near the top. It will be difficult, perhaps impossible, to find a single tree possessing sufficient symmetry of form to be worth transplanting for ornamental use. A little reflection will serve to convince us that this form of growth, so different from that of the single tree in the open ground, is the natural result of the action of the same rules under changed conditions.

When a young wood first springs up on open ground, each tree begins to grow as if it were alone, sending out lateral branches and preserving its just proportion. But whenever these laterals meet and mingle with each other, they shut out the sunlight from all below, and thence forward all lateral growth must cease, and each individual is struggling upward to keep even with its neighbors and secure its share of the sunbeams which are essential to its existence, and which can only be had at the top. It thus becomes forced out of all just proportions in the effort to keep even with its fellows. The conditions of keeping the trunk and roots in the shade, however, are even more rigidly adhered to than in the case of the single tree, growing by itself, for the whole area of the wood is shaded, and, moreover, the trees on the edges of the wood, if not interfered with by men or cattle, will be clothed on the outer side with limbs and foliage, clear to the ground, so as to check the free passage of the winds whose drying influence upon the soil is even more active than that of the sun.

If we examine more closely we shall find that nature adapts herself to these changed conditions, and avails herself of whatever advantages they afford.

The single tree when growing by itself sends its roots deep into the ground in search of the moisture which cannot be had near the surface, and thus, when it reaches mature age, it draws its supplies from sources beyond the reach of temporary changes, and, moreover, secures so firm a hold upon the ground that it suffers no injury from the storms that assail it, but fearlessly stretches forth its arms as if to challenge the gale.

In the woods, on the contrary, the surface soil never becomes parched or heated, but maintains an even degree of temperature and moisture in consequence not only of the exclusion of the sun and winds, but of the deep mulching of leaves which annually cover the ground and keep it moist, while, by their decomposition, they form a rich mould comprising all the ingredients of vegetation.

If we dig only a few inches into this mould we find it everywhere permeated by fibrous rootlets emanating from larger roots, which under these circumstances have kept near the surface where they draw nourishment from the rich material there provided. If the single tree in the open ground had tried to live by such means, it would speedily have perished for want of nourishment, or would have been uprooted by the winds as forest trees are liable to be when left alone in a clearing.

In the woods the necessity no longer exists of sending the roots to a great depth either in search of nourishment or

for support against storms, and nature always adapts herself to circumstances and attains her ends by the simplest and most economical means.

If we now consider the facts I have stated, which anyone can easily verify for himself, we shall find that all the essential principles of tree culture are comprised within their limits, and by their rational observances we may secure healthy and vigorous trees, and develop at will either such forms as will fit them for timber or for ornamental use.

The five trees I have cited—maple, chestnut, linden, oak and ash—are among the most common and yet the most valuable of our forest trees, and may be taken as representatives and proper illustrations of the facts I am stating. Either of these trees, if growing by itself in proper soil and undisturbed by other than natural influences, will attain, at maturity a height of seventy or eighty feet, with a spread of limb equal in diameter to its height, and a trunk of such massive proportions as leaves no room for apprehension of inability to uphold the wilderness of foliage it has to support. But these same trees, if growing in a wood, will send up a slender stem, straight as an arrow, fifty, sixty or seventy feet without a limb or a leaf, till it reaches the average height of its fellows, and sends out its tufts of foliage to secure the benefit of every sunbeam it can catch.

We see therefore, that if we wish to form a beautiful and symmetrical tree, or a grove of such, composed of individual specimens of majestic and graceful proportions, we must allow it free access, to sun and air, with full power of expansion on every side. While young, however, the growth will be more vigorous and healthy,

Sugar maples at edge of meadow, Marsh-Billings-Rockefeller National Historic Park, Woodstock, Vt. (Photograph by Carol Betsch.)

and we can develop the desired form more easily and successfully, by leaving a much greater number of trees than are eventually to remain, and removing from year to year all which are near enough to the final occupants to check or impede their full development.

If, on the other hand, we wish to develop the trunk or bole for use as timber we must plant, or suffer the trees to grow more thickly together, and thus extend its trunk longitudinally by forcing it to ascend in search of the sunlight on which its very existence is dependent. The indigenous growth, however, is always a great deal too thick for successful development. The trees are so crowded that many of them perish in the struggle, and those which survive are drawn up into such spindling proportions that not one in a hundred ever attains the dignity of timber, whereas by proper and reasonable thinning, and judicious culture and pruning of the trees selected for final retention, every acre of woodland might be made to yield an annual crop of fire-wood, and all the while be growing timber which eventually in many instances might be worth more than the land itself; or by a different process of management may be converted into a grove of majestic and graceful, ornamental trees.

The proper performance of this work constitutes the most important part of forest culture and for want of the knowledge of how it should be done, or from ignorance of the possibility of its application to our native forest, a vast area (in the aggregate) of woodland is running to waste; yielding no revenue and promising nothing better in the future than fire-wood, of which a very large proportion is yet susceptible of redemption and conversion into timber of great value at far less cost of time and labor than would be required for the planting and rearing of new forests, while the very process of development would be yielding an annual income instead of demanding large outlays.

Travel where we may we are never out of sight of forest, and every wood lot is a mine of wealth waiting only the application of intelligent labor for its development. In almost every tract of woodland may be found more or less of the trees I have named and in many places also hickory, walnut, butternut, elm, cherry, beech and other valuable timber trees, mingled with a great variety of those which are worthless, or fit only for fuel. In some cases they are past redemption, having been so long neglected that they have run up into mere thickets of hoop-poles. Young growth may everywhere be found, however, which are in condition to be taken in hand, and in almost all cases the work of thinning, and pruning may be entered upon with a certainty of profitable results if wisely and perseveringly conducted.

The work of thinning, as ordinarily conducted in the occasional instances in which on any account it has become desirable, is entrusted to mere laborers, who have no regard for the natural conditions which are essential to healthy growth, and which cannot be suddenly changed, without serious injury to the trees that are left.

All the small growth of shrubs, such as hazel, cornel, dogwood, elder, shad-bush, etc., is first grubbed out and destroyed under the general term of "underbrush," and this not only throughout the interior of the wood, but round its outer edges where such shrubbery is apt to spring up in thickets, which serve the very important purpose of preventing the free passage of the wind over the surface soil of the interior, besides adding incalculably to the beauty of the wood, as seen from without by connecting the line of foliage of the trees, with that of the sward below, and presenting a living mass of verdure. The trees which are considered most desirable to preserve, are then selected, and all the rest at once removed. Finally the leaves are carefully raked from the surface and carried off or burnt.

Sun and wind now have free access to the soil, and it very soon becomes parched and dry. The fine rootlets near the surface, which have heretofore been preserved by the never-failing moisture of the rich mould under its mulching of leaves, are converted into a mass of wiry fibres, no longer capable of conveying nourishment, even if it were within their reach. And while the means of supply are thus reduced, the tall, slender trunk, through which the sap must ascend to the leaves, is now exposed to the free action of the sun and winds. Now I do not presume to say, that evaporation can take place through the bark, but the provisions which nature makes to guard the inner vital tissues, from the effect of the sun's rays indicate beyond all question, that they are in some way injurious. I have elsewhere shown that in the case of the single tree growing by itself, the trunk is always shaded by the spreading foliage, when suffered to retain its natural form. In the forest, the trees shade each other, and thus affect the object by mutual action. But now let me call your attention to another provision of nature which few people observe, but the meaning of which is too obvious to be mistaken. If we examine the bark of an oak, elm, chestnut or maple, of mature age,

which has always stood by itself, exposed to the full influence of atmospheric changes, we find it to be of great thickness of very rugged character, and of a cork-like consistency, all of which characteristics make it the best possible non-conductor of heat or cold that can be imagined, under the protection of which the living tissues are safely kept from injury through the burning heat of summer and the intense cold of winter.

Now go into the forest where the trees shade each other, and wind and sun are excluded, and you will find that the bark of the trees is smooth and thin in comparison with that of those in the open ground.

Nature never wastes her energies needlessly, and the trees in the woods do not require the thick coat of those that are exposed. But the effect of suddenly admitting the sun and wind upon them is precisely the same as that of exposing any portion of the human skin which had heretofore been clothed. It is to guard against injury from this source that experienced tree-planters, when removing large trees from the woods, are accustomed to swathe the trunk with ropes of straw, which is a rational process, yet it is by no means uncommon to see the reverse of this action. I have seen, during the past winter a great many very large fine trees planted on the best avenues in Chicago, at a cost of certainly not less than fifty dollars each, from the trunks and large limbs of which all the rough bark had been carefully scraped, leaving only a thin, smooth covering over the inner tissues. This is as if a man should prepare for unusual exposure to heat or cold by laying aside all his clothing.

Few persons, even among those whose

business is tree culture, as fruit-growers and nursery men, have any just conception of the value of thorough mulching, as a means of promoting the health and vigor of growing trees. In fact, such a mulching of the whole ground as nature provides in the forest by the annual fall of the leaves, may be said to be unknown in artificial culture, so rarely is it practiced, yet its immediate effect in promoting new and vigorous growth is such as would seem almost incredible to one who had not witnessed it, and affords one of the most beautiful illustrations of nature's methods of securing the most important results by such simple and incidental means that they escape our notice, though going on right under our eyes from year to year.

Of course the richest food for plant consumption is in the soil near the surface, but if that soil is subjected to alternations of temperature and moisture, sometimes baked in clods, and at others reduced to the consistency of mire, no roots can survive the changes. In the forest, as I have elsewhere said, these changes are prevented by the shade of the foliage and the mulching of fallen leaves. The rich mould of the surface soil maintains an even temperature, is always moist, and is everywhere permeated with fibrous roots drawing nourishment from the rich sources which surround them, and this process may be artificially imitated, and the same results attained, by mulching, if properly done. It does not suffice to pile a few inches of straw or manure around each tree for a short distance from the trunk. If the tree stands singly, at a distance from others, the mulching should extend on every side beyond the spread of its branches; and in the case of an orchard, or young wood, the surface of the whole

area it occupies should be covered with leaves, straw, shavings, chip-dirt, tan-bark, or whatever material is most available, to a depth of several inches. I first learned the value of the process when a young man, on a coffee plantation in Cuba, where a portion of the hands were constantly employed in collecting refuse vegetable matter of all kinds, and spreading over the whole ground between the rows of the coffee bushes, to such depth as served to keep the surface cool and of even temperature, and also to prevent the growth of grass and weeds and thus supersede the necessity of ploughing between the rows.

Afterwards, when engaged in fruit culture in New Jersey, I practiced it in my vineyard and orchards with most satisfactory results, of which an account was published more than thirty years ago, in the *Horticulturist,* then edited by A. J. Downing.[*]

The trees and vines responded at once to my efforts in their behalf by such increased luxuriance of growth that it was easy to distinguish the portions that had been mulched as far as they could be seen, and, on digging into the surface soil under the mulching at any point, I found it filled with fibrous roots precisely as is the case in the leaf mould in the woods. No fruit-grower who has once tried this experiment will ever after forego the advantages it offers, and I have spoken of it thus at length from the obviously vital importance of its bearing on forest culture. A moment's reflection will show that in the opening and thinning of native wood which had grown thickly together, a heavy mulching of such portions of the ground as may unavoidably

[*]*Horticulturist,* vol. 3, p. 113.

become exposed may be of most essential service in preserving the health and vigor of the trees that are to be retained.

It is difficult to lay down specific rules by which a novice could be guided in the work of opening and thinning out the wood of a native forest, except by fully impressing him with the importance of preserving, so far as is possible, the conditions which nature shows to be the most favorable to vigorous growth, and proceeding very cautiously when it becomes necessary to change the relative proportions of the influences which affect the vitality of the trees. The age and condition of the wood at the time the work is begun are, of course, important elements for consideration. If the growth is not more than ten or fifteen years, and the trees have not sprung up so thickly as already to have become a mere thicket of hoop-poles, but have preserved a reasonable degree of symmetry, its management can be much more easily controlled than if it has attained a more mature age, and especially if the object is to create an ornamental grove composed of fine specimens of individual trees, a process by which the value of desirable residence sites in the vicinity of cities or large towns might often be very greatly increased.

Whether this be the object, or the development of timber, the first thing to be done is to select and place a distinguishing mark upon every tree which is ultimately to be retained. Then remove at first from its immediate vicinity only those which are actually crowding it, or impeding its growth by shading or interfering with its foliage. Those which simply shade the trunk or the ground around it are serving a useful purpose, and should not be disturbed. Indeed, if it is found that the necessary removals involve much increased exposure of the surface soil around the tree, it should at once be covered with the mulching of sufficient depth to prevent the possibility of its becoming heated and dry. All other sources of danger to the health of the trees are insignificant in comparison with that of the rude check they are liable to receive from sudden exposure of the trunks and surface roots to the influence of the sun and wind, from which they have heretofore been protected, and to which they can only become accustomed by a gradual change.

The next year it will be found that the tree has gladly availed itself of the opportunity for expansion, and has spread its limbs to fill the vacant space around it, so that more trees must now be removed, while the increased mass of foliage it has developed renders it less liable to suffer injury from their loss. The removal of the undergrowth of shrubbery, should be very cautiously conducted, and in no case should it be removed from the outskirts of the wood, which should everywhere be left with as dense a growth as possible, to prevent the entrance of the winds.

The sirocco-like wind from the S. W., which often blows with great violence for days together, especially in the spring and early summer, when the trees are full of sap, and the young shoots and leaves are tender and sensitive, is the one from which most danger is to be apprehended. The merely mechanical injury it inflicts upon the spray and foliage is often serious, but its worst effects are due to its absorption of moisture and vitality.

All experienced nursery men and fruit-growers, have learned to dread its exhausting influences especially, upon grape vines and other broad-leaved plants, and they too are aware of the fact, which comparatively few ordinary observers seem to have noticed, that its effects in giving a general trend of the spray and branches of trees in exposed situations towards the N. E., is so marked that no one who has learned to observe it, need ever be long at a loss to know the points of the compass in any parts of the country.

The fact, however, that we have it in our power to guard against the evil effects of this wind by artificial means, is not so generally known as it should be, and it was only after many years observation and experience that I came to a full realization of certain facts in connection with its action, which have a most important bearing upon the question of forest culture.

I became aware, many years since, that many shrubs, trees and plants would grow and thrive at Newport, R.I., and at Yarmouth, Nova Scotia, which in the interior were only found much farther south, and would certainly perish if removed to the latitude of those towns. The reason assigned in both cases was the warming influence of the neighboring gulf stream, which seemed a plausible explanation in which my faith remained unshaken for years, until I went to Chicago, where I found it was impossible to grow many of the finer fruits, and some of the forest trees which elsewhere are found in much higher latitudes. Neither peaches or grapes can be grown at Chicago, or at any other point on the western side of the lake without artificial protection, and the native growth of wood is very meagre, and many varieties which elsewhere are found much farther north, as the beech and the hemlock, cannot be grown; yet the eastern shore of the lake, only sixty miles distant, has no supe-

rior in the whole country as a fruit growing region. Peaches, grapes, strawberries, etc., grow most luxuriantly anywhere on that shore up to the northern extremity of the lake, three hundred miles north of Chicago, and every variety of forest tree indigenous to the country is found in the best condition of vigorous health. There is no gulf stream to account for this difference, but the relative position towards the lake of the whole extent of its fruitful shore is the same as that of Newport and Nova Scotia towards the ocean. In both cases the S. W. wind reaches the shore after passing for a long distance over water, and instead of burning and exhausting vegetation with a breath of fire, it comes laden with the moisture it has gathered up in its passage, and brings health and strength upon its wings, instead of disease and death. Further reflection served to convince me that the rule was susceptible of much wider application, and serves to explain the different vegetation of the eastern and western shores of great continents in the same parallels of latitude. Central Spain and southern Italy the lands of the orange and grape are in the same latitude as Boston, and going west on the same parallel to California, we again find ourselves surrounded with fruits and plants which in Boston can only be grown under glass. Continuing our western flight across the Pacific, we find the flora of Eastern Asia to bear, in many respects, a striking resemblance to that of Eastern America.

These facts have certainly a very important bearing upon the question of forest culture. They prove that the S. W. wind of spring and early summer is perhaps the worst enemy we have to guard against, and also that its deleterious influences are neutralized when it passes over a large body of water. It is comparatively rare, however, that a situation can be secured affording that advantage, and the question naturally arises, are there no other means of protection? I am happy to have it in my power again to summon nature as a witness that such means are within our reach.

I have said that the beech would not grow near Chicago, a fact which I was very reluctant to admit on first going there, and was only fully convinced of its truth by witnessing repeated failures, and the evidence of reliable nurserymen who had tried in vain to preserve it. Yet after I had long been satisfied that it was idle to attempt its culture, I was one day amazed, while surveying in the woods a few miles from the city, at coming upon a little group of beech trees comprising some twenty or thirty in all, of mature size and in full health and vigor. On examining the situation, to discover, if possible, an explanation of the phenomenon, I observed first that they stood in the bottom of a ravine so deep that their tops were scarcely even with its banks, while the wood which surrounded them extended more than a mile to the S. W., so that they were completely sheltered from the effects of the wind from that quarter. I have never been able to find or to hear of another beech tree anywhere in that region, and can only account for their presence by supposing the seed to have been brought from a distance by birds, probably crows, jays or wild pigeons, and dropped accidentally on a spot, which proved to be a "coigne of vantage," where they were safe from the enemy. The evidence thus afforded of the value of a screen on the S. W. side, should not be lost upon those who are selecting sites for orchards, or vineyards, and shows

the importance when thinning a wood, of leaving whatever shrubbery or foliage there may be on that side to arrest the progress of the wind.

The work of pruning the trees which are to be preserved for timber involves a careful consideration of the principles I have set forth, apart from the judgment required for the skilful performance of the mere manual labor. The object in view being the development of the bole, it is important to remove any limbs which threaten to become its rivals in size, if any such have become established before the work of improvement began. But after the trunk has attained the desired height, it is on all accounts desirable to develop the largest possible mass of foliage, because the making of wood can only be effected by the elaboration of the sap, which is the work of the leaves.

If one is rearing a new forest, in which the trees have been under his control from the time of planting, it must be the result of his own ignorance or negligence if he has failed to secure such forms as he desired, since it is easy to direct the growth of young trees, and prevent them from running into extravagances, which will unfit them for service as timber. And not unfrequently we may find a young wood of indigenous growth, which may be taken in hand and wrought into such shape that its future progress can be easily directed. But, for the most part, in woods that have been suffered to run wild till they have approached maturity, a good deal of skilful pruning will be required to bring the individual trees that are to be preserved into such form as will give them most value. Nothing but practice and careful observation can confer this power. The little treatise of DesCars on the pruning of forest and ornamental trees, translated by Mr. C. S. Sargent, of the Arnold Arboretum, and published by A. Williams & Co., of Boston (price 75 cents), contains full and explicit illustrated directions for all the manual work of pruning, and is invaluable as a guide to the novice, and a work of reference to experienced foresters. But mere manual skill in the performance of the work will be of little avail without the application of a thorough knowledge of the principles of tree growth, and a strict compliance with the requirements of their nature.

If our agriculturists will but apply to the management of their forests the same intelligence with which they direct the culture of other farm crops, they will find an equally ready response to their efforts. The farmer who should leave his field of corn or potatoes to shift for itself, or suffer his cattle and hogs to ramble through it at will, would be justly sneered at by his neighbors and punished by the loss of his crop—and trees have no more capacity for self-management than corn or other vegetables, and are quite as ready to profit by judicious culture, and to yield returns corresponding to the care bestowed upon them. They are not liable to be utterly destroyed, as corn is, by the incursions of live stock, but they do suffer serious injury from the trampling and rooting up of the ground. I have seen beautiful groves of oaks in Iowa full of dead and dying trees, and, on asking the cause, have been told that the native woods "can't stand civilization," but always die out when cattle begin to run in them; and I am told that, in Kentucky and elsewhere in the South, the young growth is found to contain only the inferior varieties of oaks, as the swine running in the

woods seek and greedily eat the acorns of the white oak, on account of their superior sweetness. Has anyone ever estimated the cost of raising hogs on such food?

I have endeavored, in the preceding pages, to confine myself to the special features of forest growth which need to be regarded in the effort to develop and improve a native wood, wherever it may be. The planting and culture of an artificial forest is quite another affair, and I have made no allusion to it because my special object has been, if possible, to urge the fact, and arouse attention to it, that we still have vast resources of latent wealth on every side, susceptible of development by proper management, which we are everywhere suffering to run to waste. The work of planting and rearing artificial forests cannot indeed be urged too strongly, and there is no danger of its being overdone. But the conviction of its necessity can be more readily and forcibly impressed upon the popular mind by an illustration of the possibilities of forest culture, when applied to our native woods, than by any other means. The need of further progress by artificial planting will speedily become obvious, and will follow in natural course.

It has been asserted, and with truth, that it is idle for us to establish schools of forestry, because there is no demand for foresters, and consequently no stimulus to the acquirement of a knowledge of the theory and practice of the art. It will be time enough to establish such schools, it is said, when we have evidence that there are people who desire to avail themselves of the advantages they offer, and that will not be till there is a demand for the services of those who have done so. This is true, so far as it goes, but the next consideration is, how to create the demand. There was no demand a few years ago for telegraph operators, and when I was a boy there was no demand for railroad employees, for there were no railroads. How was the demand created? By showing the importance of the results. Think of the time and labor expended by Morse and his associates before they could get permission to demonstrate the value of the electric telegraph by a line from Washington to Baltimore. No general interest was felt in the scheme till its advantages were thus made manifest, because there was no *realizing conviction* of its truth. And to-day we are in a similar position in reference to the question of forestry. The impending danger of the diminishing supply of timber is acknowledged by all who are familiar with the subject, but there is no realizing sense of it in the popular mind, and there is a want of confidence in the practicability of any of the proposed measures of relief. The first and most important thing to do, therefore, is to stimulate popular interest by showing what *can* be done. To create a popular demand of any kind, it is essential first to demonstrate the value of its object. The men who are familiar with forest culture, know, as well as Morse knew the capability of the telegraph, that the wealth of the nation may be enormously increased by the proper development of the native woods already standing, but they can point to no evidence of the truth of their assertion, and the fact that it has not been done is regarded as proof of its impossibility. There is no such thing in the country as an illustrative example of what may be accomplished by timber culture, and very few of our citizens who visit Europe can appreciate the works which have there been achieved. They go abroad to study works of art, with the idea that we have nothing to learn in regard to natural productions, and the comparatively small number who grasp the conception of the grand possibilities of development which our forests offer to the exercise of such artificial culture as may there be seen, can do no more on their return than express their convictions and urge the importance of acting upon them. This they have done for many years past, but they have not succeeded in arousing such a popular conviction of the necessity as should enforce the action of their representatives to the point of making needful provision. The enormous and costly scale on which the work of planting new forests must be undertaken, in order to be effective, seems to throw a damper upon every effort to bring it to pass.

If every owner of a wood lot could be convinced that its value might be enormously increased by a process which, so far from demanding an outlay, would add to his annual income, it would not be long before farmers would consider it as derogatory to their reputation to leave the forests in the wild condition they now are, as they would to have a field of corn presenting a similar appearance of slovenliness. To produce such conviction the truth must be demonstrated in actual practice, and the cost of such demonstration will be but a trifling price to pay for the returns it will bring. Let any State or city select a tract of woodland at some easily accessible point, and put it under a proper course of management, as an experimental forest, and it would very soon excite an interest which could not fail to increase. A portion of it should be suffered to remain in its original, unimproved condition. Another part should be improved as "open park," for the best development of individual trees in their fullest natural capacity of dignity and grace, and a third portion should be devoted to the production of timber by the process of thinning, pruning and proper culture. The progress of development could then be seen and watched from year to year in all its stages, and the demonstration thus afforded would touch the interest of every owner of a wood lot. The process would soon begin to be imitated, a conviction of the value and importance of a knowledge of forestry would become established in the popular mind, and the demand for the services of those who had acquired it would lead to a demand for the means of acquirement, and thus the schools of forestry would be called into existence by the natural course of events.

The inauguration of such an experimental or illustrative forest as a means of exciting public interest is surely an object that is well worth the consideration of legislative and municipal bodies, or of corporations whose interests are connected with this form of national wealth. The cost would be insignificant in comparison with that of planting and maintaining new forests, and the spur of personal interest would incite such general action as would add incalculably to the wealth of every State without further outlay than the cost of demonstration.

It is of course desirable that the experimental forest should be as conspicuous and easily accessible to the public as possible, for which reason the vicinity of a city would seem the most appropriate point. And municipal bodies would be justified in making a liberal appropriation for the promotion of such an object, since it would certainly constitute, for great numbers of people, one of the principal attractions of the city. The beneficial results which would follow, however, would add so largely to the substantial wealth and power of the State that its main support should be derived from legislative rather than municipal action.

It is not, however, my province to discuss the means of effecting the work, beyond this general suggestion.

I have aimed only to convey a conception of the rich resources which nature has placed at our disposal, if we choose to avail ourselves of her offer.

I have made no statement in regard to forest growth which will not be recognized as true by all who are familiar with the subject, and all such persons will endorse my statement that, practically, the rules which govern the process are universally ignored.

I have pointed out what I conceive to be the readiest means of awakening public attention and creating such general interest as will insure reform, and I leave to other hands the task of arranging the laws which must govern its execution.

FREDERICK LAW OLMSTED AND J. B. HARRISON

The Use of the Axe

(1889)

It has been said of our frontier settlers that they seemed to bear a grudge against trees, and to be engaged in a constant, indiscriminate warfare with them. If this were so, a strong reaction has since set in, of which a notable manifestation appears in the fact that with regard to no other matter pertaining to the public grounds of our cities has public interest taken so earnest, strenuous, and effective a form as in respect to the protection of their plantations against the axe.

It has occurred repeatedly of late years that ladies and gentlemen, seeking their pleasure during the winter in public parks, have chanced to see men felling trees, and have been moved by the sight to take duties upon themselves that nothing else short of

From *Landscape Architecture* 3, no. 4 (July 1913): 145–52. Original note: In 1889, F. L. Olmsted, Sr., and J. B. Harrison prepared, at the instance of the Park Commissioners of New York and several other organizations interested, a paper entitled, "Observations on the Treatment of Public Plantations, more Especially Relating to the Use of the Axe." The report was never given any wide publicity. We reprint excerpts from it here, as a particularly clear presentation of one side of a question on which, unfortunately, the public still needs education.

a startling public outrage would have led them to assume. Sometimes they have hastened to stand before a partly felled tree and have attempted to wrest the axe from the hand of the woodsman. Oftener they have resorted to the press and other means of arousing public feeling, and not infrequently a considerable popular excitement has resulted. At the time of such excitements a strong tendency has appeared in many minds to assume that the act of tree-cutting marks those who are responsible for it as unsusceptible to the charm of sylvan scenery, and to class them with the old indiscriminately devastating pioneers.

Naturally, an effect of such manifestations of public sentiment has been to make those in direct superintendence of public plantations, and the governing boards supervising them, extremely reluctant to use the axe. In some cases, for years not a tree has been cut down; in others, only decaying trees which were prominent eyesores or dangerous to passers-by; and, even when these were to be dealt with, the work has been done in stormy weather, when it was little likely to be observed by visitors, and care has been taken to put the fallen wood out of sight as soon as possible. To guard against the provocation of public feeling even in such extreme cases, a standing order has been made by one Park Commission that not a tree should be cut in its plantations till leave had been granted for it by a majority vote of its Board. One of the best trained and most successful tree-growers in the country having been dropped from the service of this Board, a member of it gave as the reason for his dismissal that he had been too anxious to obtain leave to cut out trees. In another case, the effect of the agitation was such that a laborer refused to fell a tree when ordered, fearing that he would be punished for it as for a crime.

While no sensible man will deliberately maintain that a tree can never be wisely removed from a public plantation, it will be seen from what has been said that a public sentiment is liable to be cultivated, the effect of which, in numerous instances, may be to keep trees standing for years that might more wisely be cut, and in a general way to prevent the free exercise of any specially competent judgment upon the question. Hence, instead of simply reporting our own view of the particular case that we have been asked to consider, we have thought it better that we should set forth by quotations what may be regarded as the Common Law view of the duty, in respect to the cutting of trees, of a professional public servant to whom has been given the direction of plantations. We venture to say that no man, however well informed he may be in other respects, can have a respectable understanding of this duty to whom such precepts as are about to

be cited are not familiar. It is greatly to be desired that knowledge of them and faith in them should be more generally diffused than it is at present among leaders of public opinion in all our cities.

1. "It is in the act of removing trees and thinning woods that the landscape gardener must show his intimate knowledge of pleasing combinations, his genius for painting, and his acute perceptions of the principles of an art which transfers the imitative, though permanent beauties of a picture, to the purposes of elegant and comfortable habitation, the ever-varying effects of light and shade, and the inimitable circumstances of a natural landscape." Repton.

2. "The old adage, 'Plant thick and thin quick,' holds as good now as centuries ago." Douglas.

3. "Fully half the number of plants inserted per acre should be removed by the time that the most valuable are twenty-five feet high." Grigor.

. . .

9. "Though they are still far short of their growth, they are (from neglect of thinning) run up into poles, and the groves are already past their prime." Whately. (Criticism on Cleremont Park.)

10. "A natural growth of pine which was thinned when six years old showed an increased rate of accretion three times as great as that of the part not thinned, which was also deficient in height growth." Fernow.

11. "Wherever systematic thinning has been applied, the crops are of nearly double the value at a given age." "We divide the several plantations into three portions, and thin one portion regularly and systematically each year successively." Brown.

12. "It is an undeniable fact that the weakly, unprofitable, and therefore unsatisfactory state of a large extent of plantations is to be attributed to the neglect of systematic thinning." "We frequently see woods growing upon the best land matured when only some sixty years old. This arises from neglect of systematic thinning." Brown.

. . .

18. Lauder (in a note upon Gilpin's *Forest Scenery*) says that, to make an artificial plantation which shall ultimately resemble a natural plantation, "the best way" is to so manage as that "by a frequent and judicious use of the axe, the best individuals, and those most calculated to associate and harmonize together, are left in permanent possession of the ground." "This mode, be it understood," he adds, "requires constant attention—an attention unremitting from the earliest years of the plantation, till nothing remains but the permanent trees; otherwise, from too long confinement or other causes, stiff and unnatural forms may be produced."

19. "Nurses are surplus trees or shrubs introduced into the plantation for a temporary purpose, for the occupancy of the ground to shelter and protect the permanent plants, and to aid in forming them into well-shaped trees." "Unless care be taken to subordinate these nurses, they will be likely to overwhelm the more valuable plants." Brisbane.

"Most trees are gregarious in extreme youth, from habit transmitted through many generations; they love company, and thrive really only when closely surrounded. Close planting is essential, therefore, to insure the best results. As the trees grow, the weaker are pushed aside, and finally destroyed by the more vigorous, and the plantation is gradually thinned. This is the operation which is always going on in the forest when man does not intervene. It is a slow and expensive operation, however, and the result is attained by a vast expenditure of energy and of good material. The strongest trees come out victorious in the end, but they will bear the scars of the contest through life. The long, bare trunk, with a small and misshapen head—the only form of a mature tree found in the virgin forest—tells of years or of centuries of struggle, in which hundreds of weaker individuals may have perished, that one giant might survive. But man can intervene, and by judicious and systematic thinning help the expenditure of vital force. Thin planting is but following the rule of nature, and thinning is only helping nature to do what she does herself too slowly, and therefore too expensively. This is why trees in a plantation intended for ornament, like those in a park or pleasure-ground, should be planted thickly at first, and why they should then be systematically thinned from time to time; and it is because this systematic thinning is altogether neglected, or put off until the trees are ruined for any purpose of ornament, that it is so rare to find a really fine tree in any public place or private grounds." Sargent.

"They are to be thinned out gradually as they come to interlock, until, at length, not more than one-third of the original number will remain; and these, because the less promising will have constantly been selected for removal with little regard to evenness of spacing, will be those of the most vigorous constitution, those with the greatest capabilities of growth, and those with the greatest power of resistance to attacks of storms, ice, disease, and vermin.

Individual tree beauty is to be but little regarded, but all consideration to be given to beauty and effectiveness of groups, passages, and masses of foliage. The native underwood is to be planted in thickets and allowed to grow in natural forms, enough of it being introduced to prevent (in connection with the grouping of trees and interspaces of groups, to be formed by the process of thinning the tree plantations) a grove or orchard-like monotony of trunks."

It will be observed that all agree that in good practice trees are planted originally much closer than it is desirable that they should be allowed to grow permanently, and that, from every well-planted large body of trees, some are removed every year up to at least eighty years.

Upon this point, we have not, with considerable search, found one man with any claim to be regarded as an authority differing from those we have quoted. Many writers on landscape gardening say nothing about it; but this evidently because they assume that their readers will be of a class not needing to be advised of a principle so well established.

The fact is, nevertheless, that until men, whether non-professional commissioners of public plantations or non-professional planters on their own private account, have learned better by costly lessons of personal experience, they are generally much indisposed to plant as thickly as is necessary, and still more indisposed to allow plantations to be thinned as is desirable. Often, therefore, plantations become and remain crowded to a degree which brings many of their trees to death, or to a decrepit and slowly dying condition, and which draws all others into such forms that, even if by a late use of the axe they are at last given

ample branch and root room, they are precluded from taking advantage of it. They come to be of senile habit, and it is no longer possible for them to contribute to broad, rich, and harmonious compositions of foliage.

The question then will often arise: What can best be done in places where trees have been more or less seriously injured by crowding; in what degree is their restoration to be wisely aimed at; to what extend will it be more judicious to clear the ground and replant? A landscape architect, who has had probably as large a private practice as any other in the country, says that no other question oftener comes to him, and no other is a greater tax upon his professional resources. It is easy, in any given case, for a shallow, conceited quack to settle it flippantly; it is easy to settle it indolently; it requires experience, close study, and sagacious foresight to determine the best practicable settlement of it. Upon this point we present a few additional quotations:

"It is very difficult to determine how to treat plantations that have been neglected in thinning. It is a bad job, and you can only hope to prevent further ruin, but not to entirely remedy that which is now so painfully apparent to anyone who knows about trees and their cultivation. The trees in some parts are so far gone that they cannot be saved to good purpose. Better cut out spaces within such groups and around the margins, fertilize the soil, trench it over, plant new trees, and, as they grow, cut away the balance of the old ones." McLaren.

At first view it will seem remarkable that complaints so specific and so sweeping as those we have considered should be made by persons of a high degree of general intelligence without any support in the actual facts of the case. It will perhaps be thought hardly credible that the common impression and sentiment of the great body of good citizens as to what is desirable in the management of plantations should be in such direct conflict with what we have shown to be the general conviction of all lovers of natural scenery to whom the question has been one of professional study.

The explanation of the mystery is to be found, we suppose, in the fact that the management of a large park is an art, the principles and methods of which are much further from being generally comprehended, even by cultivated men, than is commonly supposed. On this point we offer one more quotation bearing directly upon the particular point of management as to which expert opinion has been asked:

"To give such general rules for thinning as might be understood by those who never attentively and scientifically considered the subject would be like attempting to direct a man who had never used a pencil to imitate the groups of a Claude or a Poussin." Repton.

And yet it is most undesirable that public-spirited citizens should be led to relinquish any degree of interest that they may now feel in the management of the public grounds of our cities. It is most desirable that they should manifest still greater and more searching interest; that they should influence the management more directly, constantly, and effectively. But to do so wisely will require a seriousness of thought upon the subject such as it yet seldom obtains. It will also require a degree of respect for the technical responsibility involved that few have yet begun to realize to be its due.

CHARLES ELIOT

Landscape Forestry in the Metropolitan Reservations

(1896–1897)

Wherever Nature has herself glorified a country, and made a picture bounded only by the horizon, as in many parts of Switzerland, Italy, Southern Germany, and even our own Silesia, I am strongly of the opinion that park-works are superfluous. It seems to me like painting a petty landscape in one corner of a beautiful Claude Lorraine. In these cases we should content ourselves with laying out good roads, to make the fine points more accessible, and here and there the cutting of a few trees to open vistas which Nature has left closed.

—Pückler-Muskau

By the time the metropolitan forest reservations had been in possession of the Commission two years and a half, the removal of dead wood had been accomplished, pre-

From *Charles Eliot: Landscape Architect*, by Charles W. Eliot (1902; repr., Amherst: University of Massachusetts Press in association with Library of American Landscape History, 1999), 709–36. Passages in italics here are editorial comments by Charles Eliot's father included as explanation in *Charles Eliot: Landscape Architect*.

liminary roads on the lines of the old wood-roads had been opened to give the public and the employees of the Commission access to all parts of the reservations, and the topographical maps on a scale of 100 feet to the inch had been completed (early in 1896). Charles thought he saw in this state of things an opportunity to procure some beginning of landscape forestry work; and in January, 1896, he opened the subject to the Commission in the following letter, which proposed a small annual expenditure for supervision, and the diversion to forestry work of some of the labor regularly employed. As usual, his recommendations were moderate as regards expenditure—indeed, distinctly economical:

January 8, 1896.

We beg leave to submit the following suggestions concerning the work in the three woodland reservations:—

From the date of the acquiring of these reservations to the present time, the forces employed have been engaged in two principal works: (1) removing dead wood, both standing and fallen; (2) constructing preliminary roads on the lines of the old wood paths. Two winters have already been devoted to the first-named work, and two summers to the second. The reservations have been opened to carriages and horseback riders, and the preliminary roads are now quite sufficiently numerous. The work of the present winter ought to finally free the woods of the most dangerous part of the inflammable material. If the appropriations warrant the continuance of expenditure at the present rate, it would seem that some attention might soon be given to the restoration and betterment of the living vegetation, and we accordingly offer the following suggestions with respect to this delicate and most important work.

The existing forests of the reservations comprise both sprout and seedling woods; the former consisting of shoots sprung from the stumps of felled or fire-killed trees, and the latter consisting of woods which have grown from seeds sown without human aid in lands which once were completely cleared for pasturage or cultivation. The restoration of the burnt and sprout lands to an interesting and beautiful condition will require years of labor in accordance with a well-laid scheme of economical management. Such a scheme we may outline presently.

The work which calls for first attention is found in the reforested pastures. Here are to be seen most of the large trees and the only broad-spreading trees of the reservations. Around them press the seedling Oaks, Hickories, etc., which the birds and squirrels planted among the slow red Cedars, the short-lived gray Birches, and the beautiful wild shrubberies which were the first woody growths to appear in the old fields. If the lives of the older generation of spreading pasture trees are to be prolonged (as we hope they may be), it will be necessary to free them from the too close pressure of the trees of the younger generation, and at the same time to heal the most serious of the many wounds they have already received. The axe must be used to effect the first-named purpose, and the saw the second; but the axe must be used with discretion, and with care to retain enough of the vigorous young trees to fill the gaps when the veterans shall at last pass away.

In other smooth parts of the seedling woods, where the former pastures contained no old trees, and the present growth consists of mixed species too closely crowded, the axe ought likewise to be brought into play for the freeing of the most promising individuals, or the trees of the most desirable kinds. In valleys and glades where the surface is smooth enough and the soil good enough to grow grass when sufficient light has been admitted, it will generally, though not always, be advisable to take away all but a few trees, which will thus be encouraged to form noble individuals or groups. On rough, rocky, or steep ground where grass is unattainable, no such thinning for the development of individuals should be attempted. The axe may be used to eliminate incongruous or unsuitable kinds of trees and bushes, or to admit the sunlight necessary to the growth or increase of desirable species; but its use to produce a monotony of separated individuals regardless of soil and topography must be prohibited. Dense thickets will in many places be much more desirable than open glades.

Of the other good services in the cause

of beauty which the axe may do among the seedling growths of the reservations, it is unnecessary to write at length. Among its good works may be the removal of trees for the encouragement of shrubby ground-cover at points where distant prospects would otherwise be shut out; the similar encouragement of low ground-cover on and among some of the finer crags which to-day are wrapped from sight by mantles of leaves; the removal of conflicting species for the encouragement of the white Dogwood on this southern slope, the Winterberry by this swamp, the Bearberry on this rocky summit, or the white Pine on this ridge. We are well aware that the axe is regarded with a sort of horror by many excellent people at this time; but we are equally convinced that with the help of no other instrument, the axe, if it be guided wisely, may gradually effect the desired rescue and enhancement of that part of the beauty of the scenery of the reservations which depends upon the seedling woods and shrubberies.

Concerning the large acreage of sprout-land within the reservations, it may be sufficient at this time to point out that inasmuch as sprouts from stumps form unnatural, comparatively short-lived, and generally monotonous and unbeautiful woods, it ought to be the policy of the Commission to gradually replace the sprouts by seedlings. This work will doubtless prove a somewhat slow and arduous undertaking; but, if it is not hurried, it need not prove expensive. Sprouts which are large enough to be useful as poles, fence-posts, or railroad sleepers are always salable as they stand. Such salable sprouts should not, however, be all cut at once; but by felling a part of the crop one year and another part

a few years later, every inducement should be offered seedling trees and a suitable undergrowth to take possession and obtain a good start. On the other hand, sprouts which have sprung from the stumps in the most recent clearings or since the most recent killing fires, while unsalable, are still so small that they may be cut rapidly and without undue expenditure of tints and money. If the cutting is done in August, most of the stumps will at the same time be made incapable of sprouting again; and, if no valuable seedlings have yet come in, sheep may be pastured in such places for a year or two to complete the "killing." It is only in those places where the sprouts are so large as to make it costly to cut them, and yet so small as to be unsalable, that it seems as if it might be economical, and therefore advisable, to wait some years before the seedlings can be offered their opportunity to possess the land.

It will be noticed that these proposed works in the living woods demand uncommonly far-seeing and even artistic direction. Now that the preliminary roads have been roughed out, and the topographical maps completed, it is to be presumed that the Commission's engineer will assume charge and direction of whatever permanent works of construction may be attempted. Similarly, whenever the clearing away of dead wood shall have been practically completed, a trained woodsman ought to be placed in charge of the work in the living woods. The man who is thus placed in command of the vegetation of parks is generally called a "landscape gardener"; because he practices the operations of gardening for the sake of developing "landscapes." Such a man employed in the reservations of your Commission might more appropriately be called a "landscape forester"; but, whatever he may be called, he should be thoroughly acquainted with the fauna and flora of the woods, competent to direct all woodland work, to devise economies, to discover sources of income, and eager, at the same time, to impart to the superintendents and to a succession of younger assistants something of his own enthusiasm, knowledge, and skill. It will also be necessary that this woodsman, as well as the engineer, should be in complete sympathy with the landscape architects, and possess a good knowledge of their plans. To make a beginning, we would suggest that we be authorized to supervise, through our assistants, such work as may be suitably entered upon before long, and at the same time to draw up a scheme of work to be executed in the order of its importance during a term of years. This laying out of work and the accompanying supervising is something that we are accustomed to attend to for almost all our clients, both public and private. Our assistants (draughtsmen, plantsmen, and inspectors) take up, as we may direct, the office or field work of one client after another, the cost of their services being charged to different clients, according to the time given to the work of each. Whenever any work calling for special or novel service from our assistants is proposed, we, of course, ask for authority in advance. Work done on the Metropolitan District Map, the Guide Maps of the Forest Reservations, and the Botanical Survey has thus been specially authorized. The suggested supervision of work in the reservations is a new service, the cost of which we may estimate as $1000 for the first year. Mr. Warren H. Manning, who has been connected with our office dur-

ing eight years, would take charge of the supervising work. A more competent man cannot be found. To make his services as effective as possible, we would suggest the appointment by the Commission of at least two foremen of woodcraft, who should be men of some experience. With the aid of these men, and such of the present foremen as may be competent or trainable, we feel sure that a good general scheme of work can be mapped out during the coming year, and that valuable beginnings in the more pressing work can be assured.

It was, however, Charles's settled conviction that forestry work on a large scale, with a view to the improvement of landscape, could only be done safely after the preparation of general plans for each of the forest reservations; but the Commission was not yet ready to order such general plans. As soon as the completion of the topographical maps of the three forest reservations enabled him to get sun-prints from the full-scale tracings, he therefore organized a systematic mapping of the existing condition of the woods and ground-cover in these reservations. This work went on during the season of 1896; and Charles mentioned it in his report to the Commission for that year. It was in his mind a part of the desirable preparation for making general plans; and it also provided a permanent record of the deplorable state of the woods when the Commission took charge of them.

The completed "forest survey" was presented to the Commission on February 15, 1897. It consisted of seventy survey sheets in portfolios, accompanied by nine hundred numbered catalogue cards, each of which described the vegetation at a spot referred to by a number on one of the survey sheets. Flat tints were also used on the sheets to indicate the principal types of vegetation. The following letter accompanied this considerable piece of work:

February 15, 1897.

We hand you herewith the field notes and maps of the "forest surveys" referred to in our last annual report, —the product of studies begun soon after the "taking" of the several reservations, and continued as opportunities have offered from time to time; also a list of the trees and shrubs of the reservations, with notes on their habits and distribution. Messrs. Warren H. Manning, Percival Gallagher, J. Fred Dawson, and Charles H. Wheeler have done most of this mapping and note-taking as our assistants.

A summary report of the principal ascertained facts, with photographic illustrations, is also submitted herewith, including some account of the origin of the commoner types of woodland scenery, and some suggestions as to that control of the vegetation of the reservations which will be necessary for the preservation and enhancement of the beauty and interest of the landscape.

The "summary report" referred to in the preceding letter was illustrated by 154 photographs, 6 sketches, and 3 maps, and as a piece of exposition and argument addressed to a small Board, all of whose members could examine the highly convincing illustrations, it certainly had remarkable merit. Charles wrote it between January 11 and February 12, 1897, in the midst of many other occupations, after assembling all the various contributions of his field and office assistants, and classifying them in his own mind with his usual discrimination and perspicuity. Although intended for the Park Commission as a business report indicating a long line of executive policy, the paper is much more than an argument addressed to one park board; it shows what the charming elements of park scenery really are, and how they may be preserved. Even genuine lovers of scenery are often quite unobservant of the constituent elements of the scenes they love. Here is a concise treatise on the different types of vegetation which, in addition to the fixed "lay of the land," make New England rural scenery, and on the ways of using these types to preserve and enhance the beauty of that characteristic scenery.

VEGETATION AND SCENERY IN THE METROPOLITAN RESERVATIONS

THE OBJECT OF THE INVESTIGATION

The purpose of investing public money in the purchase of the several metropolitan reservations was to secure for the enjoyment of present and future generations such interesting and beautiful scenery as the lands acquired can supply; at all events, it is on the assumption that this was the purpose in view that the following report, with the investigation it describes, is based.

The scenery of the inland reservations may be considered as compounded of the varying forms of the ground, rocks, waters, and vegetation, and of a great variety of distant prospects, including views of the sea and of remote mountains, such as Wachusett and Monadnock. The more or less rock-ribbed masses of the Fells and the Blue Hills and the intricately carved or modeled hollows of Hemlock Gorge, Stony Brook, and Beaver Brook Reservations have life histories of their own; but the processes of their evolution are so slow that for all human purposes these smooth, rough, concave, or convex surfaces may be regarded as changeless. It is, moreover, quite unlikely that there will ever be any need of artificially modifying them in any considerable degree. Such paths or roads as will be needed to make the scenery accessible will be mere slender threads of graded surfaces winding over and among the huge natural forms of the ground.

As to the waters of the reservations, they may, indeed, be artificially ponded here and there, as they already have been in the Fells and in Lynn Woods, where the reservoirs greatly enliven the general landscape; but the numerous minor brooks and rivulets will doubtless continue to alternately dry up and rise in flood, as is their habit in our climate, without affecting more than the local scenery of the hollows or ravines in which they flow.

Thus the only changeful and changeable element in the general as well as the local landscape of the domains in question is the vegetation which clothes the surface everywhere, excepting only such bare areas as consist of naked rock or of water. Much of the most striking scenery of the world is almost or quite devoid of verdure; but here in New England we cannot escape it, even if we would. Bulrushes insist upon crowding every undrained hollow, Bearberry carpets barren rocks, and a great variety of vigorous trees and shrubs have had to be continually and forcibly prevented from reoccupying such parts of the slopes between the rocks and the swamps as men have laboriously cleared at different times for the purpose of raising food crops or grass for the feeding of cattle. The original forests disappeared long ago. Where once stood towering Pines, there are to-day perhaps thickets of scrub oak, and where great hemlocks shaded damp, mossy cliffs, there may now be sun-baked ledges with clumps of Sweet Fern in their clefts. While seedlings have been pushing their way into the clearings at every opportunity, fire and the axe have made great changes in the vegetation of the wilder woodlands during the last two hundred years; and all these changes have necessarily had their effect on the scenery.

The present investigation is not, however, an historical or even a scientific inquiry. Its purpose is simply to record the present condition of the verdure of the reservations, to note the effect in the landscape of the several predominant types of vegetation, and to inquire into the origins of these various types only so far as may be necessary to determine how best to encourage, control, or discourage the existing growth, with a view to the enrichment of that treasure of scenery which the reservations have been created to secure and preserve.

THE METHODS PURSUED

For the purpose of making a record of the present condition of the vegetation, sunprints from the original tracings of the topographical maps of the several reservations were carried into the field, together with ordinary catalogue cards. The maps used were drawn to the scale of one hundred feet to an inch, and showed roads, paths, stone walls, conspicuous rocks, and large trees, in addition to contour lines indicating every difference of five feet in elevation. Each of the seventy separate survey sheets was designated by a letter and number (for example, Fells, B. 3), the dozen or more cards bearing notes referring to each separate sheet were also numbered (for example, Fells B. 3/13), and the card numbers were entered on the survey sheets at the several points to which the corresponding notes had reference. Different observers engaged in different parts of the broad field have doubtless followed somewhat different standards in making notes; but the endeavor of all has been to record every marked variation in the existing vegetation, together with such information as to the origin of each peculiar type as could be gathered either from study on the spot or from persons acquainted with the neighborhood.

THE PRINCIPAL TYPES OF VEGETATION

On comparing and studying the returned map sheets and card notes, it gradually became clear that what at first seemed a hopeless confusion of isolated facts was after all resolvable into a rational order, and that the vegetation of the reservations can be truthfully said to be composed of some six principal landscape types or forms, the peculiarities of two of which depend chiefly on natural topographical conditions, while the distinguishing features of the other four types are principally derived from the work of men and of fire in the woodlands of the past. Perhaps the most

interesting fact established by the inquiry is just this, —that the woods of these reservations, which are commonly thought of and spoken of as "wild," are really artificial in a high degree. The peculiar growth of dwarf trees and bushes which occupies the highest summits of the Blue Hills, and the equally peculiar growth of shrubs and herbs which fills the wetter swamps, have not been worth troubling with the axe, while the bare ledges of the hill-tops have defended the summit type of growth from fire almost as effectually as the presence of water has defended the swamp type. On the other hand, all the intervening slopes and plains of the reservations have been chopped over, or completely cleared, or pastured, or burnt over, time and again since the settlement of Massachusetts. Much of the resulting vegetation, and consequently much of the scenery of the reservations, is monotonous, insipid, and unlovely, but it must be added that those parts in which men have lived longest or worked hardest are often beautiful in a high degree.

The following are the principal types of the vegetation of the reservations which are about to be reviewed in the order here set down:

Types dependent chiefly on topographical conditions: —

      The Summit,   The Swamp.

Types dependent chiefly on the interference of men: —

  The Coppice,   The Bushy Pasture,
  The Field and Pasture,   The Seedling Forest.

It is, of course, to be understood that all these types, and particularly the last three, run together more or less, and that in sketching their distribution on the accompanying maps, all that is intended is to indicate to the observer's judgment as to which type predominates in each locality.

1. *The Summit Type.* Whether the lofty or rocky summits of the Blue Hills were ever covered with high forest is not quite clear, but that the scanty soil of these hilltops is clothed to-day with an interesting and distinctive kind of vegetation is very noticeable. This vegetation is generally low, seldom exceeding five feet in height, except where wind-bent forms of pitch Pines, Hickories, Chestnut-Oaks, or other trees, occasionally rise above the dense mass of ground-covering shrubbery. This shrubbery consists for the most part of closely interlocking plants of scrub Oak, forming thickets almost as impenetrable as the chaparral of the Western States. Mixed with the scrub Oak are occasional patches of other bushes of kinds which are capable of withstanding adverse circumstances, such as Sweet Fern and Chokeberry; and where the gravelly soil is thinnest, broad mats of Bearberry are not uncommon. This growth has generally escaped destruction by fire, but where it has been killed so that raw soil has been exposed, the gray Birch has seeded itself and taken at least temporary possession. Many of the higher, steeper, and more naked crags have wholly escaped all recent fires and the axe as well; and here are found quaint stunted forms of pitch Pines and other hardy trees. The irregular upper edge of the ordinary forest in these hills (the "tree line," as it would be called in the mountains) also exhibits many more or less distorted growths of the hardier species of trees, and forms strong and sharp foregrounds for the panoramic views.

Speaking generally, this summit growth is altogether appropriate, interesting, and pleasing. It is generally low enough to enable the broad prospect of these hill-tops to be sufficiently well commanded. Its dwarfness also tends to increase the apparent height of the hills, and to set off the grand or picturesque forms of their ledges and crags. It ought to be the settled purpose of the administration of the reservations to foster the peculiar character of this vegetation by removing such few inappropriate species as may occasionally obtain a foothold on the heights, and by carefully refraining from any trimming or clearing of those crooked growths which give character to this type of scenery. It should be added that the type is in some measure imitated on even low-lying ledges and tracts of ledgy ground throughout the reservations, and that even where it is only a minor element of local scenery, it should be encouraged and helped. Rock scenery is indeed so interesting, and characteristic vegetation so enhances this interest, that it will be advisable (as is noted later) to remove much inappropriate and rock-concealing vegetation from the craggy parts of the reservations, and to induce the spreading therein of dwarf forms chiefly.

2. *The Swamp Type.* In marked contrast to the vegetation of the prospect-commanding heights is the verdure of the many sheltered and secluded swamps and wet valleys. Small, roundish swamps, generally bordered, in part at least, by ledges, are very common in the three larger reservations. The ordinary forest presses close about these hollows, but owing to lack of drainage their level floors are too wet for most trees, although the stumps of

white Pines are often found in them. Bulrushes are to-day the usual occupants of the deeper parts of these wet spots, while much beautiful shrubbery of Clethra, Azalea, Winterberry, and other sorts fringes their edges. The local scenery of these sunny openings in the monotonous woods is often extremely pleasing, as when some bold rock projects into the level of rushes, or when the encircling fringe of bushes is unbroken. It is evident that these places ought not to be meddled with, save for good reasons. Their peculiar beauty can be long preserved, if the natural drainage is not altered, and if such incongruous species as may from time to time appear are promptly removed.

According as these bowls or hollows of the surface are worse or better drained than in the typical cases just mentioned, the vegetation varies. Such high-lying or uncommonly large bowls as have not yet been completely filled by washings from the surrounding surfaces show open water in their centres, at least, and if the breadth of water is not so great as to generate waves, it is sometimes wholly or in part surrounded by a "floating or quaking bog" composed of matted roots of such low-growing woody plants as Cranberry, Cassandra, Andromeda, and the like. No shrubberies can be lovelier than some of these which, beginning with low bushes or rushes at the water's edge, increase irregularly in height as they recede from the water, until they finally merge into the margin of the surrounding woods. It is noticeable that such shrubberies are best developed where the supply of water is most constant; as at Turtle Pond in Stony Brook Reservation. Where wetness alternates with dryness, the Button-bush seems

to feel at home, and covers large areas, almost without companions. Again, where the conditions are just right and men have not cut it out, the white Cedar still holds possession, with its exceedingly dense and dark growth.

On the other hand, such hollows and valleys as have better drainage than the typical swamps first cited tend to clothe themselves with trees in addition to the usual shrubs of wet places. Where such trees thrive, the shrubs slowly disappear, and a wood results much like the ordinary forest. In any general view over the reservations these brook valleys are easily traceable by the general coloring of the trees which fill them. The gray Birch is frequent, but the characteristic tree of such wet hollows is now the red Maple, which with its haze of blossoms in early spring, its brilliant colors in early autumn, and the peculiar gray of its twigs in winter, tints all the valleys of the reservations and brings them out as on a map.

In places where the conditions are suitable for the growth of shrubs like highbush Blueberry, Clethra, and the like, the Maple often tends to intrude itself where it could well be spared. The upland woods are quite sufficiently dense, continuous, and monotonous, without filling the wet bush-covered openings with additional tree-trunks. The local scenery of such bushy openings, the bounding ledges or slopes of rocky debris, cannot be seen or appreciated, if Maples are to be allowed to crowd in. On this account trees ought eventually to be kept out of many of these places for the encouragement of the bushy ground-cover, and particularly is this the case where the removal or suppression of Maples will disclose above the bushes and between the framing woods glimpses or vistas of far blue distances.

3. *The Coppice Type.* The summit and swamp types of vegetation already reviewed have been but little molested or changed in any recent years, but, with mention of the Maples of the better drained lowlands, approach is made to the main body of the woods which, modified past recognition by both axe and fire, still occupies the smooth or ragged uplands between the swamps and the highest summits. The transition from the lowland woods of Maples to the upland forest of Oaks, Chestnuts, and other species is generally quite sharply defined, whether the dry woods consist of seedling growth or sprout-growth. Sprout-growth or coppice greatly predominates in the woodlands under consideration. It consists of trees sprung, not from seed, but from the axed or burnt stumps of the trees of a previous generation. In some parts of the reservations, as many as six or eight crops have been taken by means of the axe from the same stumps; twenty to thirty years having been allowed for the growth of each crop.

Much might be learned from study of this common practice of gathering period-ical wood-crops from lands too rough for the nicer operations of husbandry; how it tends to reduce the woods to masses of the few species which sprout with the greatest vigor and suffer the least from fire; how the extremely rapid growth of the first sprouts from old stumps strangles the small seedling trees which may have started amid the undergrowth, and thus preserves the supremacy and continuity of the coppice; and so on. Our present concern, however, is only with the appear-ance of coppice or sprout growth, and par-ticularly with the part it plays in local and broad scenery.

The interior of a high coppice wood is seldom as beautiful as the interior of a seedling forest, not to speak of an open grove. It lacks the pleasing variety of natural woods, composed as they are of numerous competing kinds of trees and underwood. The crop-like or arti-ficial nature of sprout-growth is obvious at a glance, and cannot be concealed by an occasional though rare luxuriance of undergrowth or pretty play of light and shade. Along paths and roads the monoto-nous effect of its crowded vertical lines is tedious in a high degree. It is only when some cause or condition introduces a little unwonted variety either of form or kind of tree or undergrowth, or when a dis-tant vista catches the eye, that the paths of the sprout-lands are not comparatively dull. Along the edges of old or broad roads, clearings, swamps, or ponds, and where ledges or other impediments form a defense against too near neighbors, both masses and single specimens of sprout trees naturally send out low branches and take on more interesting forms; even remarkably striking forms in many cases. On the other hand, the general appear-ance of the ordinary sprout-growth, when it is seen from a distance in any broad view over the reservations, is as dull and tame as is its usual appearance close at hand. Its crowding swarms of nearly uniform trees press closely down to the swamps, climb close up to the summit ledges and invade their slopes of debris, crowd the hollows and notches between rocks, and generally tend to wrap both the softer and the bolder features of the general land-scape in the same monotonous blanket of impenetrable twigs and leafage. A kind of vegetation which is so little beautiful in itself ought not to be permitted to take possession of those parts of public reservations which would be more interesting were the screens of close-set tree-trunks wholly or partly removed. Here, for example, is a hill on which the sprout-growth is not so thick as it often is, and yet it nevertheless conceals effectually the fine rock-buttresses of the slope, changes what would otherwise be a picturesque skyline into a level line of twigs, and in summer reduces the whole bold hillside to a soft bank of leaves. The opposing cliffs and talus slopes of the narrow valleys of the Blue Hills, many lesser knobs and ledges, and most of the elevated vista-commanding "notches" of the Hills and Fells are similarly smothered in curtains and veils of sprouts, which, in great measure, nullify the potential beauty of the scenery.

Fortunately, the one constant ally of the axe of the wood-chopper in the work of destroying the beauty of the woodlands of the reservations is now presumably under control. Ground or leaf fires have ordinarily spread through the woods almost every spring and autumn, charring the base of the trees without killing them; but about once in every ten or twelve years the dry accumulations of chopped tree-tops and fallen wood have furnished material for conflagrations hot enough to kill trees as well as ground-cover over large areas. In such cases the dead or dying trees stand for a year or two, intact but naked, while new sprouts shoot up from their roots. Later, the dead trees lose their now dry twigs and fall from time to time, forming almost impenetrable barriers of sticks, supremely well adapted to serve as kindling for new

flames. The greater part of the woodland of Blue Hills Reservation was in this dead, dangerous, and unsightly condition at the time the reservation was acquired, and the woods of the Fells and Stony Brook Reservations were largely in the same miserable state. For the sake of the safety of the living growth, it was, therefore, necessary to clear away the accumulations of dead wood, and this has been done by burning it in heaps in winter.

When full-grown coppice is thus killed by fire or felled by the axe, the stumps, as has been noted, push out many vigorous and crowded shoots at the first seasonable opportunity. If care is taken to prevent such sprouting, for example, by bruising the shoots when tender, or by sending sheep to browse on them, the stumps can be eventually killed so that they will sprout no more, and clearings, pastures, or fields may be the result. If, however, the stumps are not killed, the ground is soon so thickly covered by the new sprouts that it cannot be seen and can hardly be traversed. It makes little difference whether such new sprout follows the killing of high sprout by fire, or whether it springs from the stumps of felled trees, its appearance is equally dreary and monotonous. If the fire-killed trees are not entirely removed (as they now have been throughout most of the reservations), or if they are allowed to slowly fall to pieces amid the tangle of new sprouts, the woodland scenery becomes still more dismal and squalid. It would, indeed, be hard to exaggerate the ruined appearance of such scenes; and yet they were met with on every hand when the reservations were first acquired.

As in the case of old sprout, the presence of young sprout is particularly unwel-

Tree-clogged Notch, near the southeastern escarpment of the Fells, from *Charles Eliot, Landscape Architect*, opp. 732.

come when it screens from sight any fine rocks or any richly verdurous swamp openings, as well as when it blots out possible vistas. It sometimes springs from the stumps of such deciduous trees as once were mixed with conifers on rocky hillsides, and in such cases it ought to be suppressed at once for the encouragement of seedling Pines, or other trees known to be long-lived and appropriate in such situations. The occasional broad views obtained from "clearings" made just previous to the acquisition of the reservations, or from areas from which fire-killed old sprout has been recently removed, are often fine, but they are generally only temporary, —the growth of the young sprout will obliterate most of these prospects in a very few years, together with many now pleasing glimpses of the ponds in the Fells, of the distant sea, or of the Great

Blue Hill seen through some chance valley or ravine. The growth of the young sprout in other recent clearings will also once more shut out from view such bold hill-forms and foreground rock-masses as are temporarily visible and enjoyable just at present. Many of these chance and fleeting openings in the too continuous and too monotonous woods of high sprout ought certainly to be made more permanent, if only to illustrate how the removal of sprout-growth from large surfaces, and particularly from among the rocks, will enrich and vivify the scenery. To neither the old nor the young living coppice has any attention yet been given. The only care the previous private owners gave it was to cut the sprout-growth clean whenever the crop seemed ripe, that is, whenever most of the trees were large enough for cordwood, or sometimes for chestnut posts.

Notch after opening, view of the Malden-Melrose valley and Saugus hills, from *Charles Eliot, Landscape Architect*, opp. 733.

To thin the sprout-growth so as to develop trees of more spreading habit was never worthwhile from the wood-lot owners' point of view; but such thinning has been practiced at a few places within the limits of the reservations by persons desirous of making their lands more attractive in the eyes of purchasers of suburban house-lots, with results which, though startlingly ugly at first, serve the purpose after a few years. To treat the sprout-lands of the reservations in this manner throughout their length and breadth would, however, be inadvisable, since the result would be quite as monotonous and artificial in its way as is the present dense growth. Moreover, in most of the rough lands of the reservations no type of growth could be more inappropriate than that which consists of separated and spreading trees. In such lands there is not enough soil to grow really

fine separate or specimen trees, and again there are few sprout trees which are sufficiently sound at their necessarily deformed bases to make them likely to thrive and live more than a comparatively small number of years. In view of the uninteresting quality of sprout-growth as an element of scenery, and of these grave objections to any general thinnings, it ought to be the settled policy of the management of the reservations to gradually effect the substitution of mixed seedling growth in place of the existing sprout-growth. Now that fires are prevented from spreading, seedlings of many species of trees will soon spring up wherever the sprout trees are not too thickly set; Pine seedlings here, Hemlocks and Beeches there, Birches among these rocks, Hickories, Chestnut-Oaks, and so on. Such seedling underwood is noticeable in many places to-day; and wherever it exists and wherever it appears, it can and ought to be given possession by gradually removing the sprout trees and killing their stumps. In such cases the high sprout trees should first be severely thinned, and then wholly removed perhaps two years later, so as not to expose the seedlings to new conditions with too great suddenness. In the high vista-commanding notches, as well as on the higher slopes and in other places where few trees, whether sprout or seedling, are really desirable, it will be best to fell all the sprout-growth at once and to kill the stumps. How beautifully a level or ledgy pasture will clothe itself with seedling shrubbery and trees will be illustrated later. It is sufficient to point out here that intelligent management will find it easy to gradually replace the crop-like coppice with vegetation much more beautiful in itself, and also more conducive to beauty of scenery.

4. *The Field and Pasture Type.* The scenic value of even temporary clearings in woods has just been mentioned, but the importance and beauty of more lasting open places, such as fields and pastures, is incomparably greater. In this climate almost all treeless and grass clothed areas, if not quite all, are due to the labor of men, supplemented by the browsing of domestic animals. For a year or two the stump-studded slopes or levels destined to be converted into pastures or fields are ugly enough in themselves, though they may open to view certain previously invisible prospects, but the more or less bare earth between the now dead stumps soon springs to life and covers itself with plants of many sorts, —often with berry bushes, which will yield great crops of fruit so long as the bushes are not browsed down by animals,

or overshaded by seedling plants of taller species. Much work devoted to dragging out stumps and stones is necessary before such lands can be called even rough fields. Most of the few smooth fields of the reservations are products of the slow labors of many generations, while the hard and close sod of the old pastures is the result of many years of continuous browsing.

After traversing long stretches of monotonous coppice, to emerge into grassy openings of this sort, set with occasional spreading trees, bordered or framed by hanging woods, beyond which rises perhaps some bold hill or ledge, is like coming to a richly interesting oasis in the midst of a bare desert, save that our desert is a close-ranked wood, and our oasis a sunny opening in it. Such man-made oases are specially lovely when they lie in hollow glades or intervales where there is moisture enough to keep them fresh and green in dry seasons; and even the still wetter meadows, from which crops of only the swamp grasses are obtainable, make welcome and interesting incidents in landscape.

It seems plain that few, if any, of the existing grassy areas of the reservations can be spared without loss of scenery, and they should, therefore, be maintained by systematic mowing and pasturing. In the future, some additional grassed openings will be desirable in smooth and hollow spots where provision will be needed for the gathering of people or for the setting forth of some especially interesting local scenery; but as such grass-lands are troublesome to maintain, they ought not to be multiplied unduly. A ground-covering of bushes will serve as well as grass, when it is only a question of keeping a view open, and there is no need of providing strolling places for crowds or smooth playgrounds for boys or children.

5. *The Bushy Pasture Type.* Of the several types of vegetation thus far mentioned, the coppice type occupies by far the largest part of the new reservations, while the summit, swamp, and field types cover approximately equal, but much smaller areas. It now appears that almost all the remaining area of the reservations has been at one time or another either grassland, field, or rough pasture land, and that the growth which now covers it more or less densely results from the more or less complete abandonment of the use and care of these lands by their owners. Why these considerable areas, cleared with great labor and situated near growing towns, should have been thus abandoned, it is not for us to ask, though the subject is one of considerable historical and economical interest. It is only to be noted here that the peculiar vegetation of these lands combines with their topography to form some of the most pleasing scenery of the reservations.

Even where cattle are still pastured, it is common enough to find plants of red Cedar starting up from seed here and there. Other seedlings are bitten off as fast as they appear, but the foliage of the red Cedar, prostrate Juniper, pitch Pine, and a few other species, is not edible, and so these plants survive and spread in pastures, unless they are burnt or rooted out by men. Sometimes, as at Bear Hill in the Fells, the red Cedar takes almost complete possession of the ground, often with striking effect, as when it stands up stiffly on bare rocks, or when it clothes a stony hillside. As soon as cattle cease to browse a piece of land, the common and fast-growing gray Birch mingles with the Cedar, or takes possession of large areas by itself. Abandoned ploughed land goes the same way in time, Cedars, pitch Pines, and Junipers forming the centers of many spreading islands of low or high shrubbery. The beautiful variety and intricacy of this bushy growth is often, and, indeed, generally remarkable and delightful. With time the bushes of Sweet Fern, Bayberry, Blueberry, Viburnum, and the like grow more and more numerous and entangled, and their combination with the dark Cedars and the white Birches often helps to form even broad landscape of rare beauty. Gradually, however, this type of landscape vanishes. From the midst, perhaps, of Junipers which browsing cattle have avoided, or from clumps of crowded bushes, slow-growing Oaks and other forest trees start up from seeds brought by the winds, birds, or squirrels. Slowly but surely, as the great trees grow in height and breadth, the low-growing Birches, Cedars, Junipers, and bushes are overshadowed, and as it were suffocated, and in the end the forest of seedling trees takes full possession.

On the other hand, it is obvious that the bushy stage or type is so beautiful in itself that it ought to be preserved in many places for itself alone, while it is equally obvious that in such parts of the reservation as command broad views which would be shut from sight by trees, this bushy ground-cover will need to be encouraged in every possible way; even, if need be, by going through the natural order of felling trees, killing the stumps, and pasturing the rough ground for a limited time.

6. *The Seedling Forest Type.* That part of the total area of the reservations which is clothed with seedling woods is comparatively small. Here and there are found

groups or patches of old seedling trees, like the Hemlocks of Hemlock Gorge, Hemlock Pool, or Breakneck Ledge, which appear to be direct descendants of innumerable generations occupying the same peculiarly rocky ground. Here and there are found clusters or groves of white Pines, apparently survivors of that generation of Pines which not so very many years ago clothed the major part of the reservations. Single specimens of such surviving Pines are not uncommon even in the midst of the sprout-lands. Like the Hemlocks, they have sometimes survived in positions from which it was thought too difficult to remove them. A few of the larger Pine groves have been leased by their owners as picnic grounds, and so have been more or less cleared of undergrowth and trampled. A few other woods, for example, the Wolcott Pines, have been in some measure cared for and encouraged, without destruction of low undergrowth, during one or two generations. Here conflicting deciduous trees have been cut out, and the Pines themselves thinned in some degree; while young seedlings from the parent trees have been protected both from fire and from too vigorous neighbors. The not unusual fate of the carelessly managed Pine woods has been their ruin by fire, and the subsequent surrender of the ground to coppice or scrub Oak. Here and there, again, are found crowded groves of deciduous trees, sprung from the small seedlings which, after long struggling in the shade of Pines or Hemlocks, shot up in vigorous competition with each other when the Pines or Hemlocks were felled. On the other hand, almost all such deciduous seedling woods have long ago been cut down and con-

verted into that coppice which so shrouds the hills and valleys, and which, on being cropped, again sprouts so vigorously as to suppress such seedlings, whether evergreen or deciduous, as may have started in its shade. Beech-trees often seed the land around them very thickly; Hemlocks and Pines, also, when they have a chance; and once in a while, though by no means often, such seedlings compete successfully with the surrounding coppice, and form colonies in the midst thereof.

In spite, however, of these and other exceptions to the rule, it is true that most of the now existing seedling woods of the reservations owe their origin to the activity of the winds, and of the seed and nut eating animals, in the fields and pastures prepared by men for their own purposes, but afterwards abandoned for one reason or another. The trees which thus eventually obliterate the fields and pastures are of many species, forms, and habits, and the resulting woods are often varied, interesting, and beautiful, as no coppice can be. The varied appearance of these woods and groves has been increased also by the diversity of their history since they first sprang up in the worn-out and abandoned pastures. Where, for example, all but the largest trees have at one time been felled and removed, the sprout trees from the stumps now form, with the old seedling trees, a mixed type of vegetation common in the rougher parts of the Fells. Where pasturing has been resumed after certain trees have got a good start, and then the animals have been again removed, a secondary growth of seedling trees has subsequently mingled with the primary trees, often to the injury of the latter, but as often with pleasing effect. If, on the other hand, pasturing is resumed and continued after well-spaced trees have been developed, the open groves which result present, perhaps, the most lovely local scenery of the reservations. The extreme rockiness and poverty of soil of most of the new domains makes this preeminently "park-like" type of landscape impracticable, as well as inappropriate. Intricacy, variety, and picturesqueness of detail of rock and vegetation, combined with numerous and varied openings, vistas, and broad prospects, must serve as the sources of interest and beauty throughout the larger part of the reservations; but where smooth grass-lands and broad-spreading trees exist, or are obtainable, they should certainly be preserved or secured. Compared with the sameness and dullness of the general scenery of the sprout-lands, the wealth of variety, character, and beauty presented by the relatively small area of fields, pastures, and seedling woods is indeed remarkable, and it is to be noted that this greater beauty counts in the broad scenery of the reservations as well as close at hand. The sky-lines and what may be called the profiles of the coppice woods are flat and nearly uniform. The masses of the seedling growths are bold in outline, as well as varied in detail, all of which only adds weight to the argument that the crop-like coppice should be forced to gradually give place to seedling shrubbery and seedling trees.

CONCLUSIONS

With regard to the relation of the vegetation of the reservations to the present and future scenery, perhaps the most important conclusions to be derived from this investigation are the following: It is found that the vegetation of the reservations is an exceedingly important component part of the scenery. It is found, moreover, that the present vegetation—its variety and beauty, as well as its monotony and ugliness—has resulted from repeated or continuous interference with natural processes by men, fire, and browsing animals.

It follows that the notion that it would be wrong and even sacrilegious to suggest that this vegetation ought to be controlled and modified must be mistaken. The opposite is found to be the truth; namely, that as the beauty or ugliness and scenic appropriateness or inappropriateness of the present vegetation is due to the work of men, so also will the vegetation of the future be beautiful in itself and helpful or hurtful in the general scenery, according as it may or may not be skillfully restrained, encouraged, or modified during the next few years.

Simply to preserve the beauty of so much of this vegetation as is now beautiful, or the suitability of so much as is now suitable, —for example, the tree-fringed vales of grass, the open groves of great trees, the intricate shrubberies of old pastures, and the dwarf ground-cover of the hill-tops, —will necessarily require continual painstaking care. To restore variety and beauty in the now more or less degenerate or ruined woods will similarly demand intelligent attention. So to control, guide, and modify the vegetation generally that the reservations may be slowly but surely induced to present the greatest possible variety, interest, and beauty of landscape will particularly require skilled direction.

That such preservation, restoration,

and enhancement of the beauty of vegetation and of scenery is only to be accomplished by the rightly directed labor of men is the principal lesson taught by this study of the present condition and the past history of the vegetation of the reservations. To preserve existing beauty, grass-lands must continue to be mowed or pastured annually, trees must be removed from shrubberies, and competing trees must be kept away from veteran Oaks and Chestnuts, and so on. To restore beauty in such woods as are now dull and crop-like, large areas must be gradually cleared of sprout-growth by selling the standing crop, or otherwise, the stumps must be subsequently killed, and seedling trees encouraged taking possession. To prepare for increasing the interest and beauty of scenery, work must be directed to removing screens of foliage, to opening vistas through "notches," to substituting low ground-cover for high woods in many places, and other like operations. The sooner all these kinds of work are entered upon systematically, the finer will be the scenery of twenty and fifty years hence, and the more economically will that scenery have been obtained.

Eight days after the above report was presented, Charles wrote to the Commission making a definite proposition on behalf of his firm for beginning forest work in the reservations, and continuing it three years. If the following letter is from one point of view an asking for employment by the Commission, from another it is a public-spirited offer of valuable service. The Olmsted firm had at this time so much well-paid
work on hand that, from the strictly pecuniary point of view, the less work they did for the Metropolitan Park Commission, the better. Charles's interest in that work was so keen that he would always give time to it altogether in excess of the time which the Commission paid for. The firm never took the view that their services were to be measured carefully by the amount of compensation they received; they wanted the personal satisfaction and the professional credit of contributing to the success of a superb and beneficent public enterprise.

February 23, 1897.
. . . We have prepared and submitted a report on the existing vegetation of the reservations, together with some account of the kind of work in the living woods, which, as it seems to us, ought to be begun at once if the reservations are to serve their purpose in a manner to justify their cost.

A few reasons for making an early start in this work are these: First, there is a great deal of this work to be done; but as the nature of the work is so peculiar, it will be advisable to make haste slowly, and to train men to prosecute it rightly. This will take time. Second, the "young sprout" which now covers large areas, while easily controllable to-day, will soon be too large to be easily handled. It already begins to obliterate many valuable prospects, as well as much local scenery. The small stature of the present growth also makes it possible to discover scenic possibilities to-day which would never be dreamed of if the trees were some years older. Third, much of the work we have called "rescue work" (the saving of fine or promising trees in smooth or good land from too pressing neighbors, and the like) will not be worth attempting if it is not begun soon. Of course, the first-named reason is fundamentally the most important.

There seems to us to be a strange incongruity in the provision by the Commission of elaborate approaches to the reservations, like the Fellsway, while no attention is directed to even preparing for the work of preserving and restoring the scenery of the reservations themselves.

Accordingly, and in order that a beginning in this work may be made in an orderly way and under responsible direction, we beg leave to suggest that, in addition to such force as the superintendents of the reservations may be authorized to employ under the appropriation for maintenance, and in addition to such force as they may employ in the construction of boundary roads, they be also authorized to engage one or more foremen and one or more gangs of laborers to be assigned to work in the living woods; and that just as their work on roads is now guided by inspectors representing the Commission's engineer, so the new work in the woods should be guided by inspectors representing the Commission's landscape architects. These inspectors will not themselves be foremen—they will correspond to the men who set the line and grade stakes for the road-builders. It will not be necessary that they should give all their time to the work. Unless the work is begun on a grand scale (as we cannot recommend that it should be), the Commission would not be warranted in engaging the whole time of trained inspectors. To avoid this difficulty, we will lend inspectors from our office as often or as seldom as may be necessary, and will charge the Commission with just the cost to us of their time and travelling expenses. Our own professional and semi-annual fee, covering the responsible selection and laying out of the work which the inspectors will guide in detail, would certainly not exceed the reasonable amount which we have heretofore charged for advice and suggestions respecting the location and boundaries of the acquired reservations.

As the Commission is directed to, in some sense, complete its work by January, 1900, we would suggest that a certain part of the money now available be specially appropriated for labor in the living woods between the present time and the date named. If entrusted with the direction of the work as above suggested, we would do our best to secure the expenditure of whatever appropriation is made to the best advantage; but it would greatly assist us to lay out the work aright, if the amount to be spent in the three years, rather than that to be spent in one year, could be named at the outset.

As reported by us a year ago, and again in our last annual report, we believe the only logical and truly economical way of going about the slow development of the reservations is to begin with a general scheme for each, and then to carry out such parts of the work called for by the adopted plans as may be most pressingly demanded from time to time. It is always our custom, when we are engaged to suggest general plans, to throw in advice and guidance during the period of study without extra charge, and we should be happy to take up the planning of one or more of the Commission's reservations, with this understanding, at any time. The foregoing proposals as to the guidance of woodland work in advance of all plan-making are submitted only because it seems wrong to allow the present fleeting opportunities to accomplish valuable results in the woods to pass unused.

On March 3, 1897, the Metropolitan Commission made an appropriation of $500 for forestry inspection; and Charles welcomed the chance to begin improving the woods in well-selected spots, although he had failed to induce the Commission to order general landscape designs for the three forest reservations.

The following letter to Mr. Hemenway, who was the Committee on Blue Hills Reservation, explains the principle on which he proceeded in Marigold Valley:

March 13, 1897.

Let me report to the Committee on Blue Hills Reservation that I have (under the vote of the Board) asked the Superintendent to begin forest work at the extreme head of Marigold Valley, and to proceed southward along the eastern side of the valley as far as the Plains. I have marked with him a large number of trees for felling, most of which are to be removed (1) for the sake of seedling Beeches in one place and Hickories in another; (2) for the sake of freeing from too near neighbors certain already well-established spreading trees; and (3) for the sake of breaking up certain straight rows of trees which followed walls now removed.

Some additional trees have been marked for the sake of opening two vistas which it seemed desirable to open while we were working in the neighborhood.

I shall, of course, be glad to have your suggestions and comments on the work proposed and executed.

On the same date Charles wrote also to Mr. de las Casas, who took special interest in the Middlesex Fells, explaining where he proposed to set the Superintendent at work in that reservation. It will be noticed that all the places he mentions for forestry work are on roads sure to be permanent, —that is, existing highways and border roads.

March 13, 1897.

The extent of the forest work will, I suppose, depend on the number of men employed and the length of time they keep at it. The place for beginning the work in the Fells is a matter of choice, of course. I have proposed to Price that he should begin on Ravine Road, where Pines and Hemlocks have begun to spring up on the slope once cleared by Mr. Butterfield. This is a hillside one would like to have clothed again with evergreen, and the process can be assisted by some chopping. It is a slope practically free from ledges; so that it does not call for the nice discrimination between trees which will be required among ledges.

Beyond this I would propose to attack similar work in a few spots along Pond and Woodland streets, where young evergreens are suffering, and after that I would suggest working round the east and southeast borders of the Fells for the purpose of ensuring the better appearance of the reservation as seen from the border roads, even as far round as Highland Avenue.

There is so much work to do that it seems to me it matters little where our small beginning is made, so long as it is arranged to be as educative as possible for the foreman and laborers employed.

Charles's letters to the Commission were invariably signed Olmsted, Olmsted & Eliot; but these two letters, addressed personally to members of the Commission, were signed, Yours sincerely, Charles Eliot. They were his last words on Metropolitan work.

JENS JENSEN

Report of the Landscape Architect

(1904)

The movement for the acquisition of large forest park areas within Cook County is in embryo. This fact is evidenced by the absence of surveys defining the existing forest areas.

The study of the vegetation indigenous to the forest tracts of this county, which furnishes the basis for this part of the report, has been extensive and has covered a period of more than fifteen years. It has been made partly in the interest of botanical science and largely for the purpose of obtaining an intimate acquaintance with the distribution of the flora in this and adjoining counties.

One of the purposes for which forest parks should be acquired is to preserve for present and future generations lands of natural scenic beauty situated within easy reach of multitudes that have access to no other grounds for recreation or summer outings. A second purpose is to preserve

spots having relation to the early settlements of Chicago and which are therefore of historical significance, and still another is to preserve the flora in its primeval state for the sake of the beauty of the forest and for the benefit of those desiring knowledge of plants indigenous there.

The most conspicuous physiographic features in Chicago and its vicinity are the Lake Plain, the Valparaiso and the Lake Border Moraine.

Generally speaking, this region is a great plain, above which rise a few elevations varying from sand ridges to bluffs. Examples are found in Lincoln Park, the ancient lake beaches and in the bluff to the north and southwest known to geologists as moraines.

On the north shore these bluffs reach a height from 100 to 125 feet, at Blue Island from 60 to 90 feet and at Mt. Forest and Palos from 170 to 185 feet above Lake Michigan.

From *Report of the Special Park Commission to the City Council of Chicago on the Subject of a Metropolitan Park System*, by Dwight H. Perkins (Chicago: W. J. Hartman Co., 1904), 80–101.

GEOLOGICAL FORMATIONS IN AND AROUND CHICAGO

Chicago is situated on the lake plain, commonly called prairie. This plain, which during the latter part of the ice-period was covered with water—Lake Chicago—consists of glacial drift, the average depth of which is from 75 to 125 feet under the central part of the city. The depth increases or diminishes in accordance with the levels of the underlying limestone rock. This rock rises gradually toward the south and is plainly visible along the Drainage Canal. It also rises to the surface in several places within the city limits and is quarried for lime and for macadam. It is known as Niagara limestone and constitutes the solid foundation upon which Chicago rests.

The glacial drift is a soft blue till, beneath which are remnants of a hard till of an earlier age. Goth tills are filled with boulders of all sizes, representing the pre-cambrian, upper silurian and devonian rocks. Towards the lake the drift has been covered later with sand, varying in depth from 5 to 20 feet, which has blown into ridges.

The predominating character of the landscape around Chicago is that of the prairie. By prairie is understood a treeless plain of fertile grass lands.

Variation from this general level is almost wholly found in elevations formed by glacial drift (moraine) and shore deposits of prehistoric lakes. Erosions formed by great volumes of running water and the action of waves have left their visible marks and in places have formed abrupt banks similar to those cut by rivers. They have an interesting, and for our topography, a bold and beautiful effect. It is these bluffs and elevations that command far-reaching and beautiful prospects. In themselves they form a pleasing feature in the landscape and may be seen from distant points.

Natural drainage, uneven surface favorable for catching seeds carried by wind or weather, and comparative immunity from vast prairie fires, favored tree growth on these uneven lands.

The greater part of these lands were not as well adapted for agriculture nor as readily cultivated as were the prairies. They consequently were left untouched to a considerable degree by the early settler. With the growth and prosperity of Chicago some wooded tracts became the property of wealthy land owners and were thereby shielded from the invading ax.

We therefore find here whatever is left of forest lands in the vicinity of Chicago. It is reasonable to recommend the acquisition of lands for forest parks in such areas as above described. They may be found north of the city along the shores of Lake Michigan, in the drainage basins of the Chicago and Desplaines Rivers, in what is known as the Sag outlet and along Blue Island.

FEATURES OF THE CALUMET DISTRICT

Of an entirely different nature is the land south of Chicago, the Calumet District. Alluvial deposits formed by Lake Michigan in the work of centuries have lifted these lands above the present level of the lake and left as an indication of a previous inundation Lake Calumet. The preservation of this lake until the present day is perhaps due more to the action of the winds than to anything else.

With the exception of a few sand ridges—old beaches—the entire region presents almost one dead level, entirely devoid of scenic beauty, with the exception of that attraction afforded by the placid waters of Lake Calumet, which forms a characteristic landscape feature peculiar to this section.

In a general way the proposed areas consist of swamp and rolling lands, but there exists enough variation in the different sites to name them according to their natural features.

Thus, the Skokee suggests meadow scenery. The Desplaines Valley, river scenery, the Sag environments, hilly scenery and the Calumet District, lake scenery. Save for the interference of man these lands will remain unchanged indefinitely just as they did for centuries before the arrival of the white man.

This inquiry is chiefly based upon the character of the forest park areas as they exist to-day, both with regard to their primary vegetation and the possibilities for their preservation. Forests in the country are independent and self-perpetuating, but the encroachment of the smoky city makes them dependent upon man for preservation. Park areas are so located in this report, however, as to guarantee to large portions the permanent conditions of country parks under which they now exist.

According to the topographical conditions there are two types of vegetation, one indigenous to rolling lands, the other the swamp of marsh lands.

Taking Fort Dearborn as the first settlement of this region, perhaps little of the remaining forests can be called primeval in their entirety. Most of the lands have been cut over once and some twice, yet scattered or grouped over the entire district trees remain, showing an age extending years beyond the original settlement.

PICTURESQUE WORK OF MAN

Man's interference with the forest is visible everywhere, and this has in many instances produced a picturesqueness that has rendered some tracts, especially along the Desplaines River, most beautiful and established a precedent that should be encouraged. One thing is certain, that the present growth, if not entirely primeval, is a true descendant of the species which covered these lands before man's intervention. It is also a gratification to know that no species of any prominence has become extinct, although the introduction of new ones has not been noticeable. One species was found not indigenous to the district, the common white willow. It had been planted here to protect the river bank from erosion where presumably some previous owner had carelessly removed such protection supplied by nature. The type of vegetation distributed over the entire area varies little. Certain species may be more pronounced in one locality than in the other and a few characteristic only in certain localities, as for instance, the red cedar, white pine, common and creeping juniper that are found in the ravine and on the lake bluffs in the northern tract. These varieties, mixed with scrub pine, were indigenous to the sand ridges along the lake shore, but the building of Chicago has destroyed them there.

In the Mount Forest region oak predominates to-day. The hard maple has been entirely cut out over great areas and annual fires and browsing herds keep the under-growth down. The present growth in some instances seems to have been subjected to care in its even distribution and here represents a rather attractive forest scene.

In some sections the hard maple still forms a prominent part of the forest, but here also the ax has done its destructive work.

One owner has cleared away all trees and undergrowth with the exception of the hard maple. The stand is open enough to admit sufficient light for the full development of the trees and a beautiful grove of sugar maples will be the result. Such treatment, if not overdone, is worthy of approval.

In the Calumet tract little remains but limited stands of oak. The once dense forest further south along the little Calumet River and Thornton Creek has disappeared long ago. Only infrequent remnants remain in the form of the farmer's wood lot.

MIXTURE OF FOREST GROWTH

Outside of minor changes in the forest produced by man's intervention mentioned above, the entire forest area consists of a mixture varying from soft maple, willow, swamp oak, ash, elm, cottonwood, linden, hackberry, red maple, alder, hawthorn, elder, dogwood, ninebark, blackhaw, wild grape vine, roses, etc., on the bottom or moist lands, to oak, hard maple, hickory, butternut, walnut, mulberry, ironwood, hop hornbeam, juneberry, white ash, American bird cherry, wild red cherry, choke cherry, crabapple, arrow-wood, witch-hazel, hazel, sumach, honeysuckle, etc., on the higher level.

This happy mixture makes the forest not only more interesting with its varied vegetation, but picturesque and harmonious with the idea of a forest park. Wherever the forests have not been disturbed save by the cutting out of natural trees, a most luxuriant undergrowth results. The bad habit of some owners of annually burning down the undergrowth so they can "see through," shows its ruinous effect; but its influence in bringing about changes in the type of the vegetation is not appreciable.

Severe thinning out of the forest for pasture purposes, especially where oak predominates, has in some instances shown its damaging influences and the once luxuriant forest is gradually dying out. Such proceedings demonstrate that a removal of the undergrowth in oak forests, together with a severe thinning out, is injurious to the trees and should be discouraged. To encourage the undergrowth in such places where a greater congregation of the public is not desirable, or where on account of the location undergrowth is considered advisable, will not only enhance the beauty of the forest, but tend to preserve the great mass of beautiful and interesting vegetation that covers the forest floor. Such plants as violets, dogtooth violets, hepaticas, trillium, phloxes, anemones, spring beauty, asters, goldenrod, etc., help to enrich the forest scenery and destruction of them would deprive the forest of its greatest beauty and one of the chief reasons for which these lands are to be preserved. How quickly the forest will take possession of abandoned pasture land is noticeable in a few instances where land has been bought up for speculation and left alone. No special types seem to take hold of these fields, but a mixture of such trees as constitute the adjoining forest is here reproduced.

PROTECTION FOR
YOUNG GROWTH

Such pioneers of the forest as the hawthorn, protected from attack of browsing cattle by its thorn branches, gradually advance upon the pasture lands and under their protection, young ash, elm and maple seedlings get a foothold. How responsive vegetation is, if not molested by fire or grazing herds along our country roads, and how much it adds to beautifying these public highways, is well worth mentioning here. Crab, thorn, hazel, choke cherry are quick to take possession of the vacant space left along the roadways, and later come elm, oak, maple, ash and other trees. Cottonwood invariably finds a welcome home along the eroded sides of an open ditch, soon followed by other types brought by birds. These efforts of nature are worthy of careful study for reproduction under similar conditions.

It is fortunate that coppice woods are almost entirely absent and its mention here is due to showing the strong reproductive powers of an ash coppice. In this instance it is green ash and at an age not yet strong enough to crush out the competing seedlings that form part of the growth. It is not improbable that this piece of coppice has killed out competitors of other varieties. Its complete hold of the ground here rather tends to verify this assertion as the tree growth surrounding it is of the usual mixture and no difference exists in the character of the land. Such growth as this coppice wood pres-

ents is monotonous and ugly to the highest degree; it kills any other vegetation of interest and beauty, leaving the whole a barren and uninteresting tree cover.

The wooded banks along the Desplaines River give this stream its charm and beauty. Commencing with arrowhead and other aquatic plants fringing the water edge and followed by dogwood, hawthorn, blackhaw, silver maple, various willows, especially on the lower shore, and majestic elm, ash, linden and cottonwood, it becomes one of the prettiest landscape scenes of the entire area. However, where the industrious farmer has robbed the banks of their luxuriant vegetation, and grain fields have replaced the forest along the river, the scenery becomes less beautiful and incompatible with the forest park idea.

NECESSARY TO PRESERVE
THE RIVER VIEW

It not only becomes necessary for the preservation of the river scene to protect the tree growth on these banks, but for the preservation of the banks themselves. This growth keeps the steep banks intact and preserves them from erosion. Remove the protection afforded by vegetation and the spring-floods will soon do destructive work upon these cuts formed by the river as the work of centuries. Where the bluffs command noteworthy prospects, vegetation of low growth should be encouraged, offering the same protection to the bluffs without impairing the view of the beautiful landscape beyond.

The openings or sunny spots in the forest previously referred to are not always due to the ax, but in some instances represent hollows filled with water, or natural run-offs or drainage channels, either forming continual running creeks, which in the course of time have cut deep crevasses into the otherwise almost level surface, or run-offs caused by the accumulation of water during the spring thaws or heavy rainstorms on adjacent level lands. These prevent the growth of any vegetation except grass. The run-offs due to spring thaws prevent seeds of trees or shrubs from obtaining a foothold in dry years, which might be favorable for re-foresting such open spaces. Whatever the causes, these run-offs become a beautiful diversion from the monotonous forest and they arouse special interest in the greater variation of vegetation encouraged through the introduction of more light.

Hawthorn, crab and plum brighten up these openings during spring in a most charming manner and their fruit in autumn makes them interesting also. Filled up with tree growth, these natural drains lose their bold character and beautiful effect and prevent views over lower lying lands to great distances.

FORMATION OF BOG LANDS

Hollows or depressions on the level surface not provided with a natural outlet for the escape of the gathered water gradually fill up with decayed vegetable matter and in this condition are known as bogs. Here the oak forest has pushed itself to the very edge of the wet hollow and moisture-loving button bushes have penetrated beyond the water's edge.

Depressions of a more prominent type attributed to glacial spurs are found in the Palos region. Here a brook drains the land enough to render it fit for agriculture. In consequence the tree growth has been removed, greatly beautifying the landscape. Such scenic effects are worthy of reproduction where conditions of like nature exist.

Prevailing tree growth on the bolder slopes often shut off beautiful prospects from the higher elevation. Clearings in the wooded slope of the east side of the Skokee swamps have brought to view, from the Green Bay road, these wood-fringed plains and farm lands to the west. A similar opening into the tree-covered slope towards the lake would reveal the blue waters of Lake Michigan to the east and here create one of the grandest prospects of the entire region.

A retrenchment of the same character would command great views from the higher elevation at Palos and Mt. Forest over the Sag and Desplaines Valley and the low prairie lands toward the east.

SWAMPS AND THEIR IMPORTANCE

Almost as important as the forest covered lands are the swamps or marshes that form a considerable part of the proposed park areas in the Skokee and Sag district. Nature has here created one of the prime factors of beautiful landscape, which is unbroken distant view. Their origin is prehistoric and of glacial nature. The Skokee is known as an old back bay and the Sag the outlet of ancient Lake Chicago, formed in the ice period.

In the Calumet District these marshes are too much the controlling feature. They demand some modification.

Water and land represent almost one

dead level, only interrupted by a few tree-covered ridges—ancient lake beaches. The vegetation found in these swamps varies very little. Sedge, flag, spike-bull and bog-rush, cat-tail, reed and water plantain cover the greater part of these low and partly submerged lands, fighting for supremacy in the deeper waters with pond weed and white and yellow water lilies. A retrenchment of this swamp vegetation must necessarily become one of the important steps in reclaiming such lands for park purposes, the Calumet district especially.

In places where an open beach is not necessary, the tall reed with its feathery plume amid the stately cat-tail become an attractive and harmonious feature in the landscape, but when permitted to crowd into the lake for hundreds of feet, they lessen the beauty of the water prospect and interfere with the boating and water sports that are destined to make this lake park renowned. A reclamation of the swamp lands bordering the lake to the south and north for public utility will eventually become necessary, but their present topography should be left undisturbed.

It might be well to give the proper Indian name to this district which is "Conamic" (snow beaver). It seems that the English-speaking people took this word for Calumet (pipe), which word they received and understood from the French settlers. Calumet is a Norman word meaning reed, such as was used for the pipe-stem. Later this word was used for the whole pipe. The Indian word Conamic and Calumet sounded enough alike to make it probable that the early settlers and explorers made the mistake.

MENACE OF ARTIFICIAL SEWERAGE

Manufacturing is gradually killing out the woodlands along the north branch of the Chicago River and artificial sewerage has exterminated the beautiful groves north and south of the city. These facts stand as a lesson to be well observed. Public improvement which lowers the present level of the underground water permanently will have an injurious effect upon existing vegetation.

That the character of the vegetation depends chiefly upon topographical conditions and that these together form the most prominent part of the landscape, must be conceded. We have also seen that where one type of vegetation dominates the landscape becomes less picturesque and even monotonous, as for instance in the Calumet district and the southern part of the Skokee. But where a happy combination of the two—meadow and forest—exists, the beauty of each is perceptibly enhanced. By this we must conclude that the closer we get to the latter state the more beautiful and interesting will our forest parks become. In addition, stretches of meadow will encourage outdoor sports.

The treatment of the different sites will vary according to physical and natural conditions. Generally speaking, sunny openings are desirable. Wherever feasible, the growth of the forest should be encouraged on new cultivated or pasture lands, where it tends to beautify the scenery, and should be restricted where its introduction in the meadow will seriously impair the pastoral landscape or the natural water courses and run-offs. For the opening up of views or vistas wherever desirable distant prospects can be obtained from higher elevations, the adjoining lower lands should be acquired.

FARM LANDS NEED MODIFYING

The forest covered lands like those on the woody slopes of Palos visible from Mt. Forest, or those along the west shore of the Skokee visible from the Green Bay road on the east, constitute a beautiful setting in the landscape and should also be secured. Farm lands now under cultivation west of the Skokee will need some modification, according to their possibilities in beautifying the landscape. Here they may be treated as grassy plains and there again covered with tree growth. Even in their present state of straight edges and sharp outlines over these clearings in the forest they present a landscape picture full of interest and beauty. To change the Skokee from a wet and impenetrable marsh to a dry grass plain may eventually become necessary, yet any drainage scheme that will tend to injure adjoining forests must be avoided.

By the introduction of a few more "wooded islands" to the south and the encouraging of a dense and luxuriant growth to the very edge, this grand meadow scene would become more beautiful, but any other tree growth must be kept out of the open plain.

An attempt to preserve the tree-covered bluffs of the Desplaines River and its beautiful scenery would be in vain without possessing control over both sides of the river. This will also keep under surveillance any obstruction on the lower side that may tend to shut off distant prospects attainable from the higher bluffs.

The question of artificial drainage endangering the existence of the forest can be repeated with emphatic words: Drains of any importance must, under no circumstances, be permitted if the forest is to remain in its present state. That sewers are less detrimental to tree growth on heavy clay lands than on porous sandy grounds is not doubted, but practical conditions explain their deadly work even in the supposed waterproof sub-soil along the Desplaines. The great fertility of the soil in the Desplaines Valley has produced a tree growth not exceeded anywhere else in this part of the state, especially where the individual tree has had a chance to perfect its development.

Such beautiful growths will be well worth encouraging and will ultimately develop a forest park with special characteristics entirely its own, yet perfectly in harmony with the future plan of this valley, for it must be looked upon as a great pleasure drive and waterway, quite as much as a forest park. Again, such treatment would provide beautiful picnic grounds for the multitudes that will visit these woodlands. Such growth should be distributed over their entire length, or the continual wear and tear of human tramping may otherwise overtax the strength of the forest and cause its destruction. In the Mt. Forest tract conditions are more favorable for encouraging the forest idea. Lands now in pasture should be re-forested, except where interfering with distant prospects or detrimental to the scenic effect of the forest itself.

RESTORE THE MIXED FOREST

The mixed forest that formerly covered these hills should again be introduced, partly for scenic beauty and interest, but also to insure a forest of a more healthy character. Where erosion tends to destroy the tree growth or otherwise interfere with the beauty of the scenery, undergrowth, if encouraged, will soon cover up the damaged slopes, prevent further erosion and enhance the beauty of the landscape. Brooks and bogs must be left alone. They add variety and beauty to the scene and here supply the forest with water and drainage.

Bluffs, affording views of surrounding country, where openings are desired, may be covered with shrubbery vegetation that will not obstruct distant prospects and will help to bring out the bold form of the bluff to better advantage. As pointed out before, any modification that tends to destroy the marsh character of the Calumet district destroys forever the possibilities of preserving these lands in their natural state for coming generations.

To build a beach-like elevation around the lake for driving and promenading, covered with a harmonious and fitting tree growth, would frame the lake most beautifully and form a pleasing setting from opposite shores.

Elevating the low lands south of Lake Calumet would destroy the ancient lake beaches. Eventually these lands must be reclaimed, but a few windmills will keep them dry at a reasonable cost and preserve their present topography. With a belt of woods surrounding the great Lake Park it will form someday a beautiful oasis in one of the world's greatest manufacturing districts.

To conclude, roadways will have to be built in some instances and especially to points commanding views over the surrounding country.

Such roads as form the connecting link between the different reservations should not be walled in with vegetation which will obstruct the view of adjacent farm land prospects. Fires and grazing animals must be kept out of the forest, the flora protected from vandalism, the forest cleared of dead wood and the growth retrenched or encouraged according to its qualification for beautifying the scenery. All this should be done.

We may then succeed in encouraging and protecting the forests so that it may be restored to its original condition. We see remnants to-day—picturesque in themselves—so situated that viewed from a distance they are revealed not only as beautiful themselves, but valuable as settings for the adjacent country. They may now be seen and enjoyed from the public highways and from the homes of thousands of people.

They may and should form natural gateways to the city. They are monumental in character and should embellish the highways that enter our great metropolis.

The forest park, great in area, rich in vegetation, will ultimately become a great source of knowledge for the student of silviculture and forestry and will assist in making Chicago an educational center in such lines.

LARS PETER JENSEN

Parks as Preservers of Native Plants

(1915)

In the making of parks no material is of greater importance than plants. Even in parks, whose space is utilized for playgrounds, some trees and shrubs are essential, the trees for the purpose of providing shade and the shrubs for the relief of some of the harsh lines, which are always essentially associated with this form of a park, and for boundary plantations. Of plant material, that native to the region in which the park is located is, of course, indispensable and of the greatest importance. While we should, by all means, utilize the many splendid plants introduced from other countries, the native species should, in the main, predominate, because of their permanence and dependability. This applies particularly to our larger parks and reservations, those which are of a rural character and whose chief function is restfulness and repose, rather than exercises of a more or less strenuous nature. In such parks, in-

From *Park and Cemetery*, September 1915, 204–5. An address before the San Francisco Convention of the American Association of Park Superintendents.

troduced species of plants are very apt to appear out of place, unless unusual care and forethought is employed in their selection, whereas our native plants fit harmoniously into the surroundings.

That many of our beautiful and interesting native plants, particularly those inhabiting woodlands and those which for some natural reason, are limited in their power of perpetuation, are becoming rare, where a few years ago they could be found in abundance, everyone knows, who has paid some attention to plant study outside the laboratory.

The principal reasons for the destruction and consequent disappearance of native plants are:

1. The entire cutting out of woodlands for timber, in the wasteful American way, and for the making of land for the growing of crops.
2. The destruction of undergrowth in woodlands for the making of pasture for stock.
3. The destruction of undergrowth for no

other purpose than that of a false idea of tidiness.

4. The wanton destruction of woody flowering plants by persons gathering flowers.
5. The pulling up of entire plants when gathering flowers.
6. The removal of plants from their native habitat, for the purpose of transplanting, by persons who have no conception of their governing requirements; and
7. Last, but not least, the lack of popular education on the subject of plant preservation and protection.

I will take a few moments for a short detailed consideration of the above mentioned causes of plant extermination.

The destruction of plants caused by lumbermen, whose sole purpose is the making of money, irrespective of other considerations, is so well known that it hardly needs mention.

The elimination of wooded areas for the growing of agricultural crops must necessarily increase in a ratio corresponding to the increase of population of this country and the deficiency of such food material abroad.

Pasturing of woodland, particularly if given over to sheep and goats, exterminates practically all undergrowth of shrubs and herbs, and prevents the perpetuation of existing arboreous vegetation.

The first act of most persons coming into possession of a parcel of natural woodland is to improve it, by cleaning out all the undergrowth of shrubs and herbs. This practice is so very common that anyone who happens to have the contrary view on the matter is looked upon by his neighbors as somewhat irrational.

I have personal knowledge of many a place, whose charm consisted of its native growth of redbud, flowering dogwood, crabapple, hawthorn, native roses, varieties of viburnums, sumach, bittersweet, native grapes, intermingled with asters, golden rods, purple cone flower, butterfly weed and other attractive and desirable native plants, which have been changed, with an idea of improvement, by completely destroying these natives and replacing them with a few beds of annual flowering plants.

I have one particular instance in mind, where I had been called upon to work out a design which would adapt a ten-acre parcel of natural woodland to the requirements of a country home for a well-known St. Louis physician, who is a great lover of botany.

This parcel of land is located on the bluffs overlooking the Mississippi River, over which some splendid views were secured, simply by the removal of a few branches. By retaining most of the native growth of plants, and by careful selection of additional planting material, the result has been most pleasing and satisfactory.

One of his neighbors, who had employed the usual clearing up process in the development of his place, thereby utterly destroying its charm, asked me what he could do to make his home grounds more attractive. To this question there seemed only one answer: Restore the greater part of that which you have destroyed. Unfortunately, it would take many years and much work to do so.

A similar stretch of native growth along a public road, over which I have occasion to pass almost daily, was a source of pleasure and satisfaction to me, and undoubtedly to many other lovers of native plants, as it provided a continuous succession of interesting flowers and foliage throughout the season, until the owner, apparently for no other reason than lack of exercise in winter, completely destroyed every plant. This was about five years ago. Having been undisturbed since that time, the place in question is again becoming interesting, but will undoubtedly soon become the object of another winter's recreation for the owner, who insists that this work of destruction improves the appearance of his property.

I know of some parks of a rural character where native herbs and shrubs are being ruthlessly destroyed whenever they appear. This practice is fortunately becoming less common, owing in a large measure to the teaching of ours and similar organizations.

Woody plants, whose value consists principally in their great number of beautiful flowers, are often exterminated by thoughtless persons, who break the plants to pieces for the gathering of an armful of flowers, which in most cases wither and are thrown away along the roadside. They do not realize that their act creates wounds which seldom heal, but which give opportunities for the spread of diseases, which through the wound enter the tissues of the plant, resulting ultimately in its destruction

Other plants growing in the loose and mellow leaf mold of the woods are destroyed by gatherers of flowers, who carelessly pull out the entire plant.

The popularity of nature study is responsible for the destruction of many plants, because most authors and writers on this subject neglect to call attention to the importance of plant protection.

In the vicinities of cities the woods are denuded of their former wealth of ferns and flowering herbs by persons who wish to transplant them into their gardens, but who do not realize that these plants require a soil and situation which is not often to be found or provided on a city lot or in the ordinary garden border. The result in such cases is always the ultimate death of the plant.

Not so very many years ago the closed gentian (*Gentiana andrewsii*), the yellow ladyslipper (*Cyprepidium pubescens*), the white flowering gentian (*Gentiana flavida*), the narrow-leaved gentian (*Gentiana liniaris*), the rose pink (*Sabatia angularis*), the white flowering wake-robin (*Trillium grandiflora*), the bloodroot (*Sanguinaria canadensis*), the liver-leaf (*Hepatica triloba*) and other attractive herbs of the woods were to be found in the vicinity of the city of St. Louis; today they are only to be found in remote localities, and some of them, the gentians, cyprepidiums, trilliums and hepatica, only where guarded by some plant lover who is reluctant to reveal their location for fear of the plant hunter.

It is evident from what has been said that some of our most interesting and beautiful native plants are in need of our protection, and that the matter of their protection is of sufficient importance to be considered by everyone interested in the perpetuation of the beauties of nature.

We should consider it not only a pleasure, but a duty to our descendants, to preserve and protect our native plants. Let them not find that we have preserved only illustrations and herbarium specimens, for their gratification and use.

A popular campaign of education on plant preservation is needed, and I know that many of the members of this organization are ardent and tireless workers in this field, but we need the assistance of every member.

Teachers, writers and speakers endeavoring to popularize our native plants should always call attention to their need of protection, and how and why they should be protected. Much good might be accomplished in this manner, and all of us should come forward with a helping hand in this movement of education. Here is where the superintendent of public parks and the superintendent of large private estates may be of the greatest service to the cause, by introducing these plants into his parks whenever and wherever an opportunity presents itself. He should study the habits and requirements of those plants which are becoming scarce in his locality, and find suitable places for them in the parks, thereby giving them absolute protection. He should inform the school authorities and the public about the presence of these plants in the parks, at the same time calling their attention to interesting facts concerning these plants, their beauty, scarcity in the locality, and the importance of their protection, wherever found. Then you, Mr. Superintendent, are not only preserving the plants, but also educating the public to an appreciation of our native flora.

The time is rapidly coming, if not already here, when to the numerous responsibilities of the park superintendent is to be added the great responsibility to posterity, of the preservation of our natural scenery, the protection of those mammals, birds and plants which modern civilization is gradually, but nevertheless surely, exterminating and destroying.

The following list of plants which seems to need protection, in the vicinity of St. Louis, Missouri, is merely sugges-

tive, because plants which may be nearing extinction in one locality may be abundant in another:

TREES:
Juniperus virginica, Red Cedar;
Betula nigra, Black Birch;
Carya olivaeformis, Pecan;
Gymnocladus canadensis, Kentucky
    Coffee-tree;
Juglans cinerea, Butternut;
Juglans nigra, Black Walnut;
Pyrus coronarius, Western Crabapple;
Prunus americana, Wild Plum;
Prunus serotina, Wild Black Cherry;
Crataegus, all species, over thirty of which
    are found in Missouri;
Cornus florida, Flowering Dogwood;
Amelanchier canadensis, Shad-bush;
Viburnum prunifolium, Black Haw

SHRUBS:
Ceanothus americana, New Jersey Tea;
Celastrus scandens, Shrubby or Climbing
    Bittersweet;
Cornus paniculata, Panicled Dogwood;
Corylus americana, Hazel;
Euonymus atropurpurea, Strawberry Bush;
Ilex decidua, Deciduous Holly,
Species of native roses;
Viburnum lentago, Sheep-berry.

HERBS:
All species of native ferns;
Acorus calamus, Calamus;
Cyprepidium pubescens and *parviflorum,*
    Lady-slipper;
Erythronium albidum and *americanum,*
    Dog-tooth Violets;
Iris hexagona and *versicolor,* Flags;
Lilium canadense, philadelphicum and
    superbum, Lilies;

Orchis spectabile, Showy Orchid;
Smilacina racemosa, False Solomon's Seal;
Trillium grandiflora, Large-flowered
    Wake-Robin;
Aquilegia canadensis, Columbine;
Aster novae-angliae, New England Aster;
Gentiana andrewsii, flavida, liniaris, quin-
    quefolia and *saponaria,* Gentians;
Dodecatheon medea, Shooting Star;
Hepatica triloba and *acutiloba,* Liver-leaf;
Lobelia cardinalis, Cardinal Flower;
Physotegia virginiana, False Dragonhead;
Sabatia angularis, Rose Pink;
Sanguinaria canadensis, Blood-root and
Viola pedata, Bird's-foot Violet.

Each one will be required to study his own locality, to determine which plants are becoming scarce, which are already extinct, and which are apt to become exterminated in the near future. Certain plants should be protected everywhere, for example, the orchid family, the members of which, owing to the peculiar form of their flowers, are adapted to fertilization by but few insects, and consequently many of these plants, not being fertilized, fail to produce seeds, which results in slow perpetuation of the species.

JENS JENSEN

The Dunes of Northern Indiana

(1917)

The world is full of things that add to human intellect and life. Perhaps least consideration and least appreciation are given to those things that form an interesting part of Mother Earth herself. We give first consideration, it seems, to things that have a commercial value; in other words, man-made things. The fine arts are of the man-made variety; but the inspiration or source from which they spring is found in the great outdoors. All art has its root in the primitive, unadulterated beauty made by the hand of the Great Master. Without this source creative art would be impossible.

The dunes of northern Indiana are one of the great expressions of wild beauty in our country. They are the greatest of nature's expressions of this beauty in the Middle West and as a type of landscape they are unequaled anywhere in the world. They are to us what the Adirondacks and the Catskills are to our eastern and the Rocky Mountains to our western friends.

From *Report on the Proposed Sand Dunes National Park, Indiana*, by Stephen T. Mather (Washington, D.C.: National Park Service, 1917), 98–100.

Their beauty of wildness and romance must be measured by comparison with the level plains of the Middle West. They are less severe and less melancholy perhaps than the dune countries of the Italian coast or the western coasts of France and Denmark. They are more poetic, more free, more joyful, something that appeals more, to the average human being and which has a greater influence on him than the colder, more severe and overwhelming forms of landscape. Those of us who feel the necessity of paying homage to this interesting region they not only charm with their hidden mysteries, but give us—who are imprisoned as it were in the brick and stone of a great city—a greater and clearer vision of the great out-of-doors. Few can imagine the magnificent outlook over Lake Michigan from the tops or ridges of the dunes, especially at sunset, and the wonderful view of Indiana and the blue haze of the State of Michigan.

From an artistic standpoint, the color expressions of spring and autumn are not equaled anywhere. Added to this is the movement and history of the dunes, dating back into geological ages thousands of years ago.

The dunes represent a book of the great outdoors which man can never fully comprehend; but it is not the great dramatic things, which appeal perhaps more to the eye than the more intimate and hidden treasures, that gives the real charm to this bit of nature's landscape. It is among the sand hills that the real mystery of the dunes is to be found. In the dune meadows, in the bogs or tamarack swamps, or along hidden trails one feels the exquisite homily of the hidden shrines of nature's great work. Carpets of flowers cover the hills and valleys of the dunes during spring and early summer—in fact during the entire season. Here the lupine brings the first joy of spring to the visitor, with its beautiful handlike leaves upon which the rays of the rising sun turn the dew of early morning, glistening in its palm, into millions of diamonds. Later a sea of blue covers the forest floor, and in late autumn we have the same expression in its beautiful leaves as in spring. Also in late autumn the gentian puts its color on the dune meadows, holding out until the winter blasts shrivel up the last flower. Along the trail asters stand in a blaze of glory as so many candles lighting up the way of the pilgrim who ventures into the woods on dark and gloomy autumn days, and in the wind rustling through trees that have seen generations pass below one fancies he can hear the chanting song of the Red Man, or the cradle song of the Indian squaw when listening to the murmuring waves breaking over the sandy beach of this dune country.

Man becomes small and insignificant, indeed, in such environment. He should be thankful for being able to enjoy and understand, at least in a small way, this wonderful beauty that lies all around him, and grieve that millions have to live and die without knowing anything of its wonders. Perhaps he thinks about the millions that are growing up and are debarred from the enjoyment of this the greatest of all books. He thinks, no doubt, about the necessity of this balance of mind, the need of knowing something about mother earth, her great beauty, mysterious life, and never-ending change. No one has more need of an intimate acquaintance with out-of-door life and the always changing charms of nature than those who grind away their lives in our mills, our factories, our shops, and our stores. The man in the factory turning out the same kind of work day after day during his entire lifetime needs something as a balance, something that will make his work more endurable, more cheerful, something that will broaden his vision and save him or his descendants from the destruction sure to follow the endless grind of his daily life. The people of the mills, the shops, and the stores are the backbone of the great cities. They are the producers of wealth and the human species; and the opportunity for those people to get the full value of the out-of-doors is made almost impossible. The great national reservations of the West are beyond their reach and the parks of the cities, valuable as they are, do not possess the wild beauty of the Master's hand nor do they inspire the soul in the same degree. There is no other place in our country where this wild beauty lies so close to great industrial communities. The dunes of northern Indiana are almost within a stone's throw of perhaps one of the greatest industrial communities of the world. It is the only landscape of its kind within reach of the millions that need its softening influence for the restoration of their souls and the balance of their minds.

Of all the national parks and monuments donated by Congress to the American people, there is none more valuable and none more useful to the people of the Middle West than the dune country of northern Indiana. It is today the Mecca of the artist and the scientist. No one knows what the future has in store. Possibly the influence of these wild and romantic dunes may be the source from which America's greatest poets and artists get their inspiration. Who can tell?

HENRY CHANDLER COWLES

Testimony at the Hearing on the Proposed Sand Dunes National Park

(1917)

Mr. Secretary, ladies, and gentlemen, I certainly heartily second all that has been said in regard to Mr. Mather's very large part in making our national parks useful. I feel, however, that if we do not cease making parks outside of the periphery of our country, the name of the department may have to be changed from "Department of the Interior" to "Department of the Exterior." [Laughter and applause.] Therefore I second very heartily the move toward the establishment of a national park in this great Central West. For 20 years I have been studying the dunes more than anything else, more than everything else combined. In fact, that has been my chief reason for existence, perhaps, for those 20 years. During those 20 years I have studied not only the dunes of Lake Michigan but nearly all the dunes of the world, having personally visited most of them and read about the others. And so this meeting here today seems to me almost the culmination

From *Report on the Proposed Sand Dunes National Park, Indiana*, by Stephen T. Mather (Washington, D.C.: National Park Service, 1917), 43–46.

of a lifetime of scientific effort, though I hope that my lifetime is not coming to an end just now, because I want to enjoy this great national park when it becomes such, together with all of the thousands and hundreds of thousands of people who are likely to go there when it is created into such a park. Three years ago I had the great privilege of conducting through our continent, or through our country, perhaps I had better say, a large number of the greatest scientists of Europe, the greatest botanists of Europe, men representing all the countries which are now at war with one another. As there was so much in our country to see in the brief time that we had to see it in, I asked these people who had come here to indicate what they wanted to see in the United States in two months. They mentioned things, of course, that it would have taken dozens of months to witness, even briefly; but there were three or four things that all of them mentioned as highly worth seeing, even in the briefest trip to the United States. One of those was the Grand Canyon of the Colorado; another was the Yosemite; another was Yellowstone Park; and the fourth was the Lake Michigan dunes. [Applause.] Those were the only four things that were mentioned by all of those European scientists, regardless of whatever else they wished to see. In other words, in Europe, among the scientific men, our Lake Michigan dunes are rated with the wonders of the West that already have been set aside, with the exception of the Grand Canyon, for national parks. Now, my studies for all these years have mostly been, as has been indicated, along the line of plant life, botany. Now, I am not going to read this manuscript to you of course; that would be a crime. But I am going to merely call your attention briefly to one or two of the things that have impressed me in those 20 years. The botanical features of the dunes may be considered under two heads; first, the dunes as a common meeting ground of trees and wild flowers from all directions; and second, the dunes as a picturesque battle ground between plant life and the elements. Botanically the Indiana dunes are a marvelous cosmopolitan preserve, a veritable floral melting pot.

There are few places on our continent where so many species of plants are found in so small compass as within the area suggested for conservation. This is in part because of the wide diversity of conditions prevailing there. Within a stone's throw of almost any spot one may find plants of the desert and plants of rich woodlands, plants of the pine woods, and plants of swamps, plants of oak woods and plants of the prairies. Species of the most diverse natural regions are piled here together in such abundance as to make the region a natural botanical preserve, not only of the plants that are characteristic of northern Indiana, but also of the plants of remote outlying regions. Here one may find the prickly pear cactus of the southwestern desert hobnobbing with the bearberry of the arctic and alpine regions. The commonest pine of the dunes, the jack pine, is far out of its main range, reaching here its farthest south. One is almost startled at the number of plants of the far north, many of which, like the jack pine, are not found to the southward of our dunes. Among such plants of the Canadian forest and tundra are the twin flower, the glandular willow, the poverty grass, and the northern rose. Northern plants are particularly characteristic of the dune swamps, and embrace such interesting species as the larch, bunchberry, dwarf birch, sage willow, numerous orchids, cranberry, leather leaf, and many more. Many of these species are found nowhere for many miles outside of the dune region, so that the failure to conserve the dunes would result in the extinction of this wonderful flora for all time.

The picturing of the beauties of the dune wild flowers may perhaps belong to an artist rather than to a botanist, but I cannot forbear noting that in the dunes, as nowhere else in our part of the world, is there a procession from April to October of beautiful flowers. Our woodlands in spring and our swamps and prairies in summer are favorite haunts for flower lovers, but the dunes are beautiful the season through. In early spring one finds in the dunes the trailing arbutus (found nowhere else in our region), the sand cherry, the bearberry and hepatica. In May there are splendid displays of the lupine, puccoon, phlox, trillium, and the magnificent bird's-foot violet. Somewhat later come many of the orchids, among which may be noted four species of ladies' slipper, the roses, columbine, twin flower, spiderwort, rock rose, and coreopsis. In midsummer there occur a bewildering number of attractive flowers, as the harebell, goat's rue, butterfly weed, flowering spurge, and the incomparable prickly pear cactus. In late summer one sees numerous kinds of golden rod and aster, and also sunflowers and yellow gerardias. Perhaps the culmination of this wonderful display comes in the autumn with the gentians, grass of Parnassus, witch hazel, and various golden rods and asters. One should not neglect mentioning here the display of autumnal color, which nowhere else in this part of the country reaches the magnificence seen in the dunes. The sour gum, sassafras, sumac, oak, red maple, and many vines and shrubs contribute to the fascinating blaze of color.

The struggle for existence always interests, because our life is such a struggle. Nowhere perhaps in the entire world of plants does the struggle for life take on such dramatic and spectacular phases as in the dunes. A dune in the early days of its career is a moving landscape, a place that is never twice alike; it is a body of sand which under the influence of wind moves indifferently over swamp or town or forest. Perhaps nothing in all nature except a volcano with its lava flow is to be compared with such a moving dune as is to be seen at Dune Park, Tremont, or Furnessville, in the Indiana dunes. In my 20 years of study of the Indiana dunes I have many times watched the destruction of forests by sand burial. But the plants do not yield supinely. Many species, such as the oaks and pines, give up very quickly, but others, such as the cottonwood, various willows, wild grape, and dogwood, display an aston-

ishing resistance, growing up and up as the sand advances over them, and often succeeding in keeping pace with the advance of the sand. The power to respond in such a way depends upon the possession of a capacity for the rapid extension of stems and roots; in such plants new roots develop freely from the buried stems. Even such a lowly plant as the common horsetail can extend its stems sufficiently fast to keep above a rapidly advancing dune. Some species can even start on a moving sand dune and flourish where all life conditions seem impossible. The average visitor to a moving dune would say that such a place is bare of life; not so a botanist, who finds small and scattering plants in almost every situation. To almost every condition, no matter how severe, some plants are found adapted.

Now, in closing, I believe that there is one particular reason why, as a student of the dunes for 20 years, and a student during that time of dunes in all parts of the world, I can make a special plea for the preservation of these particular dunes as a national park. There is only one Yellowstone Park in this or any other country, and it we have well conserved. There is only one such Crater Lake as we have set aside. There is only one such place as the Mesa Verde, which has been set aside, and there is only one such canyon as that of the Colorado, which is likely to be made a national park. It is well known that there are many dunes in the world, and many Americans, even, who know nothing of the marvelous dunes of Lake Michigan, have heard about the relatively insignificant dunes of Germany, France, and Belgium, or those of our own Cape Cod or Cape Henry. It is not so well known as it should be that the dunes of Lake Michigan are much the grandest in the entire world. Not necessarily the highest, though some of them reach up 400 feet and more above the lake, but more than any other anywhere, our dunes show magnificent and contrasting types of plant life, everything from the bare dunes to magnificent primeval forests. No other dunes than ours show such bewildering displays of dune movement and struggle for existence, such labyrinths of motion, form, and life; just because its uniqueness preserved the Yellowstone—there are no such geysers elsewhere, so should their uniqueness preserve our dunes, for they are without a parallel. I thank you. [Applause.]

ALDO LEOPOLD

The Last Stand of the Wilderness

(1926)

How many of those whole-hearted con-servationists who berate the past genera-tion for its short-sightedness in the use of natural resources have stopped to ask themselves for what new evils the next generation will berate us?

Has it ever occurred to us that we may unknowingly be just as short-sighted as our forefathers in assuming certain things to be inexhaustible, and becoming conscious of our error only after they have practically disappeared?

Today it is hard for us to understand why our prodigious waste of standing tim-ber was allowed to go on—why the exhaus-tion of the supply was not earlier foreseen. Some even impute to the wasters a certain moral turpitude. We forget that for many generations the standing timber of Amer-ica was in fact an encumbrance or even an enemy, and that the nation was simply unconscious of the possibility of its becom-ing exhausted. In fact, our tendency is not

From *American Forests and Forest Life*, October 1925, 599–604.

to call things resources until the supply runs short. When the end of the supply is in sight we "discover" that the thing is valuable.

This has been true of the latest natu-ral resource to be "discovered," namely the group of things collectively called Outdoor Recreation. We had to develop tenements and tired business-men before Outdoor Recreation was recognized as a category of human needs, though the use of the out-doors for recreational purposes is as old as the race itself. This "discovery" that we need a national policy on Outdoor Rec-reation is in fact so new that the ink has barely dried on its birth certificate. And, as usual, we are becoming conscious of thou-sands of wasteful errors in the past han-dling of recreational resources which an earlier discovery might have avoided.

I submit that this endless series of more or less postmortem discoveries is getting rather tedious. I for one am piqued in my sense of national pride. Cannot we for once foresee and provide? Must it always be hindsight, followed by hurried educational work, laborious legislative campaigns, and then only partially effective action at huge expense? Cannot we for once use foresight, and provide for our needs in an orderly, ample, correlated, economical fashion? The next resource, the exhaustion of which is due for "discovery," is the wilderness. The purpose of this article is to show why the wilderness is valuable, how close it is to exhaustion and why, and what can be done about it.

Wild places are the rock-bottom foundations of a good many different kinds of outdoor play, including pack and canoe trips in which hunting, fishing, or just exploring may furnish the flavoring matter. By "wild places" I mean wild regions big enough to absorb the average man's two weeks' vacation without getting him tangled up in his own back track. I also mean big areas wild enough to be free from motor roads, summer cottages, launches, or other manifestations of gasoline. Driving a pack train across or along a graded highway is distinctly not a pack trip—it is merely exercise, with about the same flavor as lifting dumbbells. Neither is canoeing in the wake of a motor launch or down a lane of summer cottages a canoe trip. That is paddling—and the supply is unlimited.

Is the opportunity for wilderness trips valuable? Let us apply the test of the market price. Any number of well-to-do sportsmen are paying from $3,000 to $10,000 for a single big-game trip to the wilderness regions of British Columbia, Alaska, Mexico, Africa and Siberia. It is worth that to them. Now how about the fellow who has the same tastes for wilderness travel but a lesser pocketbook, and who probably has more real need of recreation? He simply has to do without, subsisting as best he can

on polite trips to summer resorts and dude ranches. Why? Because the old wilderness hunting grounds, formerly within his reach, no longer exist, having been opened up by motor roads.

Right here I had better explain that motor roads, cottages, and launches do not necessarily destroy hunting and fishing, but they destroy the wilderness, which to certain tastes is quite as important.

Neither do I imply that motors, cottages, summer resorts, and dude ranches are not in themselves highly valuable recreational assets. Obviously they are. Only they are a different *kind* of recreation. We need to preserve as many different kinds as we possibly can. The civilized kinds tend to preserve themselves through the automatic operation of economic laws. But wilderness travel is a kind that tends to disappear under the automatic operation of economic laws, just as the site for a city park tends to disappear with the growth of a city. Unlike the city park, however, the wilderness cannot be re-created when the need for it is determined by hindsight. The need for it must be determined by foresight, and the necessary areas segregated and preserved. Wilderness is the one kind of playground which mankind cannot build to order.

Since the pilgrims landed, the supply of wilderness has always been unlimited. Now, of a sudden, the end is in sight. The really wild places within reach of the centers of population are going or gone. As a nation, however, we are so accustomed to a plentiful supply that we are *unconscious* of what the disappearance of wild places would mean, just as we are unconscious of what the disappearance of winds or sunsets would mean. The opportunity to disappear into the tall uncut has existed so long that we unconsciously assume it, like the wind and sunset, to be one of the fixed facts of Nature. And who can measure the influence of these "fixed facts of Nature" on the national character? In all the category of outdoor vocations and outdoor sports there is not one, save only the tilling of the soil, that bends and molds the human character like wilderness travel. Shall this fundamental instrument for building citizens be allowed to disappear from America, simply because we lack the vision to see its value? Would we rather have the few paltry dollars that could be extracted from our remaining wild places than the human values they can render in their wild condition?

A national policy for the establishment of wilderness recreation grounds would in some instances be easy to put into operation if we act at once. The National Forests and Parks still contain a few splendid areas of relatively low value for other purposes, which could be readily segregated as roadless playgrounds. Wilderness areas in the National Forests would serve especially the wilderness-hunter, since hunting is not and should not be allowed in the Parks. On the other hand, wilderness areas in the National Parks would serve all kinds of wilderness-lovers except the hunter. In general, I believe that both the Forest Service and the Park Service would be receptive to the wilderness idea, but neither can be expected to execute it with the vigor and dispatch necessary to save the situation, unless they can point to a definite crystallized public demand for such action. The public being still largely unconscious that the end of the wild places is in sight, there is as yet no articulate public expression for or against the wilderness plan. Meanwhile the remaining wild areas in both the For-

ests and Parks are being pushed back by road construction at a very rapid rate, —so rapid that unless something is done, the large areas of wilderness will mostly disappear within the next decade.

This paper is a plea for a definite expression of public opinion on the question of whether a system of wilderness areas should be established in our public Forests and Parks. Let me illustrate what I mean by saying that administrative officers cannot effectively execute a wilderness policy without the help of a definite public demand. District Forester Frank C. W. Pooler has already tentatively designated the headwaters of the Gila River, in the Gila National Forest, New Mexico, as a wilderness area. It is the last roadless area of any size in the Southwest containing all the best types of mountain wild life and scenery, and by reason of its exceedingly broken topography is the logical location for a wilderness playground. It is Mr. Pooler's belief that the Forest Service should withhold extending its road system into the Gila Wilderness, and should withhold granting permits for summer homes in it, until the whole wilderness idea has had an opportunity to crystallize into a definite policy, under which a final plan for handling the Gila Wilderness can be laid down.

Now suppose that a timber operator were to apply to build a railroad into this area thus tentatively reserved for wilderness purposes. Suppose the District Forester were to reply: "No. This area is being held for public recreation as a wilderness hunting ground." The lumber operator answers: "I haven't heard of the public wanting wilderness hunting grounds. Where is this public, and just what does it want?"

Obviously, unless there existed some clear expression of public need, and a definite official policy for meeting it, the District Forester's position would be untenable, no matter how certain he felt that it was right. The point is that governmental policies cannot be actually applied without many decisions by administrative officers involving the adjustment of conflicting interests. In such conflicts individual or economic interests may always be counted upon to be articulate. Group or public interests must likewise be made articulate, else they place the government executive in the thankless and often untenable position of being at once judge of the conflict and counsel for an absentee. The public interest must "speak up or lose out." The dangers of delay in formulating a national policy for the establishment of wilderness recreation grounds are strongly emphasized in the present situation of the Lake States. In the last few years many people have begun to realize that wilderness canoe trips are about to become a thing of the past in the Lake States, because of the extension of tourist roads and summer resorts into the remnants of wild country.

The proximity of the Lake States to the centers of population in the Middle West, and the fact that canoe-travel is a distinctive type of wilderness life not to be found elsewhere south of the Canadian border except in Maine, adds to the vital need for such a project.

But what to do about it is a difficult problem. The national land holdings consist of three little National Forests, The Superior, Minnesota, and Michigan. Their combined area is woefully inadequate. Moreover, they are more or less riddled with private holdings which, until eliminated by land exchanges, constitute serious obstacles to any and all future plans for developing the full public value of the Forests. The Isaac Walton League and the Superior National Forest Recreation Association, with a foresight for which they deserve much credit, have insisted that at least one wilderness area be established in the Lake States on these national lands. But this is easier said than done. An incredible number of complications and obstacles, too intricate to be here discussed, arise from the fact that the wilderness idea was born after, rather than before, the normal course of commercial development had begun. The existence of these complications is nobody's fault. But it will be everybody's fault if they do not serve as a warning against delaying the immediate inauguration of a comprehensive system of wilderness areas in the West, where there is still a relatively unimpeded field for action.

A start toward such a system has already been made at the initiative of the Forest Service. The hinterland around Jackson Hole, including the Grand Tetons and Two-Ocean Pass, are entered as "roadless" in the recreational plans for the future. Likewise, that part of the Absoraka Forest between Boulder Creek and Yellowstone Park, the Middle Fork of the Salmon River in Central Idaho, and parts of the Clearwater country in Montana are so classified. The Gila area in New Mexico has been already mentioned. What now seems to me important is for the government to undertake and the public to support the establishment of similar areas in every state that still contains National Forest or Park lands suitable for wilderness purposes.

The big thing that stands in the way of such a program is the well-nigh universal assumption that advance action is unnecessary. "Why, this area never will be opened up!" That was said ten years ago about many an area that has since been broken up. I know of five in the Southwest alone. It is being said today, and unless we clearly realize the danger, it will continue to be said until the chances for adequate action are gone.

Let us now consider some of the practical details of how the proposed system of wilderness areas should he administered. It is, for instance, a moot question whether regulated timber cutting should be allowed in them. If the conditions are such that the cuttings would leave motor roads in their wake, I would say "no." But in the Lake States much logging can be done over the lakes, without any trunk roads, so that it seems to me possible, by skillful planning, permanently to use much of the remaining wild country for both wilderness recreation and timber production without large sacrifice of either use.

Another question is that of fire. Obviously the construction of trails, phone lines, and towers necessary for fire control must be not only allowed but encouraged. But how about roads? Wherever the opponents of the idea can argue that unless the country is opened up it will burn up, there is no chance for the wilderness. Let us take the Gila as an example. I think it can be confidently asserted that on the Gila, extension of roads is not necessary for good fire protection. The Forest Service, with its system of lookouts, telephone lines and trails, is successfully handling the fires, even during the bad years. The percentage of lightning as compared with man-caused fires on the Gila is very high (65 per cent lightning; 35 per cent man-caused). As a

rule the greater the percentage of lightning fires, the more serious is the handicap of inaccessibility. The reason for this is that man-caused fires are usually increased by building roads and letting in more transients, whereas lightning fires remain the same. Therefore a heavy lightning region like the Gila ought to be a severe test of the practicability of controlling fires in roadless areas. As already stated, that test has been thus far successful.

I do not imply, however, that this one case disposes of the argument. The game of fire-control is too complicated to be comprehended in "rules of thumb." There may be regions here and there where fire control is impossible without roads. If so, we must have roads in such regions, wilderness or no wilderness. But there may with equal likelihood be other regions where the reverse is true. The whole fire question in its relation to the wilderness plan is one of skill in selecting and administering each particular area. Such skill is already available among the forest officers who have devoted years of study to fire control as well as a dozen other related forest problems.

The acceptance of the idea of wilderness areas entails, I admit, a growth in the original conception of National Forests. The original purposes were timber production and watershed protection, and these are and must always remain the primary purposes. But the whole subsequent history of these Forests has been a history of the appearance and growth of new uses, which, when skillfully adjusted to the primary uses and to each other, were one by one provided for and the net public benefit correspondingly increased. Public recreation was one of these. When the forests were first established, recreation did not exist in the minds of either the foresters or the public as an important use of the public Forests. Today it has been added to timber production and watershed protection as an important additional public service. It has been proven that skillful administration can provide for both in the same system of Forests without material sacrifice of either.

One wilderness area could, I firmly believe, be fitted into the National Forests of each State without material sacrifice of other kinds of playgrounds or other kinds of uses. Additional wilderness areas could, it seems to me, be fitted into the various National Parks. As far as I can see there would usually be necessary neither new costs nor new laws nor new work—simply a well-pondered administrative decision delimiting the areas, and in such areas establishing a permanent "closed season" on roads, cottages, or other developments inimical to wilderness use.

To urge that wilderness playgrounds are unnecessary because ample forest playgrounds of other kinds are already being established is just as idle as to urge that there is no need for public tennis courts because there are already public golf links. The two things represent differing needs of different people, each entitled to recognition in due proportion to their numbers and importance. The people in need of wilderness areas are numerous, and the preservation of their particular kind of contact with Mother Earth is a national problem.

The National Conference on Outdoor Recreation is the official agency for extending recognition to new needs of this kind. Through the generosity of the Laura Spelman Rockefeller Memorial a joint committee of two member organizations, the American Forestry Association and the National Parks Association, has received a grant and a field study of the recreational values of Federal lands is under way. This committee will give particular attention to the need of a wilderness policy. If any individual or group believe in a wilderness idea, or have any one place where they believe it should be applied, now is the time to make known their belief.

PAUL B. RIIS

Ecological Garden and Arboretum at the University of Wisconsin

(1937)

*Man sees in each of the millions of living forms
with which the earth is teeming, the action
of many of the laws which are operating in
himself; and has learned to a great extent his
welfare is dependent on these seemingly insignificant relations; that in ways undreamed of
a century ago they affect human progress.*

—Clarence Moores Weed

*He who knows what sweets and virtues are
in the ground, the waters, the plants, the
heavens, and how to come at these enchant-
ments, is the rich and royal man.*

—Ralph Waldo Emerson

PART I
A LAST CENTURY IDYLL

Fair and fruitful, Wisconsin ranks high
among the best of the agricultural states
in the union. Abundantly blessed with
fertile soils, productive valleys, matchless

From *Parks & Recreation* 20, no. 8 (April 1937): 382–89,
and no. 9 (May 1937): 451–57.

lakes, forested ridges, rolling hills and
prairies, a land attractively warm with
promises, it held out cordial welcome
to thrifty pioneers, who were happy to
settle amid these pleasant surroundings
and till their fruitful soil. Its present day,
well-ordered civic and industrial life are
eloquent testimonials of splendid achievements, of hopes realized. Well balanced
and rich stores of natural resources, rest-
ing upon a solid foundation laid in the
mist of ages, millions of years ago, abundantly contributed to inevitable success.
Nature patiently continued her persistent
labors through infinite aeons, gently applying those impelling forces, that culmi-
nated in this favored land, Wisconsin, as
pioneers found it a hundred years ago.

Those curious to pierce the veil of mystery shrouding those years of long ago,
seem to glimpse primeval Wisconsin as
a small, granite island, steadily emerging
from an ancient sea. Mountains lined its
shores, which yielded slowly and inexorably
to the forces of erosion and a continental
icesheet, leveling them and filling the val-

leys and lowlands with drift. In due time, plant life became established thereon and through its well-known processes, tediously built up the fertile soils of today.

Others interpret Wisconsin's earliest history from its geological records somewhat differently. They point to the presence of a large, central mass of Archaean rocks in the northern part of the state as the foundation, and stumps of former mountains which were gradually reduced by erosion to near-base level. This wearing process finally resulted in a peneplain that contained few hills and upward accents to relieve its flatly undulating surface. Still later, this plain, in turn, became submerged and then elevated through the slow process of sedimentation during the Paleozoic. In this manner Wisconsin assumed the rough outline and ground conformation, which later glacial and erosional action sculptured and refined into its present mature topography. And, lastly, the Wisconsin Drift Sheet came along and carved the Rock River Drainage, in which the Arboretum, the University, Madison and Dane County are situated. Dane County in itself is of much geological interest; its outstanding feature is that of four large lakes of transcending beauty—Mendota, Monona, Wingra and Waubesa. Distinctive morainic character marks the topography much emphasized by typically rounded drift hills. Its streams, marshes, lakes and geological formations clearly reveal the path of glacial forces. Crystaline erratics of gneiss, granite, diorite, red porphyry and felsite, and gneissoid syenite are scattered everywhere. Adjoining counties to the north and west, also, contain superlative examples of erosion and glaciation, as those of Devils Lake, the Baraboo Bluffs, the Wisconsin Dells and the unglaciated Driftless area to the west.

The Arboretum and ecological garden have been established on the east, west and south shores of Lake Wingra, a body of water now of about a hundred acres, or one-fourth of its former area; a fact, which in itself may serve as a yardstick of time for the maturity of local drainages. Deep layers of peat, remnants of former extensive tamarack swamps, also marl, have filled this lake to its present level, the orderly progress of ultimate maturity assured in the mass presence of decaying cattail and moontail, further hastened by erosional sedimentation.

Originally, Dane County was covered by oak-hickory forests, interspersed with small prairies, with bur-oak savannas or "oak openings" and with tamarack swamps. The "oak openings" marked the transition from prairie to forest, stimulated and facilitated early agriculture; clearings, drainage and their attending fires wrought environmental changes, influencing its present flora and fauna. When the first settlers arrived a hundred years ago, native grasses covered the prairies in billowing rhythm; grasses, whose mature color intensify in the fall, vied with the glory of the autumn foliage of trees. Inured as they were to fire and drought they could not withstand hard grazing and plowing. Now, these native grasses are rare and all but extinct, and their places filled with their exotic successor, blue grass, which will ever remain a stranger, out of step with the climate and, hence, caught yearly by fall frosts in a green, rather than a ripened condition. The once rich mesophytic flora has fared similarly. Fires and cultivation have destroyed much of its native habitats and exterminated many species until today, there are mere fragments of their former number and species left.

Wingra Marsh, formerly a tamarack forest, with its understory of leatherleaf, bog rosemary, poison sumach, dwarf birch, chokecherry, marsh ferns, pitcher plants, clintonias, orchids, and sphagnum moss today bears only grasses, rushes, weeds, willows and dogwood. Repeated burning, grazing and mowing have destroyed the tamarack forests and replaced it with hay-meadow species. The lake too, has shared in this general decline. Formerly a rice lake, and a waterfowl paradise, its future for ducks and geese looks uncertain. Carp supposedly accounted for the rice, and at no time since its original destruction has the lake been attractive to ducks. Ten years ago its waters were still clear enough for fly-fishing. Since that time they have become more roiled and muddy and the larger game fish scarcer, presumably due to the increase of carp.

The Arboretum covers approximately eight hundred acres. Two spots of marsh still retain nearly their full assortment of native vegetation. Much of the area has been seriously disturbed, and some marsh burned so deeply, that the native plant life has been exterminated and replaced by nettles. These nettle fields are biological deserts and occur frequently on southern Wisconsin peats as the infallible results of severe burning. Recurring fires and drought, also have left telling marks in the oak forest and disturbed its orderly successions. White oak, for example, has been much reduced through fire damage and replaced by black oak and popple. Inroads of civilization and destructive agriculture have not only affected the original composition of flora and fauna, but, also, have changed the capacity of the soil. Some of these soil changes are temporary, others permanent. Human agencies, in their blind conflict with natural forces are, also, responsible for the modification of the landscapes. This is strikingly exemplified in certain floral transformations situated between the Arboretum and Madison, less than a mile away. Here, a single glance encompasses sterile patches poisoned by economic waste, ascendingly flanked by stinging nettles and brambles. These in turn are bordered with thickets of dogwood, willow and aspen and adjoined by towering oak.

THE ECOLOGICAL GARDEN AS A RESEARCH PROJECT

The injury to prodigality leads to this, that he who will not economize, will have to agonize. —*Confucius*

Conservationists have been profoundly impressed with the steady vanishing and, also, the dwarfing of our native flora and fauna. They feel real concern in the sustained dwindling of a former richly diversified wildlife, today perhaps most discernible in mass replacement of choice plant life with lowly weeds. They rightfully sense in the decline of wildlife resources, a dilution and decline of a former abundance and richness of human existence. Meager crops and undernourishment inexorably follow soil impoverishment; introduction of exotics succeed vanishing and extinct species, exotics that impair native beauty and lower national ideals. Conservationists view with alarm the consistent increase of new deserts and note apprehensively, "that the tools of civilization are too potent and destructive and out of time and rhythm with the natural process of rebuilding."

When the first settlers arrived in Dane County they found soil, flora and fauna in perfect balance. Virgin soils supported a hardy and well-rounded-out plant life, which in turn sustained a balanced fauna, typical of the country and its environmental influences. Together, soil, flora and fauna formed an interdependent, organic structure, in which the smallest, related unit contributed its unconscious part toward that essential balance, which made life possible for all. Into this earthly paradise stepped man, the supreme creature; a paradise apparently to his way of thinking, created for his especial benefit. Settled agriculture supported his growing people and industries. He multiplied and filled the land, until the population grew into millions. The land was good to him, yet, with that same deadly regularity of older cultures in other lands, he lowered its productivity for his own enrichment; he sapped the soil of its stores of fertility with a speed beyond the pace of natural or artificial replacement. In geological reckoning of time, things happened with the suddenness of catastrophies. Wholesale and destructive changes of native environment extirpated some species, and reduced others to pitiful remnants. Weeds, barrenness and sterility followed in the wake of fires; erosion ravaged the stripped land; hectic cultivation impaired soil productivity. Cultural attainments seemed impotent to stem the ebb of abundance, the gradual loss of soil fertility and with it the basic richness of life. The reward is found in "Culture Deserts" instead of well-ordered "Culture Steppes."

The University of Wisconsin has sensed the impotence and futility of purely cultural equipment to adequately, and alone, cope successfully with the complexities of Nature's basic laws and with ecology in its intricate mutual relations that exist between organisms and their environment; laws that fundamentally support the complete structure of all life. The University has come to realize that cultural knowledge alone is insufficient to deal intelligently with this major problem and touches but lightly and superficially, if not one-sidedly, on the existing relationship between plants, animals, soils and man. Present continued methods of land use indicate a lack of appreciation of soil as a precious heritage, easily dissipated. Erosional deserts in many forms, increasing soil sterility and the avoidable losses from present agricultural practices, chargeable to an unplanning civilization, are a challenge to the University that must be met with changes in instruction to fit its students to adapt agricultural methods to a cooperative, harmonious land use. It finds itself faced with the problem of supplementing cultural theorems with a demonstration area that its visual land history and actual contact with soil, will impart both an intelligent and practical knowledge and, also, enable the students to personally analyze complexities responsible for that marvelously adjusted balance and harmony that existed in Dane County and Wisconsin a hundred years ago. Faculty and students in natural history have, in the ecological garden, a practical outdoor laboratory for botany, zoology, entomology, limnology, game management and landscape gardening.

Cultural students in Nature History are handicapped without such a laboratory and because of it, are rarely able to

Native Plant Garden, designed by Darrel Morrison, University of Wisconsin, Madison. (Photograph by Darrel Morrison.)

practically understand the things all about them or are able to explain their places in the scheme of things and to isolate their specific functions; they are not intellectually equipped to see what is taking place under their own eyes. The Ecological Garden supplies this deficiency and will give cultural interpretation of the common and everyday things they see, but do not understand. This practical knowledge will enable them to appreciate harmonious land use that they may constructively cooperate with plants, animals, soils and man. Thus equipped, these new disciples of intelligent land use will spread the good gospel in their respective fields of labor, throughout the land, to the end that our growing "Cultural Deserts" will diminish in size and numbers, their places filled with "Cultural Steppes" in acceptance of native values as the source for the fullness of life. The Ecological Garden is the answer to the chal-

lenge, as a research project rather than a social or recreational enterprise, dedicated to the reconstruction of a fragment of early Wisconsin rather than a boarding place for alien plant life.

Unlike other arboreta, attempting to portray native and exotic plant life in ecological, systematic and structural order, Madison will devote practically all of its garden to ecological and geographic groups of Wisconsin. This policy finds inspiration in plant behavior itself, since plant life removed from natural environment to alien soils rarely develops its typical characters and, hence, much of its value is lost. Equally unsatisfactory are other attempts to show the inter-relation of plants in their associations, and this fact has prompted the management to the conclusion that it can serve its own purpose and science best and more constructively by a sincere portrayal of the native Wisconsin flora. To attain this end consistently, the groundwork has been laid to reconstruct the native landscape as a basic approach to all related problems to follow. This procedure avoids and removes every semblance of affectation and of man dominance and in its place accepts in all humility nature's own concepts, and her guidance.

Topography and ground cover favor reconstruction of the more valuable forest, marshland and prairie types of Wisconsin's original animal and plant communities. It is, however, to be expected, that it will take fifty years for the plantings to fill in their respective places to again represent a typical portion of the original landscape of the state, and more significantly that of Dane County in its earliest days. Those privileged to view the matured project will have the rare opportunity to glimpse the past glory of Wisconsin's native landscape, as originally evolved by natural forces, since those dark days of the last glacial period from 10–20,000 years ago. Thus, again robed in its original attire the ecological garden will inspire literature and art, biology and agriculture, geography and the sciences and men professionally engaged in land uses. It will stimulate professional training through further research and lead to a more profound study of plants, insects, birds, mammals, aquatic life and soil in their little understood inter-relations. Its scenic, archaeologic, geologic and bionomic moods and tenses will constitute a living library as a visual teaching aid toward a true perspective of life.

Effigy mounds on the Arboretum grounds link the present more intimately with a remoter past and the cultures of a vanished race. These mounds are qualified endorsements and significant of the native landscape, imparting thereto much archaeological interest. Their presence here, as elsewhere in Wisconsin, suggest that the region had age-old attractions for human abode. Menomenee Indians of a more recent culture named it Weese-coh-seh, "a good place to live." The French pronounced this Quise-con-sen, which through other modifications first became Quisconsin and then the present Wisconsin. The University of Wisconsin, through research work in its Arboretum, hopes to be helpful in perpetuating the qualities of its native appellative, that the state may continue forever as "a good place to live."

Administration of the Arboretum is in the hands of an able faculty committee, whose members are specialists in their chosen lines. It is composed of the following: Prof. E. M. Gilbert, chairman; Prof. G. W. Longenecker, director; Prof. Aldo Leopold, research director.

PART II
RESTORATION OF THE NATIVE FLORA

In this world of plants, which, with its magician, chlorophyll, conjuring with sunbeams, is ceaselessly at work bringing life out of death, —in this quiet vegetable world, we may find the elementary principles of all life in almost visible operation. —John Fiske

Browsing through the 1913 edition of Britton and Brown's excellent three-volume work, Illustrated Flora of the Northern United States, Canada and the British Possessions, the botany student is struck with such recurring remarks on plant nativities, as, "Troublesome weed, naturalized, from Europe . . . Native of Europe or Asia . . .

Fugitive from Europe, etc." These notations naturally create the impression that the native flora has been greatly disturbed throughout North America at least. A check-up confirms this and lays bare the startling truth that 99% of the native flora has been replaced by exotics.

Attempts, therefore, by the University of Wisconsin to restore the state's native flora within the Arboretum, appears to be a task of some magnitude. In the absence of its original plant life, the University finds guidance in making sincere replacement through meager records of former flora and extant species, and, also, an island in Lake Wingra, protectively situated, which contains a nearly unspoiled remnant of typical, native plant life. Its source of information is further supplemented by well preserved pollen grains, uncovered from the deep layers of sphagnum moss which compose the peat beds of former tamarack swamps. These pollen grains at once reveal both the kind and abundance of post-glacial plant life.

It, however, becomes necessary to make preliminary and specific studies of the soil beforehand, in order to determine its suitability. The soil is no longer what it was. During the comparatively short period of man's habitation, it has been unnecessarily exploited and mined out and seemingly is unsuited now to receive its original plant life. These soil changes are not entirely incidental to economic use. Some of them are traceable to severe burning; fire specifically is responsible for mixed stands of oak and, in its severer forms, for the large patches of stinging nettles. As a monotype, these nettles form biological deserts; nothing subsists on them and they have no value as food or cover. Their mission is that of soil builders, requiring about three years

to prepare for higher species. In the light of this knowledge, the refusal of Arboretum neighbors to assist in putting out a fire they themselves had started to get rid of the nettles, seems amusing, since in the natural order of things these lowly plants were forced to start all over again from the beginning. The fire prolonged their stay rather than curtailed it.

Restoration of soil fertility by natural means is a slow process on burned peat. Nettles usually cover severe burns with its pioneer plant growth, just as ragweed and smartweed form the first stage of cultivated fields. A three year tenure of these weeds usually suffices to improve the soil sufficiently for the succeeding second stage of milkweed, asters, golden rod and Joe Pye weed. These, too, require about three years to prepare the soil for their successors, the grasses. The dominant plant life is reached in the fourth stage, composed of shrubs, as those of dogwood, aspen and willows. Occasionally, for reasons now unknown, nature makes a short cut and eliminates stages one, two and three and in their places, covers the barren ground with black raspberries, aspen and willows. In the total or near absence of parent trees and seed-bearing brambles, the presence of dense stands of above species are a revelation of constancy and thoroughness of nature's agents in the dispersal of seeds.

Physiographically, the Arboretum is featured with rolling prairie land, copious springs, brooks, marshes, lagoons, oak forests and a lake. Detail drawings indicate widely varying habitats, adapted to a rich, native flora, harmoniously grouped within associated environment. There are plants for water and bog gardens, for pools and islands, lagoons and marshes, for open marsh islands and tamarack swamps, for grasslands and Wisconsin prairies, for woodlands and forests. There will be stands of native trees, with natural associations, oak, red and hard maple, red and white pine, white spruce, hemlock, nut trees, birch, willows, crab-apples and hawthorns.

The central feature of the Arboretum is the prairie basin, a large tract of undulating grassland, that rises imperceptibly into ascending upland and gentle hills. Its commanding expanse will be the focal point of the proposed development into a reconstructed Wisconsin prairie. Its present stands of exotic grasses will be replaced with the former native species, the tall prairie bluestem, *Andropogon,* which, it is hoped, will eventually crowd out the exotics and pave the way for other associated prairie species. Plantings made of this species during the spring of 1936 suffered greatly during the ensuing heat and drought of that year. Undaunted, the management will continue other plantings under more favorable conditions. The slopes surrounding the prairie basin, will be planted to stands of various native trees, and oak openings will again form the transition from prairie to forest. There will be plantings of Norway pine, interspersed with under-plantings of aspen, white birch and hemlock. Dry knolls, rising above the floor of the interior marsh, will be planted to white birch and creeping juniper. A plot of native willows form an interesting exhibit near the west entrance. A tamarack forest will be planted in its former habitat, the peat beds of the interior marsh. Its modification from former expanse and outline is a natural one, and a harmonious coordination with the bogs, lagoons and pools established for the wildlife reserve.

A compromise planting of horticultural varieties of shrubs, trees and evergreens has been established near the prairie as an exhibit of interest and guidance to those engaged in the beautification of home grounds. Adjacent thereto, is an indispensible nursery, depended upon to furnish a wealth of the material necessary to plant the Arboretum. Existing roads will be screened out to soften their utilitarian aspect into that of rural lanes. Shrub thickets and tangles of vines, eventually, will completely cover all fences, placed against trespass and straying dogs; these thickets to provide native food and cover for the resident faunal wildlife. Lagoons and waterways have been designed as moats and supplementary protective features against undesired trespass. To more completely and effectively protect more vulnerable exhibits, several tourist protected areas have been set aside and restricted to guided parties only. Yet, a complete urban expression of welcome manifests itself in the presence of two modest picnic areas, invitingly furnished with camp ovens and small shelters.

RECONSTRUCTION OF WILDLIFE HABITATS

Given, then, the knowledge and the desire, this idea of controlled wild culture or "management" can be applied not only to quail and trout, but to any living thing from bloodroots to Bell's vireos. A rare bird or flower need remain no rarer than the people willing to venture their skill in building it a habitat.
—Aldo Leopold

Research within the Arboretum, also, interests itself constructively with its faunal wildlife. The range composition within its boundaries is typical of the region, and also shows vivid economic scars. Hence, the management has no undue advantages and is obliged to begin from scratch. It is, however, most fortunate in its personnel and in having the services of an outstanding research director and wild life technician, Aldo Leopold, to guide its destinies. Contained in the Arboretum area are habitat opportunities for varied wild life, the exploitation of which will be of international interest. Naturally, the methods of strengthening bruised environment for occupation by specific species, solution of problems with interlocking interests, through research, assembling of basic facts on seasonal requirements of food and cover, vulnerability to competition and predation and carrying capacity of conditioned ranges, will be looked for with general interest. But the management intends to go further and demonstrate the possibility of increasing both number of species and carrying capacity within a given range through a directly applied technique. It is fully aware of the fact, that artificial propagation of wildlife in its early stages is fraught with liabilities. Likewise, it appreciates that artificial remedies in game questions are expensive, ecologically and otherwise. To this end, several projects of more than passing interest are moving forward simultaneously. These projects introduce planned construction for specific faunal purposes. Dredging operations in the marl marsh, located in the easterly part of the Arboretum, are now well under way. This project contemplates deliberate construction of this marsh into a shorebird beach, an innovation never before attempted. When completed, ornithologists will have opportunity to study shorebirds throughout the open season, within walking distance of the city.

A heron rookery will also be attempted. This undertaking, without a resident nucleus, is more difficult than it may appear and calls for not only ingenuity in planning, but also infinite patience. The exhibit is needed to round out the typical native bird life and to widen the scope of the outdoor laboratory. Carp in Lake Wingra, as pointed out before, are considered a menace to both floral and faunal species. The lake now is practically spoiled as a waterfowl lake, assumedly because of the elimination of the native food by carp. In Germany, this fish is approved of and considered desirable. The knowledge of what environmental influences contribute to its status of acceptability there would be of great interest to American anglers. The University, therefore, hopes to make a special research project of the carp in Lake Wingra for the purpose of unraveling the causes of deterioration of plant and fish life.

Experiments at the Arboretum have conclusively shown that the weeds and grasses of the marsh and upland, which ordinarily are suitable to hold quail and pheasants, were of little value as cover during heavy snows. Ecologically there seems to exist a general principle that the intermediate stages of plant growth contain the richest plant and animal features of interest to man. As seen, stage one, —nettles, ragweed and smartweed, also, stage two, —asters, Joe Pye weed, golden rod and milkweed, were devoid of game during the heavy snows of 1935–1936. On the other hand, the carrying capacity of stages three and four, —weeds, grass, dogwood, willow, and aspen, was ten times greater than that of stages one and two. The answer thereto is found in the supporting shrubs, that supplied cover and kept open the food below and in consequence, held both quail and pheasants throughout the severe winter.

The University of Wisconsin is striving in the sincere application of biological science to biological problems and proceeds to uncover facts, that it may be in a position to train the students professionally. It seeks to avoid too much conservation with its infallible effacing of esthetic values and, instead, evolves and tests and measures every environmental control and factor necessary for a balanced integration of utility and beauty. It aims to combine esthetic, scientific and economic interest as the approach and goal for professional training, and uses uncovered facts, that they may be applied in man's relation to land and soil with its diverse problems of soil maintenance, forestry, water resources and wildlife. Thus, the University hopes that its fragmentary findings and its research projects will form the beginning for an integrated program of nation-wide action toward a return to naturalism.

Epilogue

By teaching people to see the common things you will add to their joy in living.
—O. C. Simonds, "Open Your Eyes" (1913)

This collection of writings about the native landscape is by no means complete. In making my selection, I strove to represent a diversity of ideas and people who advocated for greater appreciation, understanding, and conservation of our native landscape heritage in North America. Some of the ideas express biases and attitudes prevalent in the nineteenth and early twentieth centuries, but many are equally relevant today. In this closing section, I want to reflect briefly on the key themes and offer thoughts for the future.

Many of the authors included in *The Native Landscape Reader* regarded our native landscape as something to celebrate, to respect, and as Liberty Hyde Bailey proposed in *The Outlook to Nature*, "as one of the means of restoring the proper balance and proportion in our lives." Psychologists have repeatedly confirmed the value of nature to our mental and physical well-being; time spent in natural settings can reduce stress and restore cognitive function. In *The Experience of Nature: A Psychological Perspective* (1989), Rachel Kaplan and Stephen Kaplan demonstrate the effect of nature—from small fragments near the places people live and work to wilderness tracts likes those visited on vacation—in providing mental and physical enjoyment, reducing stress levels and fatigue, and improving health and well-being. In more recent articles, they have emphasized the role of nature in contributing to people's reasonableness and ability to function in an often confusing world.[1] Other researchers have documented the role of nature—views, plantings of trees, and nearby pockets of natural surroundings—in patient recovery in hospitals, in reducing crime, aggression, and violence in public housing blocs, and in encouraging neighborliness and community pride.[2] Participating in nature-based activities—gardening as well as volunteering in environmental stewardship programs—has

Students in Nichols Arboretum, Ann Arbor, Mich. (Photograph by Robert E. Grese.)

been shown to have tangible restorative benefits.[3]

Connecting people to nature is seen as valuable for all ages, but it is regarded as particularly critical for young children and adolescents. Again, this concern is not new. Several of the authors included in this volume wrote eloquently about the need for children in cities to have access to nature. H. W. S. Cleveland, for example, in "Influence of Parks on the Character of Children," framed the issue as one of social justice, noting that tenement children were denied exposure to scenes of natural beauty. In 1909, O. C. Simonds proposed that the Illinois Out-Door Improvement Association champion the incorporation of nature study in the curriculum for children in the state of Illinois.[4] The loss within his lifetime of places that had shaped his own love of nature and had led him to a career in landscape gardening motivated his desire to preserve or create such places for others.[5] "I wish that all the children of the present day," Simonds once told an audience, "as well as their fathers and mothers, could have some place to go where they could sit quietly and enjoy nature, or where they could romp about and play on the grass, or go in wading or swimming; a place where they could become acquainted with the shapes of all the leaves and their habits of growth; with the perfume of the linden and lilac, with the songs of the thrushes and cat-birds, with the motions of the chipmunk, and, in short, all the charms of the country."[6]

Today's children are frequently described as suffering from "nature-deficit disorder" owing to their lack of direct contact with the natural world and over-programmed lives.[7] The Alliance for Childhood states that children today spend 50 percent less time in unstructured outdoor activities than they did in the 1970s. They also report that, on average, ten- to sixteen-year-olds daily spend only 12.6 minutes in vigorous exercise and more than ten waking hours relatively motionless either in the classroom or in front of a TV or computer monitor.[8]

There is as well a deepening concern that today's children do not have sustained informal interactions with the natural world. Such interactions are thought to be especially critical during middle childhood, roughly ages seven through twelve, for developing deeper connections with nature which may affect the way these children will care about environmental issues later in life.[9]

The recent documentary *Where Do the Children Play?*, filmed in Michigan, examines the impact of sprawl and suburban development, time spent on computer games and television, and overscheduling on children's opportunities for creative outdoor play.[10] The film contrasts children growing up on Beaver Island, with its rural community and undeveloped open spaces, with children in suburban neighborhoods in Ann Arbor and in inner city neighborhoods in Detroit. The children on Beaver Island clearly spend more time outdoors and develop a rich attachment to the cycles of nature around them. Urban and suburban children spend considerably more time indoors. However, contrary to prevailing assumptions, children from the urban neighborhoods seem to fare better than their suburban counterparts. This is partly because of a better-developed community network whereby neighbors watch out for each other's children, so they have a relatively high degree of freedom within the bounds allowed by their parents. The importance of children's territories within which they can explore freely and create their own places has been widely recognized as important to childhood play and development.[11]

Many advocates believe that native gardens can make a big difference, not only ecologically, but by integrating nature back into our lives. Native gardens acquaint us with local plants and animals, connecting us to our region's unique natural history.

Bringing nature home can, in turn, foster deeper awareness and concern about local conservation issues. In "Going Native: Bringing Biodiversity into Your Own Backyard," the writer Janet Marinelli suggests that creating native gardens at home can help reconnect people and the larger landscape: "Human habitat becomes a part of the larger ecological community. We nurture nature and nature nurtures us. In our own backyards, as we plunge our hands into the soil and struggle to balance human and ecological needs, one of the great philosophical and scientific tasks of our time, the long-ruptured link between nature and daily life is restored."[12]

Others have pointed to the need to rebuild nature-based environments to allow children a deeper and richer connection to the natural world. In *The Geography of Childhood: Why Children Need Wild Places,* the ecologist Gary Paul Nabhan and the naturalist Stephen Trimble demonstrate that children need simple, intimate spaces in nature to which they can retreat, as well as trees for climbing and places where they can store and study the objects they collect—parts of plants, stones, bones, and other treasures. These "wild places" need not be pristine—the corner of a yard, a nearby vacant lot, an old woodlot will do. Such places can afford moments of wonder and awaken a child's curiosity and excitement about the environment.[13] Many ecologists acknowledge the importance of wild places in their own childhood lives. Access to such places was critical in nurturing my attachment to nature, and I find that many of my students in landscape architecture and natural resources feel the same way.

Richard Louv's *Last Child in the Woods: Saving Our Children from Nature-Deficit Disorder* (2005) has become a rallying force for reconnecting children with the natural world. Louv carefully chronicles children's growing separation from nature through personal narrative, studies on children's lives and how they spend their time, and stories of families who are trying to reconnect with nature. New alliances are emerging among health and conservation organizations to encourage outdoor play, to work for legislation that supports stronger connections between children and nature, and to foster research on the significance of those connections.[14] The North American Association for Environmental Education has proposed "no child left inside" federal legislation to support programs providing outdoor recreation and environmental education for all children.[15] Several states, including Connecticut, Illinois, Massachusetts, Michigan, and Wisconsin, have proposed their own versions of the bill. To see that these efforts mirror those of reformers in the late nineteenth and early twentieth centuries is a striking reminder that we need to be vigilant to ensure that this basic need of connecting children with nature is not forgotten.

Conservation and management of remnant wilds as well as the restoration of damaged lands is a second key theme throughout the volume. The conservation of native landscapes today is increasingly difficult, and perhaps even more challenging than in the period most of these authors were writing. Our landscape today is considerably more degraded than in the nineteenth and early twentieth centuries. Our cities are now sprawled across great expanses, rivers dammed and wetlands drained, prairies plowed and forests fragmented. We have introduced hundreds of new species, some of which have become invasive and have greatly damaged native ecosystems. We have lost many key species—the American chestnut, the American elm, the passenger pigeon, the Carolina parakeet are just a few.

In addition, the future holds many unknowns, including dramatic shifts in climate. However, the work to conserve our native landscape is being carried on. Scientists and land managers continue to build on the ecological studies by pioneers such as Henry Cowles, and the environmental inventories initiated by Victor Shelford and his colleagues at the University of Illinois have become integral components of natural heritage programs found in most states and Canadian provinces. The inspiration of Aldo Leopold continues to guide efforts in land preservation and pioneering organizations—the Wilderness Society, the Nature Conservancy, the Ecological Society of America—continue to provide strong leadership.

Early experiments in ecological restoration are recounted by some of the authors here: Aldo Leopold and his colleagues' work at the University of Wisconsin Arboretum in Madison; Edith Roberts and Elsa Rehmann's project to create an out-door ecological laboratory at Vassar College; Jens Jensen's attempt to "restore" the landscape of Lincoln Memorial Garden to what Abraham Lincoln would have experienced. Since then, hundreds of efforts to restore woodlands, prairies, wetlands, rivers, alpine meadows, and other landscapes have been undertaken. Restoration ecology is an evolving science: we learn as much from our mistakes as from our successes.

The process of ecological restoration has drastically challenged our ideas about wild lands and the human relationship to nature. One of the most intensely debated issues in ecological restoration centers around defining the role that humans play in the process and whether we refer to the result as "nature," "garden," or something in between. In his article "Faking Nature," the philosopher Robert Eliot likens efforts to restore nature to forging works of art. He maintains that the human "origin" of the decisions relating to the restoration of a site renders it artificial and clearly less valuable than a place that has evolved under what is considered to be less human influence. Similarly, in "The Big Lie: The Human Restoration of Nature," Eric Katz maintains that restored nature "is an artifact created to meet human satisfactions and interests" and an ultimate expression of attempts at human dominance.[16] Others, however, have argued a more benevolent view of the restoration process, centering on our obligation to restore nature we have damaged and noting that the practice of restoration helps to build a new human relationship with nature, one based on stewardship ideals rather than dominance.[17]

The ways in which the process of ecological restoration relates to the process of creating designed landscapes such as those promoted by authors in *The Native Landscape Reader* deserves discussion and clarification. Some people have suggested that restoration and native gardens fall along a continuum, with attention to historical and ecological fidelity being a target of ecological restoration and increased attention to human use resulting in "wild design" or more of a "garden."[18] The late landscape architect and planner John Lyle championed the term "regenerative landscape" to describe designs that merge natural processes and culture. He suggested that regenerative landscapes evoke qualities of a particular place (both its human culture and biological characteristics), showcase fecundity (that is, attention to the natural processes that sustain a system), emphasize diversity, and reflect continuity, respecting change and evolution in the landscape over space and time.[19]

Many of the values expressed by the designers represented in *The Native Landscape Reader* fit squarely within this discussion. For most of them, achieving historical or ecological fidelity to the native landscape in their designs was not a goal. Jensen described the process as one of idealization rather than making a facsimile: "A landscape architect, like a landscape painter, can't photograph; he must idealize the thing he sees . . . in trying to make a garden natural, we must not make the mistake of copying Nature."[20] The creation of parks and gardens that are at once expressive of local nature and of the art of the designer provides a rich opportunity for re-integrating the native landscape into our cities and towns and celebrating the unique natural heritage of a region.

Much of the literature promoting native gardens written over the last several decades has emphasized these themes. In "Restoring the Midwestern Landscape," published in 1975, the landscape architect Darrel Morrison describes how a garden designed to restore prairie in the Midwest helps to reinstate differences "between regions and between micro-habitats within regions," provides "educational value" about regional natural heritage, provides an experiential dynamic that is often lacking in more static gardens, and offers garden experiences that are both visually and ecologically complex. In addition, such gardens may have value in helping to "perpetuate or even increase the numbers of a species that otherwise might become extremely rare or locally extinct."[21] In Chicago, this idea of using native gardens as a conservation mechanism has led to the Native Seed Garden Project, a collaborative effort involving urban gardeners in growing and gathering seed from rare plant species for use in region-wide restoration efforts.[22]

The value of native gardens for wildlife has also been a compelling argument for their creation. If homeowners across the country used a portion of their yards as wildlife habitats and these were connected to larger parks and preserves in their communities, the result could greatly benefit many wildlife species that are rapidly losing habitat options. Over the past thirty-five years, the Certified Wildlife Habitat program of National Wildlife Federation has enlisted thousands of homeowners to create wildlife habitat. Similar programs target schools, college campuses, and other community spaces, and Audubon International sponsors a Cooperative Sanctuary program for golf courses.[23]

Sara Stein's popular book *Noah's Garden: Restoring the Ecology of Our Own Back Yards* makes a strong case for the potential value of a linked network of many backyard preserves. Crediting Mrs. William Starr Dana, author of *How to Know the Wild Flowers* (1893), as one of her inspirations, Stein proposes the reshaping of suburban lots to include a variety of native plants and wildlife habitat.[24] In *Bringing Nature Home: How Native Plants Sustain Wildlife in Our Gardens,* the entomologist Douglas Tallamy eloquently pleas for insect diversity in our parks and gardens, noting that the trend toward "pest free" plants in ornamental horticulture has had a high ecological cost.[25] Reducing insect populations can trigger cascading declines in other wildlife species that feed on them. Focusing instead on a region's native species and plant communities and habitat structure that provides for a diversity of wildlife would greatly aid broader conservation efforts. Tallamy argues that gardening with native plants "is an important part of a paradigm shift in our shaky relationship with the planet that sustains us—one that mainstream gardeners can no longer afford to ignore."[26]

At one level, the future prospects for sustaining our native landscape are bleak. The challenges of global climate change, species loss, an increasingly fragmented landscape, and growing threats from invasive species are daunting indeed. To some degree, however, the authors gathered in *The Native Landscape Reader* faced many of the same issues and found a way to champion nature in their parks, gardens, and preservation efforts. They helped awaken people to the beauty and the value of what was being lost. The key was—and is—getting people to care.

Today, there is growing interest in native gardens and ecological restoration efforts at a variety of scales. Region-wide initiatives by conservation organizations and state and federal agencies to prevent the spread of invasive species and restore native ecosystems are increasing. The most successful are collaborative and connect with individual and community efforts.[27] Further, there is greater recognition of the need to integrate cultural dimensions with the physical components of restoration and landscape management. In *Nature by Design,* the philosopher Eric Higgs proposes a model for ecological restoration that incorporates both ecological history and cultural memory and invites cultural imagination in making sense of the ecological future.[28] Many advocates of ecological restoration emphasize the value and necessity of integrating people into the process. In his article "The Gardenification of Wildland Nature and the Human Footprint," the ecologist Daniel Janzen makes a convincing case for changing our perspective on wildland conservation to recognize it as another form of gardening. He argues that gardening is something we humans have done for thousands of years, whereas wildland preservation is relatively new to us: "If we label conservation wildlands with what feels good and normal to our genes, maybe they will have some chance of survival. Then maybe we can feel good about applying what we know to them. . . . Restoration is the key to sustainable gardening. Restoration is fencing, planting, fertilizing, tilling, and weeding the wildland garden: succession, bioremediation, reforestation, aforestation, fire control, prescribed burning, crowd control, biological control, reintroduction, mitigation, and much more."[29]

Student volunteers collecting prairie seed, Nichols Arboretum, Ann Arbor, Mich. (Photograph by Jim Lempke.)

This idea, of a continuation of gardening that extends from the backyard to regional conservation efforts, is what several of the authors in *The Native Landscape Reader* envisioned. Jensen and Simonds, for instance, saw the parks and gardens they designed as part of a larger process of conservation.[30] Through the careful tending of nature in gardens, they worked to inspire larger conservation efforts. Similarly, Harold Caparn, Charles Eliot, Warren Manning, Wilhelm Miller, Paul Riis, Elsa Rehmann, Edith Roberts, and Frank Waugh saw their work reaching beyond the local to the regional scale of conservation. Others of the authors here, in particular Liberty Hyde Bailey and Aldo Leopold, sought a change in our mindset which would make conservation a basic ethical value and way of living.

Working on this book, I have been inspired by many of the authors. I now feel even more motivated to learn what I can about the regional natural heritage of southeastern Michigan, my current home. I arrived much too late to experience "the earthly paradise" described by Cadillac in 1702 or the prairies and oak openings around Ann Arbor that J. W. Wing wrote of in 1838 as "beautiful beyond description." Fortunately, however, we do have fragments of those landscapes that provide glimpses of what our region once was like. Following the lead of many of the writers in *The Native Landscape Reader*, I can join with others to conserve and restore what remains and create gardens that embrace the distinctive beauty and ecological processes of the region. Doing so not only helps celebrate the past but also helps us prepare for the challenges that lie ahead.

Notes

INTRODUCTION

1. Pollan, "Against Nativism."
2. Patell, "The Language of Pests"; Peretti, "Nativism and Nature"; Gobster, "Invasive Species as an Ecological Threat."
3. Subramaniam, "The Aliens Have Landed!," 34.
4. Gröning and Wolschke-Bulmahn, "Some Notes on the Mania for Native Plants"; see also Gröning and Wolschke-Bulmahn, "Response."
5. Gröning and Wolschke-Bulmahn, "Some Notes on the Mania for Native Plants," 121–24; see also Wolschke-Bulmahn, "The 'Wild Garden' and the 'Nature Garden.'"
6. Wolschke-Bulmahn, "The Mania for Native Plants in Nazi Germany," 68.
7. Ibid.
8. Egan and Tishler, "Jens Jensen, Native Plants, and the Concept of Nordic Superiority."
9. Jens Jensen, speech to the Women's International League for Peace and Freedom meeting, Chicago, May 31, 1924, Anita McCormick Blaine Papers, box 765, Wisconsin Historical Society, Madison. I thank William Tishler for sharing this source with me.
10. Jensen to Frank A. Waugh, April 13, 1936, Jensen archives, Sterling Morton Library, Morton Arboretum, Lisle, Illinois (hereafter cited as Morton).
11. Egan and Tishler, "Jens Jensen, Native Plants, and the Concept of Nordic Superiority," 23.
12. Jensen to Genevieve Gillette, undated, Morton.
13. Jensen and Eskil, "Natural Parks and Gardens,"

18. Stephen Christy, in "Jens Jensen: The Metamorphosis of an Artist," noted Jensen's gradual evolution in abandoning non-native species to emphasizing native plants in increasing ecologically based patterns. See also Grese, *Jens Jensen*, 151–52.
14. In *Siftings*, Jensen spoke of preserving lilacs and apple trees near the house of a client (69–70). Similarly, in "Some Gardens of the Middle West," Jensen described hollyhocks, lilacs, flowering almond, Chinese cherries, and sweetbrier roses planted along a garden wall.
15. Jensen, untitled undated manuscript, Jens Jensen Drawings and Papers, Bentley Historical Library, University of Michigan, Ann Arbor (hereafter cited as Bentley).
16. Jensen to Camillo Schneider, March 11, 1937, Bentley.
17. Egan and Tishler, "Jens Jensen, Native Plants, and the Concept of Nordic Superiority," 13; Marinelli, "Natives Revival"; U.S. Environmental Protection Agency, "Landscaping with Native Plants"; Burrell, Marinelli, and Harper-Lore, *Native Alternatives to Invasive Plants*, 8–10; Waitt, "Reply to 'What Constitutes a Native Plant?'"
18. In *Bringing Nature Home*, 58–63, Douglas Tallamy suggests that there be some flexibility in moving a plant outside its native range for garden planting, setting the criterion of whether it can "still perform some or even most of its evolutionary roles within its new ecosystem"

(62). Accordingly, planting native azaleas from the southern Appalachians within the range of other native azaleas may be reasonable, given that there would be native insects and wildlife that are adapted to a similar species; planting Douglas fir in the eastern United States, far outside its native range of the West, would not be appropriate.

19. Gould, "Evolutionary Perspective," 9.

20. Reichard and White, "Horticulture as a Pathway of Invasive Plant Introductions," 110.

21. Simberloff, "Confronting Introduced Species," 189.

22. Marinelli, "Introduction: Redefining the Weed," 5–6.

23. Gobster, "Invasive Species."

24. Waugh, *The Natural Style in Landscape Gardening*, 16–24, 39; Jensen and Eskil, "Natural Parks and Gardens"; Jensen, *Siftings*, 39–61, 63–87.

25. Tufts, "Introduction to the Environmental Benefits of Landscaping with Native Plants."

26. Novak, *Nature and Culture*, 4.

27. Ibid., 7.

28. Nash, *Wilderness and the American Mind*, 44–83; Huth, *Nature and the American*, 21–53.

29. Nash, *Wilderness and the American Mind*, 54–55. The full title of Bartram's book is *Travels through North and South Carolina, Georgia, East and West Florida, the Cherokee Country, the Extensive Territories of the Muscogulges or Creek Confederacy, and the Country of the Chactaws. Containing an Account of the Soil and Natural Productions of Those Regions; Together with Observations on the Manners of the Indians.*

30. Elman, *First in the Field*, 40–44.

31. Huth, *Nature and the American*, 50–51.

32. Nash, *Wilderness and the American Mind*, 76.

33. Ibid., 38; H. F. Smith, "The Spell of Nature in Irving's Famous Stories."

34. Callow, *Kindred Spirits*, 3–37, 63–69.

35. Greenough, *Form and Function*, 58–59, 60.

36. Cranz, *Politics of Park Design*, 5–7.

37. Beveridge, "Regionalism in Frederick Law Olmsted's Social Thought," 212–14.

38. Ibid., 221–23; Wilson, *The City Beautiful Movement*, 23–25.

39. Beveridge, "Frederick Law Olmsted's Theory on Landscape Design." Carol Grove provides an excellent comparison of the gardenesque and picturesque approaches to landscape design and the philosophy behind them in her discussion of Tower Grove Park, St. Louis, Missouri, in *Henry Shaw's Victorian Landscapes*, 124–27.

40. Frederick Law Olmsted Sr., *Notes on the Plan of Franklin Park and Related Matters* (1886), quoted in Beveridge, "Frederick Law Olmsted's Theory on Landscape Design," 40.

41. Nadenicek, Tishler, and Neckar, "Horace William Shaler Cleveland"; Nadenicek and Neckar, "Introduction"; Karson, *A Genius for Place*, 6–7.

42. Lubove, "Introduction," x–xii; Neckar, "Fast-Tracking Culture and Landscape," 85–94.

43. Connor, "Historical Background"; Anderson, "'Master of a Felicitous English Style'"; Carr, "*Garden and Forest* and 'Landscape Art.'"

44. Clayton, "Wild Gardening and the Popular American Magazine."

45. Barnard, "Commercial Value of the Wild," 766.

46. Simonds, *Landscape Gardening*, 22–23.

47. Ibid.

48. Cowles, "Ecological Relations of the Vegetation on the Sand Dunes of Lake Michigan."

49. Jensen, "Soil Conditions and Tree Growth around Lake Michigan."

50. Perkins, *Report of the Special Park Commission*.

51. Cranz, *Politics of Park Design*, 63–65.

52. McArthur, "Parks, Playgrounds, and Progressivism"; and Tippens and Sniderman, "Planning and Design of Chicago's Neighborhood Parks."

53. Beveridge, "Frederick Law Olmsted's Theory," 39; Jensen, *Siftings*, 71–73, 91–92.

54. R. Kaplan, "Nature of the View from Home"; Kaplan, Kaplan, and Ryan, *With People in Mind*; Kaplan and Kaplan, "Preference, Restoration and Meaningful Action"; S. Kaplan, "Restorative Benefits of Nature."

55. Grese, "Jens Jensen: The Landscape Architect as Conservationist"; Grese, "Conservation: Roots of the Prairie Style, Part I."

56. Grese, *Jens Jensen*, 120–21.

57. Ibid., 122–36; Grese, "Conservation: Roots of the Prairie Style, Part III," 7.

58. Jensen, *Siftings*, 57; Jensen, "Naturalistic Treatment in a Metropolitan Park," 35; Jensen to Henry and Clara Ford, October 4, 1944, Henry Ford Papers, box 58:14, Correspondence with Jens Jensen, Benson Ford Research Center, Dearborn, Michigan.

59. Frank Waugh wrote a book devoted to the

design of outdoor theaters which featured Jensen's "players green" at Columbus Park. Waugh, *Outdoor Theaters,* 125–27.

60. Crewe, "Rural Landscapes of Frank Waugh."
61. Seeley, "Liberty Hyde Bailey."
62. Roberts and Rehmann, "Plant Ecology I," 805.
63. Roberts, "Development of an Out-of-Door Botanical Laboratory."
64. *American Plants for American Gardens* was republished by the University of Georgia Press in 1996 with an introduction by Darrel Morrison.
65. C. H. Smith, "Shelford."
66. Rotenberk, "Remembering May Watts"; Morton Arboretum, "History."

EPILOGUE

1. R. Kaplan and S. Kaplan, *Experience of Nature,* 121–74; S. Kaplan and R. Kaplan, "Health, Supportive Environments, and the Reasonable Person Model"; R. Kaplan and S. Kaplan, "Bringing Out the Best in People."
2. Ulrich, "View through a Window"; R. Kaplan, "Nature of the View from Home"; Kuo and Sullivan, "Environment and Crime in the Inner City."
3. R. Kaplan, "Some Psychological Benefits of Gardening"; Miles, Sullivan, and Kuo, "Ecological Restoration Volunteers"; Kaplan, Kaplan, and Ryan, *With People in Mind;* Grese, Kaplan, Ryan, and Buxton, "Psychological Benefits of Volunteering in Stewardship Programs"; Schroeder, "The Restoration Experience"; Ryan and Grese, "Urban Volunteers and the Environment"; Stuart, "Lifting Spirits."
4. Grese, Introduction to Simonds, *Landscape Gardening,* xxvi.
5. Ibid., xiv–xv.
6. Simonds, "Lecture #5: 'Parks,'" given at the University of Michigan, Ann Arbor, 1909. Bentley Historical Library, University of Michigan, Ann Arbor.
7. Richard Louv brought the term "nature-deficit disorder" into common use with his book *Last Child in the Woods, Saving Our Children from Nature-Deficit Disorder.* See also Pandey, "Child Participation for Conservation of Species and Ecosystems."
8. Alliance for Childhood, "The Loss of Children's Play."
9. See Cornell, *Sharing Nature with Children;* Kellert, "Attitudes toward Animals"; Kellert, "Experiencing Nature"; and Sobel, *Children's Special Places.*
10. A companion book has also been published: Goodenough, *A Place for Play.*
11. See Moore, *Childhood's Domain;* and Hart, *Children's Experience of Place.* In 1998, Elizabeth Goodenough organized a symposium focused on the "secret" places that children create; many of them found places in nature. Essays related to the symposium are collected in Goodenough, *Secret Spaces of Childhood.* For a historical perspective on children's play in New York City, see Dargan and Zeitlin, *City Play.*
12. Marinelli, "Going Native," 28–29.
13. See Putz, "A Breeding Ground for Conservation Biologists"; Uhl, "Conservation Biology in Your Own Front Yard"; and Pyle, "Eden in a Vacant Lot." For discussion about a schoolyard transformed into a semi-natural habitat for play, see Moore and Wong, *Natural Learning.*
14. An example of this type of alliance is the Outdoor Alliance for Kids, formed by the National Parks and Recreation Association, the Sierra Club, the Outdoor Foundation, the Children and Nature Network, the National Wildlife Federation, the Izaak Walton League, the YMCA, and REI, Inc. See www.sites.google.com/site/outdoorsallianceforkids.
15. Examples include a national initiative supported by the North American Association for Environmental Education; see www.naaee.org/ee-advocacy.
16. Katz, "The Big Lie," 84.
17. See Light, "Ecological Restoration and the Culture of Nature"; and Jordan, "Restoration, Community and Wilderness."
18. See Hall, *Earth Repair,* 212–17.
19. Lyle, "Landscape: Source of Life or Liability."
20. Jensen and Eskil, "Natural Parks and Gardens," 169.
21. Morrison, "Restoring the Midwestern Landscape," 398.
22. See McGee, "The Roots of Things."
23. See www.nwf.org; http://auduboninternational.org.
24. Stein, *Noah's Garden,* 34–51.
25. Tallamy, *Bringing Nature Home,* 42–57.
26. Ibid., 14.
27. For several examples, see Doyle and Drew,

Large-Scale Ecosystem Restoration; and Foreman, *Rewilding North America.*

28. Higgs, *Nature by Design,* 259–61.
29. Janzen, "Gardenification of Wildland Nature," 1312–13; for further discussion of these ideas with regard to ecological restoration, see Allison, "What Do We Mean When We Talk about Ecological Restoration?"
30. Grese, "Roots of the Prairie Style, Part I."

Works Cited

Alliance for Childhood. "The Loss of Children's Play: A Public Health Issue." Policy Brief no. 1, November 2010. www.allianceforchildhood. org.

Allison, Stuart K. "What Do We Mean When We Talk about Ecological Restoration?" *Ecological Restoration* 22, no. 4 (December 2004): 281–86.

Anderson, Phyllis. "'Master of a Felicitous English Style': William Augustus Stiles, Editor of *Garden and Forest.*" In *Historical Essays on "Garden and Forest,"* www.loc.gov/preserv/prd/gardfor /essays/andersen.html.

Ashe, W. W. "Forest Types of the Appalachians and White Mountains." *Journal of the Elisha Mitchell Scientific Society* 37, nos. 3–4 (March 1922): 183–98.

———. "Reserved Areas of Principal Forest Types as a Guide in Developing an American Silviculture." *Journal of Forestry* 20 (March 1922): 276–83.

Bailey, Liberty Hyde. *The Nature-Study Idea: Being an Interpretation of the New School-Movement to Put the Child in Sympathy with Nature.* New York: Doubleday Page, 1903.

Barnard, Charles. "The Commercial Value of the Wild." *The Craftsman* 10 (September 1906): 763–66.

Bartlett, Peggy, ed. *Urban Place: Reconnecting with the Natural World.* Cambridge: MIT Press, 2005.

Bartram, William. *Travels through North and South Carolina, Georgia, East and West Florida, the Cherokee Country, the Extensive Territories of the Muscogulges, or Creek Confederacy, and the Country of the Choctaws. Containing an Account of the Soil and Natural Productions of Those Regions; Together with Observations on the Manners of the Indians.* Philadelphia: James and Johnson, 1791.

Beakes, Samuel W. *Past and Present of Washtenaw County, Michigan: Together with Biographical Sketches of Many of Its Prominent and Leading Citizens and Illustrious Dead.* Chicago: S. J. Clarke, 1906.

Beveridge, Charles E. "Frederick Law Olmsted, Sr." In Birnbaum and Karson, *Pioneers of American Landscape Design,* 277–81.

———. "Frederick Law Olmsted's Theory on Landscape Design." *Nineteenth Century* 3, no. 2 (Summer 1977): 38–43.

———. "Regionalism in Frederick Law Olmsted's Social Thought and Landscape Design Practice." In *Regional Garden Design in the United States,* ed. Therese O'Malley and Marc Treib (Washington, D.C.: Dumbarton Oaks Research Library and Collection, 1995), 209–42.

Birnbaum, Charles A., and Robin Karson, eds. *Pioneers of American Landscape Design.* New York: McGraw-Hill, 2000.

Bray, William L. *Development of the Vegetation of New York State.* Technical Publication no. 29. Syracuse: New York State College of Forestry, 1930.

Burrell, C. Colston, Janet Marinelli, and Bonnie

Harper-Lore. *Native Alternatives to Invasive Plants*. Brooklyn, N.Y.: Brooklyn Botanic Garden, 2006.

Callow, James T. *Kindred Spirits: Knickerbocker Writers and American Artists, 1807–1855*. Chapel Hill: University of North Carolina Press, 1967.

Carr, Ethan. "*Garden and Forest* and 'Landscape Art.'" In *Historical Essays on "Garden and Forest*," www.loc.gov/preserv/prd/gardfor/essays/carr.html.

Chapman, Charles C. *History of Washtenaw County, Michigan: Together with Sketches of Its Cities, Villages and Townships*. Vol. 2. Chicago. Charles C. Chapman, 1881.

Chicago Public Library Special Collections Department and the Chicago Park District. *A Breath of Fresh Air: Chicago's Neighborhood Parks of the Progressive Reform Era, 1900–1925*. Chicago: Chicago Public Library, 1989.

Christy, Stephen. "Jens Jensen: The Metamorphosis of an Artist." *Landscape Architecture* 66, no. 1 (January 1976): 60–66.

Clayton, Virginia Tuttle. "Wild Gardening and the Popular American Magazine, 1890–1918." In Wolschke-Bulmahn, *Nature and Ideology: Natural Garden Design in the Twentieth Century*, 131–54.

Cleveland, Horace William Shaler. *Culture and Management of Our Native Forests for Development as Timber or Ornamental Wood*. Springfield, Ill.: H. W. Rokker, 1882.

———. *Landscape Architecture as Applied to the Wants of the West*. Chicago: Jansen, McClurg, 1873; repr., Amherst. University of Massachusetts Press in association with Library of American Landscape History, 2002.

———. "Suggestions for a System of Parks and Parkways for the City of Minneapolis." In Board of Park Commissioners of the City of Minneapolis, *First Annual Report for the Year Ending March 13, 1884*. Minneapolis: Johnson, Smith & Harrington, 1884.

Connor, Sheila. "Historical Background." 1999. In *Historical Essays on "Garden and Forest*," www.loc.gov/preserv/prd/gardfor/essays/connor.html.

Cornell, Joseph. *Sharing Nature with Children*. Nevada City, Calif.: Dawn Publications, 1979.

Cowles, Henry C. "The Ecological Relations of the Vegetation on the Sand Dunes of Lake Michigan." *Botanical Gazette* 27, no. 2 (February 1899): 95–117; no. 3 (March 1899): 167–202; no. 4 (April 1899): 281–308; no. 5 (May 1899): 361–91.

Cranz, Galen. *The Politics of Park Design: A History of Urban Parks in America*. Cambridge: MIT Press, 1982.

Crewe, Katherine. "The Rural Landscapes of Frank Waugh." *Landscape Journal* 22, no. 2 (2003): 126–39.

Dargan, Amanda, and Steven Zeitlin. *City Play*. New Brunswick, N.J.: Rutgers University Press, 1990.

Dion, Mark, and Alexis Rockman. *Concrete Jungle: A Pop Media Investigation of Death and Survival in Urban Ecosystems*. New York: Juno Books, 1996.

Doyle, Mary, and Cynthia Drew, eds. *Large-Scale Ecosystem Restoration: Five Case Studies from the United States*. Washington, D.C.: Island Press., 2008.

Egan, Dave, and William H. Tishler. "Jens Jensen, Native Plants, and the Concept of Nordic Superiority." *Landscape Journal* 18, no. 1 (Spring 1999): 11–29.

Eliot, Charles W. *Charles Eliot, Landscape Architect*. 1902; repr., Amherst: University of Massachusetts Press in association with Library of American Landscape History, 1999.

Elliot, Robert. "Faking Nature." *Inquiry* 25 (March 1982): 81–93.

Elman, Robert. *First in the Field: America's Pioneering Naturalists*. New York: Van Nostrand Reinhold, 1977.

Foreman, Dave. *Rewilding North America: A Vision for Conservation in the 21st Century*. Washington, D.C.: Island Press, 2004.

Gobster, Paul H. "Invasive Species as an Ecological Threat: Is Restoration an Alternative to Fear-Based Resource Management?" *Ecological Restoration* 23, no. 4 (December 2005): 261–70.

Gobster, Paul H., and R. Bruce Hull, eds. *Restoring Nature: Perspectives from the Social Sciences and Humanities*. Washington, D.C.: Island Press, 2000.

Goodenough, Elizabeth, ed. *Secret Spaces of Childhood*. Ann Arbor: University of Michigan Press, 2003.

———, ed. *A Place for Play: A Companion Volume to the Michigan Television Film "Where Do the Children Play?"* Ann Arbor: National Institute for Play, 2010.

Gould, Stephen Jay. "An Evolutionary Perspective on Strengths, Fallacies, and Confusions in the Concept of Native Plants." In Wolschke-Bulmahn, *Nature and Ideology: Natural Garden Design in the Twentieth Century,* 11–19.

Greenough, Horatio. *Form and Function: Remarks on Art.* Edited by Harold A. Small. Berkeley: University of California Press, 1947.

Grese, Robert E. "Conservation: Roots of the Prairie Style, Part I." *The Living Green* 1, no. 2 (Fall 2000): 1, 6–7. Available at www.jensjensen.org /Fall2000/RootsI.htm.

———. "Conservation: Roots of the Prairie Style, Part III." *The Living Green* 1, no. 4 (Summer 2001): 1, 6–7. Available at www.jensjensen.org /Summer2001/RootsIII.htm.

———. Introduction to *Landscape Gardening,* by Ossian Cole Simonds. Amherst: University of Massachusetts Press in association with Library of American Landscape History, 2000.

———. "Jens Jensen: The Landscape Architect as Conservationist." In *Midwestern Landscape Architecture,* edited by William Tishler, 117–41. Urbana: University of Illinois Press in cooperation with Library of American Landscape History, 2000.

———. *Jens Jensen: Maker of Natural Parks and Gardens.* Baltimore: Johns Hopkins University Press in association with the Center for American Places, 1992.

Grese, Robert E., Rachel Kaplan, Robert L. Ryan, and Jane Buxton. "Psychological Benefits of Volunteering in Stewardship Programs." In Gobster and Hull, *Restoring Nature,* 265–80.

Gröning, Gert, and Joachim Wolschke-Bulmahn. "Response: If the Shoe Fits, Wear It." *Landscape Journal* 13, no. 1 (Spring 1994): 62–63.

———. "Some Notes on the Mania for Native Plants in Germany." *Landscape Journal* 11, no. 2 (Fall 1992): 116–26.

Grove, Carol. *Henry Shaw's Victorian Landscapes: The Missouri Botanical Garden and Tower Grove Park.* Amherst: University of Massachusetts Press in association with Library of American Landscape History, 2005.

Hall, Marcus, *Earth Repair: A Transatlantic History of Environmental Restoration.* Charlottesville: University of Virginia Press, 2005.

Hart, Roger. *Children's Experience of Place.* New York: Irvington Publishers, 1979.

Higgs, Eric. *Nature by Design: People, Natural Process, and Ecological Restoration.* Cambridge: MIT Press, 2003.

Huth, Hans. *Nature and the American: Three Centuries of Changing Attitudes.* 1957; repr., Lincoln: University of Nebraska Press, 1957.

Janzen, Daniel. "Gardenification of Wildland Nature and the Human Footprint." *Science* 279, no. 5355 (February 27, 1998): 1312–13.

Jensen, Jens. "The Naturalistic Treatment in a Metropolitan Park." *American Landscape Architect* 2, no. 1 (January 1930): 34–38.

———. *Siftings.* 1939; repr., Baltimore: Johns Hopkins University Press, 1990.

———. "Soil Conditions and Tree Growth around Lake Michigan," *Park and Cemetery* 14, no. 2 (April 1904): 24–25; no. 3 (May 1904): 42.

———. "Some Gardens of the Middle West." *Architectural Review* 15, no. 5 (May 1908): 93–95.

Jensen, Jens, and Ragna B. Eskil. "Natural Parks and Gardens." *Saturday Evening Post,* March 8, 1930, 18–19, 169–70.

Jordan, William R. III, ed. *Our First 50 Years: The University of Wisconsin–Madison Arboretum, 1934–1984.* Madison: University of Wisconsin Arboretum, 1984. Available at http://digital .library.wisc.edu/1711.dl/EcoNatRes.ArbFirstYrs.

———. "Restoration, Community and Wilderness." In Gobster and Hull, *Restoring Nature,* 23–36.

Kahn, Peter H., Jr., and Stephen R. Kellert, eds. *Children and Nature: Psychological, Sociocultural, and Evolutionary Investigations.* Cambridge: MIT Press, 2002.

Kaplan, Rachel. "The Nature of the View from Home: Psychological Benefits." *Environment and Behavior* 33, no. 4 (July 2001): 507–42.

———. "Some Psychological Benefits of Gardening." *Environment and Behavior* 5, no. 2 (June 1973): 145–62.

Kaplan, Rachel, and Stephen Kaplan. "Bringing Out the Best in People: A Psychological Perspective." *Conservation Biology* 22, no. 4 (August 2008) 826–29.

———. *The Experience of Nature: A Psychological Perspective.* New York: Cambridge University Press, 1989.

———. "Preference, Restoration and Meaningful Action in the Context of Nearby Nature." In Bartlett, *Urban Place: Reconnecting with the Natural World,* 271–98.

Kaplan, Rachel, Stephen Kaplan, and Robert L. Ryan. *With People in Mind: Design and Man-*

agement of Everyday Nature. Washington, D.C.: Island Press, 1998.

Kaplan, Stephen. "The Restorative Benefits of Nature: Towards an Integrative Framework." *Journal of Environmental Psychology* 15, no. 3 (1995): 169–82.

Kaplan, Stephen, and Rachel Kaplan. "Health, Supportive Environments, and the Reasonable Person Model." *American Journal of Public Health* 93, no. 9 (September 2003): 1484–89.

Karson, Robin. *A Genius for Place: American Landscapes of the Country Place Era.* Amherst: University of Massachusetts Press in association with Library of American Landscape History, 2007.

———. *The Muses of Gwinn: Art and Nature in a Garden Designed by Warren H. Manning, Charles A. Platt, and Ellen Biddle Shipman.* Sagaponack, N.Y.: Sagapress in association with Library of American Landscape History, 1995.

———. "Warren Henry Manning." In Birnbaum and Karson, *Pioneers of American Landscape Design,* 236–42.

Katz, Eric. "The Big Lie: The Human Restoration of Nature." In *Environmental Restoration: Ethics, Theory and Practice,* edited by William Throop, 83–94. Amherst, N.Y.: Humanity Books, 2000. Originally published in *Research in Philosophy and Technology* 12 (1992): 231–41.

Kellert, Stephen R. "Attitudes toward Animals: Age-Related Development among Children." *Journal of Environmental Education* 16, no. 3 (Spring 1985): 29–39.

———. "Experiencing Nature: Affective, Cognitive, and Evaluative Development in Children." In Kahn and Kellert, *Children and Nature: Psychological, Sociocultural, and Evolutionary Investigations,* 117–52.

Kerner von Merilaun, Anton. *The Natural History of Plants: Their Forms, Growth, Reproduction and Distribution.* Translated from the German by F. W. Oliver. 2 vols. London: Gresham, 1903.

Kuo, Frances E., and William C. Sullivan. "Environment and Crime in the Inner City: Does Vegetation Reduce Crime?" *Environment and Behavior* 33, no. 3 (May 2001): 343–67.

Lange, Willy. *Die Gartengestaltung der Neuzeit.* Leipzig: J. J. Weber., 1907.

Light, Andrew. "Ecological Restoration and the Culture of Nature: A Pragmatic Perspective." In Gobster and Hull, *Restoring Nature,* 49–70.

Louv, Richard. *Last Child in the Woods: Saving Our Children from Nature-Deficit Disorder.* Chapel Hill, N.C.: Algonquin Books of Chapel Hill, 2005.

Lubove, Roy. Introduction to *Landscape Architecture as Applied to the Wants of the West,* by H. W. S. Cleveland. 1873; Pittsburgh: University of Pittsburgh Press, 1965.

Lyle, John Tillman, 1999. "Landscape: Source of Life or Liability." In *Reshaping the Built Environment: Ecology, Ethics, and Economics,* edited by Charles J. Kibert, 151–75. Washington, D.C.: Island Press, 1999.

Marinelli, Janet. "Introduction: Redefining the Weed." In *Invasive Plants: Weeds of the Global Garden,* edited by Janet Marinelli and John M. Randall, 4–6. Brooklyn, N.Y.: Brooklyn Botanic Garden, 1996.

———. "Going Native: Bringing Biodiversity into Your Own Backyard." *The Amicus Journal* 14, no. 3 (Fall 1992): 28–29.

———. "Natives Revival—Is Native-plant Gardening Linked to Fascism?" *Plants and Gardens News* 15, no. 2 (Summer 2000): 1–4, available at http://v1.bbg.org/gar2/topics/wildflower/1995fa_native.

McArthur, Benjamin. "Parks, Playgrounds, and Progressivism." In Chicago Public Library Special Collections Department and the Chicago Park District, *A Breath of Fresh Air,* 9–14

McGee, Lindsay. "The Roots of Things—The Wild Garden Project." In *North Branch Prairie Project: 16th Year Report,* edited by Karen Holland, 29–31. Chicago: North Branch Prairie Project, 1994.

Miles, Irene, William C. Sullivan, and Frances E. Kuo. "Ecological Restoration Volunteers: The Benefits of Participation." *Urban Ecosystems* 2, no. 1 (1998): 27–41.

Miller, Wilhelm. *The Prairie Spirit in Landscape Gardening.* 1915; repr., Amherst: University of Massachusetts Press in association with Library of American Landscape History, 2002.

Moore, Robin. *Childhood's Domain: Play and Place in Child Development.* London: Croom Helm, 1986.

Moore, Robin C., and Herb H. Wong. *Natural Learning: The Life History of an Environmental Schoolyard.* Berkeley: MIG, 1997.

Morrison, Darrel G. "Restoring the Midwestern Landscape." *Landscape Architecture* 65, no. 4 (October 1975): 398–403.

Morton Arboretum. "History." www.mortonarb.org /donor-resources/history.html.

Nabhan, Gary Paul, and Stephen Trimble. *The Geography of Childhood: Why Children Need Wild Places.* Boston: Beacon Press, 1994.

Nadenicek, Daniel J., and Lance M. Neckar. Introduction to H. W. S. Cleveland, *Landscape Architecture as Applied to the Wants of the West.* Amherst: University of Massachusetts Press in association with Library of American Landscape History, 2002.

Nadenicek, Daniel J., William H. Tishler, and Lance M. Neckar. "Horace William Shaler Cleveland." In Birnbaum and Karson, *Pioneers of American Landscape Design,* 61–64.

Nash, Roderick. *Wilderness and the American Mind.* New Haven: Yale University Press, 1967.

Neckar, Lance M. "Fast-Tracking Culture and Landscape: Horace William Shaler Cleveland and the Garden in the Midwest." In *Regional Garden Design in the United States,* edited by Therese O'Malley and Marc Treib, 69–98. Washington, D.C.: Dumbarton Oaks, 1995.

Novak, Barbara. *Nature and Culture: American Landscape and Painting, 1825–1875.* New York: Oxford University Press, 1980.

Pandey, P. D. "Child Participation for Conservation of Species and Ecosystems." *Conservation Ecology* 7, no. 1 (2003), www.ecologyandsociety.org /vol7/iss1/resp2/.

Patell, Shireen R. K. "The Language of Pests." In Dion and Rockman, *Concrete Jungle,* 62–64.

Peretti, Jonah. "Nativism and Nature: Rethinking Biological Invasions." *Environmental Values* 7, no. 2 (May 1998): 183–92.

Perkins, Dwight Heald. *Report of the Special Park Commission to the City Council of Chicago on the Subject of a Metropolitan Park System.* Chicago: W. J. Hartman, 1905.

Pollan, Michael. "Against Nativism." *New York Times Magazine,* May 15, 1994, 52–55.

Putz, Francis E. "A Breeding Ground for Conservation Biologists." *Conservation Biology* 11, no. 3 (June 1997): 813–14.

Pyle, Robert Michael. "Eden in a Vacant Lot: Special Places, Species, and Kids in the Neighborhood of Life." In Kahn and Kellert, *Children and Nature: Psychological, Sociocultural, and Evolutionary Investigations,* 306–27.

Reichard, Sarah Hayden, and Peter S. White. "Horticulture as a Pathway of Invasive Plant Introductions in the United States." *Bioscience* 51, no. 2 (February 2001): 103–13.

Riis, Jacob A. *How the Other Half Lives: Studies Among the Tenements of New York.* New York: C. Scribner's Sons, 1890.

Roberts, Edith A. "The Development of an Out-of-Door Botanical Laboratory for Experimental Ecology." *Ecology* 14, no. 2 (April 1933): 163–223.

Roberts, Edith A. and Elsa Rehmann. *American Plants for American Gardens.* 1929; repr., Athens: University of Georgia Press, 1996.

———. "Plant Ecology I: The Contributions to Naturalistic Planting of This Study of Plants in Relation to Their Environment." *House Beautiful* 61, no. 6 (June 1927): 805, 842–45.

———. "Plant Ecology II: Seaside Planting." *House Beautiful* 62, no. 1 (July 1927): 46, 81–84.

———. "Plant Ecology III: Natural Water Gardens." *House Beautiful* 62, no. 2 (August 1927): 133, 168–70.

———. "Plant Ecology: IV: The Open Field." *House Beautiful* 62, no. 3 (September 1927): 247, 294–300.

———. "Plant Ecology V: The Juniper Association." *House Beautiful* 62, no. 4 (October 1927): 399, 448–54.

———. "Plant Ecology VI: Oak Woodlands." *House Beautiful* 62, no. 5 (November 1927): 533, 578–82.

———. "Plant Ecology VII: The Pine Association." *House Beautiful* 62, no. 6 (December 1927): 652.

———. "Plant Ecology VIII: The Hemlock Ravine." *House Beautiful* 63, no. 1 (January 1928): 74, 103–4.

———. "Plant Ecology IX: Beech-Maple-Hemlock Association." *House Beautiful* 63, no. 2 (February 1928): 190, 238–40.

———. "Plant Ecology X: Gray Birches." *House Beautiful* 63, no. 3 (March 1928): 324.

———. "Plant Ecology XI: The Stream-Side Planting." *House Beautiful* 63, no. 4 (April 1928): 464, 500–503.

———. "Plant Ecology XII: The Bog." *House Beautiful* 63, no. 5 (May 1928): 626.

Roberts, Edith A., and Margaret F. Shaw. *The Ecology of the Plants Native to Dutchess County, New York.* n.p.: The Conservation Committee of the Garden Club of America, n.d.

Rotenberk, Lori. "Remembering May Watts." *Chicago Wilderness Magazine,* Winter 1999, https://

chicagowildernessmag.org/issues/winter1999 /maywatts.html.

Ryan, Robert L., and Robert E. Grese. "Urban Volunteers and the Environment: Forest and Prairie Restoration." In Bartlett, *Urban Place: Reconnecting with the Natural World,* 173–88.

Schroeder, Herbert W. "The Restoration Experience: Volunteers' Motives, Values and Concepts of Nature." In Gobster and Hull, *Restoring Nature,* 247–64.

Schuyler, David. *Apostle of Taste: Andrew Jackson Downing, 1815–1852.* Baltimore: Johns Hopkins University Press in association with the Center for American Places, 1996.

Seeley, John G. "Liberty Hyde Bailey—Father of American Horticulture." *HortScience* 25, no. 10 (October 1990): 1204–10.

Shintz, H. L., and R. L. Piemeisel. "Fungus Fairy-rings in Eastern Colorado and their Effect on Vegetation." *Journal of Agricultural Research* 11, no. 5 (October 1917): 191–245.

Simberloff, Daniel. "Confronting Introduced Species: A Form of Xenophobia?" *Biological Invasions* 5 (2003): 179–92.

Simonds, Ossian Cole. "Open Your Eyes." *Country Life in America,* January 1913, 55.

———*Landscape Gardening.* 1920; repr., Amherst: University of Massachusetts Press in association with Library of American Landscape History, 2000.

Smith, Charles H. "Shelford, Victor E(rnest) (United States 1877–1968)." *Some Biogeographers, Evolutionists and Ecologists: Chrono-biographical Sketches* (2005), www.wku.edu/~smithch /chronob/SHEL1877.htm.

Smith, Herbert F. "The Spell of Nature in Irving's Famous Stories," in *Washington Irving Reconsidered: A Symposium,* ed. Ralph M. Aderman (Hartford, Conn.: Transcendental Books, 1969), 18–21.

Sobel, David. *Children's Special Places: Exploring the Role of Forts, Dens, and Bush Houses in Middle Childhood.* Tucson: Zephyr Press, 1993.

Stein, Sara. *Noah's Garden: Restoring the Ecology of Our Own Back Yards.* New York: Houghton Mifflin, 1993.

Stuart, Susan M. "Lifting Spirits: Creating Gardens in California Domestic Violence Shelters." In Bartlett, *Urban Place: Reconnecting with the Natural World,* 61–88.

Subramaniam, Banu. "The Aliens Have Landed! Reflections on the Rhetoric of Biological Invasions." *Meridians: Feminism, Race, Transnationalism* 2, no. 1 (2001): 26–40.

Tallamy, Douglas W. *Bringing Nature Home: How Native Plants Sustain Wildlife in Our Gardens.* Portland, Ore: Timber Press, 2007.

Tippens, William W.. and Julia Sniderman. "The Planning and Design of Chicago's Neighborhood Parks." In Chicago Public Library Special Collections Department and the Chicago Park District, *A Breath of Fresh Air,* 21–27.

Tufts, Craig. "Introduction to the Environmental Benefits of Landscaping with Native Plants." www.for-wild.org/land/tufts_op.htm.

Uhl, Christopher. "Conservation Biology in Your Own Front Yard." *Conservation Biology* 12, no. 6 (December 1998): 1175–77.

Ulrich, Roger S. "View through a Window May Influence Recovery from Surgery." *Science* 224 (1984): 420–21.

U.S. Environmental Protection Agency. "Fact Sheet: Landscaping with Native Plants." www .epa.gov/greenacres/nativeplants/factsht.html.

Waitt, Damon. Reply to "What Constitutes a Native Plant?" Lady Bird Johnson Wildflower Research Center website, www.wildflower.org /expert/show.php?id=972.

Waterston, Robert C., ed. *Memoir of George Barrell Emerson, LL.D.* Cambridge, Mass.: J. Wilson and Son, 1884.

Waugh, Frank A. *The Book of Landscape Gardening.* 1926; repr., Amherst: University of Massachusetts Press in association with Library of American Landscape History, 2007.

———. "Ecology of the Roadside." *Landscape Architecture* 21, no. 2 (January 1931): 81–92.

———. *Everybody's Garden.* New York: Orange Judd, 1930.

———. *The Landscape Beautiful.* New York: Orange Judd, 1910.

———. *The Natural Style in Landscape Gardening.* Boston: Richard G. Badger, 1917.

———. *Outdoor Theaters: The Design, Construction and Use of Open-Air Auditoriums.* Boston: Richard G. Badger, 1917.

Where Do the Children Play? Directed by Christopher Cook. Ann Arbor: Michigan Television, 2008.

Wilson, William H. *The City Beautiful Movement.*

Baltimore: Johns Hopkins University Press, 1989.

Wolschke-Bulmahn, Joachim. "The Mania for Native Plants in Nazi Germany." In Dion and Rockman, *Concrete Jungle,* 65–69.

———, ed. *Nature and Ideology: Natural Garden Design in the Twentieth Century.* Washington, D.C.: Dumbarton Oaks Research Library and Collection, 1997.

———. "The 'Wild Garden' and the 'Nature Garden': Aspects of the Garden Ideology of William Robinson and Willy Lange." *Journal of Garden History* 12, no. 3 (1992): 183–206.

Index

as preservers of native plants, 259–63; Jens Jensen's conservation values, 18; Leopold on preserving the last wilderness, 271–76; native gardens as mechanism of, 292; nature appreciation articles lay groundwork for, 23; of roadside vegetation, 161; Visher on the importance to geography of the preservation of natural areas, 78–79; wild gardening as, 15. *See also* restoration

consociations, 148

Cook County (Illinois) Forest Preserves, 11, 18, 206

Cooper, James Fenimore, 12

Copeland, Robert Morris, 14

coppice-type vegetation, 238–42

Cornell Nature-Study Leaflets, 19

Cornell Plantations, 19

council rings, 197

Country Life in America (magazine), 15, 16, 61, 164

Cowles, Henry Chandler, 206; and Chicago Playground Association, 18; "The Ecological Relations of the Vegetation on the Sand Dunes of Lake Michigan," 206; on ecology, 157n; Jensen influenced by, 17; Roberts studies under, 20; Shelford studies under, 21; "Testimony at the Hearing on the Proposed Sand Dunes National Park," 206, 267–70; Watts studies under, 21

Craftsman, The (magazine), 15

Cropsey, Jasper Francis, 11, 23

cultivated landscapes, 128–29

Culture and Management of Our Native Forests for Development as Timber or Ornamental Wood (Cleveland), 15, 205, 209–23

Curtis, John, 17, 207

Cyclopedia of Horticulture (Bailey), 89

Dana, Mrs. William Starr, 293

Dandridge, Danske, 24; "In the Company of Trees," 24, 37–39

Dawson, J. Fred, 233

descriptive geography, 78

disk-type group, 147

Dolobran (near Philadelphia), 163, 165–70

Downing, Andrew Jackson: anti-straight-line theory of, 121; "A Few Hints on Landscape Gardening," 12, 107, 109–11; *Horticulturist* edited by, 217; Hudson River background of, 12; "Neglected American Plants," 12, 83, 85–87

"Dunes of Northern Indiana, The" (Jensen), 264–66

Durand, Asher B., 11, 23

Earth Day, 3, 4

"Ecological Approach, An" (Rehmann), 20–21, 108, 157–61

"Ecological Garden and Arboretum at the University of Wisconsin" (Riis), 277–86

ecological geography, 78–79

ecological motives, 140–41

"Ecological Relations of the Vegetation on the Sand Dunes of Lake Michigan, The" (Cowles), 206

Ecological Society of America, 21, 25, 291

Ecologist's Union, 21

ecology: applications in landscape gardening, 19–21; Cowles on the ecological relations of the vegetation on the sand dunes of Lake Michigan, 206; ecological motives, 140–41; Jensen on design based on, 164; other branches of biology and, 80; Rehmann on ecological approach to landscape gardening, 157–61; restoration, 291–93

Ecology of the Plants Native to Dutchess County, New York, The (Roberts and Shaw), 20, 158

economic geography, 79

effigy mounds, 282

Egan, Dave, 5

Eldredge, Arthur: "Making a Small Garden Look Large," 164, 183–85

Eliot, Charles, 206; Boston park system, 15, 70, 206; as contributor to *Garden and Forest,* 15; "Landscape Forestry in the Metropolitan Reservations," 229–49; and regional scale of conservation, 294

Eliot, Charles W., 71

Eliot, Robert, 291

Emerson, George Barrell, 205

Emerson, Ralph Waldo, 11, 277

English gardens, 122, 159

equilibrium, 131, 132, 138

"Essay on American Scenery" (Cole), 10, 11, 27–36

Ewell, Hazel Crow, 164

Experience of Nature, The: A Psychological Perspective (Kaplan and Kaplan), 287

extinction, economic consequences of, 79

"Faking Nature" (Eliot), 291

farming. *See* agriculture

"Few Hints on Landscape Gardening, A"
(Downing), 12, 107, 109–11
field-and-pasture-type vegetation, 242
fires, 239, 275
fisheries, Pearse on value of aquatic preserves to,
76–77
Fiske, John, 282
Florida, Nehrling on native plants for gardens in,
91–93
flowers. See wild flowers
Ford, Edsel and Eleanor, *116, 145*
Ford, Henry and Clara, 18, *195*
foreign species. See non-native plants
forest cure, 128
forests: American, 34–35; Ashe on value to
silviculture of reserved areas of natural forest
types, 73–75; characteristics of work of art of,
133–34; in Chicago area, 251–58; Cleveland
on culture and management of our native,
209–23; Eliot on landscape forestry in the
Metropolitan Reservations, 229–49; farmland
displaces, 128, 260; fires, 239, 275; forest
landscapes, 127–28; Hill on prairie woodlands,
97–98; in Indiana Dunes, 269; wilderness
areas in national, 273–76
formal gardens: in America, 165; axes in, 132;
Italian gardens, 121, 165, 181; Jensen on, 187;
natural style opposed to, 119, 122, 132, 181;
poetry compared with, 122
*Form and Function: Remarks on Art by Horatio
Greenough,* 12
Franklin Park (Boston), 14
free association, 148
French, William M. R., 14, 18
Freneau, Philip, 67
Friends of Our Native Landscape, 18, 206

Gager, C. Stuart, 136
Gallagher, Percival, 233
Garden and Forest (journal), 15, 24, 83, 206
Garden Club of America, 158
gardenesque style, 13
"Gardenification of Wildland Nature and the
Human Footprint, The" (Janzen), 293
gardens: bog gardens, 171–75; domestic gardening,
126–27; Eldredge on making a small garden
look large, 183–85; gardening as wildland
preservation, 293; gardening for preserving
love of nature, 42–43; Japanese, 120–21;
Jensen on natural, 186–99; Jensen's designs,

18; McFarland on Dolobran, 165–70; natural,
163–203; "nature garden" concept, 4; Nehrling
on native plants for Florida, 91–93; as out-of-
door museums, 104; rock gardens, 194, 198;
small, 197–99; for small homes, 194–97; as
stiff and graceless, 111; wild, 15–16, 164, 170.
See also formal gardens; landscape gardening;
native gardens; wetland gardens
Garfield Park (Chicago), 186, 188–90
Garland, Hamlin, 68
geography, Visher on importance of preservation of
natural areas to, 78–79
*Geography of Childhood, The: Why Children Need
Wild Places* (Nabhan and Trimble), 290
Gifford, Sanford Robinson, 11, 23
Gila National Forest (New Mexico), 273, 274, 275
Gilbert, E. M., 282
Gillette, Genevieve, 5
global warming, 293
Gobster, Paul, 8–9
"Going Native: Bringing Biodiversity into Your
Own Backyard" (Marinelli), 290
Gould, Stephen Jay, 7–8
Graceland Cemetery (Chicago), 14, 16, 117
grading, 152–53
"Gramp" (Buckham), 61
Gray, Asa, 18
Great Lakes: American scenery, 31; aquatic
preserves, 76. *See also* Lake Michigan
Greene, Henry, 207
Greenough, Horatio, 12
Griffin, Walter Burley, 16, 18, 118
Griscom, Clement A., 163, 165–70
Gröning, Gert, 4
ground: nature in shaping of, 152–53; soil, 73, 279,
280, 283; studying, 63–64
Gwinn (Michigan), 164

Harrison, J. B., 224–28
Harshberger, John W., 159
Haynes, Frank J., 23
Higgs, Eric, 293
Hill, E. J., 83; "Prairie Woodlands," 97–98
hills: nature in shaping of, 152; rolling, 128. *See
also* mountains
historical geography, 78
Holy Earth, The (Bailey), 19, 21
House Beautiful (magazine), 15, 20
houses: revealing, 194; siting, 198
How the Other Half Lives (Riis), 17

economic laws manifest in, 134–36; knowing, 60–66; looking on with "loving eye," 28; mental and physical well-being affected by, 287–88; "nature garden" concept, 4; parks founded on love of, 49; Sargent and Stiles on love of, 40–43; Shelford on importance of natural areas to biology and agriculture, 80; Simonds on natural beauty, 44–47; Simonds on nature as the great teacher in landscape gardening, 151–56; as source of planting design, 131–34; studying, 61–66, 155–56; Visher on the importance to geography of the preservation of natural areas, 78–79; Whitcomb on value of natural areas to literature and art, 67–69; writing on, 54–60

"Nature Afoot" column (Chicago Tribune), 21

"Nature as the Great Teacher in Landscape Gardening" (Simonds), 16–17, 108, 151–56

Nature by Design (Higgs), 293

Nature Conservancy, The, 21, 291

"nature garden" concept, 4

"Nature in Early American Literature" (Shelford), 81

Nature-Study Idea, The (Bailey), 19

"Neglected American Plants" (Downing), 12, 83, 85–87

Nehrling, Henry: experimental garden of, 83; "Native Plants for Florida Gardens," 91–93

Nelson, Swain, 16

Niagara Falls, 33

Nichols Arboretum (Ann Arbor), 16, 135, 288, 294

Noah's Garden: Restoring the Ecology of Our Own Back Yards (Stein), 293

non-native plants: Downing on, 12, 110; "fear" and "threat" factor in discussions of, 8–9; invasive qualities of, 7, 8; Jensen on, 7, 187; Manning's use of, 164; Nazi attitude toward, 5; Olmsted's use of, 13; in silviculture, 74; xenophobia and opposition to, 4

North American Association for Environmental Education, 290

Norton, Charles Eliot, 60

Olmsted, Frederick Law: anti-straight-line theory of, 121; on calming influence of nature, 18; Cleveland and, 48; conservation efforts of, 205–6; Eliot works for, 206; as Garden and Forest contributor, 15; Manning works for, 163; naturalistic design of, 12–14; on natural parks, 70; scientific forestry methods of, 205;

Simonds on, 46; "The Use of the Axe," 205, 224–28

"On Improving the Property" (Watts), 21, 164, 202–3

"Open Your Eyes" (Simonds), 287

outdoor recreation, 271–73, 276

Outlook to Nature, The (Bailey), 18, 19, 24–25, 51–66, 287

painting: Hudson River School, 11–12, 23; landscape gardening compared with, 155, 191

Parker, Edward J., 117

parks: Boston Metropolitan Reservations, 15, 70, 206, 229–49; in Chicago, 17, 18, 118, 132, 164, 181, 186–87, 188, 189, 190, 191–92; Cleveland on influence on children of, 48–50; Cowles's testimony on making Indiana Dunes a national, 206, 267–70; Jens Jensen on natural, 186–99; Lars Peter Jensen on preservation of native plants in, 259–63; naturalistic design for, 161, 163–203; of Olmsted and Vaux, 13; Olmsted on thinning trees in, 224–28; as out-of-door museums, 104; White on value of natural preserves to landscape architecture, 70–72; wilderness areas in, 273, 276

Parks and Recreation (magazine), 207

"Parks as Preservers of Native Plants" (Jensen), 259–63

pasturing of woodland, 98, 260

Pearse, Arthur S.: as contributor to A Naturalist's Guide to the Americas, 25; "The Value of Aquatic Preserves to Fisheries," 76–77

peat, 171, 278

Percival, James Gates, 68

Perkins, Dwight, 18

Pinchot, Gifford, 205

Pinckney State Recreation Area (Michigan), 6

plains: plains landscapes, 127; savanna, 8, 104. See also prairie

plant associations, 157

"Plant Ecology" series (House Beautiful), 20

planting composition, Caparn's thoughts on, 130–39

Plant Physiology and Ecology (Clement), 159

plants, native. See native plants

plants, non-native. See non-native plants

poetry: on American flora and fauna, 67; formal gardens compared with, 122; nature, 57–60

Pollan, Michael, 4